Vol. I only (oop) $40.—
" II " (oop $32.—

# WORLD CROP PROTECTION

*Volume 1*

PESTS AND DISEASES

# WORLD CROP PROTECTION

## *Volume 1*

PESTS AND DISEASES

J. H. STAPLEY, B.SC., A.R.C.S.
and
F. C. H. GAYNER, M.A., PH.D.

With Foreword by Dr. Lee Ling
Head of Plant Protection and Plant Production Department
Food and Agriculture Organisation of the United Nations

LONDON ILIFFE BOOKS LTD

ILIFFE BOOKS LTD
42 RUSSELL SQUARE
LONDON, W.C.1



First published in 1969

592 00035 4

Filmset by Photoprint Plates Ltd., Wickford, Essex
Printed in England by
J. W. Arrowsmith Ltd., Bristol

# CONTENTS

# FOREWORD

by Dr. Lee Ling, Head of Plant Protection and Plant Production Department, Food and Agriculture Organisation of the United Nations

Studies conducted over the past twenty years in the fields of entomology and plant pathology in the most advanced countries have developed much useful information, through which considerable improvements in pest and disease control methods have evolved. These studies and the experience gained, especially in the use of pesticide chemicals, have directed attention toward new control principles as well as to the need for more fundamental knowledge in all fields closely related to plant protection sciences. As a result, such fields as biochemistry, biophysics, genetics and cytology have received increasing attention and have contributed toward a better understanding of the mechanics of pest and disease control.

While these remarkable advances were being made in the most advanced countries, little or no progress took place in less favoured countries where pressing needs for raising agricultural production existed and where all kinds of obstacles retarded the turn of progress. Quite often in these countries pests and diseases have continued to be regarded by farmers as acts of God and taken for granted. Likewise, quite commonly pests and diseases have continued to be considered of importance by Governments only when they caused serious destruction. While this attitude towards pests and diseases could be justified before the scientific revolution of a century ago, nowadays, with the available knowledge and means of control, there is no longer any reason or excuse for this. Farmers in developing countries as elsewhere when properly educated and guided, could do much for their crops in avoiding losses caused by pests and diseases. Recognition of these pests and diseases and of their importance is the first step in doing something about them, and the authors of this book are fully aware of this. It is for this reason that they make a very serious attempt to bring together under "one roof" the descriptions of pests and diseases of important crops and of their methods of control. Even a long journey starts with a first step; and this is indeed a good step in the very right direction.

Rome, 1968.

# PREFACE

This book has been prepared in an attempt to survey the principal pests and diseases which occur on the main cultivated crops in the world today. As far as is known, no previous attempt has been made to cover the whole field of pests and diseases in this way although many excellent accounts have been written on the problems on different crops. It is hoped that, by bringing together the whole subject within the confines of one single volume this book will be of value to agricultural research institutes, university departments of agriculture, agricultural colleges and to students of agriculture and horticulture in different parts of the world. It is also intended to be useful to industrial firms in this field of activity when they want a quick reference to pests and diseases of crops, their distribution and importance.

Many influences have been at work during the past twenty years which have stimulated the science of crop protection. In particular, the ever growing need for increased food production, the improvements in plant breeding and the development of many new and potent pesticides have all contributed to rapid advances. It is, therefore, difficult to keep knowledge completely up-to-date, but the basic facts of the life cycles of pests and diseases have been known for many years and change infrequently.

The book is illustrated by photographs and line-drawings. Most of the photographs have been chosen to show what the farmer would see if his own crop were attacked and the attendant losses. The line-drawings are not intended to be diagnostic but are included to give the reader a visual idea of pests and diseases described.

All authors on biological subjects have to deal with the problem of scientific nomenclature which is complicated by the changes made on the grounds of priority. Usually the most up-to-date name has been used and a reference made to the usual latin name. Common chemical names have been given throughout and sometimes the trade names in brackets where these are better known as is frequently the case with well-established products.

The English system of measurement has been generally used but on occasions the metric system has been introduced, especially where the investigations have been carried out in countries using this system. Conversion from one system to the other is very easy using the tables published by some of the international spray chemical companies.

In conclusion it should be said that the science of crop protection is relatively young and is likely to continue its rapid development. As well as the influences mentioned earlier, the greater ease of travel, the ready exchange of information and more accurate assessments of losses caused by pests and diseases all stimulate research. They also encourage the adoption of improved methods of protecting the different crops. It is hoped that this book will contribute to a better understanding of the importance of crop pests and diseases in the world today and will assist in their control.

1969

J.H.S.
F.C.H.G.

# ACKNOWLEDGEMENTS

The authors have individually submitted their accounts of different crops pests and diseases to friends and colleagues who have some special knowledge on the subjects discussed.

Mr. J. H. Stapley wishes to acknowledge with thanks the assistance received in the account of crops pests from: F. G. W. Jones, C. P. Kennard, J. H. Proctor, H. P. Allen, J. W. Drummond, G. H. L. Dicker, A. B. M. Whitnall, I. M. Burnet, F. S. Downing, R. L. Burgess, E. H. Hainsworth. He also wishes to thank Plant Protection Limited for permission to write the book and for the use of their excellent library while a member of their staff.

Dr. F. C. H. Gayner thanks the following for the advice on plant diseases which they have so generously given to him: G. E. Ainsworth, R. S. Elias, G. H. Brenchley, M. J. Geoghegan, R. L. Burgess, E. Hainsworth, I. W. Callan, A. C. Hayward, J. M. Hirst, J. C. F. Hopkins, R. Hull, F. T. Last, E. B. Martyn, H. C. Mellor, M. H. Moore, G. Watts Padwick, R. W. Rayner, R. H. Springett, J. M. Waterson, N. Wright, F. Valenza, and the late L. R. Reed, and E. A. Riley.

He also is greatly indebted to Plant Protection Limited and to the Commonwealth Mycological Institute for the use of their libraries and to their librarians, Miss A. P. Weller and Miss S. Daniels for their skill in dealing with his enquiries.

The line-drawings have been based on sketches by Miss Joanna Stapley and original resources. The photographs accompanying the pests section mostly came from Mr. J. H. Stapley's own collection, secured during many overseas assignments while working as senior entomologist for Plant Protection Limited, to whom his grateful thanks are due. Many of the photographs of plant diseases were made available by Imperial Chemical Industries Limited and by the Shell International Petroleum Company Ltd., and are greatfully acknowledged. In addition, the authors wish to thank all those friends and acquaintances who have kindly allowed their photographs to be reproduced in this book.

# I INTRODUCTION

## GENERAL INTRODUCTION

### THE WORLD FOOD PROBLEM

From the earliest times man has struggled against famine and disease. It is ironic that in recent times the great advances made in medicine have aggravated the world food problem for lower infant mortality, increased longevity and the control of such tropical diseases as malaria and smallpox have contributed to the startling increase in world population. Man's own fertility has now become one of the greatest threats to progress, and even to survival in certain areas, and it is difficult to visualise how in the next few decades the production of food and fodder can be increased to keep pace with the rising population. Food is man's primary need, yet its production is limited both by the surface of the earth and the ability of mankind to utilise the land area and the oceans to the maximum advantage.

In recognition of this problem, the United Nations in 1945 established the Food and Agriculture Organisation (F.A.O. in Quebec, Canada, and in 1951 it moved into its permanent headquarters in Rome. F.A.O. promotes the publication of information on all aspects of agriculture as a step towards achieving its objective of increasing world food production. The annual statistics and publicity booklets of F.A.O. have drawn attention to the present and probable future shortages of food, particularly in Asia, and to a lesser extent in the tropical areas of Africa and Central America. The population of India, for example, is increasing at the rate of about 2% per annum, so that in 15 years it will exceed 600 million people. The increase in food production over the last 10 years is only about 0·4% in this part of the world. Such a population, growing rapidly, will become increasingly under-nourished.

In advanced countries, techniques which lead to increased food production are widely accepted. These include the use of high-yielding varieties of crops, of fertilizers to ensure adequate plant nutrition, and of irrigation (Richardson, 1963). Educated farmers are well aware of the necessity for controlling pests, diseases and weeds, but in agriculturally less advanced parts of the world knowledge is often lacking and the economic conditions are often not conducive to successful farming. The farmers in these areas are mainly peasants, often lethargic through poor health, caused through malnutrition and disease. Religious prejudices, superstition and traditional conservatism may hinder change towards better farming methods—as do inadequate transport, poor implements and educational backwardness. Together, these factors may amount to a situation of hopelessness, from which escape is impossible and provide a vicious circle which rotates around the hub of poverty.

This book attempts to give a readable account of the major pests and diseases which damage world crops and the methods which are being used to combat them. The field is so vast that it has been essential to select the subjects which were the most important. The choice has usually been made on the basis of the acreage occupied by the crop, or by its economic importance. In the same way the pests and diseases which cause the greatest losses have been chosen.

The descriptions of the pests and diseases are not diagnostic, but are intended to give a general picture of the insect or pathogen responsible, its distribution, the damage it does, its life history and the methods of control.

## PRINCIPAL CROPS

In order to keep the book within a reasonable compass, discussion has been limited to the principal crops of the world. Of these, the group producing carbohydrates is easily the largest. In the temperate regions, it includes wheat, barley, oats, potatoes and sugar-beet and, in the tropics and sub-tropics, rice, maize, sorghum, bananas and sugar-cane. Although fruits occupy a much smaller area, they are high-value crops and of considerable economic importance to the countries which grow them. Those dealt with are apples, pears, peaches, vines, olives and citrus fruits. Finally, there are two small groups comprising crops of great importance in world trade. The first produces industrial raw materials such as cotton, tobacco, rubber, coconuts and oil palms. The second produces the beverages, coffee, cocoa and tea.

## CROP LOSSES

The figures for crop losses caused by pests and diseases are essential to governments to justify expenditure on research. They are also needed by farmers who have to decide whether or not control measures are worth while.

The total estimates of losses are often enormous. F.A.O. has published world figures which indicate that 35% of the wheat which could theoretically be harvested is lost as a result of pests and diseases. The corresponding figure for potatoes is 40%, for sugar-beet 24%, for apples 30%, for cotton 60% and for tobacco 62%. Even in the most advanced countries, losses are still very heavy in spite of the adoption of modern methods of crop protection. For example, in the United States it is believed that the farmers annually lose £1,000 million due to pests and a similar amount due to plant diseases (Anon. 1962).

Various methods of expressing crop losses have been used. The percentage of the potential crop which has been lost, and the monetary value of the loss are the two most commonly employed. In many cases, more efficient production would enable the farmer to produce the saleable output from a smaller acreage. The extra acres which have to be planted to compensate for losses represent the 'untaken harvest', as a survey by Ordish (1952) has demonstrated. The whole subject of crop losses caused by insect and allied pests, diseases and even weeds has been discussed at a recent Symposium held in Rome and organised by the F.A.O. (1967). A comprehensive survey has also been prepared by Cramer (1967), whose work should be consulted by all interested.

Years ago, no difficulties were experienced in deciding what were the most important sources of loss. The devastation caused by locusts, the defoliation of potatoes by Colorado Beetle, and by potato blight, were only too obvious but, as protective methods have advanced, so has the necessity for more refined methods of measuring losses arisen. With more accurate measurement, the problems can then be put in their correct order of priority.

From the practical aspect, it is important to remember that it is usually the farmer who makes the final reckoning of the probable loss and who decides what must be done about it. He must estimate how much he is likely to lose, how much the treatment will cost, and how much he will gain by employing control measures. Farmers only use pesticides if they think it will be a profitable operation. On the other hand, the control of certain pests and diseases is sometimes of benefit to the nation as a whole in order to preserve the economy; in such a case, government subsidies may be given. The measures adopted to minimise the losses of cotton over the last 15 years in Uganda by dressing the whole of the seed are an example of this type of action.

## METHODS OF PEST AND DISEASE CONTROL

Many methods of controlling pests and diseases have been devised. They can be conveniently classified into five groups:

1. *The use of resistant varieties*
Over the centuries, those crop varieties which are particularly susceptible tend to be superseded by the more resistant types. The introduction of plant breeding techniques in the twentieth century has made this one of the most important methods of defending the world's crops, e.g. the raising of new cereal varieties which resist the rust diseases.

2. *Cultural methods*
Probably the most important of these methods is crop rotation, particularly in the control of insect pests, e.g. for the control of cereal leaf miner and of root diseases such as take-all.

3. *Biological control*
When natural control ceases to operate, an insect species becomes a pest. The supplementation of existing natural parasites or the introduction of a new species from another country has occasionally proved effective, e.g. in the control of Levuana moth in Fiji (Ordish, 1967).

4. *Government action*
Legislation has an essential part to play in preventing the spread of pests and diseases by the operation of quarantine regulations and by the carrying out of programmes such as the eradication of alternate hosts. A good example of government action is to be found in the measures taken to eradicate the virus disease bunchy top of bananas from Queensland during the 1930's.

5. *The application of pesticides*
Pesticides are of great importance when the four methods noted above are not applicable. Many of the more valuable crops such as apples, bananas, citrus fruits, cotton, potatoes and vines are given routine treatments to protect them from the ravages of insects and fungi. In addition, treatment with pesticides may be the only way of saving crops in such emergencies as unexpected attacks by locusts or by armyworm.

REFERENCES

ANON., WLD. CROPS, **14**, 247 (1962)
ORDISH, G., *Biological Methods in Crop Pest Control,* Constable, London (1967)
ORDISH, G., *The Untaken Harvest,* Constable & Co. Ltd., London (1952)
RICHARDSON, G. L., *Out. Agr.*, **4**, 3 (1963)
*F.A.O. Symposium on Crop Losses Rome 1967*
CRAMER, H. H., *Plant Production and World Crop Production,* Farben Fabriken Bayer, Leverkusen (1967)

# BIOLOGICAL INTRODUCTION

## THE EFFECTS OF PESTS AND DISEASES

The earliest farmers, who in all probability were the cereal-growers in the Near and Middle East, must have noticed that the effect of locusts and rust diseases on their crops, but many years elapsed between the observation of what happened and a proper understanding of the cause and its effect.

Recognition of the importance of insect pests dates from about 100 years ago. The early writers were really unable to do more than describe the life cycles of insects as there were few, if any, means of dealing with them. Early twentieth century attempts to take direct action against pests were limited to control scale insects on citrus with oil sprays in the U.S.A. and in Europe Codling Moth control with lead arsenate. Few other chemicals were available and the means of applying them in sprays to trees was, by modern standards, quite primitive. Fumigation of citrus trees also was practised in the U.S.A. and in the Mediterranean region by tenting trees and releasing HCN gas into the tents. HCN, one of the most deadly and speedy poisons known to science, was handled freely by operators, but would never have been approved in any country today.

Early entomological work tended to concentrate on the medical and public health problems rather than on agriculture. Spectacular discoveries were waiting to be made, such as the transmission of diseases by insects. These tended to overshadow developments in the control of pests of crops, as in 'The Insect Menace' by L. O. Howard, 1931.

As knowledge about pests and diseases gradually accumulated, so did an awareness that this knowledge should be made available to the farming community. The U.S.A. was the leader, for in 1887 the Hatch Act made provision for Agricultural Experiment Stations in each State and for the information to be passed on to the farmers and agricultural students.

The organisation of an Advisory Service for farmers in England began about 1911. It was revised and reinforced after the First World War so that many Agricultural Colleges and Institutions found a place for a recognised adviser on their staff. During the period from 1920–39 this service, working in England together with official research stations and other bodies, gave much advice over the whole range of insect pests and allied problems; the control of insect pests and diseases became organised into an orderly body of knowledge.

During this period much research into insect problems was carried out. The investigators, however, were invariably unable to make effective recommendations for control because of the absence of suitable chemicals capable of eliminating the insects. The range of insecticidal sprays materials was limited to:

Lead arsenate—against caterpillars and Codling Moth on apples
Nicotine—against aphids
Derris—against aphids and caterpillars
Lime-sulphur—against red spider
Tar oil—as a winter wash against aphids on fruit trees
Mineral oil—against apple capsid bugs and San José scale
White oil—against citrus scales and red spider

The situation at the beginning of the Second World War can be summarised by saying:

1. Crop losses from insect and allied pests were now recognised. Their importance during fifty years has been assessed.

2. The ways of combating insect pests was limited by the lack of chemicals and by the absence of suitable machinery for the application of those available.

## METHODS OF DISEASE CONTROL

Although the early farmers noticed the effects of diseases on their crops, many centuries elapsed before plant diseases were studied scientifically. Empirical methods have, however, long been in use.

Probably the most important effect has come from the preference for the best yielding varieties. Many factors contribute to high yields, disease resistance among them, so that over the years the susceptible varieties tend to disappear. Farmer selection has thus operated in the same direction as natural selection in the survival of the varieties which are fittest for their particular purpose.

Crop rotation has also contributed to disease control. It is not applicable to every disease, but is of much value in cases where the fungus is present on the roots or persists on the crop residues.

The first scientific recommendation for the control of plant disease was made in 1755 when a study of bunt of wheat was published. Slow progress was made during the succeeding hundred years, but two occurrences during the nineteenth century focussed attention on the necessity for methods of controlling plant diseases. The first was the appearance in 1845 of potato blight in Europe, and the second was in 1878 when the first outbreak of vine downy mildew occurred in France.

The attack on the vines was so serious that much effort was spent in finding a remedy. The search culminated in the discovery of a new fungicide, Bordeaux Mixture, which was effective for the control not only of downy mildew but also potato blight.

The knowledge that plant diseases were controllable encouraged the hunt for improved fungicides and seed dressing materials.

*How New Pesticides have Solved Old Problems*
The problem of wireworm control in the ploughing up of old grassland was encountered during the First World War when grassland was converted to arable land to increase crop production. Wireworm caused total and partial failure to crops grown in ploughed-up grassland, especially in the first and second years. No advice could be given except the growing of more resistant crops. Obviously, everyone who converted grassland to arable could not grow such crops. The same problem was again encountered in the Second World War but the Advisory Service was now better organised to meet it, but could only do so by estimating wireworm populations in the soil of fields before cropping (Miles, 1944).

The problem was solved very simply by the discovery of the insecticide BHC (benzene hexachloride). At first this chemical was applied broadcast to the soil as a $3\frac{1}{2}\%$ dust, but later was used as a seed-dressing in the form of the gamma isomer. Seed-dressing of all cereals and sugar-beet became possible with gamma BHC, a treatment which was cheap and effective. The solution to the wireworm problem has awaited the discovery of a chemical with the right properties. In the present day, about 15 years after launching of the first commercial seed-dressing against wireworm (1949), many growers and advisers are thinking that seed-dressing with insecticides on cereals against wireworm can be omitted.

Many other examples of the immediate solution of insect problems by the discovery of synthetic insecticides could be given. Here are some of them.

Apple Blossom Weevil was a pest of fruit in northern Europe, including the United Kingdom and was often so severe that some apple trees never came into bloom. The details of the life-cycle had been meticulously worked out but the problem could not be solved. Growers were advised to put bands of sacking round the trunks of their trees to catch the weevils when they looked for a place to hibernate. Such bands were taken off in the autumn and burnt, but other bands were produced containing B-naphthol which asphyxiated the weevils which entered them. In spite of all these efforts, the Apple Blossom Weevil remained in English apple orchards until after the Second World War and the release of DDT as an insecticide for use in agriculture. Application of DDT to apple trees as a spray at bud-burst eliminated the Apple Blossom Weevil so that nowadays growers no longer consider it in their fruit-spraying programme.

The same fate awaited the Apple Capsid Bug, a severe pest of apples. DDT eliminated it simply and cheaply whereas formerly growers were compelled to spray in the winter with a wash containing mineral oil—an expensive and laborious procedure. The grower had been faced with the need to spray his apple trees twice in winter—once with tar oil against aphids, and once with mineral oil against capsids. This was a time-consuming undertaking even supposing it were possible as, in many winters, conditions were totally unfavourable for spraying. Spring spraying, with DDT and BHC and certain other chemicals, eliminated the need for winter sprays completely—all spraying could be done in the spring and summer.

Overseas in the tropics and sub-tropics, insect pests are even more important than in the temperate climate. Little direct action could be taken against species which caused enormous crop losses. For example, in Egypt one of the principal cotton-producing countries of the world, a serious pest and a constant threat to the crop was the leaf worm. This insect, a voracious caterpillar, lived in the winter on berseem, the Egyptian clover, which dried up in the spring and the caterpillar moved into the cotton. Vast numbers of moths swarmed into the cotton fields and deposited eggs on the undersides of the leaves. The fellahin mustered all the village lads and girls to comb the cotton fields and pick off the egg masses on the leaves. In some years, such measures were successful, but in years of severe attack the egg-laying of the moths outstripped the vigilance of the pickers and caterpillars appeared and devoured the cotton crop. Today, not only are insecticides available to assist or replace the young leaf pickers, but also the machines to apply them.

In Japan, the basic food is rice derived from the paddy plant. As would be expected, the paddy is attacked by insect pests of which none is more important than the Rice Stem Borer. Japan is a country of many millions with a severe shortage of land for paddy growing as the centre of the mainland is mountainous and paddy can only be cultivated on the coastal strip. Naturally, all efforts are made to produce as much rice as possible from the inherently infertile soil by using the highest yielding varieties and the liberal use of fertilizers. The Japanese also combat the Rice Stem Borer with the new organo-phosphorus insecticide, parathion, which is far superior to any previously used insecticide for this purpose. In spite of the toxic hazard to humans from the insecticide 1,000 tons of 50% liquid and 15,000 tons of dust were used in 1960. Likewise, 47,000 tons of 3% gamma BHC dust was also used. A new chemical, less toxic than parathion, known as fenitrothion is already under trial.

In other countries, little action is taken against rice and paddy borers but in these countries the agriculture is less well organised than in Japan and there is more land available for paddy cultivation.

Locusts have always been a problem, especially in the Middle East and parts of Africa. Little action could be taken against them in the past but where necessary and possible, the use of bait was practised. The bait preferred consisted of a food material, such as crushed maize or wheat bran, mixed with a poison—sodium arsenite. While this method of killing locusts was quite successful, the bait was also attractive and poisonous to domestic animals, especially camels and goats. Post-war, the aeroplane was introduced in the fight against locusts by direct spraying of locusts in flight with DNOC (dinitro-ortho-cresol) in oil. DNOC was also poisonous to the operators, especially as it was formulated in oil and it also stained the skin and clothes bright yellow. BHC was found to be very toxic to locusts and could be used in baits as was sodium arsenite but it was non-toxic and could be used without hazard to domestic animals. BHC, as the gamma isomer, could be formulated for aerial spraying in oil. Sprays containing 15% gamma BHC could be used and caused a heavier mortality per gallon than DNOC. The product also stung the skin and eyes and so was handled with more care but was in fact safe to use. Other advances of this kind will be made as new chemicals are discovered (Rainey, 1958).

While some of the new insecticides have conquered pests which the older ones did not, the new fungicides have not markedly expanded the range of fungi which can be controlled. The main reason for this is that the older fungicides based on sulphur, copper and mercury compounds are all wide spectrum materials. Between them they covered a good proportion of the parasitic fungi with a few exceptions, such as those living in the vascular system or on the roots. The existing gaps are thus small and it so happens that the post-war discoveries have not filled them.

The new organic fungicides have been welcomed for two reasons, reduced phytotoxicity and improved control. For example, under certain conditions copper compounds have a deleterious effect on the yield of potatoes, whereas the dithiocarbamates, zineb and maneb, have none. Similarly, sulphur and lime-sulphur when used on some of the sulphur-sensitive varieties of apples have an adverse effect on the crop. Their replacement by materials such as captan and dinocap has led to a marked increase in the amount of fruit harvested. Examples of improved control are not so common, but there can be little doubt that the use of captan and dodine has enabled fruit-growers to obtain a better control of apple scab than ever before.

REFERENCES

HOWARD, L. O., *The Insect Menace,* Century Press, New York (1931)

MILES, H. W., *Bull. No. 128. Mins. Agric. & Fish.,* H.M.S.O. (1944)

RAINEY, R. C., *J. Sci. Fd. Agr.,* **9,** 677 (1958)

## THE STUDY OF ENTOMOLOGY AND PLANT PATHOLOGY

The principal pests of crops in the world are insects. Other pests certainly exist including allied pests not true insects such as plant feeding acarina (mites) and plant parasitic nematodes (eelworms). Likewise birds, rodents and even elephants and monkeys can all assume importance as pests if their breeding is allowed to progress unchecked. All cause the destruction of crops which someone has carefully cultivated. All plants, certainly all crop plants, are natural targets for insects which have inhabited and colonised all parts of the earth's surface except the sea. Insects can live on a wide variety of food substances. Consider the large numbers of species which use wood as a source of food, including the whole of the order *Isoptera* or termites, and the Death Watch Beetle which lives on the oldest and driest of wood. Insects can make use of the smallest quantity of food material, and in doing so materially destroy plants, seeds, fruit and so on.

The insect species have unlimited powers of reproduction but fortunately the insect house is divided against itself and many groups live by preying upon other insects. Even so, insects which feed on crops frequently outstrip their natural enemies and so become ranked as pests. The importance of insects in public health has long been recognised both as direct parasites, such as lice and fleas, and also as carriers of human disease.

Many excellent books are available on the basic principles of entomology and plant pathology. There are also many books dealing with the pests and diseases of different crops to which reference is made under each crop heading.

There are no recent books dealing with the history of entomological studies, but a most readable account of the growth of plant pathology has been written by Large (1940). It describes how plant diseases have affected man, and his efforts to protect his crops.

ENTOMOLOGICAL BOOK LIST

BRAUN, H. and RIEHM, E., *Krankheitén und Schädlinge der Kulturpflanzer,* Paul Parey, Berlin (1957)

FAES, H., STAEHELIM, M. and BOVEY, P., *La Défense des Plantes Cultivées,* Librairie Payot, Lausanne (1947)

GHOSH, C. C., *Insect Pests of Burma,* Supdt. Govt. Printing-Stationery, Rangoon (1940)

IMMS, A. D., *Outline of Entomology,* 3rd Edn., Methuen & Co. Ltd., London (1942)

JONES, F. G. W. and JONES, M., *Pest of Field Crops,* Edward Arnold Ltd., London (1964)

METCALF, C. L. and FLINT, W. P., *Destructive and Useful Insects,* 3rd Edn., McGraw-Hill Book Co. Inc., New York (1951)

RIVNAY, E., *Field Crop Pests in the Near East,* Der Haag, Uitgeverij Dr. W. Junk (1962)

STAPLEY, J. H., *Pests of Farm Crops,* E. and F. N. Spon, London (1948)

WEGOREK, W., *Ochrona Roslin,* Panstwowe Wydawnictwo Rolnicze I Lesne, Warsaw (1963)

PLANT PATHOLOGICAL BOOK LIST

AINSWORTH, G. C. and BISBY, G. R., *A Dictionary of the*

Kew (1961)

BAWDEN, F. C., *Plant Viruses and Virus Diseases,* 4th Edn., Ronald Press Co., New York (1964)

BROOKS, F. T., *Plant Diseases,* 2nd Edn., Oxford University Press, London (1953)

BUTLER, E. J. and JONES, S. C., *Plant Pathology,* Macmillan & Co. Ltd., London (1949)

C.M.I., *Descriptions of Pathogenic Fungi and Bacteria* (Series started in 1964), Commonwealth Mycological Institute, Kew

DOWSON, W. J., *Plant Diseases due to Bacteria,* 2nd Edn., Cambridge University Press, Cambridge (1957)

LARGE, E. C., *The Advance of the Fungi,* Jonathan Cape, London (1940)

SMITH, K. M., *A Textbook of Plant Virus Diseases,* 2nd Edn., J. and A. Churchill Ltd., London (1957)

STAKMAN, E. C. and HARRAR, J. G., *Principles of Plant Pathology,* The Ronald Press Co., New York (1957)

WALKER, J. C., *Plant Pathology,* 2nd Edn., McGraw-Hill Book Co. Inc., New York (1957)

JOURNALS

The number of research reports on pests and disease control published every year is expanding due to the growing importance of the subject. Fortunately, there are abstract journals which make this knowledge more accessible to the student and the specialist.

*Review of Applied Entomology,* Series A. Published monthly by the Commonwealth Entomological Institute, Queen's Gate, London, S.W.7.

*Review of Applied Mycology.* Published monthly by the Commonwealth Mycological Institute, Ferry Lane, Kew, Surrey.

## GENERAL DESCRIPTION OF PLANT INJURIES

In the pages which follow, the very varied ways in which pests and diseases damage plants are depicted. Pests, using the term in the wider sense to include insects, red spider mites and nematodes, feed on all parts of the plant, particularly those above-ground.

The biting insects, mainly caterpillars, but occasionally larvae or adults of other genera, consume the foliage, thus causing varying degrees of defoliation. They may also feed on the shoots, the flowers and the fruits, all or any of such actions reducing the yield. The sucking insects such as the aphids and the plant bugs live on the sap of plants. This may cause direct injury, but they are probably of even greater importance as the vectors of virus diseases. Mites are also sap feeders. A few individuals do little harm, but their powers of rapid multiplication give rise to enormous populations whose feeding causes the foliage to turn brown and make it ineffective. Nematodes which can live on both the leaves and the roots are particularly destructive when they damage the roots as normal development is inhibited.

There are four major causes of disease in plants; the fungi, bacteria, viruses and mineral deficiencies. The first three are true pathogens and come within the province of the plant pathologist, but although mineral deficiencies give rise to pathological symptoms, the subject is usually regarded as part of plant nutrition.

Fungi are undoubtedly the most important cause of disease in plants, with viruses in second, and bacteria in third place. Their effects on the host plant are most varied. Dealing first with the fungi, many attack most of the above-ground parts, but some only occur on specific organs. It is the foliar injury which is probably the chief cause of crop reduction due to fungal attack, but in addition there are serious losses from seedling blights, vascular wilts, grain smuts and fruit rots.

The plant viruses upset the metabolism, causing such symptoms as leaf mottling, stunting or the death of the plant. Their presence usually results in a reduction of the crop.

The bacteria which cause the heaviest losses are those which inhabit the vascular tissue where they may become so numerous that the vessels become blocked or necrosis may result from the production of toxic substances.

# II CEREALS

## TEMPERATE CEREALS

The cereals of the temperate zones of the world are wheat, barley, oats and rye, as distinct from the tropical and subtropical cereals, namely rice, maize and sorghum. The acreage figures given below show that wheat is the most important food crop grown by western man (F.A.O., 1964):

| | |
|---|---|
| Wheat | 515,000,000 acres |
| Barley | 176,000,000 acres |
| Oats | 82,000,000 acres |
| Rye | 65,000,000 acres |

The principal wheat lands are found in Europe, the U.S.A., the U.S.S.R., Canada, India, Australia, Argentina and Turkey. Barley is grown in the same countries but on a smaller scale. It is an important crop in the United Kingdom, but bigger areas occur in the U.S.A., India, Canada and Turkey. The biggest European producer is Spain. The distribution of oats is somewhat similar, but as it is more tolerant of a cool climate more is grown in the northern countries. Rye is also suited to a cool climate and is extensively grown in Poland, Germany and the U.S.S.R.

The cereal diseases are particularly important as they are a potential threat to the main energy foods for man and beast. The rust diseases can cause very serious losses of grain and have therefore received much attention from plant pathologists. Bunt, or stinking smut, was responsible for considerable losses of wheat until the end of the eighteenth century, but since then methods of controlling it have become so efficient that it is now rarely seen. Closely related smuts attack both barley and oats. In addition to the diseases mentioned, there are others which attack the roots, the stems, the foliage and the ears. That cereal diseases are being held in check is demonstrated by the gradual increase in yields per acre which have come from the use of scientific methods of farming.

The principal cereal insect pest is the wireworm. It is more important in the northern regions, its place being taken by cutworms and white grubs in the southern regions, such as Turkey. In Anatolia, the near and middle east, new pests are found in the form of cereal Hemiptera, such as *Eurygaster,* the notorious 'Sunni' pest, similar in the tropics to the rice bugs *Leptocorisa* spp.

Aphids occur on all cereals but are relatively unimportant as pests of these crops. On the whole, cereals are remarkably free from pest troubles now that the wireworm problem has been effectively solved by insecticidal seed dressings. Local pests, of course, are to be found, such as the Hessian fly in the U.S.A. and *Zabrus tenebrioides* in central Europe.

The literature on cereal pests and diseases is vast, but Peterson's (1965) book on wheat provides a most welcome summary of the subject. The major diseases are described in the standard text books on plant pathology and in addition there are excellent accounts of the fungi attacking cereals by Moore *et al.* (1961), McKay (1957) and Dickson (1947).

REFERENCES

DICKSON, J. G., *Diseases of Field Crops,* McGraw Hill Book Co. Inc., New York (1947)

*F.A.O. Production Yearbook 1963–64,* **18,** F.A.O., Rome

MCKAY, R., *Cereal Diseases in Ireland,* Arthur Guinness Son & Co. (Dublin) Ltd. (1957)

MOORE, W. C. and MOORE, F. JOAN, *Cereal Diseases* (3rd Edn.), Bull. 129, H.M.S.O., London (1961)

PETERSON, R. F., *Wheat,* Leonard Hill Books, London (1965)

## COLEOPTERA

### *Agriotes spp. (Elateridae)*

The larval or immature stages of certain species of *Agriotes* are known as wireworms. The most common in Europe are *A. lineatus* L., *A. obscurus* L., and *A. sputator* L. Their larvae are yellow to brown, hard, smooth and wirelike. The smaller forms are about one-tenth of an inch in length and are seldom seen but the older larvae are almost an inch in length. In the U.S.A., other species predominate such as *A. mancus* Say. and there are yet other species which resemble *Agriotes* and their larvae behave as wireworms. Among these are species of *Athous* and *Limonius* but these are usually less numerous than those of *Agriotes.*

Wireworms are pests in northern Europe, Russia and Canada but they are less important and often absent in the southern and subtropical cereal growing regions such as Turkey, Spain, Argentine, South Africa, and Australia. The beetles are of no importance as pests. They are known as 'Click Beetles', elongate, dark in colour with the ability to jump into the air by means of a projection and socket beneath the thorax. Some species fly readily but not *Agriotes* which seldom takes to wing. The average life-cycle takes five years, almost wholly occupied by the larval stages. Eggs are deposited in soil well covered with vegetation especially grass. The larval stages feed slowly, moving up and down in the top few inches of the soil according to the season. Pupation occurs in the soil and the new beetles emerge in the summer. Some species go through a shorter cycle but none an annual one.

Wireworms usually inhabit grassland, feeding on the stems which are mascerated and consumed in liquid form. Permanent grassland can support 3 million or more per acre. Wireworms become pests of crops when grassland is converted to arable as happened in the two World Wars. Wireworms turn their attention to the crop which is unable to withstand the feeding and damage occurs either in the first year after ploughing from grassland or in the second, or in both. Seeds, germinating seedlings and later, the stems just below ground, are attacked often causing total loss of crop. Wireworms also inhabit arable land especially if cereals are common in the rotation. After fallowing, crops are heavily attacked as the food supply becomes exhausted during the fallow period but most crops can tolerate small populations of wireworms without suffering. The tolerance limit is about 600,000 per acre but cereals and other crops can often withstand such populations. Injury occurs in the spring as the soil warms up and the wireworms move into the surface layers where they remain until it becomes too dry and feeding ceases.

Many investigations into wireworm behaviour have been done and it was found that certain crops are more susceptible than others. Soil type has little influence on wireworm prevalence and while wireworms are usually more numerous on heavy land more damage usually occurs on light soils (Cockbill *et al.*, 1945).

#### METHODS OF CONTROL

The problem of wireworms defied the efforts of all investigators in many different countries to solve it although much was known about

*Plate 2.1. Wireworm control with 20% gamma BHC seed dressing. Treated area on left, untreated on right*

the insects. Much advice had also been given about ways to avoid damage to crops, usually of a negative character; positive advice seemed confined to recommendations to roll the crop and harrow to stimulate growth. All known chemicals appear to have been tried but few were cheap enough to be used on a field scale. Naphthalene possessed some insecticidal action and was relatively cheap but ineffective. The first chemical which could be applied to the soil and was both cheap and effective was benzene-hexachloride (BHC) discovered in 1942 in the United Kingdom. The toxic effect of BHC to wireworms was first reported by Jameson and his fellow workers in 1947. They showed that 6 lb BHC per acre decreased wireworm injury to wheat, improved plant establishment and increased the yield of grain and straw. The number of wireworms also decreased to about 25% of the original population.

BHC could be applied with a combine drill which deposited the insecticide in the same furrow as the seed but Jameson used a purified form containing 40% of the gamma isomer of BHC as a seed-dressing applied to the seed. Both these methods of application gave similar protection but the seed-dressing required only 2 oz of gamma BHC per acre whereas the broadcast method needed 12 oz of gamma BHC per acre. Obviously the line of development lay with seed-dressings. Commercial seed-dressings became available for cereals in the United Kingdom in 1949 as a standard product containing 1% mercury and 20% gamma BHC. The rate of application was 0·2% by weight for wheat and barley seed and 0·3% for oats (Jameson *et al.*, 1951) (Plate 2.1).

Similar lines of research were being pursued in other countries, notably in the U.S.A. where Lange (1949) investigated the use of seed-dressings on a variety of seeds against wireworms of the species *Aeolus, Limonius* and *Anchastus.* Commercial treatment of cereal seed with the combined dressing is now practised in many countries, especially in Europe and North America (Faber, 1952). Sometimes the farmers themselves overdress the mercury-treated seed with insecticide.

Attempts have been made to introduce liquid seed-dressings containing mercury and an insecticide especially where central seed-dressing is carried out. Gamma BHC cannot be used in this type of formulation and aldrin, dieldrin and heptachlor have taken its place as they are less phytotoxic to seed. Unfortunately, seed-dressings containing these insecticides proved toxic to wild birds and game birds in the United Kingdom and, it is expected, that their use will be discontinued (Cook, 1964).

### *Zabrus tenebrioides* Goeze *(Carabidae)*

This insect occurs in Europe as a pest of cereals in the central and more southern regions spreading to the countries bordering the Black Sea. It is known as the Cereal Ground Beetle and is one of the few examples of members of this family, normally carnivorus, feeding on plants (Kadocsa, 1941). The adult beetle appears in June and July and develops a fondness for plant food, ascending the stalks of wheat and feeding on the ears. The larvae, which occur in the soil, feed on the roots and foliage, especially in the autumn. The damage from *Zabrus* is not very important unless the insects are numerous when total losses are possible (Stankovic and Ilic, 1951). Like wireworms, *Zabrus* is more common in cereals taken after grass fields and in fields near grassland.

#### METHODS OF CONTROL

Damage from *Zabrus* can be decreased by insecticides applied to the soil but there is no evidence that seed-dressings, as used against wireworms, are effective. Against the adults a 10% DDT dust is sometimes used applied to small areas.

### *Anisoplea spp. (Lamellicornia)*

This is an important insect pest in Turkey and neighbouring countries where the adults feed on the grain when it is in the milky stage. The insect is similar in habits to *Zabrus,* the larval stages occurring in the soil, feeding on the roots, and may be controlled in the same way.

### *Heteronychus consimilis* Kolbe. *(Lamellicornia)*

This insect which occurs in Kenya, resembles the Black Maize Beetle (see p. 56) and the adults feed on the shoots of wheat as these are coming through the ground. The larval stages are passed in the soil where they feed on roots.

Seed-dressings containing gamma BHC are effective.

REFERENCES

COOKBILL, G. F., HENDERSON, V. E., ROSS, D. M. and STAPLEY, J. H., *Ann. appl. Biol.,* **32,** 148 (1945)

COOK, J. W., *Rep. Adv. Ctte. Poisonous Subs. in Agric.,* 29, H.M.S.O. (1964)

FABER, W., *R.A.E.,* **40,** 216 (1952)

ILIC, B. and STANLOVIC, A., *R.A.E.,* **41,** 297 (1953)

JAMESON, H. R., TANNER, C. C. and THOMAS, F. J. D., *Ann. Appl. Biol.,* **38,** 121 (1951)

JAMESON, H. R., THOMAS, F. J. D. and WOODWARD, R. C., *Ann. Appl. Biol.,* **34,** 346 (1947)

KADOCSA, A., R.A.E., **33,** 11 (1941)

LANGE, W. H., CARLSON, E. C. and LEACH, L. D., *J. Econ. Entomol.,* **42,** 942 (1949)

## DIPTERA

The most important species of the two-winged flies which attack cereals are as follows:

*Cecidomyidae* Gall Midges
  *Contarinia tritici* Kirby. The Wheat Blossom Midge
  *Sitodiplosis mosellana* Gehin

*Cecidomyia destructor* Say. The Hessian Fly

*Chloropidae*

*Oscinella frit* L. The Frit Fly

*Meromyza saltatrix* L.

*Chlorops pulminionis* Bjerk. The Gout Fly

*Opomyzidae*

*Opomyza florum* Fab.

*Geomyza tripunctata* Fall.

*Anthomyidae*

*Leptohylemyia coarctata* Fall. The Wheat Bulb Fly

*Phorbia genitalis* Schn. The Late Wheat Shoot Fly

Very few species of the above are of economic importance especially if their occurrence is known and precautions are taken. Probably the Hessian Fly causes more loss than any other, but attention to sowing dates can avoid such losses. Likewise, the Frit Fly can be avoided by the early sowing of oats. Wheat Bulb Fly is also partly controllable by attention to rotations. Losses from Wheat Midges are small and seldom exceed 1–2%.

### *Cecidomyia (Mayetiola) destructor* Say.

The Hessian Fly is a very important pest in the U.S.A. and Canada. It is, however, a European insect, occurring on wheat throughout Europe including Russia but appears to be absent from the United Kingdom. It is relatively unimportant as a pest in Europe and it is said to have been introduced into the U.S.A. in the eighteenth century in straw from Russia. The name comes from the German troops from the province of Hesse who evidently used this straw. The Hessian Fly attacks wheat, barley and rye but it is as a pest of wheat that it has become one of the best documented among insect pests. Most crop losses appear to occur in the U.S.A. The lower part of the plant stem is injured, usually below ground. Sap is withdrawn from the stems so that the plant is weakened and falls over before harvest. Plants may also be attacked in the autumn and spring. They become bluish in colour and stand up more stiffly.

The adult flies are seldom seen, being tiny insects. All the injury is caused by the feeding of the larvae, which are white, headless and legless. The winter is passed in this stage, concealed in a brown puparium found underneath the leaf sheath. These puparia are called 'flax seeds', which they resemble. The adult flies emerge in the spring and the females deposit large numbers of eggs on the wheat but only on plants with two or more leaves. The larvae descend into the ensheathing leaf where they feed—they never bore into the shoot but soon become fully fed and pupate and are flax seeds again. The new adults occur in August and eggs are again laid on winter wheat there being usually two generations in a year.

#### METHODS OF CONTROL

In the U.S.A., a method of avoiding losses from Hessian Fly has been worked out. Sowing is timed to take place after the adults, which have emerged in the summer, have disappeared, that is sowing on 'fly free dates'. If no wheat or alternative cereal is available for egg laying, the adults cannot deposit any eggs. Wheat plants, which germinate from shed grain, provide oviposition sites for the females and therefore should be destroyed. Infested stubble after harvest, should be ploughed under immediately to prevent the flax seeds from giving rise to summer adults. By adopting these measures, losses from Hessian Fly can be avoided. In Europe, the same methods of control could be practised but they are unnecessary.

### *Contarinia tritici* Kirby<br>*Sitodiplosis mosellana* Gehin

These two species of gall midges occur in the inflorescences of wheat in all the wheat growing countries, although it is doubtful if both species occur in the U.S.A. where midges of this type are not important pests. The larvae of both species feed on the developing grain, which subsequently shrivels. Although midge larvae are always found in wheat ears, it is doubtful how much injury they cause. Barnes (1941) recorded ear infestation over several years showing that the percentage grain attack seldom exceeded 2%. The number of larvae per ear is about 5 and seldom exceeds 40.

The life-cycle is annual, starting with the deposition of the eggs in the flowers. After becoming fully grown, the larvae drop to the soil where they remain until the following year when they pupate. Every year a partial second generation occurs, which lives on grasses, particularly couch grass *(Agropyron repens)*. The life-cycle of *Sitodiplosis* is similar to that of *Contarinia* but the actual larvae are easily distinguished, those of the former are orange in colour whereas those of the latter are lemon-yellow. *Sitodiplosis* never has a second generation as has *Contarinia* and larvae may remain many years in the soil before pupating and emerging as adults.

### METHOD OF CONTROL

There are no control measures against these insects. Probably it is best practice to use resistant varieties but, at present, only degrees of resistance are known. In any case, it is unlikely that resistant varieties would be grown on these grounds alone. Attempts to use insecticides against the ovipositing females in the summer months, mainly DDT, have been successful only on a pilot scale. In Eire, field spraying has been tried following certain bad years but it is doubtful if it is economically or practically feasible to take action against wheat midges.

### *Leptohylemyia coarctata* Fall.

The Wheat Bulb Fly is an important pest in Europe, especially in the United Kingdom. It occurs throughout the northern wheat-growing lands to a greater or lesser extent and is primarily a pest of wheat, but can attack barley and rye. Oats are immune. The Wheat Bulb Fly is a shoot-boring insect which destroys complete plants or ear bearing shoots. Crops in badly attacked fields may be totally destroyed.

The life-cycle of the Wheat Bulb Fly is peculiar in that eggs are deposited during the summer months in bare soil, which is either uncropped or incompletely covered by a crop. Eggs are deposited in fields some of which may not carry a crop suitable for attack, and remain unhatched in the soil until the following year by which time many have died. Hatching usually takes place in February. The larvae move through the soil and bore directly into the stems of wheat seedlings. Often, the plant possesses at this time, only a single shoot which is killed by the attack. Pupation takes place in the soil about two months later and the new flies emerge in the summer. Egg numbers in the soil have been assessed from time to time, usually with a view to advising if the field is safe for wheat growing. Over 1 million eggs per acre is not uncommon and Raw and Lofty (1957) showed that over 2 million can occur. Very severe losses occurred in England in 1953 when over 200,000 acres were affected (Gough, 1957) largely from a combination of heavy egg deposition and poor winter growing conditions.

### METHODS OF CONTROL

It is well known that Wheat Bulb Fly damages wheat when it is taken after a fallow but the insect occurs in wheat when this crop is taken after potatoes. Such fields are selected by the flies for egg laying as the soil is exposed and in Germany, the insect is known as the Fallow Fly. With this knowledge, it is easy to avoid Wheat Bulb Fly by taking a crop other than wheat but this simple procedure is not always possible as fallowing is a common preparation of the land for winter wheat and probably was the reason for the development of the peculiar life-cycle of the fly. Wheat is frequently taken after potatoes, as the crop will make use of the residues of heavy fertilizers whereas the soil would be too rich for either oats or beans.

Wheat, when it is well grown, can withstand heavy attack from Wheat Bulb Fly, in fact, Raw and Lofty (1957) state that tillered wheat showed no loss from infestations up to 30% and even an infestation of 80% gave a reasonable yield. Therefore, wheat should be sown early in England, that is before November 15th. Wheat sown after this date has not tillered before the time of the attack the following year and can be totally destroyed.

In recent years, seed-dressings have been introduced to minimise losses from Wheat Bulb Fly. Early dressings contained 40% gamma BHC used at 0·2% by weight on the seed. In England, such dressings were widely used as they also controlled wireworm and, because they also contained mercury, fungal diseases. Heptachlor, aldrin and dieldrin were also used as seed-dressings (Way, 1959). The insecticides could be introduced into the soil by means of combine drilling but this method was more wasteful and expensive (Maskall and Gair, 1961).

*Oscinella frit* L.

The Frit Fly is a shoot-boring insect, widely distributed throughout Europe. It also occurs in Canada but is absent from the U.S.A. It is primarily a pest of oats occurring every year to a greater or lesser extent. Thomas (1954) states that 5–10% of the shoots are attacked every year and Frit Fly also attacks grasses, particularly *Lolium pratense* in which it passes the winter. Losses occur either from the first generation attacking the shoots of oats or from the second generation attacking the ears. A third generation occurs in the autumn and sometimes attacks wheat.

Frit Fly has three generations a year. Starting with egg laying on the leaves of oats at the end of May, the larvae bore downwards into the ensheathing leaf and enter the main stem. This induces tillers to be produced to take the place of the damaged shoot so that attacked plants assume a tufted appearance as more shoots are attacked. The larvae pupate in the stems and the flies emerge to start the second generation in July. Eggs are deposited on the glumes of the ears and the larvae feed on the kernels while they are soft and milky. Not only the ears are attacked by the second generation but also the shoots if these are available. Sometimes the larvae boring downwards affect the rachis of the ears so that they emerge 'blind' containing no grains at the top. The flies of the third generation appear in September and deposit eggs on grasses. Eggs are laid on cereals if available as may arise from grain shed at harvest. These larvae overwinter in these plants.

METHODS OF CONTROL

Early sowing is the simplest way to avoid damage from Frit Fly. Oats sown before the end of March in England, suffer little because the larvae fail to gain entry to the stem as the internodes have elongated and hardened. Late sown oats should be avoided and replaced by either barley or spring wheat. The attack on the ears is quite distinct from that on the shoots and early sown oats are also less liable to ear attack. Winter oats and wheat are seldom attacked by the third generation unless they are sown after a grass ley already infested with Frit Fly when the larvae change over from one plant to another. Some varieties of spring oats are said to be less susceptible than others but there are few real differences between varieties.

Direct action against Frit Fly is scarcely possible on a field scale although Jepson (1959) showed that spraying with DDT or parathion eliminated Frit Fly attack. The ear attack could also be decreased, but such measures are hardly practical or economic and the gain in yield is not great (Empson, 1958). Many attemps have been made to use insecticidal seed-dressings against Frit Fly and those containing aldrin, dieldrin and gamma BHC have all given positive but variable results. Seed-dressings have not therefore been adopted as routine measures against Frit Fly.

REFERENCES
BARNES, H. F., *J. Anim. Ecol.,* **10,** 94 (1941)
EMPSON, D. W., *Plant Pathol.,* **7,** 76 (1958)
GOUGH, H. C., *Bull. Entomol. Res.,* **48,** 447 (1957)
JEPSON, W. F., *Ann. Appl. Biol.,* **47,** 463 (1959)
LEGOWSKI, T. J. and GOULD, H. C., *Bull Entomol. Res.,* **52,** 443 (1961)
MASKELL, F. E., and GAIR, R., *Bull. Ent. Res.* **52,** 683 (1961)
RAW, F., and LOFTY, J. R., *Plant Pathol.,* **6,** 51 (1957)
THOMAS, J. D., *Plant Pathol.,* **3,** 55 (1954)
WAY, M. J., *Ann. Appl. Biol.,* **47,** 783 (1959)

## LEPIDOPTERA

### *Syringopais temperatella* Ld. *(Tineoidea)*

This little insect is known as the Cereal Leaf Miner (Fig. 2.1). The caterpillar feeds between the upper and lower leaf surfaces of cereals, particularly wheat, and it is especially common in the eastern Mediterranean region including Cyprus, Turkey, Syria, and Israel. It also lives on barley, oats and grasses. If the attack is severe, the entire leaf area is destroyed and the plant shrivels in dry weather.

The life-cycle is unusual in that the larval stage, immediately after emergence from the egg, does not feed but shelters in a cocoon in the surface soil where it remains until January. As the weather becomes warmer the larvae become active and enter the leaf blades of the cereals, feeding on the tissues. Many larvae may be found in a single leaf. When the larvae are fully grown, they pupate in the stubble or soil. The adult moths, which are golden and black in colour, appear in April and again deposit eggs in the soil, each female laying about 100. The abundance of the insect is much influenced by the weather and large numbers appear after rain.

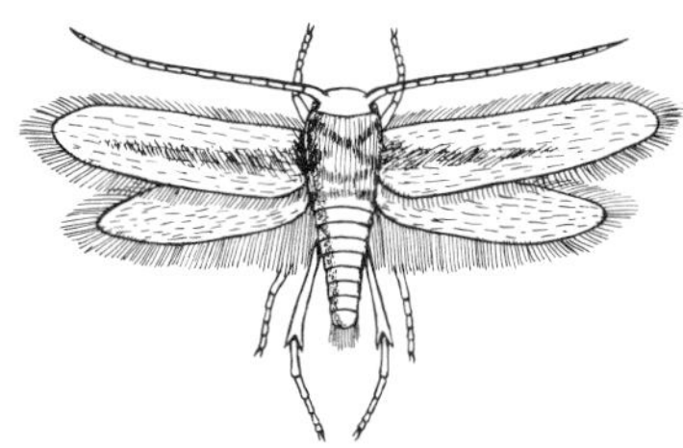

*Fig. 2.1.* Syringopais temperatella *(adult)*

METHODS OF CONTROL

Formerly, ploughing to desiccate exposed larvae was the only method known and several ploughings were necessary to ensure that most were killed. Many larvae, however, were so deep in the soil that they escaped exposure. The frequency of ploughing was also determined by the previous crop. Nowadays, BHC and aldrin are applied to the attacked foliage as dusts or sprays. Gamma BHC at the rate of 500 gm per hectare in January is often applied with hormone weedkillers (Rivnay, 1956).

REFERENCE
RIVNAY, E., *R.A.E.,* **46,** 417 (1956)

## HEMIPTERA

### *Eurygaster integriceps* Put. / *Aelia rostrata* Boh. *(Pentatomidae)*

These large bugs occur on wheat in the eastern Mediterranean region. *Eurygaster* (Fig. 2.2), known as the 'Sunni' pest, occurs in Turkey, Persia, Syria and adjoining countries and in small numbers, in Russia where it borders Turkey. *Aelia* is also found in Turkey on the central Anatolian plateau. Both pests injure wheat by feeding on the young leaves but also on the grains when they are milky.

*Eurygaster* is a large bug about 15mm long, brown to grey in colour with black markings. The adults hibernate in the mountains, move down to the fields in April and appear in the wheat. Small clusters of eggs are deposited on the leaves, each female laying 150–200. New adults occur in June. The adults and

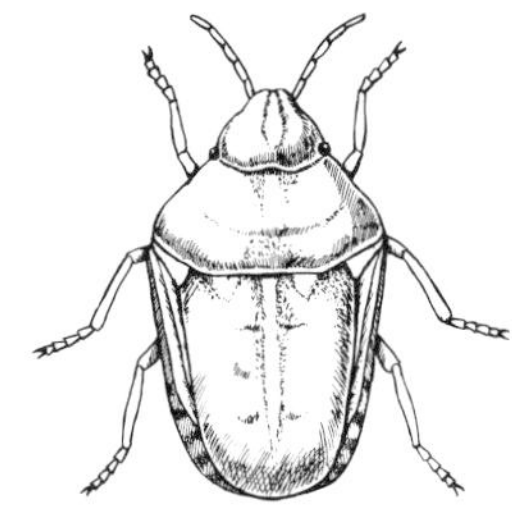

*Fig. 2.2.* Eurygaster integriceps *(adult)*

later instars feed on the developing ears causing the grain to shrivel so that both the quality and yield is reduced. In due course, the adults move back to the mountains (Brown, 1962 and Zoebelein, 1962). Barley, rye and maize are attacked and the bugs can also survive on grasses. *Aelia* is a red bug, smaller than *Eurygaster* but similar in life cycle and habits. Several species of *Eurygaster* and *Aelia* have been recorded and the dominant species in Russia is said to be *A. sibirca* Reut.

### METHODS OF CONTROL

Abundance depends on the weather, especially on there being some rain in spring during the feeding period of the nymphs. Normally, the insect occurs in pockets where severe injury to wheat can be caused and it is in these areas that action against the pest must be taken. Formerly, hand picking the adults was the only control but recently attempts have been made to employ insecticides, especially applied from the air. The most effective insecticide against *Eurygaster* has been parathion applied as a 0·75% dust but recently, newer and less hazardous insecticides have been tried. DDT/BHC dusts and sprays are effective against the young bugs but against the later instars an effective material is trichlorotipon (Dipterex) sprayed at 1 lb per acre. *Aelia* is more susceptible to insecticides. Treatment is necessary at the very beginning of the invasion before adults spread out and egg laying begins.

## Aphids on Cereals *(Aphididae)*

*Sitobium avenae* F. (= *Macrosiphum granarium* Kirby) is the most common aphid on cereals and is found throughout northern Europe, America, parts of Africa and in all countries bordering the Mediterranean. It is a large aphid, usually green but also light brown. The cornicles are long and black. The sexual females deposit eggs on grasses in the autumn. This aphid inhabits the ears of cereals but the damage caused has not been assessed and control measures are seldom, if ever, taken against it.

*Schizaphis graminium* Rond., the cereal green bug, is also extremely common on cereals and is generally distributed throughout the world except the United Kingdom. The aphid overwinters either as an egg, deposited on cereals and grasses, or as an aphid reproducing slowly. If numerous, it can destroy cereal crops especially wheat, more often, however, only patches in the crop fail. The abundance of *Schizaphis* depends on the availability of food, mild winters enable numbers to build up in the early part of the year on self-sown plants. If necessary aerial application with insecticides can be carried out and has proved effective. Demeton-Methyl (Metasystox) is the best at 12 fl oz. per acre and has been used with success in South Africa (Snyman, 1959). BHC dust was successful formerly (Dahomy, 1951).

*Rhopalosiphum* species occur on cereals in summer. The egg stage is on fruit trees but the exact identity of different species is in doubt. *R. cratagellum* Theob. (= *insertum* Wlk.) is one species which over-winters on apples and transfers to cereals, mainly oats, in summer and is an important pest in some years. It is a green aphid, with rusty patches at the base of the cornicles.

*R. padi* L. ( = *Aphis avenae* Theob.) is a dark green species. The eggs occur on cherry and the summer forms fly to cereals. This species transmits Barley Yellow Dwarf—a virus disease in New Zealand.

*R. maidis* Fitch (= *Aphis maidis*) is the Cereal Leaf Aphid which occurs throughout the world, principally in the warmer regions. The life cycle occurs wholly on cereals and grasses. It is found also on maize, sorghum, and sugar-cane. It overwinters as an aphid, no eggs having been found, but some observers state that it descends to the roots of plants in the winter. In Australia, it also transmits Barley Yellow Dwarf. It is a greenish-grey aphid with black cornicles.

METHODS OF CONTROL

Where necessary, insecticides can be used, especially where aerial spraying is possible. A quick acting product is needed in order to eliminate the infestation immediately. Lowe (1962) reported that the control of aphids did not necessarily lead to a reduction of losses from Barley Yellow Dwarf virus. Application of insecticides with hormone weedkillers for the treatment of cereals has been suggested to cut cost.

REFERENCES

BROWN, E. S., *Bull. Entomol. Res.*, **53**, 445 (1962)
DAHOMY, R. G., *J. Econ. Entomol*, **44**, 954 (1951)
LOWE, A. D., *New Zealand J. Agr.* **105**, 173 (1962)
SNYMAN, A., *Veld*, **19**, 12 (1959)
ZOEBELEIN, G., *Pflanzenschut Nachr*, **15**, 198 (1962)

NEMATODA

*Heterodera major* O. Schm.

This species is known as the Cereal Root Eelworm. Early records of attacks by a *Heterodera* type eelworm on cereals were thought to be by *H. schachtii* and were reported in many northern European countries. More recently, attacks causing losses in cereals have been recorded from South Africa, Australia and Canada and the eelworm is also known in America.

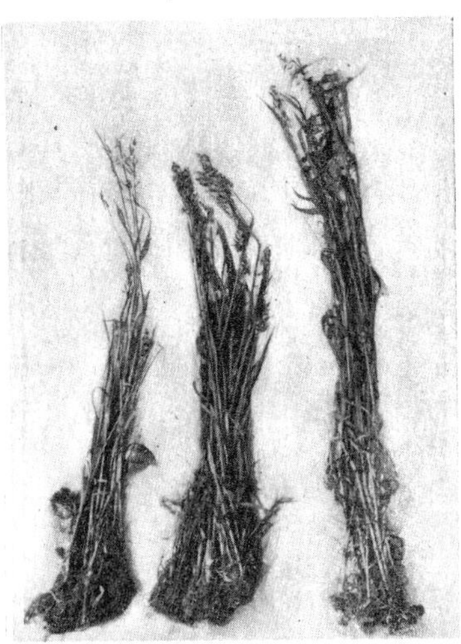

*Plate 2.2 Cereal root eelworm on oats—heavily attacked on left, normal oats on right*

The cyst is lemon shaped but with a less tapering vulva than in the Beet Eelworm, *H. schachtii*. The larvae begin to escape from the cyst as the soil warms up but not all escape in one season. Oats are severely attacked and barley and wheat stunted in growth on some soils (Plate 2.2). The roots of the plants are invaded by the nematodes and they become matted and are unable to penetrate into the deeper soil. Attacked plants are dwarfed and the foliage discoloured. The host range appears to be restricted to the *Graminae*.

METHODS OF CONTROL

In the United Kingdom, the eelworm is widely distributed but appears to cause most losses in regions of light soils, particularly in Shropshire on the Bunter sandstone. It is in such regions that oats form an important part of the rotation. The numbers of eelworms have increased because of the tendency to grow oats in forage mixtures as well as short term leys containing a high proportion of rye-grass which is susceptible to the Cereal Root Eelworm. The best control is to return the land to grass for a longer period in order to decrease the eelworm numbers in the soil, to build up the humus content and the general level of fertility.

*Ditylenchus dipsaci* Kuhn.

The Stem Eelworm is not a cyst forming species and is of minor interest as it attacks mainly oats and rye which are not cereals of much importance. All races of this eelworm are polyphagous, attacking a wide range of weeds on which they are able to maintain themselves between more susceptible crops. The oat race causes the base of the stems to swell and a distortion of the tillers. Such plants produce few ears. Cool moist weather favours its development, as do clay soils and wet areas such as river valleys.

### METHODS OF CONTROL

Fortunately, certain oat varieties are resistant to Stem Eelworm. In the United Kingdom, the winter varieties Grey Winter, Manod, Penant, Picton and Milford are resistant and should be grown in fields known to be subject to Stem Eelworm.

## RUST DISEASES

Although the rust diseases of wheat occasionally caused severe damage in Europe, it was the opening up of the enormous wheat-growing areas in the U.S.A. and Canada in the last century which provided the rusts with perfect conditions for their multiplication and spread. The total losses due to the three major rusts have been put at 10% of the crop (Stakman *et al.*, 1957).

Of the three, black stem rust is, without doubt, the most destructive of all the wheat rusts, and it does more harm in the world than all the other diseases put together (Beaumont, 1959). Yellow rust is common in the more temperate wheat-growing areas, particularly Europe, but it is unimportant in the U.S.A.s wheat belt. The third disease, brown rust is very widespread, but it only causes losses of economic importance in wheat areas which have high humidity and high temperatures during the summer, such as parts of the U.S.A. and India.

Barley is not as susceptible to the rust diseases as wheat, but occasionally it suffers from severe attacks of black stem rust. The same fungus can also attack oats, but crown rust, which is specific to oats and some grasses, is usually the more damaging.

REFERENCES

BEAUMONT, A., *Diseases of Farm Crops*, 33, W. H. & L. Collingridge Ltd., London (1959)

STAKMAN, E. C. and HARRAR, J. G., *Principles of Plant Pathology*, 345, The Ronald Press Company, New York (1957)

### Black Stem Rust *(Puccinia graminis* Pers.*)*

It is both convenient and logical to start a description of world crop diseases by considering black stem rust, known in the U.S.A. as stem rust, because it is the major disease of wheat, the world's major crop, and is also of importance on both barley and oats. It is a dramatic story which has been told by Large (1940).

The life history of black stem rust was first unravelled by De Bary who published his results in 1865. The disease makes its appearance on the wheat during the summer. There are numerous reddish-brown spots, roughly oval in shape, scattered about on the leaves and stems. These spots are composed of the uredospores (summer spores) (Fig. 2.3a) which are vegetative single-celled spores capable of spreading the disease rapidly from plant to plant, and if conditions are favourable, an epidemic may quickly result.

In the autumn the teleutospores (winter spores) are produced in the pustules (Fig. 2.3f). These are dark brown spores which are double-celled (Fig. 2.3b). They remain attached to the wheat debris and are the means by which the fungus overwinters.

De Bary who was investigating the life cycle of the fungus by growing it on wheat plants had had no difficulty in sowing the summer spores on the wheat. They germinated readily and produced more summer spores and the winter spores later in the season. But when he sowed the winter spores on wheat in the spring, they germinated but no infection took place. This was a detective problem worthy of a mycological Sherlock Holmes. De Bary realised that there must be another or alternate host on which the teleutospores could develop and remembering the farmer's long-held belief that there was some association between the barberry and black stem rust, he tried sowing the winter spores on barberry. The winter spores germinated (Fig. 2.3c) and produced sporidia (minute spores) which then infected the barberry leaves. In due course the barberry leaves became covered in rust spores. De Bary did not succeed in getting the spores from the

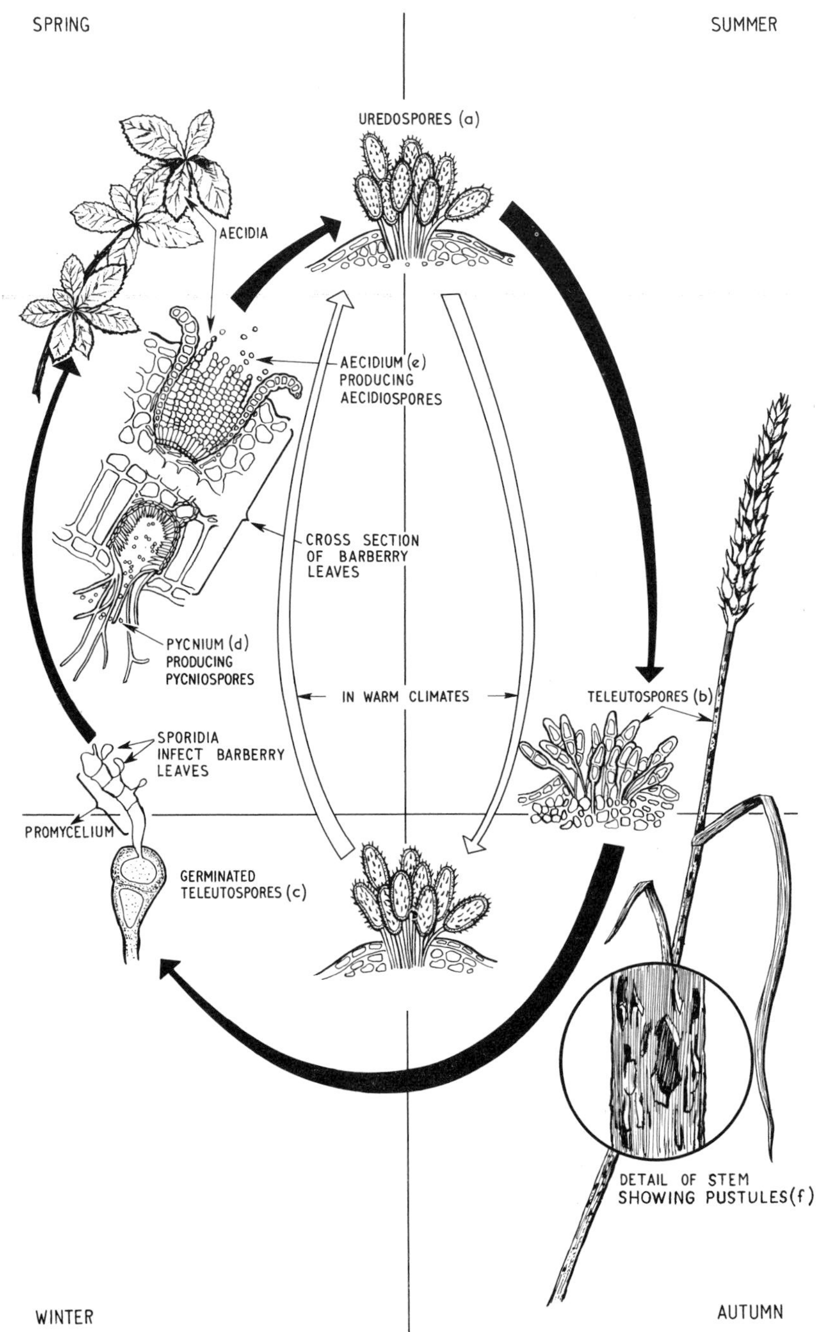


*Fig. 2.3. Life Cycle of Black Stem Rust. (a) Uredospores, (b) Teleutospores, (c) Germination of teleutospore with development of promycelium and sporidia, (d) Pycnium and pycniospore, (e) Aecidium and aecidiospore, (f) Teleutospore pustules on the stem*

barberry to infect the wheat, but the oft repeated observation that black stem rust was worst in the neighbourhood of barberry bushes made him certain that he had discovered the host plant for the winter spores and the way in which the disease started up again in the spring.

It was not until 1927 that further investigation showed that the life of the fungus on the barberry bush was more complicated than at first appeared. It will be recalled that the teleutospores germinate and produce minute spores called sporidia. Careful observation showed that the sporidia infected the barberry leaf, and that this was followed by the development of another type of fruiting body, with a flask-like shape, known as a pycnium (Fig. 2.3d). Each pycnium produces spores with either male or female characteristics, which are exuded in a sticky mass. After union of the spores of opposite sexes has taken place, the fungus penetrates the barberry leaf producing a second type of fruiting body, the aecidium (Fig. 2.3e), the cluster cup stage of the fungus. These cups produce quantities of orange-yellow aecidiospores which are carried by the wind. Those which alight on a susceptible crop, such as wheat, germinate and start the summer cycle of the disease.

The life-history of the fungus appears complicated because of the numerous names used to describe the different fruiting bodies and their respective spores. The subject is shown diagrammatically in Fig. 2.3.

## METHODS OF CONTROL

The enormous losses of grain due to black stem rust eventually spurred the plant pathologists to look for some way of minimising them. The part played by the barberry bushes as the alternate host made it obvious that the first improvement would be their removal. This idea was followed up in Denmark in 1903 and by 1917 when most of the bushes had gone, the results were most favourable. The demand for wheat in the U.S.A. was stimulated by the First World War and made increased production imperative. Consequently, when the U.S. Department of Agriculture was considering ways of encouraging this, the eradication of the barberry, the value of which had been shown in Denmark, was the obvious first step. The campaign which started in 1918 involved the tracking down and destruction of the bushes over millions of acres. By 1930, when the work had been practically completed, no less than 18·5 million barberry bushes had been destroyed. The elimination of the alternate host reduced the losses due to black stem rust from 57 to 9 million bushels of wheat.

But the victory, for victory it was, was a limited one, due to the ability of the fungus to overwinter on wheat plants growing in the warmer climates of Mexico and southern Texas. Each spring, southerly winds carry the spores northward, so that the disease moves steadily further and further north, until the whole wheat belt is infected.

Other methods of defence were therefore necessary, and these were provided by the plant breeder. Biffen in Cambridge had observed that the wheat plants in his plots showed marked variation in resistance to the yellow rust. Breeding experiments started in 1900 had shown that the inheritance of resistance to the yellow rust was due to a single factor which behaved according to Mendel's laws. His results, published in 1907, made it clear that the plant breeder had a vital part to play in producing plants which resisted disease. This lead was followed by the initiation of a rust-resistant wheat breeding campaign by the U.S. Department of Agriculture in 1904 and eventually by the setting up of a special wheat-breeding department at the Minnesota Experiment Station. Canada was also vitally interested and set up a Rust Research Laboratory at Winnipeg in 1925.

Meanwhile, in 1916, Stakman had observed that varieties of wheat differed in their reaction to rusts collected from various places. This lead was followed up and it was eventually found that the black stem rust fungus produced many strains, which could be typed by their effect on twelve varieties from five species of wheat. Using this technique, no less than 250 physiological races have been detected, with the probability of many more still to the typed.

This discovery made it likely that the plant breeder would be faced with difficulties, a forecast which has indeed been borne out in practice. The first important resistant wheat variety introduced by the Minnesota Experiment Station was Thatcher in 1934, while the Winnipeg workers released Renown in 1936 (Hanna, 1957).

During the years from 1938 to 1950, the spring wheats in the North American Wheat Belt flourished with the minimum of damage from black stem rust due to the eradication of the barberry and the culture of resistant varieties. The plant pathologists and plant breeders might indeed be pleased by the results of their joint labours. The first cloud on the horizon appeared in 1950 when a new race of the fungus appeared, which could attack the resistant varieties and, as had so often happened in the past, it rapidly multiplied until in 1953 and 1954 it destroyed about 25% of the bread wheat.

The programme for breeding new varieties of rust-resistant barley and oats has encountered the same difficulties as that for wheat. Their introduction has been followed by the appearance of new races of the rust fungus which are capable of attacking them. Fortunately, the continued raising of new varieties has prevented any reduction in crop yields.

It is clear that the fungus has not been beaten. It is likely that the contest between the plant breeder and the fungus will be a never-ending one.

Fungicides have, of course, been looked at as possible methods of control. Sulphur dusts were under trial between 1925 and 1931 and it was demonstrated that the disease could be checked by chemical means and an increase both in yield and grade obtained.

Since then, trials of other fungicides have taken place and some of the newer fungicides have been found most effective. For example, zineb alone and mixtures of nickel sulphate and dithiocarbamate sprays have given excellent results, but the cost of treatment is high relative to the value of the increased yield. There is an obvious opening here for a new fungicide, probably with systemic properties, but although many of the large chemical companies must be looking for such a compound, it has not yet been found.

The black stem rust story is a record of a fascinating struggle of man versus a fungus, in which each side has scored remarkable victories. With two powerful opponents in the ring, the future rounds will be of great interest to plant pathologists, and of vital importance to mankind.

REFERENCES

HANNA, W. F., *Plant Protection Conference 1956*, 37, Butterworths Scientific Publications, London (1957).

LARGE, E. C., *The Advance of the Fungi*, Jonathan Cape, London (1940)

## Yellow Rust (*Puccinia striiformis* Westend. [Syn. *P. glumarum* Erikss. and E. Henn.])

While black stem rust is the dramatic and dominant rust in North America, yellow rust is the most important of the rusts attacking wheat in Europe (Butler *et al.*, 1949). Yellow rust is occasionally destructive, but in most seasons the crop loss in not severe.

Although yellow rust has a very widespread distribution, it does most damage in the cooler areas where wheat is grown, such as Europe, high altitude areas in North and South America, northern Canada, and Japan (Stakman *et al.*, 1957).

The fungus is easily seen when the attack starts as it produces elongated orange-yellow stripes on the leaves parallel to the leaf veins, hence the American name stripe rust. The stripes contain the uredospores (summer spores), which spread the disease during the summer and being winter hardy, are the means by which the fungus survives from one year to the next. It also overwinters as an infection on grasses such as couch and cocksfoot, and when conditions become more favourable in the spring, produces the summer spores which infect those grasses which are susceptible. Temperature controls the rate at which the disease spreads, cool weather favouring it, hot and dry weather arresting.

Teleutospores (winter spores) are also produced but they appear to be functionless. No alternate host is known.

### METHODS OF CONTROL

In dealing with black stem rust, mention was made of Biffen's early breeding work on rust resistance having been carried out with yellow rust. Biffen, in the course of his work, made crosses between Square Head's Master and a Russian rust resistant variety, and from this cross selected a variety which was named Little Joss. Its excellence may be judged from the fact that for many years it was the most important wheat grown in England.

The discovery of physiological strains of the yellow rust fungus makes it clear that the problem of breeding a rust resistant wheat variety is more complex than it was at first thought to be. Fortunately, the strains are, as yet, few in number, but it does mean that a potential new variety must be tested against the known strains to make sure that it is not susceptible to them. As with black stem rust, fungicides are at present of no practical value, hence the farmer is dependent on the wheat breeder to keep this disease in check.

REFERENCES

BUTLER, E. J. and JONES, S. G., *Plant Pathology*, 352, Macmillan & Co. Ltd., London (1949)

STAKMAN, E. C. and HARRAR, J. G., *Principles of Plant Pathology*, 347, The Ronald Press Company, New York (1957)

## Brown Rust (*Puccinia recondita* Desm. [Syn. *P. triticina* Erikss.])

Brown rust, known as leaf rust in the United States, has a world-wide distribution and is common wherever wheat is grown. Its relative importance as a source of loss is debateable. Chester (1946) in his monograph on this disease claimed that it caused even greater losses than black stem rust. The more generally accepted view is that brown rust is comparatively unimportant in the temperate parts of the world, but is responsible for serious crop losses in areas with high humidity and high temperatures, for example, in parts of the United States, particularly the south-eastern States, the Ohio and Mississippi Valleys, and in India (Stakman *et al.*, 1957).

Brown rust pustules are mainly confined to the leaves, but occasionally occur on the leaf sheaths and stems. The pustules are distributed irregularly over the leaf, a character which distinguishes the disease from yellow rust where the pustules typically run parallel to the veins, forming stripes.

The uredospores (summer spores) are bright orange at first, but darken with age, and eventually turn brown. They are winter hardy and provide the usual means by which the disease carries over from one season to the next. Black teleutospores (winter spores) occur but appear to be unimportant. The alternate hosts, some of the meadow-rues (*Thalictrum* spp.), were not discovered until 1921 but like the teleutospores, do not seem to play an important part in the life cycle. There are, however, at least 140 physiological strains of the fungus, and it is possible that the sexual cycle may be of importance in producing new strains (U.S.D.A., 1953).

### METHOD OF CONTROL

The breeding programme for brown rust resistance began in 1926 in the Botany Department of Kansas Station and was in addition to its earlier work on resistance to black stem rust. The plant breeder has produced a number of varieties which are less susceptible than the older ones. Research on similar lines has also been carried out in both Australia and the Argentine.

A consideration of the qualities now regarded as desirable in a good wheat, such as high yield, strong straw, etc., combined with resistance to both fungi and insects shows how complex wheat breeding has become, and how much the world owes to those who raise new varieties to meet these needs.

REFERENCES

CHESTER, K. S., *The Nature and Prevention of the Cereal Rusts as exemplified in the Leaf Rust of Wheat,* Chronica Botanica Co., Waltham, Mass. (1946)

STAKMAN, E. C. and HARRAR, J. G., *Principles of Plant Pathology,* 347, The Ronald Press Company, New York (1957)

United States Department of Agriculture, *Plant Diseases, the Yearbook of Agriculture,* 332, The U.S. Government Printing Office, Washington, D.C. (1953)

## Crown Rust of Oats (*Puccinia coronata* Corda)

Crown rust is to be found in most parts of the world where oats are grown and attacks the foliage, severely affected leaves appearing golden yellow at first glance. Inspection of a rusted leaf will show that the pustules containing the uredospores (summer spores) are orange-coloured, and are present on both surfaces of the leaf. It is probably the most serious disease of oats.

Early attacks, which occur more frequently in the warmer oat-growing areas, may injure the foliage so severely that the grain does not fill out normally, thus causing serious crop losses. Late attacks such as those experienced in the more northerly regions do not do much harm.

The fungus is restricted to members of the oat family and certain grasses, but it does not infect either wheat or barley. There does not appear to be much cross infection from oats to grasses or vice versa due to physiological specialisation of the numerous races.

The life-cycle of crown rust has many similarities with black stem rust. The uredospores of *P. coronata* are produced in enormous numbers during the summer and spread the disease throughout the crop. The telutospores (overwintering spores) appear in the autumn and are clustered together in black pustules. The fungus persists from one season to the next in two ways, as a living mycelium on winter oats, and as teleutospores on the oat stubble.

In the spring the teleutospores germinate giving rise to sporidia which can only infect buckthorn (*Rhamnus* spp.) the alternate host. The fungus grows rapidly on the buckthorn and forms the cluster cups and their offspring, the aecidiospores, which are dispersed by the wind and carry the disease back to the oats. The alternate host stage can be important in areas where the oats are spring sown, but where winter oats are grown, it is obviously not essential to the survival of the fungus.

### METHODS OF CONTROL

Campaigns to eradicate buckthorn have been organised in those parts of the world such as Wisconsin, U.S.A., where the presence of the alternate host is responsible for the spring infection. This has its limitations so that the main defence against crown rust comes from the use of resistant varieties, a development which has already had considerable success.

## HEAD SMUTS

The head smuts are caused by a group of closely related fungi which produce their spores inside the cereal grains. They can be conveniently divided into two groups, the covered smuts in which the spore masses are enclosed within the seed coat, and the loose smuts where the spores are exposed so that the blackened heads are readily seen.

Bunt, or stinking smut of wheat, is the best-known of the group. Not only has it been responsible for serious crop losses and for contamination of the flour, it has also been the subject of investigation for more than 200 years.

The damage done by the smut diseases is now relatively small, thanks to the labours of plant pathologists, plant breeders and organic chemists who have devised efficient methods of controlling them.

The world's smut fungi are described in the textbook by Fischer *et al.* (1957).

REFERENCE

FISCHER, G. W. and HOLTON, C. S., *Biology and Control of the Smut Fungi,* The Ronald Press Company, New York (1957)

## Bunt (*Tilletia caries* [Dc.] Tul.)

To our forefathers, a disease known as bunt or stinking smut was a serious threat to their bread supplies, for bad attacks could destroy half the crop. Today, the methods of controlling it are so effective that bunt has become so rare that it is almost a museum curiosity. How this has been achieved has been described by Large (1940).

The disease is seen in the ears of infected wheat plants, where the attacked grains, known as bunt balls, are filled with a fishy smelling black powder (Plate 2.3). The diseased and healthy grains ripen at the same time and when the wheat is threshed, the bunt balls break up releasing the black powder which contaminates the sound grain. In earlier days when there was a poor harvest, this contaminated grain had to be used for milling, producing a discoloured and unpleasant smelling flour. It is probable that the ginger in gingerbread was originally added to mask the odour of the bunt.

The earliest scientific investigations of this disease were carried out by a remarkable Frenchman, Mathieu Tillet, who was Master of the Mint at Troyes, about 90 miles west of Paris. His hobby was agriculture in which he must have achieved a considerable reputation, as he was approached by the Royal Academy of Literature, Science and Arts of Bordeaux, with the proposal that he should investigate the cause and possible cure of bunt.

In 1750 when the work began, there were various beliefs about the reason for the bunted grains. It was reported as being due to the use of certain manures, the malignity

*Plate 2.3. Bunt of wheat. Healthy ear on the left, diseased on the right (A Plant Protection photograph)*

of fogs, the failure of the fertilization of the grain, excessive humidity or violent sunstroke on the water-soaked heads.

It was part of Tillet's philosophy that problems such as this could only be solved by experiments. Accordingly, he laid out a trial to test the effects of different treatments such as manuring and contaminating clean seed with bunt dust and their interactions. He did this by dividing a rectangular area of ground into five large blocks, each block receiving a different manurial treatment. Each block was then sub-divided into small plots and sown with grain treated in four different ways. Some of the grain was clean seed mixed with bunt dust, some treated with salt and lime, some with lime only, and the remainder untreated seed.

This ingenious layout enabled him to study the effect of all possible combinations which he thought might be responsible for the disease, while the untreated seed provided a standard with which the other treatments could be compared.

The result was much more clear-cut than Tillet could have expected. Contrary to the accepted belief, the type of manure had no effect on the amount of bunt. The ears with the most bunt were always those from grain which had been intentionally contaminated with bunt dust. It was also clear that the treatment of the grain with a solution of lye reduced the amount of infection. Although the result of the first year's work was so definite, the investigation was continued for three years more in order to verify the findings.

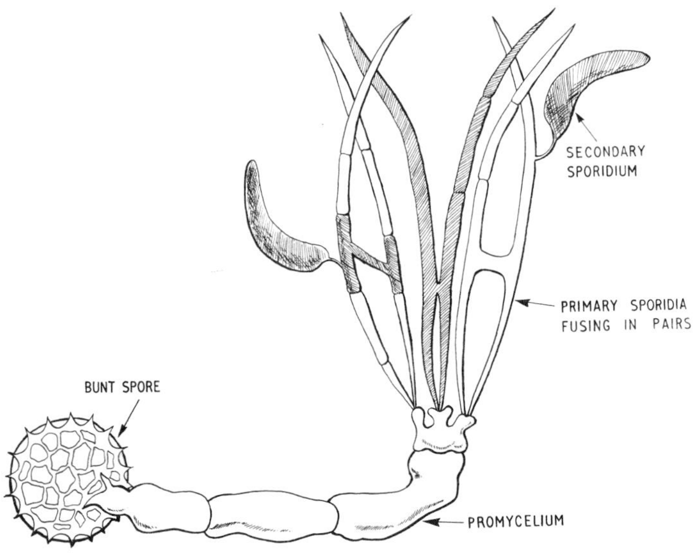


*Fig. 2.4. Bunt of Wheat. Germination of spore and development of promycelium and sporidia*

Monsieur Tillet's 'Dissertation on the cause of the corruption and smutting of the kernels of wheat in the head' was published in 1755. His scientific methods and the results he obtained entitle him to be regarded as the father of experimental plant pathology. The work demonstrated the need for learning more about bunt and the value of treating the seed with a lye solution to reduce the losses from the disease.

The next advance in the study of bunt was also made by a Frenchman, Bénédict Prévost, who published his results in 1807. Prévost made two notable discoveries, that bunt was caused by a fungus, and that the black powder was composed of a mass of fungus spores. He watched the spores germinating in water with his somewhat primitive microscope, and followed the unexpectedly complex process by which sporidia (secondary spores) were formed from the large black mother spore (Fig. 2.4). He surmised that the mycelium of the fungus must penetrate the collar of the young wheat plant and thread its way up the growing stem to the ear, but he was unable to find it in the plant. His forecast was, however, confirmed some fifty years later. His observations made it clear that bunt could be prevented by killing the spores on the surface of the grain.

## METHODS OF CONTROL

Now that the objective was known, it was relatively simple to carry out tests to find substances which would kill the spores. The spores germinated in clean water, but the effect of the chemicals could be determined by adding small quantities of them to the water, and watching the result. Shrewd observation suggested that copper might poison the bunt spores. The hypothesis was tested using various copper compounds. The experiments showed that copper sulphate was most effective. As a result of his researches, Prévost recommended that the wheat should be steeped in a dilute copper sulphate solution for half-an-hour, and then after it had been allowed to drain, it was ready for sowing. Handling damp wheat is an awkward task, and it was not long before farmers were adding lime to the heap of damp grain to dry it before sowing.

The copper sulphate treatment was most effective for the control of bunt, and was so successful that it continued in use for over one hundred years. It is also of historic interest as being the first use of copper as a fungicide. But the steep treatment had two great disadvantages, the difficulty of handling large quantities of wet grain, and the necessity of sowing it soon after treatment.

The steep treatment was eventually superseded by the simple device of mixing powdered copper carbonate with the grain. Grain so treated could be bagged and stored ready for use, a marked advance over the wet process where the grain had to be sown after it had been treated.

A German, Dr. Riehm, working in the agricultural research service, was responsible for the next major advance with his discovery of the effectiveness of an organo-mercurial compound against bunt. The Bayer Company, who had synthesised the 'Chlorphenol Mercury', marketed it in 1915 under the trade name 'Uspulun' for use as a wet steep. The introduction in 1917 of the copper carbonate treatment demonstrated the manifold advantages of a dry treatment, and it was not long before a powder containing the same active ingredient as 'Uspulun' was sold as 'Tillantin' R.

In practice, the new mercury compounds were better than copper in many ways. On wheat, not only did they control bunt, but also gave a partial control of other diseases such as brown foot rot (*Fusarium* spp.). The outstanding success of the mercurial seed dressings was on the main seed-borne diseases of barley and oats, which were unaffected by the copper treatment. The early trials showed that the organo-mercury compounds gave a very high degree of control of barley leaf stripe and covered smut of barley, and also three diseases of oats—leaf spot, covered smut and loose smut. It is not surprising that the mercurial dressings steadily replaced copper in the twenties and thirties and now completely dominate the market.

Since the original introduction of the mercury fungicides, some fifty years ago, many organic compounds of mercury have have been synthesised and tested as seed dressings. The phenylmercury compounds such as phenylmercury acetate are widely used in powder form on account of their safety in use, linked with their low volatility and ease of manufacture. The methyl and ethyl analogues are also very effective compounds due to their volatility which gives them a fumigant action.

All mercury compounds must be handled with care on account of their toxicity to man. In general, the greater the volatility, the greater the risk. In practice, the powder seed dressings based on compounds of low volatility have proved reasonably safe to those handling them, but the more volatile compounds were very dangerous until special machines were developed for applying them to the seed. In these special seed treating machines (see Plate 2.4), all the poisonous vapours are extracted and blown into the air, thereby avoiding any contamination of the atmosphere for those operating the machine.

The more volatile compounds can be formulated in liquid form for seed treatment. This can only be carried out in special machines which mix the grain and the liquid very thoroughly. Due to the small volume of liquid used, the grain remains dry and can be bagged and stored after treatment in just the same way as with powder dressings.

It is fashionable in some circles to decry the use of chemicals in agriculture. To those who take a balanced view, it is marvellous that 1 gramme of mercury can be used to disinfect the wheat required to sow an acre. To it we mainly owe the bunt-free crops of wheat—something which was unknown and unattainable two hundred years ago.

Much effort has been put into the search for a non-poisonous replacement for the mercury seed-dressings, particularly in countries such as France where most of the seed treatment is carried out on the farm where it is not possible to use adequate safety precautions. The search was rewarded by the discovery of the fungicidal properties of hexachlorobenzene (HCB) which was announced in 1945 (Lhoste *et al.*, 1949). HCB is highly specific for the control of *Tilletia* species and has little effect on any of the other seedborne fungi. Its use has developed in places such as Australia where bunt is the major disease on the seed and in western North America and parts of Europe where a very cold winter allows the bunt spores to survive in the soil during the interval between combine harvesting and seed sowing in the spring.

The concentration of HCB required to kill the bunt spores is 200 p.p.m. compared with 16–20 p.p.m. for mercury. Seed dressings containing HCB are formulated as 10% dusts for use at 2 oz per bushel, the usual European rate, and as 40% dusts for application at $\frac{1}{2}$ oz per bushel which is preferred in North America.

More recently, it has been found that maneb is a good wide-spectrum cereal seed-dressing,

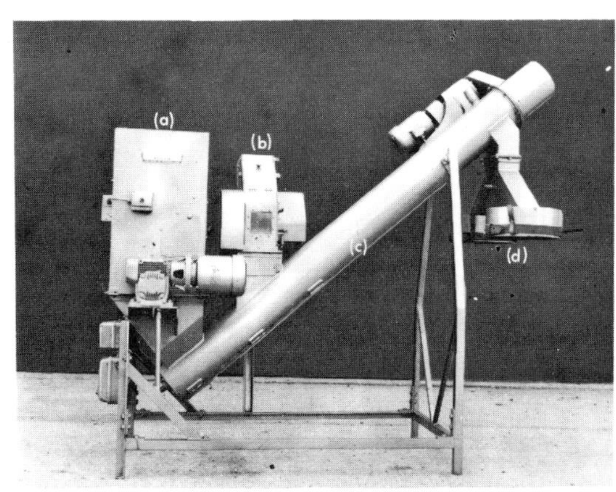


*Plate 2.4. A seed dressing machine (a) seed hopper, (b) seed dressing dispenser, (c) mixing chamber, (d) twin bagging spouts (A Plant Protection photograph)*

effective against bunt and as efficient as the mercurials against glume blotch (*Leptosphaeria nodorum* Müller) and certain species of *Fusarium* (Ponchet *et al.*, 1963). The discovery has been quickly exploited in France where the new seed-dressing has become popular.

The maneb has to be used at the rate of 1,000 p.p.m., about fifty times stronger than that for mercurials, and at the required concentration it is more expensive per bushel of seed than products based on the organo-mercurials. The higher cost of the maneb treatment makes it unlikely that it will replace the standard materials where properly designed seed-treating machinery is available.

Mention must also be made of dual-purpose seed-dressing containing both an insecticide and a fungicide. These were introduced in 1949 (Price Jones, 1956) and have the advantage of greatly increasing the protection of the seedling, virtually ensuring a full stand of wheat under almost all conditions. The majority of dual-purpose materials are formulated as dusts, but small quantities are used as liquids.

The seed-dressing industry has developed in different ways in various parts of the world to suit particular needs. Variations occur in the use of powder and liquid dressings and in the method of application, whether by the farmer, agricultural merchant, or contractor.

The powder seed-dressings in Europe and Australia are used at the rate of 2 oz per bushel of wheat. In North and South America, the lower rate of $\frac{1}{2}$ oz per bushel is preferred and consequently more concentrated powders have to be used. The pattern is similar for liquid seed-dressings, 2 fl oz per bushel in Sweden and the United Kingdom, $\frac{3}{4}$ fl oz in North America.

The powder treatment is the predominant method in Europe, South America, South Africa and Australia. The liquid treatment is popular in North America, where approximately half the grain is treated in this way.

Seed treatment is still done by the farmer himself in some countries such as France, Italy and the Argentine, but it is gradually becoming an industrial process as for example in the United Kingdom where it is mostly done by the agricultural merchant. In other parts of the world the work is carried out by contractors specialising in seed treatment. This can either be done on the farm, as in the U.S.A., Canada and Australia, or at seed treating centres, as in Germany.

The ease with which the seed-dressing can be applied, the small cost and the high efficiency, have resulted in its being used in all the wheat-growing areas of the world. France may indeed be proud of Messieurs Tillet and Prévost who were responsible for introducing a technique which is now accepted as good husbandry wherever wheat is grown.

REFERENCES

LARGE, E. C., *The Advance of the Fungi*, Jonathan Cape, London (1940)

LHOSTE, J. and ROUALT, L., 'Contribution a l'étude de l'Hexachlorobenzene produit actif contre les spores de *Tilletia tritici* Berk.', 251, *Proc. 2nd. Intern. Congr. Crop Protect.* (1951)

PONCHET, J. and VENTURA, E., *Phytiat.-Phytopharm.*, **12**, 57 (1963)

PRICE JONES, D., *J. Sci. Food Agr.*, **7**, 62 (1956)

TILLET, M., *The Cause of the Corruption and Smutting of Wheat,* translated from the French by H. P. Humphrey. Classic No. 5, American Phytophathological Society

## Covered smut of barley and oats (*Ustilago hordei* [Pers.] Lagerh.)

The covered smut fungus attacks both barley and oats. With barley the black spores are retained inside the seed coat (Plate 2.5), but this is not invariably so with oats so that it is sometimes difficult to distinguish between the covered and loose smuts of this crop in the field.

The disease is practically world-wide in its distribution, oats being particularly susceptible in the higher rainfall areas.

The covered smut spores are dispersed at threshing time and adhere to the grain ready for infection when it germinates. As might be expected from its close resemblance to the life-cycle of wheat bunt, the disease is readily controlled by mercurial seed dressings used at the standard rates.

*Plate 2.5. Covered smut of barley. Healthy head on the left, infected on the right (A Plant Protection photograph)*

### Loose smut of wheat and barley (*Ustilago nuda* [Jens.] Rostr.)

The loose smut fungus destroys the heads of both wheat and barley, and as the name indicates, the spores are exposed so that the blackened heads are conspicuous in the field.

It was not until 1888 that the life-history of the loose smut fungus was described. The spores are blown about when the cereals are in flower and some are caught by the feathery stigmas. The spores germinate and produce hyphae which penetrate into the ovule. The mycelium remains dormant inside the seed, and then, as the seed germinates, it puts out hyphae which gradually travel up the stem to the developing ovaries. The embryo grains become a black mass of spores which are ready to start the cycle again.

#### METHODS OF CONTROL

It should be added that the mycelium within the seed is protected from any fungicide so that seed dressings have no effect on the disease. The commercial wheat and barley-grower keeps loose smut in check by only using seed taken from smut-free crops.

Techniques have been worked out for the disinfection of small quantities of special seed using either heat treatment or the anaerobic method. The schedules for the two cereals differ slightly.

To treat wheat, the sack of grain is warmed up in water at 32°C for four hours and then transferred to the hot-water tank for 10 min. The hot water must be maintained between 52°C and 54°C, the temperature range being critical, because below this the fungus is not killed, while temperatures above the maximum are likely to damage the grain.

With barley, the winter barleys must first be soaked in cold water for four hours and then kept for 10 min in hot water at 51–52°C. With the spring-sown varieties, the initial soak must be made in warm water at 32°C followed by the heat treatment in water at 51–52°C for 10 min.

The anaerobic treatment kills the fungus by suffocation. The grain is first soaked in warm water to stimulate the fungus into growth and then put into a sealed container such as a plastic bag to deprive it of oxygen. Finally, the seed must be dried if it is to be stored.

### Loose smut of oats (*Ustilago avenae* [Pers.] Rostr.)

Loose smut of oats is a common disease with a world-wide distribution. It has caused serious losses on susceptible varieties, but the introduction of more resistant kinds has been one of the ways of checking it.

As with the other loose smuts, the spore masses are naked turning the head black (Plate 2.6). The spores are dispersed when the oats are in flower and some lodge between the

*Plate 2.6. Loose smut of oats (A Plant Protection photograph)*

glumes. Exactly what happens next is uncertain. The spores may either germinate, leading to the development of mycelia within the glumes and on the seed coat, or they may remain dormant until the spring. At this stage there is no penetration of the seed, unlike the loose smut of wheat and barley. The fungus remains dormant until the oats are sown, when it again becomes active and infects the seedlings. The mycelium grows up the developing stem and enters the ear with the eventual production of the smutted head.

### METHODS OF CONTROL

As the mycelium of the loose smut fungus does not get inside the grain, it is not protected from fungicides. Thus both covered smut and loose smut of oats can be controlled by seed disinfection, a treatment which is so effective that both diseases have become scarce where it has been used (Beaumont, 1959).

The mercurial seed dressings are very efficient against the seed-borne diseases of oats. The normal rate is 2 oz per bushel for the European type of powder product, and $\frac{1}{2}$ oz for the North American one. Maneb has been shown to be an effective alternative to the mercurials for the control of loose smut (Ponchet *et al.*, 1963).

REFERENCES

BEAUMONT, A., *Diseases of Farm Crops*, 47, Collingridge Ltd., London (1959)

PONCHET, J. and VENTURA, E., *Phytiat.–Phytopharm.*, **12**, 57 (1963)

## LEAF STRIPE DISEASES

Barley and oat seedlings are liable to be attacked by two closely related fungi which may either kill or cripple them. The diseases take their name from the discoloured stripes on the leaves of infected plants.

### Leaf Stripe (*Pyrenophora graminea* Ito and Kuribay.)

Leaf stripe was one of the more important barley diseases until effective methods of controlling it were introduced in the 1930s. The fungus attacks the young seedlings, killing many of them, and also damages the foliage of the surviving plants where the symptoms appear as small, pale spots. On older plants the affected leaves show pale, yellowish stripes which darken with age and eventually die (Plate 2.7). The dead stripes break readily so that the leaves can become very tattered.

The fungus overwinters on the seed, as a dormant mycelium under the glumes. When the infected grain is sown, the mycelium starts into growth and produces hyphae some of which penetrate the coleoptile and subsequently the leaves. The fungus produces numerous conidia, which do not appear to infect other leaves, but they do infect the

*Plate 2.7. Leaf stripe of barley →*
*(A Plant Protection photograph)*

flowers which are very susceptible. The fungus spreads through the seed head and those parts of the mycelium which penetrate beneath the glumes eventually become dormant, providing the means by which the fungus survives.

Infection of the seedlings by the leaf stripe fungus is favoured by low soil temperatures. The disease, which is widespread, is thus at its worst in the northern part of its range. It has caused serious damage in parts of the U.S.A., in northern Europe and in the north and east of Asia.

METHODS OF CONTROL

The early trials with the mercurial seed dressings in 1927 were remarkably successful and gave almost complete control of this disease (Large, 1940). The powder seed-dressings are applied at their standard rates, namely 2 oz per bushel for the European formulations, and $\frac{1}{2}$ oz per bushel for the North American ones. If it is inadvisable to use the organo-mercurial products, the maneb seed dressings can be substituted as they are reported as being effective against this fungus (Ponchet *et al.*, 1963). The seed-dressing treatment is so effective that leaf stripe has become a rare disease, but like smallpox with human beings, ready to return should the prophylactic measures be dropped.

REFERENCES

LARGE, E. C., *The Advance of the Fungi*, 386, Jonathan Cape, London (1940)

PONCHET, J. and VENTURA, E., *Phytiat.–Phytopharm.*, **12,** 57 (1963)

## Leaf Spot and Seedling Blight (*Pyrenophora avenae* Ito and Kuribay.)

Leaf spot and seedling blight of oats, sometimes called leaf stripe, is caused by a close relative of the fungus responsible for leaf stripe of barley and gives rise to similar symptoms. The disease is particularly damaging in the colder, wetter areas such as parts of Scotland and Ireland. The fungus is at its most destructive in the seedling stages of the oat (Plate 2.8), when it can either kill the seedling before it emerges (pre-emergence blight), or destroy the plant after it has emerged (seedling blight). Attacked seedlings have brown stripes and spots on the leaves.

*Plate 2.8. Leaf spot and seedling blight of oats (A Plant Protection photograph)*

The fungus can overwinter on the seed in two ways, as a resting mycelium on the husks and seed coat, and as a spore on the outside of the grain. After the seed has been sown, the mycelium and spores start growing, putting out hyphae which penetrate the coleoptile and then the developing leaves. Spores are produced on the infected leaves and spread the disease to neighbouring plants. The fungus is not very active during mid-summer, but in late summer spreads to the upper green leaves and panicles. This phase does not cause much loss of crop, but it does result in the infection of the seed (McKay, 1957).

There is a close similarity in the life cycles of the leaf stripe fungi attacking barley and oats, the main difference being that the conidiospores of *P. graminea* do not spread the disease to healthy foliage, whereas in *P. avenae* their dissemination results in widespread infection of the plants in the field.

### METHOD OF CONTROL

The early trials with the mercurial seed dressings on oats quickly demonstrated their effectiveness in preventing this disease. Instead of having to sow eight to ten bushels of oats per acre, three to four bushels of dressed seed were adequate. These Scottish trials made a great impression on all those who took part in them, particularly the plant pathologists who were previously unaware of the extent of the damage caused by the leaf spot and seedling blight fungus (Large, 1940).

REFERENCES

LARGE, E. C., *The Advance of the Fungi,* Jonathan Cape, London (1940)

MCKAY, R., *Cereal Diseases in Ireland,* 119, Arthur Guinness Son & Co., (Dublin) Ltd. (1957)

## MISCELLANEOUS DISEASES

The rust and smut diseases which have been described are of such obvious importance, that they have been studied by plant pathologists from the earliest days of the science. There are in addition many other fungi which can attack the temperate cereals and cause losses of varying importance.

Many of these are well-known, such as powdery mildew, take-all, eyespot and scab. A brief description of these fungi is followed by an account of recent work on the estimation of the losses some of them cause in England.

Mildew *(Erysiphe graminis DC.)* is very widespread, attacking wheat, barley and oats. As a rule the fungus on each cereal is a specialised race, so that mildew does not normally spread from one type of cereal to another. The disease survives from one season to the next as mycelial patches on the winter varieties. Fresh infections make the foliage look as though it had been lightly dusted with flour, but as the disease progresses, the mycelium darkens and the foliage eventually dies.

The disease is spread by two types of spores. During the spring and summer months the asexual conidiospores are produced in enormous numbers on the mycelial patches. Later on the sexually produced ascospores are discharged from the perithecia (black spore cases) which develop among the fungal mats.

The fungus which causes take-all (*Ophiobolus graminis* [Sacc.] Sacc.) lives on the roots of wheat, barley and certain species of grasses, but not oats. It is found in most parts of the world where cereals are grown under temperate conditions, and is sometimes very destructive when there are insufficient breaks between susceptible crops. Severe take-all attacks can destroy the roots of young plants and thus kill them, but more typically root damage results in stunted plants which die somewhat prematurely. The affected plants are whitish in colour while the ears contain shrivelled grain, hence the popular name take-all. The disease quickly responds to crop rotation as the absence of the host plants for a year reduces the amount of inoculum to a low level.

The eyespot fungus (*Cercosporella herpotrichoides* Fron.) is a parasite of wheat, barley and oats. It occasionally kills seedlings, or some of the tillers, leaving a poor stand, but more typically it weakens the stem, with the result that it falls over when the grain starts to ripen. The stem is liable to fall in any direction, making the mixture of upright and fallen straw very difficult to harvest. The fungus survives on debris from the previous cereal crop and produces spores which infect the leaf sheaths near soil level. The mycelium penetrates through the sheaths and enters the stem, where the symptoms of a dark central spot surrounded by a brown ring can be seen. Crop rotation is the best defence against eyespot.

Scab or ear blight is caused by one of the *Fusarium* fungi, but the existence of the perfect stage is responsible for its classification as a species of *Gibberella* (*G. zeae* [Schw.] Petch). The fungus has been found in many parts of the world. It is a parasite of wheat, barley and oats, and has been a frequent cause of damage to both yield and quality, particularly in the central and eastern cereal growing areas of the U.S.A.

The fungus can survive from one season to the next both on cereal remains and on the seed. The seed-borne phase is thought to be the most important source of infection of the barley seedlings.

Each of the three main ways in which the fungus damages the crop are distinguished by particular names. Seedling blight describes the results when the young plants are killed, brown foot rot when the root system is attacked, and scab for the infection of the ears. Warm, humid weather is necessary for the infection of the heads, and consequently this stage is only common in regions where the climate favours it.

Grain from infected ears is shrivelled and sometimes has a pink or reddish colour at the germ end. The presence of the disease has a great effect on the value of the barley because contaminated grain has an emetic effect when ingested by pigs, dogs or human beings. Fortunately, such grain is not entirely useless as cattle, sheep and poultry tolerate it.

Scab has not proved easy to control but it can be kept down by the use of clean seed, treating the seed with one of the organomercurial seed dressings and by a crop rotation which prevents an excessive accumulation of diseased crop residues in the soil.

## ESTIMATION OF CROP LOSSES DUE TO FUNGI

It will be noted that there are various methods by which cereal diseases can be kept in check, such as crop rotation, seed-dressings and even fungicidal sprays in exceptional cases, but the main defence has been provided by the plant breeder.

The selection of the objectives for a breeding programme can best be made if the losses caused by each disease are known. Work of this kind is going on at the National Institute of Agricultural Botany (N.I.A.B.) at Cambridge. Two methods of measuring crop losses are being used: by experiments with small plots which are either naturally or artificially infected, and by surveys of the intensity of disease attack in the field. The correlation between disease intensity and crop loss can be measured. In this way, surveys of the amount of disease present in the field can be used to determine the amount of grain lost.

The results are of considerable interest. For example, mildew, which is normally disregarded by the farmer, has been calculated as causing a loss of 60,000 tons of wheat in the United Kingdom, worth £1,500,000. Losses due to take-all have not yet been estimated, but eyespot over a 19-year period at Rothamstead was responsible for a mean loss of 12·5% or about 3½ cwt per acre. It must be added, however, that the eyespot losses occurred with Yeoman—a susceptible variety. The popular variety Capelle-Desprez is moderately resistant so that the national loss from this disease is now much less.

Observations have also been made on loose smut. Normally, this does not rise above 1% of infected ears but figures as high as 17% have been recorded. On the experimental plots the disease has been found to double itself in two years out of five. In the worst case recorded, loose smut reduced the yield by 23%.

The research workers, however, do not expect that final victory over cereal diseases is near, for they forecast that victory over one disease opens the way for another. For example, the use of mildew-resistant cereals would provide good foliage, which might be susceptible to brown rust in wheat, leaf blotch (*Rhynchosporium secalis* [Oudem.] J. J. Davis) on barley and crown rust on oats (Doling, 1963). The defence of our cereal crops calls for continual vigilance.

REFERENCE

DOLING, D. A., *Proc. 2nd Brit. Insecticide Fungicide Conf.*, 27 (1963)

Rice is one of the most productive cereals grown by mankind, the yield per acre being nearly double that of wheat. Some 257 million tons of paddy rice are produced from the 310 million acres devoted to its culture throughout the world (F.A.O., 1964).

Paddy, which is the rice plant, is cultivated in many countries of the world but by far the greatest area occurs in the Far East. The largest area is to be found in India with about 88 million acres. Elsewhere in the world, paddy is grown in the U.S.A., Brazil, and to a limited extent, in Europe.

Rice is mainly a peasant crop, in contrast to wheat which is most economically grown by the large-scale farmer. The education of peasant farmers in the use of modern techniques is a slow process, but that it can be done has been demonstrated with outstanding success in Japan.

The principal pests of rice occur in all the areas of the Far East although the dominant species is often different. These pests have their counterparts in other rice-growing countries, even in Spain and Italy. The most important pests are the Pyralid shoot borers, but losses from these seldom exceed 20%. Obviously, in a country like Japan, where all losses must be prevented owing to the shortage of land suitable for the cultivation of paddy, considerable effort is devoted to the control of these insects. It is in Japan therefore that most work on insect pests has been carried out.

Fungous diseases are considered to have been responsible for two relatively recent rice famines in Asia. The Bengal famine in 1942 was due to damage done by brown spot disease, while another disease called blast caused a partial famine in Japan in 1941 (Grist, 1959). These two diseases have a wide distribution and are the most important ones affecting the crop. The other diseases tend to be of local importance, but have nevertheless been responsible for serious crop losses.

The total loss due to fungal attacks has been estimated as being between 5% and 10%. This may not seem large to a small peasant cultivator, but the total amount lost is obviously enormous (Padwick, 1956).

A description in English of rice culture in Japan has recently been published (Matsubayashi *et al.,* 1965). There are excellent chapters on both pests and diseases in this book, and in that by Grist (1959).

The standard English monograph on rice diseases has been written by Padwick (1950) while the subject has been briefly described by Dickson (1956).

REFERENCES

DICKSON, J. G., *Diseases of Field Crops* (2nd Edn.), McGraw-Hill Book Co. Inc., New York (1956)

*F.A.O. Production Yearbook 1963–64,* **18,** F.A.O., Rome

GRIST, D. H., *Rice* (3rd Edn.), Longmans, Green & Co. Ltd., London (1959)

MATSUBAYASHI, M., *et al., Theory and Practice of Growing Rice,* Fuji Publishing Co. Ltd., Tokyo (1965)

PADWICK, G. WATTS, *Manual of Rice Diseases,* The Commonwealth Mycological Institute, Kew (1950)

PADWICK, G. WATTS, 'Losses caused by Plant Diseases in the Colonies', Phytopath Paper No. 1, The Commonwealth Mycological Institute, Kew (1956)

## LEPIDOPTERA

### *Schoenobius incertellus* Wlk. (= *bipunctifera* Wlk.) *(Pyralidae)*

The Rice Borer or Yellow Stem Borer (Fig. 2.5) occurs in Japan, Taiwan, India and China where it is the principal paddy pest. It is also found in many other paddy-growing areas where it is also a prominent pest as in Malaya, the Philippines and Australia.

Two generations occur a year. The moth is pale in colour. It lays 120–150 eggs in several clusters which are covered with scales from

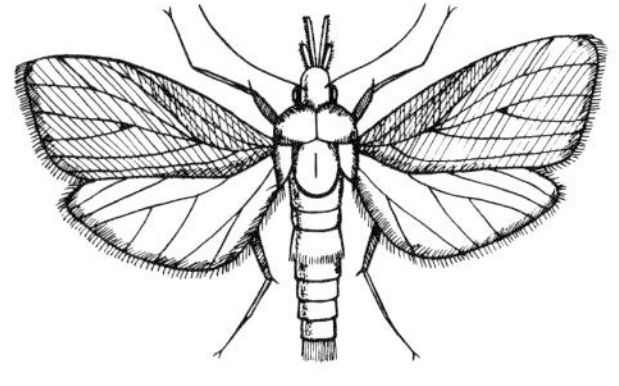

*Fig. 2.5.* Schoenobius incertellus *(adult)*

the body of the female. Only about 10% of the larvae survive after egg hatch and these enter the ensheathing leaf of the paddy plant and thereby the main stem. The damage causes the central shoot to die and turn yellow either before or after the ear has appeared. Several stems may be attacked by the migrating caterpillar, which either are blown by wind, trailing silken threads or float on the water surface, sometimes on a piece of leaf. Pupation occurs after about 2–3 weeks feeding and takes place in the base of the stem.

The second generation is similar but the caterpillars feed higher up in the stem and cause a loss of nutrient to the developing ear. Pupation occurs in the stubble in which the insect spends the winter, usually as a caterpillar.

More generations may occur in a warm climate such as the Philippines and Malaya than in Japan where there are two. The insect lives principally on paddy but can occur in some grasses. *Schoenobius* tends to increase where two crops of paddy are taken in a year.

*Chilotraea suppressalis* Wlk. *(Pyralidae)*

Striped Stem Borer occurs principally in Japan and South Korea. The moth is pale colour similar to other Pyralids (Plate 2.9).

*Plate 2.9. Adult of* Chilotraea suppressalis, *Japan (T. Suzuki, Tokyo)*

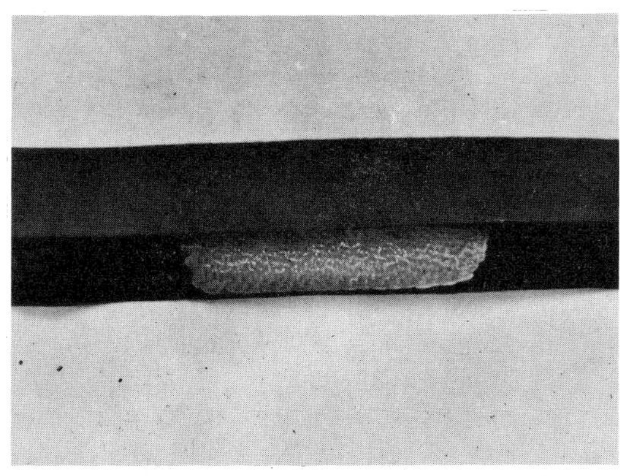

*Plate 2.10. Egg mass of* Chilotraea suppressalis, *Japan (T. Suzuki, Tokyo)*

Its life-cycle is similar to *S. incertellus* but deposits fewer eggs in the clusters, usually 50–60 in 5–6 clusters (Plate 2.10). The larvae enters the stalks of the paddy plant often as many as 10 being attacked by a single caterpillar. In Japan, two generations occur, one in June and one in August. The insect can also live on grasses, sorghum and maize. *C. suppressalis* also occurs in Malaya and certain other countries in south-east Asia and this insect is reported from other parts of the world including the paddy fields of Spain and Portugal. It has also been found to be present in Hawaii.

*Chilo simplex* Butler (= *oryzae* Fletcher = *zonellus* Swinh.)

There is little doubt that these insects, which have been described in many publications, are in fact *Chilotraea suppressalis* Wlk.

*Chilotraea polychrysa* Meyr.
*(Chilotraea = Proceras) (Pyralidae)*

This is the principal stem borer of paddy in Malaya. Egg masses of 60–70 are deposited as with other stem borers. The main attack occurs just before flowering as the insect has been living on other plants earlier in the year, especially grasses (Nair, 1958).

*Scirpophaga innotata* Wlk. *(Pyralidae)*

This is the White Borer of Indonesia which appears to be the main paddy borer in Java (Fig. 2.6). It also occurs in the Philippines where it is second in importance to *Schoenobius*. Eggs are laid in clusters of 200, usually

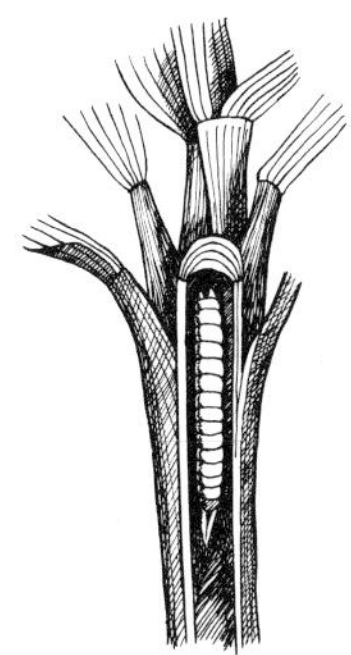

*Fig. 2.6.* Scirpophaga innotata *(larva in paddy stem)*

on the lower side of terminal leaves. Two or more generations are completed in a season. It occurs in many countries in south-east Asia and also in Australia. Recently renaming of *Schoenobius* and *Scirpophaga* has included both genera under one new generic name *Tryporyza* (Common, 1960).

*Elasmopalpus lignosellus* Zell. *(Pyralidae)*

This insect is not an important pest of paddy but is rather a maize pest. It is a green caterpillar and bites into the paddy stems in dry land paddy. It is not a wet paddy pest. It occurs in U.S.A. and South America.

*Sesamia inferens,* Wlk. *(Noctuidae)*

This insect in paddy is called the Violet Stem Borer but it is really a pest of maize. It occurs all through the Far East but does not rank as an important paddy pest. It has many alternative host plants.

REFERENCES

COMMON, I. F. B., *Australian J. Zool,* **8,** 307 (1960)

NAIR, M. R. G. R., *Indian J. Entomol.,* **20,** 136 (1958)

METHODS OF CONTROL

*Cultural Methods.* Flooding of land has always been regarded as a worthwhile practise for the control of *Schoenobius* to reduce the number of larvae hibernating in the stubble. Flooding should be maintained for at least three months and is better carried out after the stubble of the previous crop has been ploughed (Liu and Cheng, 1937) from evidence in China.

Alteration of the time of sowing so that it takes place after the first flight period of the moth has been recommended, especially for *Scirpophaga,* the emergence of which is dependent on rain. Sowing should take place at the time of the flight. Khan and Murthy (1955) found that dry-season early (December) sowings in the Hyderabad State of India were more heavily infected than late sowings. Wet-season (July) infestations were not influenced by sowing date. In Indonesia, delayed sowing has always been practised against *Scirpophaga,* sowing is carried out after the flight period is finished (van der Goot, 1948).

Trapping of moths by light has been suggested for *Schoenobius* and *Chilo* but there is no evidence that this does in fact give a reduction in damage. Natural control by means of insectivorous birds has been recommended by placing perching or resting places for the birds in paddy fields. Collection of egg masses has also been practised.

*Chemical Control.* Most work with insecticides against paddy borers has been carried out in Japan where measures are widely adopted. Trials have also been carried out in Taiwan, China, Malaya and India but little adoption of insecticides has taken place in these countries.

In Japan two insecticides are in common use, namely parathion as a spray and gamma BHC as a 3% dust. Parathion, in spite of its poisonous nature, has been widely used in Japan against *Chilo* applied at about 50 gal per acre at the relatively strong dose of 0·1%.

Other insecticides have been tested and found effective in laboratory and plot trials including endrin and EPN 300. Malathion, demeton and azinphos-ethyl have been found to be less effective (Liang and Liu, 1958) in Taiwan. Dusts containing 1–5% gamma BHC at 30–40 kg per hectare have also been found to be effective. DDT at 1 lb per acre has been found effective in Malaya (Wyatt, 1957).

Tao (1958) in experiments over four successive seasons in Taiwan showed that the insecticides parathion, dieldrin, endrin, aldrin, azinphos-ethyl and diazinon all gave some control of *Schoenobius* when used as sprays at 800–1,200 litres per hectare (about 100 gal per acre) applied about 2–3 weeks after transplanting. Yield increases of up to 80% were recorded in some years, in others only 10%. Sengupta and Rout (1957) reported good control of *Schoenobius* with endrin 19·5% emulsion at 12, 16 and 32 oz per acre applied about four weeks after planting in India.

A recent Japanese insecticide has been developed for use against *Chilo* namely fenitrothion ('Sumithion'), an organo-phosphate of low mammalian toxicity. This is recommended at 0·1% and is said to be equal in effect to parathion. The insecticide is also non-toxic to fish—an important perquisite in insecticides for paddy. DDT and gamma BHC are also relatively non-toxic to fish but parathion, endrin and EPN 300 are all fish poisons.

Application of insecticides should be directed against young newly hatched larvae. At this time the greatest mortality of insects will be achieved. When the caterpillars have scattered and entered into the plants the insecticides are not likely to be effective. Toxic action and persistence are both desirable. The time of application should coincide with the peak of egg-laying. Eggs hatch in a few days, the peak should be ascertained and passed before application is made. More than one application may be necessary.

Treatment of paddy is not difficult in the seedling stage or just after transplanting but for larger plants with later generations of shoot borers attacking the ear stage, application is more difficult. Knapsack sprayers and dusters are suitable but useful only for small plots. Large areas of paddy are best treated on a communal basis with more effective machines.

Mist-blowers, either for low volume sprays or for dusts, are suitable but the concentration on the insecticide in sprays need be increased to about x5 or x10 and application made at about 50–100 litres per hectre (5–10 gal per acre).

Aerial application of sprays and dusts has also been carried out with success against the shoot borer of paddy in Japan. Successful aerial application of gamma BHC/DDT mixed dust for the control of *Chilo* is also reported from Spain (Planes and del Rivero, 1956).

*Natural Enemies.* These seem to be of little value against shoot borers which spend much of their life enclosed and protected by the plant. The egg parasites *Trichogramma spp.* appear to have been recorded from most shoot borer eggs. Attempts to introduce a larval parasite into Malaya against *Chilotraea* were unsuccessful during 1952–55 (Lever, 1956).

REFERENCES

KHAN, M. G. and MURTHY, D. W., *Indian J. Entomol.*, **17**, 175 (1955)
LEVER, R. J. A. W., *R.A.E.*, **46**, 73 (1956)
LIU (CHI-YUNG) and CHEN (CHENG LIANG), *R.A.E.*, **27**, 613 (1937)
LIANG (TUNG-TING) and LIU (HSIEN-LSIA), *R.A.E.*, **49**, 102 (1958)
PLANES, S. and DEL RIVERO, J. M., *R.A.E.*, **45**, 287 (1956)
SENGUPTA, G. C. and ROUT, G. D., *J. Econ. Entomol.*, **50**, 221 (1957)
TAO CHIA-HWA, *J. Econ. Entomol.*, **51**, 571 (1958)
VAN DER GOOT, P., *R.A.E.*, **40**, 150 (1948)
WYATT, I. J., *R.A.E.*, **46**, 276 (1957)

## ARMYWORMS

### *Spodoptera mauritia* Boisd. *(Noctuidae)*

This insect is known variously as the Paddy Swarming Caterpillar and the Rice Armyworm (Fig. 2.7). It occurs principally in India, Pakistan and Ceylon but has also been recorded in Indonesia, the Philippines, parts of Africa and in Hawaii.

The moth is a nocturnal and in colour mainly dark. The caterpillars are green and measure about 3 cm when fully grown (Fig. 2.8). Eggs are laid in batches on the leaves and the caterpillars feeding on the foliage of the plants. If numerous, entire seedbeds or planted fields can be grazed to the water surface. Considerable mortality occurs to caterpillars by drowning. In order to survive they must reach the dry soil of the bank of the field in order to pupate. More than

*Fig. 2.7.* Spodoptera mauritia *(adult)*

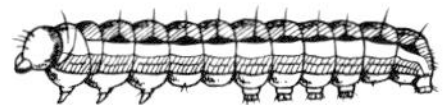

*Fig. 2.8.* Spodoptera mauritia *(caterpillar)*

one generation a year can occur but it is doubtful if more than one attack on paddy takes place.

The insect can live on other plants especially grasses and cereals.

### *Cirphis unipuncta* Haw. *(Cirphis = Pseudaletia) (Noctuidae)*

This insect is variously known as the Rice Armyworm or Rice Cutworm but in India it is usually called the Paddy Climbing Cutworm (Fig. 2.9). This moth is also nocturnal and is widely distributed in both Asia, South and North America and Australia. It is well-known in India and Thailand where it is a pest. The moths are brown and the caterpillar green and brown. Eggs are in larger batches, usually in the enfolded leaf. The caterpillar feeds on the foliage of the paddy plant. They are typical armyworms in habit appearing in large numbers often following flooding (Puttardriah and Usman, 1958). They have a fondness of climbing up to the ear and cutting it off just below the node. There are usually

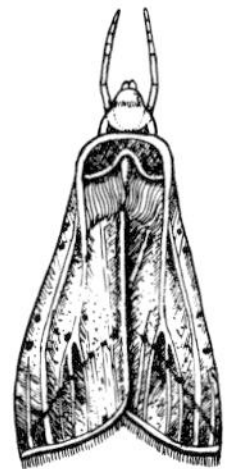

*Fig. 2.9.* Cirphis unipuncta *(adult)*

two or three generations per year. The insect attacks a variety of crops, especially grasses and cereals. Pupation occurs in the soil.

In the U.S.A. *Cirphis* is heavily parasitised by *Apanteles militatis* Walsh (Braconid), (Marcovitch, 1957).

Other species of this type of moth are:
*Laphygma frugiperda* Sm. and Abb.—which occurs in U.S.A. and South America
*Borolia venalba* Mo. in Burma, India and Ceylon
*Prodenia litura* Fab. in Formosa
*Naranga aenescens* Moore in China
*Crambus melacellus* in Mauritius
*Mocis repanda* Fab. in Brazil
all species of *Noctuidae*.

### *Nymphula depunctalis* Guen. *(Pyralidae)*

Reference must be made to the insect known in India as the Rice Case Worm as the caterpillar rolls itself in a portion of paddy leaf and lives within, attaching itself to the leaf blade with its thoracic legs only (Figs. 2.10, 2.11). Other species also occur in Malaya, Philippines, Borneo, Japan, Korea and many other countries, e.g. *N. fluctuosalis* Zell. in Malaya. *N. vittalis* in Japan.

The moth is a small insect. The caterpillar strips the epidermis from the leaves. Pupation occurs within the folded leaf on the plant

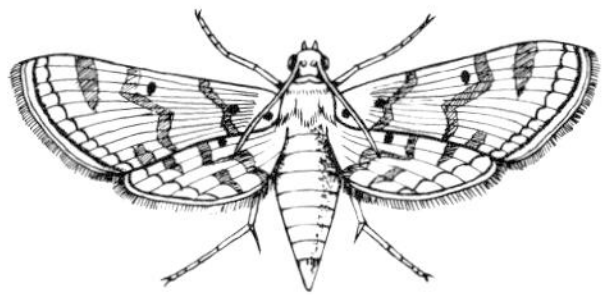

*Fig. 2.10.* Nymphula depunctalis *(adult)*

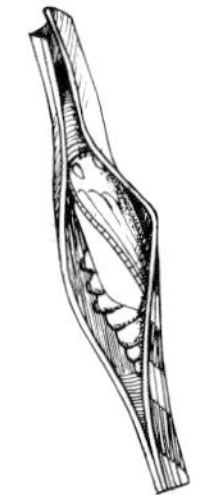

*Fig. 2.11.* Nymphula depunctalis *(pupa in folded leaf)*

but overwinters in the straw and stubble as a caterpillar. The larvae can breathe even if submerged through gills but normally they float on the water surface in their leaf-tubes. It is said that these leaf-tubes contain water from which the caterpillar receives its supply of oxygen. It seems doubtful if these insects are of particular importance as pests in comparison with the others.

## METHODS OF CONTROL

*Cultural Method.* Flooding is always popular for paddy pests and is recommended for *Spodoptera.* The procedure is to allow egg laying to take place and then flood to drown young larvae at egg hatch. Flooding is not recommended for *Cirphis* because the insect feeds high up on the plants. Dislodging the larvae with long canes or ropes is often suggested. Flooding would be useless against *Nymphula.* Noctuid moths are also attracted to light but it is doubtful if such responses can be put into practice for control.

*Chemical control.* The standard method of armyworm and cutworm control is to use a poison bait of bran, formerly Paris Green (an arsenical compound) or sodium fluosilicate were used, but baits are not very useful in wet paddy. Arsenical dusts have also been used.

These practices have been superseded by modern insecticides which are superior. The best insecticide is DDT, either as a spray or dust (Gannon and Decker, 1955). A 5% dust is suitable, sprays need 1 lb of DDT per acre by ground and aerial application.

Other insecticides can also be used, especially suitable being endrin at $\frac{1}{4}$–$\frac{1}{2}$ lb per acre and toxaphene at 2 lb per acre. Application is made at the first sign of an outbreak. Application of DDT using 2 pt per acre of an 18% emulsion has been made by aircraft in Ceylon against *Spodoptera* with success on paddy (Fernando *et al.,* 1954). Wei (1959) has recommended the use of mixed DDT 5%/gamma BHC 0·5% dust at 20 lb per acre in China against *Spodoptera.*

New methods for the control of the rice stem borer have recently been developed in the Philippine Islands and consist in the application of BHC to the surface of the irrigation water. BHC is an insecticide of the slight systemic properties which enable the insecticide to enter into the rice plant, translocate in the sap stream and kill the rice borer larvae within the stem. A granular formulation containing gamma BHC is an ideal way in which the insecticide can be applied as the product can simply be broadcast over the crop and the granules will fall into the irrigation water. The correct rate of gamma BHC is 3 kg per hectare. Application should be made to the surface of the water approximately 25 days after transplanting the rice. The time of application should coincide with the peak flight period of the moth of the stem borer. The duration of the action of the insecticide is about 30 days and a second treatment should be made 20 days after the first.

A very high degree of stem borer control can be achieved by this method against *Chilotraea suppressalis* and also against *Schoenobius incertellus.* The application is estimated to give a concentration of gamma BHC in the water of 6 ppm. Such a concentration if achieved will give 100% kill of the young stem borer larvae. It is possible by repeat applications to protect the rice during a 3 months period to harvest. Trials in the Philippines have shown that the yield by this method can be increased by 50% and in some cases doubled (Pathak, 1967).

REFERENCES

FERNANDO, H. E., WEERAWARDENA, G. W. and MANICKAVASAGAR, P., *R.A.E.,* **45,** 36 (1954)

GANNON, N. and DECKER, G. C., *J. Econ. Entomol.*, **48**, 260 (1955)
MARCOVITCH, S., *J. Econ. Entomol*, **50**, 112 (1957)
PATHAK, M. D., *PANS.*, **13**, 45 (1967)
PUTTARDRIAH, M. and USMAN, S., *R.A.E.*, **47**, 179 (1958)
WEI HUNG-CHEN, *R.A.E.*, **49**, 256 (1959)

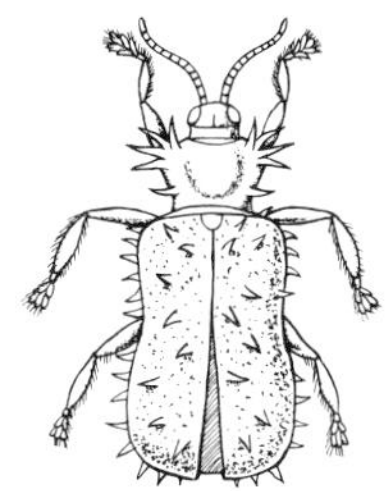

*Fig. 2.12.* Hispa armigera *(adult)*

## COLEOPTERA

### *Hispa armigera* Ol. ( = *aenescens* Baly) *(Chrysomelidae)*

This little beetle, blue-black in colour with marked projections on the thorax and elytra, occurs in India, especially in Bengal (Fig. 2.12). It is also reported from Indonesia, China and Formosa. In India it is called the Rice Hispa. *H. stygia* Chap. also occurs in India and H. *similis* in Formosa.

*Fig. 2.13.* Hispa armigera *(on leaf of paddy)*

*Hispa* is a Chrysomelid leaf beetle, both adults and larvae feeding on the leaf blades of paddy from which the epidermis is eaten in strips (Fig. 2.13). The whole life-cycle occurs on the leaves—several generations take place in a season. The winter is passed on grasses and the beetle flies into the paddy fields in March. Considerable injury to plants can be caused if the beetles are numerous.

Other species of leaf-feeding beetles occur but appear to be of lesser importance. These are: *Lema oryzae* Knw. in Japan; *Lema flavipes* Suffr. in Korea.

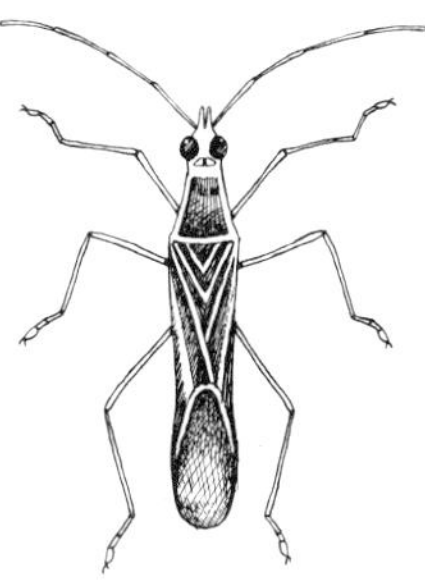

*Fig. 2.14.* Leptocorisa acuta *(adult)*

#### METHODS OF CONTROL

The only satisfactory method of dealing with *Hispa* is by the application of insecticides. Both DDT and BHC can be used either as sprays or dusts; DDT is usually employed as a spray at 0·5% and BHC as a 5% dust. Both are very effective.

## HEMIPTERA

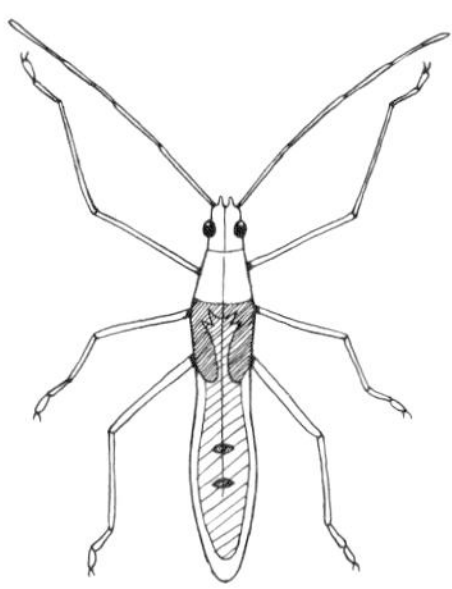

*Fig. 2.15.* Leptocorisa acuta *(nymph)*

Various species occur as pests of paddy but probably the most important are the ear-bugs (Figs. 2.14, 2.15): *Leptocorisa acuta* Thubs; *Leptocorisa varicornis* Fab.

These Coreids are variously known as ear-bugs, rice-bugs, paddy-bugs and so on. The species occur in south-east Asia but are especially important in Ceylon. They also are numerous in Thailand, India, Indonesia, the Philippines and Malaya. Other species no doubt occur also.

The adults survive for up to six months but the duration of the immature stage is only about 20–30 days. The bugs are attracted to the paddy fields when these begin to flower. The population increases as more paddy fields come into flower and the bugs move on to new fields.

The bugs, both mature and immature, feed on the developing grains when these are in the soft stage. Attacked grains are sucked and tend to shrivel with consequent loss of yield. When no flowering paddy is available the bugs live on grasses (Shugaatul, 1958). The whole life-cycle can be spent on paddy. Several hundred eggs are laid by the females on the leaves.

### METHODS OF CONTROL

The only worthwhile control is by chemicals because of the abundance of alternative plant hosts. Furthermore, the insect appears on paddy at flowering and so can be watched for and treated. The bugs are very susceptible to both DDT and BHC which can be used either as sprays or dusts. Dusting with 5% BHC dust is widely practised in Ceylon (Baptist, 1947). Only small amounts of dust, about 10 lb per acre are needed, drifted over the fields.

Other insecticides are also effective. Previous methods of control have been traditional and include catching adults in nets, attracting them to flares at night and so on. The most practical method seems to have been restricting the flowering period of all the paddy in the district (van der Goot, 1949).

REFERENCES

BAPTIST, B. A., *Trop. Agr. London,* **103,** 12 (1947)

SHUGAATUL AKBAR, S., *R.A.E.,* **47,** 385 (1958)

VAN DER GOOT, P., *R.A.E.,* **41,** 30 (1949)

## *Scotinophora lurida* Burn. *(Pentatomidae)*

This is known as the Black Paddy Bug and occurs in Ceylon, Thailand and Malaya where *S. coarctata* F. also occurs. *S. lurida* also occurs all over Japan. This insect is also called a stink bug on account of its glands, carrying a strong-smelling fluid which is used in protection. It is a large compact bug.

Damage to paddy is caused by massed feeding by the bugs on the leaves which turn brown. Egg masses of about 10–20 are deposited and the nymphs feed until they are mature. When the crop increases in size, the bugs return to alternate with host plants, usually grasses. Several generations occur in a year.

Other bugs of this type have been recorded from various parts of the world as follows:

*Nezara viridula* L. in Australia
*Solubea pugnax* Fab. in U.S.A.
*S. poecilus* Dall., British Guiana, Brazil.

### METHODS OF CONTROL

Chemical control is seldom practised against these insects which are known to be susceptible to many insecticides. Probably the most toxic is gamma BHC (Fernando, 1960) from work in Ceylon.

Normal procedure in dealing with an outbreak of these insects is to raise the water level in the field to drive the bugs off the plants and to put in ducks. The bugs are readily attracted to light.

## *Nephotettix bipunctatus* Fab. *(Jassidae)*

This is the Rice Leaf Bug, a small green insect (Fig. 2.16) which occurs in India, Pakistan, Philippines, Burma and south-east

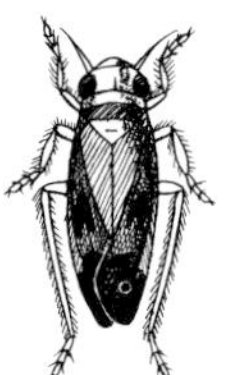

*Fig. 2.16 (a).* Nephotettix bipunctatus *(adult male)*

*Fig. 2.16 (b).* Nephotettix bipunctatus *(adult female)*

Asia. The species in Japan is *N. cincticeps* Uhler which is said to transmit the virus disease of paddy called 'dwarf'. Leaf-hopper epidemics occur in some countries and action is necessary. The insects fly and hop readily.

Several generations occur. The eggs are laid in slits in the leaf tissue. The nymphs and adults suck the cell sap (Alam and Islam, 1959).

### METHODS OF CONTROL

Chemical control is the only satisfactory method of dealing with an outbreak. Either DDT or BHC are suitable and can be applied as sprays or dusts. Probably the best and cheapest insecticide is DDT as a spray at 0·1%. Miscible liquid formulations of DDT can be applied from the air.

### *Delphacoides striatella* Fall. *(Fulgoridae)*

This insect occurs in Japan. It is said to transmit 'stripe' disease.

Other species are:

*Sogata pallescens* Dist. in Vietnam

*S. furcifera* Horv. in Japan, Formosa and Malaya

*Nilaparvata oryzae* Melz. in Formosa

## DIPTERA

### *Pachydiplosis oryzae* Wood-Mann *(Cecidomyidae)*

This insect is called the Paddy Gall Fly and occurs in India, China (Yen, Lin, Kno, 1949), Ceylon, Indonesia and Burma. This insect causes the 'silvery shoot' of paddy by the larval feeding low down in the stem, also called the Oman Shoot Disease, as the attacked shoot becomes swollen like an oman leaf. Eggs are laid in the leaf sheath. Several generations occur, some of which attack grasses. It is not an important pest. No method of control is known.

*Chlorops oryzae* Matsumura occurs as a shoot borer in Japan.

## ORTHOPTERA

Various species of grasshoppers attack paddy. They live on grasses and cereals including paddy, eating large pieces from the foliage. The abundance of grasshoppers is usually associated with rains. Eggs are laid in the soil and may remain many months before hatching.

### *Hieroglyphus banian* Fab. *(Acrididae)*

This is called the Paddy Grasshopper in India, especially in the Bombay province. The insects occur in waste land and move into paddy. The cycle lasts about 2–3 months.

*Colemania sphenariodes* Bol. The Deccan Wingless grasshopper, also in India.

*Oxya velox.* F. This grasshopper attacks paddy in Japan and Formosa.

### METHODS OF CONTROL

Grasshoppers can be readily controlled by means of insecticides as sprays and dusts. Probably the best is BHC which is very effective as a 5% dust.

REFERENCES

ALAM, Z. and ISLAM, A., *R.A.E.*, **48**, 532 (1960)

FERNANDO, H. E., *Bull. Entomol. Res.*, **50**, 7 (1960)

YEN, C., LIN, C. and KNO, K., *R.A.E.*, **34**, 119 (1949)

## Blast (*Pyricularia oryzae* Cav.)

Blast, or rotten neck, occurs wherever rice is grown, with the exception of a few areas such as California where the air is sufficiently dry to prevent its development (C.M.I., 1954). The disease is of particular importance in Japan where much attention has been devoted to its control.

The fungus occurs on the foliage, first appearing as small dark green flecks which gradually change to brown spots with grey centres (Fig. 2.17). The foliage phase of the disease is occasionally responsible for serious losses, but generally it is the later damage to the stem which has the worst effect on yield. In the stem phase, the fungus penetrates the leaf sheath and attacks the stem, particularly the neck just below the head. After infection the stem continues to develop and the head emerges from the sheath in the normal way. If the infection of the neck was early, the panicle is quickly bleached, making an obvious contrast between the healthy green heads and the pale diseased ones. If the neck infection takes place a few days later, a small number of grains develop, the weight of which causes the stem to bend over at the point of infection, hence the name rotten neck (Fig. 2.18). In addition, some blasting of individual spikelets can take place, and if this is extensive, crop losses can be quite severe.

The carry-over of the fungus from one crop to the next can take place in three distinct ways, the importance of the survival method varying in different parts of the world. The fungus can survive on other species of grass which are also hosts of the fungus, on the seed and on trash from the previous crop. The relative importance of the method of

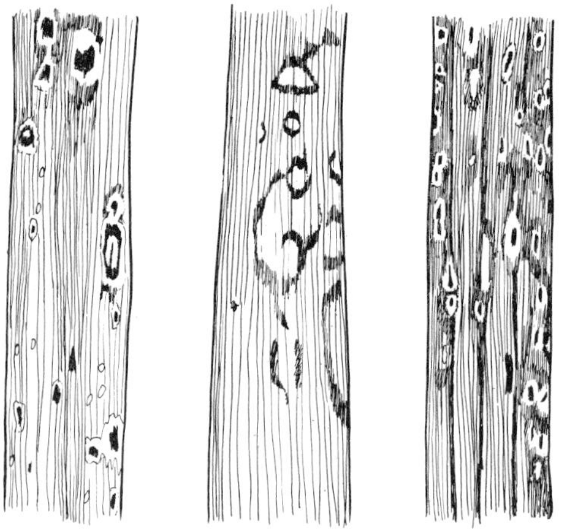

*Fig. 2.17. Rice Blast. Lesions on the leaves*

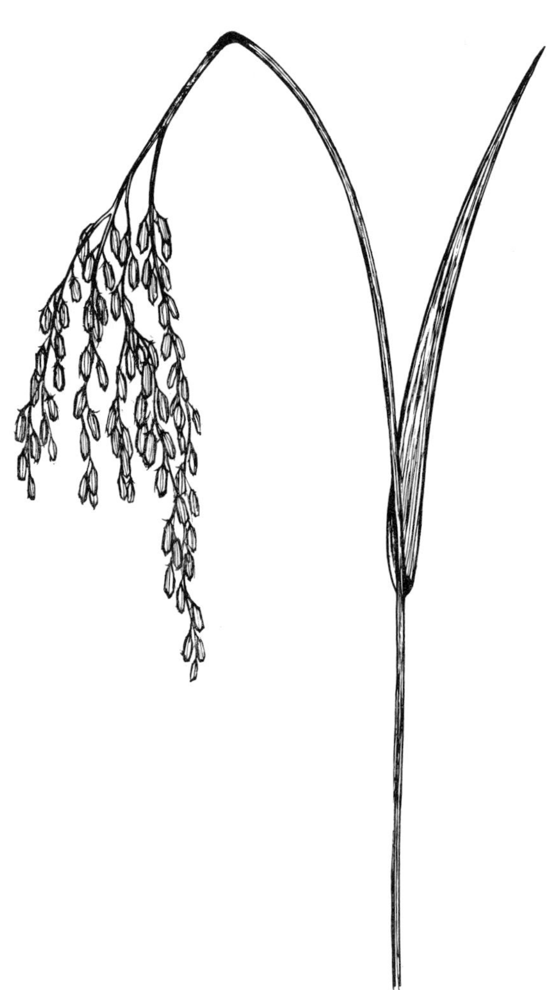

*Fig. 2.18. Rice Blast. Rotten Neck phase*

carry-over is dependent on the climate and on the farming methods used.

From a world-wide aspect the grasses, which grow on the bunds dividing the fields, are undoubtedly the most important source of infection of the rice. In India, the bunds are wide and produce large quantities of fodder, essential for feeding the cattle. It is therefore not practicable to control the disease by removing the other host plants.

In colder areas, such as Japan, the picture is quite different. Here the bunds between the rice fields are narrow mounds of mud with very little grass. Consequently, the fungus can only overwinter either on the seed or on the trash from the previous crop.

### METHODS OF CONTROL

The differences in the source of infection govern the methods of controlling the fungus. When, as in Japan and Taiwan, the grass is absent as a host plant, the seed-borne phase becomes most important. In these two countries, treating the seed with a mercurial dust or steep has been found most effective in postponing the onset of the disease and hence its final intensity. In Japan it is the usual practice to soak the seeds in a solution containing 25 p.p.m. of mercury (organically combined) for 6–12 hrs. If the temperature falls below 18°C, the steeping time must be increased.

With two sources of infection checked, the third source, the trash left in the rice fields, becomes important. In Japan this phase is dealt with by using foliage fungicides to prevent the disease establishing itself on the leaves. Although copper fungicides have some effect, the organomercurials are much better. The preferred fungicide is a dust containing 0·15–0·25% of organically combined mercury.

The optimum time of application has been determined by studying the effect of the weather and spore release on the outbreaks of the disease. This knowledge has made it possible to forecast the onset of an infection period and to warn the farmers of this. The programme usually involves the application of two rounds of dust at the rate of 27–36 lb per acre. Huge quantities of dust are required, by 1954 no less than 31,000 tons were being used (Padwick, 1956).

Mercury fungicides, however, are far from ideal due to the risk of poisoning. Research work has been proceeding in Japan looking for alternative materials and an antibiotic, which has been given the name 'Blasticidin' S, was first used commercially in 1961. This is still in the development stage, but it is of particular interest as being the first large-scale use of an antibiotic for control of a plant disease.

Finally, as with so many crops, the plant breeder has a part to play. Rice varieties resistant to blast have been reported from India, Japan and the U.S.A. Obviously in countries such as India the only hope of minimising the losses caused by blast is the use of resistant varieties.

REFERENCES

C.M.I. *Distribution Maps of Plant Diseases,* No. 51 (3rd Edn.), Commonwealth Mycological Institute, Kew (1954)

PADWICK, G. WATTS, *Outl. Agric.,* **1,** 20 (1956).

### Brown Spot (*Cochliobolus miyabeanus* [Ito and Kuribay.] Drechsl. ex Dastur syn. *Helminthosporium oryzae* Breda de Haan)

The brown spot fungus is found wherever rice is grown. The spots which it causes appear on the foliage and on the glumes surrounding the seed. The first spots on the leaves are small and purplish brown. As the spots age they grow larger, while the centre turns grey with a brown ring round it. On the seed the spots vary in size from small ones to entire coverage of the glumes (Fig. 2.19a) with a dark brown velvety felt composed of sporophores and spores (Fig. 2.19b).

The fungus can cause damage at three growth stages, during germination, when the plant is young, and also to the grain itself. Heavily infected seeds germinate poorly, but as rice is sown under conditions which favour

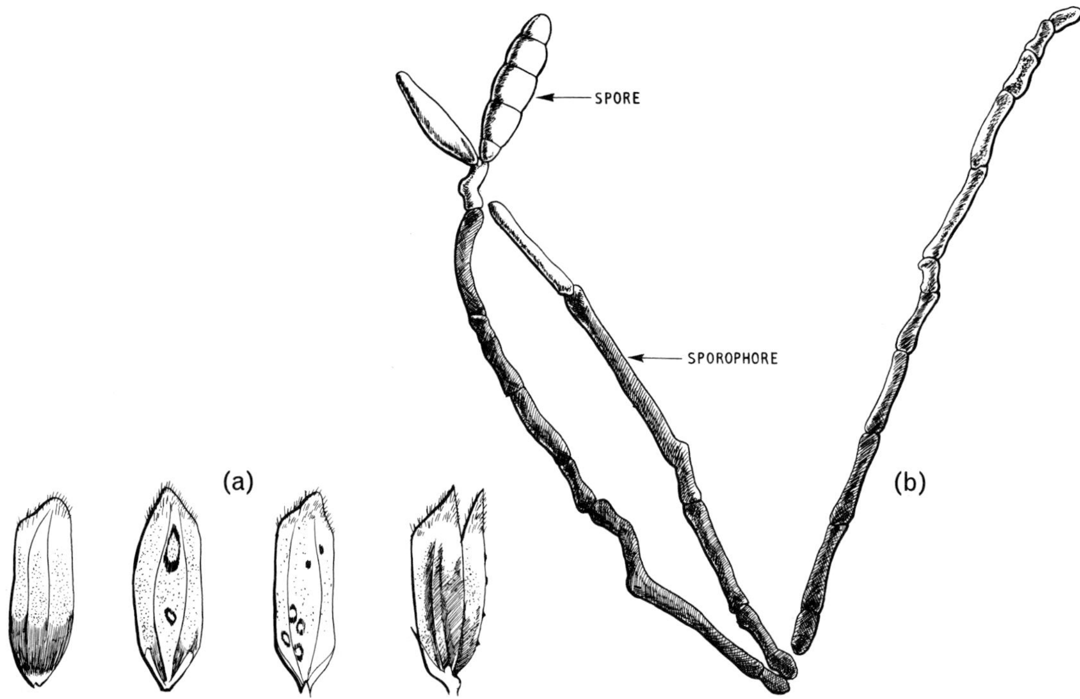


*Fig. 2.19. Brown Spot of Rice, (a) infections on kernels, (b) sporophore and spores*

rapid germination, losses from this source are usually of minor importance. The major losses occur during the seedling stage when the seed beds become infected and the young foliage is crippled. When this happens the plant is weakened and the yield seriously reduced. It was this kind of damage which was responsible for the Bengal famine in 1942. The grain itself is also attacked, the intensity varying from a few small spots to overall coverage of the glumes. The importance of this phase is unknown as the loss of yield caused by it has not been measured.

The fungus reproduces itself by means of spores which arise in large numbers on the leaves and in the later stages on the panicles. It is thought that the majority of the spores after being released quickly fall either on to other leaves or on to the water in the rice field or on to the ground because in experiments the number of spores caught on sticky glass slides placed above the crop was small. The spores which alight on the water may be carried to other rice plants and infect them.

The fungus is well equipped to survive from one season to the next, as it can do so in three ways. It is known that infection can take place from the soil and it has been suggested that this may be due to spores persisting there. The mycelium of the fungus is often present on the seed. In both cases the seedling can become infected and provide the inoculum for the later spread of the disease. The fungus also lives on other grasses and spores from this source may infect rice plants, but the relative importance of this is uncertain.

## METHODS OF CONTROL

Very good control of brown spot disease has been obtained in Japan by steeping the seed in a mercurial dip. Rates of infection of the seed as high as 60% are reduced to 4% by immersing the seed in a 0·5% Uspulun solution for 12 hrs. In Japan the disease has been brought to a low level; as long ago as 1956 it was reported that 85% of all the seed sown was treated with an organo-mercurial dip (Padwick, 1956).

REFERENCE
PADWICK, G. WATTS, *Outl. Agric.*, **1**, 20 (1956)

## Foot Rot (*Gibberella fujikuroi* (Saw.) Ito ap: Ito and Kimura)

Foot rot is potentially a serious rice disease, particularly in Japan and other parts of the Orient. It has caused losses of up to 40% of the crop (C.M.I., 1964). Its presence is readily seen in the field when the tillers are about 2 ft high, as the infected plants are markedly taller and paler than the healthy ones. The increased growth, however, comes to nothing as the plants which show these symptoms soon die afterwards. The Japanese name for the disease 'bakanae', which means foolish seedling, is thus appropriate.

The very odd effect of the foot rot fungus on the growth of the rice plant aroused the curiosity of plant physiologists. In 1926 it was shown that an extract from the fungus applied to a rice plant caused similar symptoms to those seen on naturally infected plants. From this it could be inferred that the fungus produced a chemical, or group of chemicals, which increased the rate of growth of both leaves and stem. Research on this problem was limited to Japan until 1952 when it was taken up in both the United Kingdom and the U.S.A. It was subsequently shown that gibberellic acid was the most abundant gibberellin present. With plentiful supplies of the active material, plant physiologists the world over rapidly explored the wide range of effects produced by this surprising by-product of a rice fungus (Brian, 1961).

The foot rot fungus can survive from one rice crop to the next both on the seed and in the soil, but the seed is undoubtedly the more important of the two. The grain becomes infected at flowering time and experiments have shown that this takes place readily. The appearance of the infected kernels after they have been harvested may vary from complete discoloration to brown spotting or to no obvious symptoms, depending on the degree of infection. The sowing of such seed gives a high proportion of diseased seedlings.

### METHODS OF CONTROL

In Japan where so much of the rice seed is treated for the control of blast, a very useful bonus has been the simultaneous control of foot rot, with the result that 'bakanae' has become uncommon (Padwick, 1956).

The descriptions of the three major rice diseases have each emphasised the value in Japan of the mercurial seed dressings in their control. The maximum benefits of seed treatment are most likely to occur in countries such as Japan where yields of 3 tons or more to the acre are obtained. In other countries where the yields are lower, often in the region of 1 ton per acre or less, the benefits are proportionately smaller. In India, for example, there is insufficient economic justification for their use except in the winter rice-growing areas where slow germination encourages seedling diseases (Callan, 1965).

REFERENCES
BRIAN, P. W., *Sci. Progr., London,* **49,** 1 (1961)
CALLAN, I. W., Personal communication (1965)
C.M.I., *Descriptions of Pathogenic Fungi and Bacteria,* No. 22, Commonwealth Mycological Institute, Kew (1964)
PADWICK, G. WATTS, *Outl. Agric.*, **1**, 20 (1956)

## VIRUS DISEASES

The most important virus disease of rice is dwarf or stunt, with the stripe disease in second place. They have received particular attention in Japan where the dwarf disease used to be very destructive before the introduction of control measures.

Rice plants suffering from dwarf disease are stunted in growth and develop numerous tillers, so that they have a tufted appearance. The general colour of the affected plants is rather darker green than that of a healthy plant. Closer inspection of a diseased leaf will show that there are interrupted streaks along the length, the individual dashes being yellowish-white.

The virus is spread by two species of leaf hopper, the chief vector being *Nephotettix apicalis*. It is a measure of the losses from the dwarf virus that it pays to prevent its dissemination by killing the vectors with insecticides, now widely practised in Japan (Padwick, 1956).

The stripe disease which is only found in Japan takes its name from the effect on the leaves which have one or more yellowish-green longtitudinal stripes. The virus also causes young leaves to grow abnormally with twisting, elongation and drooping. The yield of grain from affected plants is negligible.

The stripe virus is carried by a leaf hopper, *Delphacoides striatella,* but specific control measures to deal with it are not undertaken, as its importance is overshadowed by the vectors of dwarf virus.

REFERENCE

PADWICK, G. WATTS, *Outl. Agric.*, **1**, 20 (1956)

The production of maize, *Zea mays*, reached a figure of 226,200,000 tons metric (F.A.O., 1964) in 1963–4. It becomes, therefore, the third most important cereal crop in the world, being exceeded in quantity by only wheat and rice. Maize is used mainly for animal feeding but much is also used for diet, especially in Africa, India, Brazil and certain Central and South American countries; a little is used for industrial purposes.

Maize originated at one or more places in equatorial America. In the centuries following the discovery of the New World, it has been dispersed through the tropical and subtropical agricultural areas. As might be inferred from its origin, the major producing areas are in the Americas, particularly the U.S.A., which produces approximately 75% of the world's maize. As might be expected from the dominance of the U.S.A., much of the work on maize culture, pest and disease control, has been done there, with contributions from the other maize-growing countries.

Yields vary very much from country to country. The average yield in the U.S.A. is 3,783 lb per acre but in India is only 892 lb per acre. Higher yields are obviously to be found in countries where more artificial fertilizers are used.

The main pests of maize are few considering the very many different countries in which maize is grown. The two main pests are stalk borers and soil pests, principally wireworm. Stalk borers are present wherever maize is grown but wireworms occur mainly in the more northern latitudes of Europe and in the U.S.A. There is no collected account of pests of maize.

The pattern of disease control in maize is remarkably similar to that in wheat, dependence on the plant breeder for raising varieties which resists the foliage diseases and an extensive use of seed dressings to ensure maximum germination.

The maize diseases of international significance have been described briefly by Stakman (1957) and in greater detail by Dickson (1956). The incidence and relative importance of the various maize diseases occurring in the United States is dealt with in their Department of Agriculture's publication 'Plant Diseases' (U.S.D.A., 1953). A bibliography on maize with a section on its diseases has been published by the Research Station at Turrialba (Martinez *et al.*, 1960).

REFERENCES

DICKSON, J. G., *Diseases of Field Crops* (2nd Edn.), McGraw-Hill Book Co. Inc., New York (1956)

*F.A.O. Production Yearbook 1963–64,* **18,** F.A.O., Rome

MARTINEZ, A. and JAMES, C. N., *Maize: Bibliography of the publications available in the Institute Library, Turrialba* (2 vols. Diseases, Vol. II), 521–596 (*Rev. Appl. Mycol.,* **41,** 595)

United States Department of Agriculture, *Plant Diseases,* 377, The U.S. Government Printing Office, Washington, D.C. (1953)

STAKMAN, E. C. and HARRAR, J. G., *Principles of Plant Pathology,* The Ronald Press Company, New York (1957)

## LEPIDOPTERA SHOOT BORERS

### *Pyrausta nubilalis* Hubn. *(Pyralidae)*

This is the European Stalk Borer (Fig. 2.20). It occurs throughout the more southern latitudes in Europe, including Russia, but has now spread to the New World where it is an important pest in the U.S.A. and Mexico. It occurs in the Far East, where it appears to be of lesser importance than *Heliothis*.

The moths are light yellow-brown with darker markings. Eggs are laid in small groups of up to 50, usually on the undersides of leaves; females may deposit up to 1,000 eggs. The young caterpillars attempt to enter the plant after some feeding externally. When half-grown they make their way into the stalk and eventually damage the ear. The cater-

*Fig. 2.20.* Pyrausta nubilalis *(adult)*

pillar, which is pale and spotted, is at this stage $\frac{1}{2}$–1 in. in length. Pupation occurs in the stem in a cocoon. Overwintering takes place as a fully-fed caterpillar in the base of the stems of maize. Other plants are also attacked, particularly sorghum.

More than one generation can occur. In the U.S.A., two generations per season are normal but in some regions only one. In the Far East, three to four generations occur.

*Heliothis armigera* Hubn. *(Noctuidea)*

This is the Corn Earworm of the U.S.A. where it is usually called *Heliothis zea* Boddie (= *obsoleta* Fab.). It occurs all over the world wherever maize is grown. It is recorded as a pest in South America, Europe, India and the Far East, Africa and Australia. In many countries it is considered a more severe pest than *Pyrausta*.

Being a member of the *Noctuidae* the life-cycle differs from that of *Pyrausta*. The insect over-winters as a pupa in the soil. The moths, which emerge in spring, are of the Noctuid type, dull, with rounded wings and heavy bodies. Moths are nocturnal and females lay enormous numbers of eggs, usually 1,000 or more, not always in patches. At first, the caterpillars feed on the maize plant, particularly the 'silk' where eggs are usually laid. Later they enter the ear. When fully fed they drop to the soil for pupation.

Several generations occur in a season. The caterpillar is a general feeder, occurring also especially on tomato, tobacco and cotton.

Other species of *Heliothis* are also pests, notably *H. zea* Boddie. on cotton, *H. virescens* Fab. on tobacco, but these species also feed on maize and other cereals.

*Sesamia inferens* Wlk. *(Noctuidae)*

This is the Pink Shoot Borer of sugar-cane occurring in India and the Far East (Fig. 2.21). It also occurs in paddy. The moths are white in colour and the caterpillars pink (Fig. 2.22). On maize, eggs are deposited under the leaf

*Fig. 2.21.* Sesamia inferens *(adult)*

*Fig. 2.22.* Sesamia inferens *(caterpillar)*

in batches of 50–100, each female moth laying up to 500 eggs. The caterpillar bores down into the ear as in the case of *Heliothis*. Pupation occurs in the plant. Other species have similar cycles. Many plants are attacked, especially sorghum. Several generations occur in the course of the year, the stage of the plant determining the type of attack. Maize can also be attacked shortly after germination, leading to killing of the centre shoot. The insect over-winters in the base of the stalk.

There are numerous species of stalk boring *Sesamia* :

*Sesamia botanephaga* Tams or Bowden in West Africa, probably = *S. nonagriodes* Lef.
*S. calamistris* Hamps. in Uganda.
*S. nonagriodes* Lef. in Morocco and France.
*S. cretica* Led. in Kenya and the Sudan.
*S. poephaga* Tams. and Bowden in East Africa.

*Chilo zonellus* Swinh. *(Pyralidae)*

This insect is probably identical with *C. suppressalis* Wlk. which is primarily a pest of paddy. On maize, sorghum and other cereals and grasses it is usually called *C. zonellus*. It is a pale coloured moth with dark spots on the wings. The caterpillar is also pale pink. Eggs are laid in parallel rows in batches. The female laying about 500 in all. Pupation occurs in the stem of the plant and the caterpillar overwinters in the base of the stalk.

*Chilo* is not the most important maize stalk borer but occurs widely, usually mixed with a more dominant species. Two or sometimes more generations occur in a season.

*Elasmopalpus lignosellus* Zeller *(Pyralidae)*

This is the Lesser Corn-stalk Borer of the U.S.A. It appears to be more important and perhaps the dominant borer in Central and South America occurring in several countries, including Brazil and Peru. Eggs are laid in batches on the food plant. Caterpillars are bluish-green and eat the centres of the plant including the ear. Two generations a year occur.

*Diatraea saccharalis* Fab. *(Pyralidae)*

This is really a pest of sugar-cane but it occurs frequently on maize in South and Central America. Other spcies of *Diatraea* also occur in maize in this part of the world.

*Busseola fusca* Fuller *(Pyralidae)*

This is the maize-stalk borer of Africa. It is abundant in South Africa, the main maize-growing region, but also occurs in East, Central, and West Africa. Large numbers of eggs are laid between the leaves under the sheath, a few days after the maize appears above ground. The larvae enter the funnel of the leaves. A second generation occurs and attacks the ear (Plate 2.11).

*Plate 2.11. Damage to maize by stalk borer, South Africa (A.E. & C.I. Ltd., Johannesburg)*

METHODS OF CONTROL

*Cultural Methods.* It is usual to remark on methods of stalk borer control other than the use of insecticides. The methods usually suggested are either ploughing under of all stubble and trash or collecting the trash and burning it. The object in both cases is to prevent successful overwintering of the insect either by burying it or destroying it. Other suggestions are the use of resistant varieties and rotation of crops. It is doubtful if the former is of much value but rotation of crops has some merit as it means that moths emerging from old maize fields need to find the new ones to continue breeding. Probably the most useful measure is to time the sowing of maize so that it does not coincide with moth emergence. This usually means late sowing. As the date of sowing in many countries is determined by the rains it is unfortunate that rain also starts the emergence of the moths so that the two events run parallel.

*Chemical Methods.* Early attempts to use DDT against stalk borers showed that this insecticide could reduce the damage at relatively low cost. The accepted practise is to use 5% DDT dust applied to the plants by hand either from a tin or with a proper dust gun. As application is made direct to individual plants surprisingly low rates of 10–20 lb insecticide per acre are needed. Sprays can also be used of DDT at 0·1% dilution.

A good deal has been written about the use of DDT for the control of stalk borers, especially in the U.S.A. (Kulash, 1948), but probably one of the best accounts is that by Walker (1960) who published several papers dealing with the control of *Busseola fusca* in East Africa. Walker showed that sprays and dusts of DDT were equally effective but he tested other insecticides, endrin and isodrin, which were also effective. Yields of maize were increased about x2½ as a result of insecticidal treatment which was an ample return to pay for the cost of treatment at ruling prices of maize. The first application of DDT was made nine days after germination. Two more applications were necessary—the insecticides lasting for about ten days. The third application coincided with the 'silk' stage which is the second generation flight of moths. A single application of DDT was not good enough but endrin 2% dust was more effective in that only two applications were necessary. Walker showed that effective control could also be achieved with DDT at a 1% and 2·5% dust. DDT 5% dust at 10 lb per acre was, however, more economically justified than 2·5% dust at 20 lb per acre. Sprays were used at 10 gal per acre and gamma BHC as a spray at ·02% was also effective. Walker pointed out that yield increases in maize could also be achieved by using more suitable varieties and adequate manuring. Stalk borer control was essential when these factors had been omitted.

*Busseola* has in fact been the subject of insecticidal treatment since 1920 (Malley) when derris was used. Derris, however, was less lasting and was replaced by DDT in 1946. Derris liquid was used but success depended on the caterpillars being adequately soused in the derris solution. Derris dusts were no good.

Swain (1957) investigated the timing of the first application and suggested this should be related to egg hatch. Application should be made three days after egg hatch when plants were about 1 ft high. This is about three weeks after sowing and about two weeks after germination. Delayed application after this interval was less effective.

In the U.S.A. treatment of maize against *Heliothis* has been described by Anderson and his colleagues (1952) with DDT. He described the use of 5% DDT dust applied at the 'silk' stage by means of a shaving brush using 10 lb of dust per acre, usually coinciding with egg hatch. Over 80% control can be obtained. Aeroplane dusting with 5% DDT at 30–40 lb per acre was much less effective. Likewise aeroplane-spray treatment was no better. Field equipment using power dusters are again not very effective but a specially designed boom sprayer with paint-spray guns for individual treatment were much more effective. Anderson describes such a sprayer with stilts and a high boom carrying air-hose to spray guns for individual plant application by hand. U.S.A. recommendations always state that three to four applications at short intervals are needed. A mixture of mineral oil and DDT emulsifiable concentrate in water giving 0·75–1% DDT is recommended for spray-gun application. Fixed boom sprayers with four nozzles per row using 50 gal per acre are less effective.

Many trials have been carried out in the U.S.A. with DDT for stalk borer control, both against *Pyrausta* and *Heliothis*. These insects have also been test material for very many other insecticides during their development.

The recently introduced insecticide carbaryl ('Sevin') has been found very effective for *Heliothis* (Anderson and Reynolds, 1960), and as a 2% dust applied to the 'silk'. These investigations found carbaryl superior to other insecticides including endrin, endosulphan ('Thiodan'), heptachlor, trichlorophon ('Dipterex') and DDT. Semel (1959) also found carbaryl very effective, 0·5 lb per acre being equal to DDT at 1·5 lb per acre. He also found other insecticides including endosulphan, malathion, azinphos-ethyl and phosdrin much less effective.

Other investigators have found dieldrin and parathion very effective. Lespes (1957) reports trials against *Sesamia* with dieldrin ·06%, DDT ·25% parathion ·02% and derris ·02% rotenone. Dieldrin was very effective but was phytotoxic and tended to reduce yields. Parathion has never been adopted for stalk borer control, presumably on account of its toxic hazard.

A more recent development has been in the use of granular formulations of insecticides. Evidently the type of formulation can be employed at the whorl stages and also at the silk stage. Many trials have been carried out with granular formulations in the U.S.A. against stalk borers, principally with 5% DDT using 20 lb per acre (Cox *et al.*, 1957).

There is little doubt that insecticides can reduce damage especially from *Busseola, Pyrausta,* and *Heliothis.* Some information on the control of other species also exists. Isa (1958) reports control of *Sesamia cretica* Led. and *Chilo suppressalis* Wlk. in Egypt with DDT 50% at 10 lb per 100 gal sprayed four times on maize. Harding (1960) reports control of *Elasmopalpus* with granular insecticides. Bowden (1956) controlled *Sesamia botanephaga* in West Africa with 5% DDT dust and Lespes (1957) of *Sesamia nonagrioides* in Morocco.

*Control by parasites.* This aspect of control by biological means has been thoroughly investigated, especially with regard to *Pyrausta* and *Heliothis.* Very many records of parasites of these species have been made. Some attempts to multiply and introduce parasites into the U.S.A. have not been particularly successful in reducing populations. Conrad (1959) states that the Coccinellid beetle *Ceratomegilla maculata* Deg. reduced the eggs of Pyrausta by 15%. Probably the most successful parasite in the U.S.A. is the Tachinid fly *Lydella stabulans grisescens* R. and D. which attacks the larval stages of *Pyrausta.* An account of the introduction of *Lydella* is given by Baker and Bradley (1940).

*Pyrausta* is also attacked by the protozoan *Perezia pyraustae* which is transmitted by the female moth to eggs and thence destroys the larvae (Kramer, 1959). This disease frequently reduces the number of caterpillars. Infection also occurs with the fungus *Beauveria* but only against small larvae (York, 1958). The bacterium *Bacillus thuringiensis* is ineffective against *Pyrausta* (Hofmaster *et al.*, 1960). It does not appear that control either by parasites or by diseases is likely to be either reliable or effective.

*Resistant Varieties.* The problem of resistance of maize to *Pyrausta* has also been thoroughly investigated. Certain hybrid varieties are less severely attacked by *Pyrausta* (Chiang and Holdaway, 1960). This resistance takes the form of the inability of the very young larvae to survive in some varieties. Loomis, Back and Stauffer (1957) claimed this was due to a factor inhibitor which was identified as 6-methoxy-2(3)-benzoxazolinone.

REFERENCES

ANDERSON, L. D. and BACON, O. G., *Calif. Agri.*, **6** (1952)
ANDERSON, L. D. and REYNOLDS, H. T., *J. Econ Entomol.*, **53**, 22 (1960)
BAKER, W. A. and BRADLEY, W. G., *R.A.E.*, **31**, 288 (1940)
BOWDEN, J., *New Gold Coast Farmer*, **1**, 23 (1956)
CHIANG, H. C. and HOLDAWAY, F. G., *J. Econ. Entomol.*, **53**, 910 (1960)
CONRAD, M. S., *J. Econ. Entomol*, **52**, 843 (1959)
COX, H. C., LOVELY, W. G. and BRINDLEY, T. A., *J. Econ. Entomol.*, **49**, 834 (1957)
HARDING, J., *J. Econ. Entomol*, **53**, 664 (1960)
HOFMASTER, R. N., BRAY, D. F. and DITMAN, L. P., *J. Econ. Entomol.*, **53**, 624 (1960)
ISA, A. L., *Agri. Res. Rev.* **36**, 73 (1958)
KRAMER, J. P., *R.A.E.*, **49**, 94 (1959)
KULASH, W. M., *J. Econ. Entomol.* **41**, 387 (1948)
LESPES, L., *R.A.E.*, **46**, 295 (1957)
LOOMIS, R. S., BACK, S. D. and STAUFFER, J. F., *R.A.E.*, **46**, 458 (1957)
MALLEY, C. W., *Bull. Dept. Agri. S. Africa*, **3**, 111 (1920)
SEMEL, M., *J. Econ. Entomol.*, **52**, 1111 (1959)
SWAIN, G., *Bull. Entomol. Res.*, **48**, 711 (1957)
WALKER, P. T., *Bull. Entomol. Res.*, **51**, 321 (1960)
WALKER, P. T., *East Af. J. Agr.*, **25**, 165 (1960)
YORK, G. T., *R.A.E.*, **49**, 232 (1958)

## ARMYWORMS

Maize is attacked by several species of *Noctuidae* known as armyworms. The synonymy of the names and the identity of the species is confused. The following are important species.

*Cirphis unipuncta* Haw. This is the Rice Climbing Caterpillar, Rice Armyworm or Rice Cutworm of the Far East.

*Laphygma frugiperda* S. and A. is the Fall Armyworm of the U.S.A. It occurs also in Central and South America and the West Indies.

*Laphygma exempta* Wlk. is the African Armyworm but is probably identical with *Cirphis unipuncta* of the Far East and with *L. exigua* Hubn. called the Beet Armyworm in the U.S.A.

*Laphygma frugiperda* S. and A. *(Noctuidae)*

This insect is found in the southern part of the U.S.A. attacking many different plants especially cereals and grasses (Fig. 2.23). The moths are dark coloured, the female depositing up to 1,000 eggs. The caterpillars are at first gregarious but later spread out and consume vegetation everywhere. They usually pass unnoticed until they are about 1 in long. Pupation takes place in the soil. The armyworm habit arises from the tendency of the caterpillar to move in a body to new feeding grounds.

*Fig. 2.23.* Laphygma frugiperda *(adult)*

*Laphygma exempta* Wlk. *(Noctuidae)*

This insect is described from Africa by Whellan (1954) and has a similar life-cycle. Whellan states that the caterpillars change colour from green to black when it migrates in armyworm fashion. Outbreaks occur from 5 to 6 years. It also feeds mainly on cereal and grasses.

Other species of armyworms are often described but appear to be the same insect differently named. For example: *Pseudaletia australis* is described from New South Wales, Australia and in Asia generally but it is probably identical with *Cirphis unipuncta* Haw. and with *P. separata* Wlk.

Other species are *Persectania ewingii* Westw. also in Australia, *P. aversa* Wlk. in New Zealand probably identical with *P. composita* Guen. *Chorizagrotis auxiliaris* Wlk. occurs in the U.S.A.

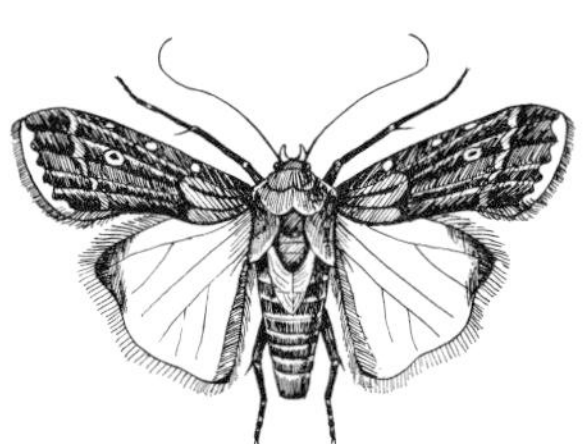

*Fig. 2.24.* Agrotis ypsilon *(adult)*

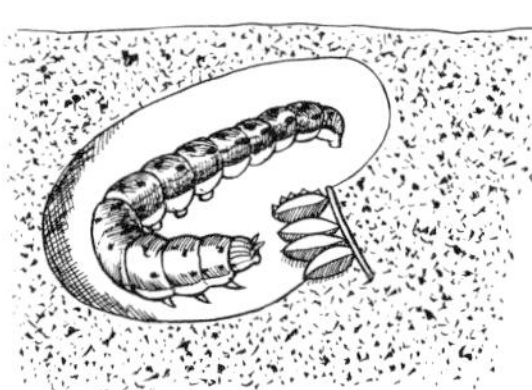

*Fig. 2.25.* Agrotis ypsilon *(caterpillar in soil)*

CUTWORMS

The cutworms are also very injurious to maize. Many species exist, usually of *Agrotis* or *Euxoa,* all *Noctuidae.* The Black Cutworm, *Agrotis ypsilon* Rott. (Fig. 2.24), appears to be one of the most injurious and widely distributed. Cutworms and armyworms both belong to the *Noctuidae* and are in fact indistinguishable in habit. Cutworms, as a rule, live in the soil surface (Fig. 2.25) rather than on the plant and do not normally migrate as a group in search of food. Both these events can, however, occur so that there is really no distinction. The moths deposit large numbers of eggs, usually 1,000, on plants and weeds. The caterpillar overwinters usually about one-third grown. One generation occurs in the more northern latitudes but several generations occur in warmer climates. Fully grown the caterpillars reach nearly 2 in in length. Pupation occurs in the soil.

Many species are listed from different countries but the pattern of life-cycle is much the same. The cutworm generally lives in the soil attacking plants at soil level as distinct from stalk borers and leaf feeding caterpillars. Several plants may be attacked by one insect. The moths appear to be attracted to flood land and it is in such regions that outbreaks of cutworms occur again similar to armyworm habits.

## METHODS OF CONTROL

General advice is usually given such as discing to destroy pupae or overwintering larvae. It is also recommended that fields should not become weedy. It is doubtful if such measures are either worth while or effective.

*Chemical Methods.* Insecticidal baits are standard methods of cutworm control. Early baits consisted of bran, as an attractant, and Paris Green as poison. Usually the ratio was 25 pt bran to 1 pt toxicant, usually with water and even sometimes molasses were added (Brooks and Anderson, 1947). The bait was broadcast over the field at 25 lb per acre.

Later experiments used DDT, BHC, chlordane and other synthetic insecticides as toxicants but more modern methods employ the toxicant directly as a spray or dust to the caterpillars. There is now ample evidence that both against armyworms and cutworms direct application at the time of attack is the most effective method. DDT and mixtures of DDT and BHC were first used. Kulash (1948) used 5% DDT plus 3% gamma BHC at 30–35 lb dust per acre direct application against *L. frugiperda*. Kulash (1949) showed that pre-planting soil treatments were of little value unless made just before planting. Soil application of chlordane 5%, DDT 10%, gamma BHC 1%, all at 20 lb per acre, were effective against *Agrotis ypsilon*. Nirula (1961) in India found pre-planting application effective with gamma BHC at 2 lb per acre.

Many experiments have been carried out, especially in the U.S.A., against *Laphygma*. Most insecticides are effective but probably the most widely tested and used is DDT at about 1 lb per acre, preferably as an emulsifiable concentrate. Good results with DDT have been reported from Australia (Zack, 1954) against *Pseudaletia* and New Zealand (Lowe, 1956; Hamblyn, 1959) against *Persectania*, both DDT dust and sprays were used. Application of DDT by aeroplane at 5–10 gal per acre of wash was also successful. The consensus of opinion seems to be against the successful use of granular formulations (Harrison *et al.*, 1959). New insecticides have also been tried in many experiments and carbaryl ('Sevin') has proved remarkably good at 1·5 lb per acre (Henderson *et al.*, 1962) (Ganett and Reed, 1960).

Application should be made as soon as the caterpillars are seen. On upstanding plants, such as maize, this should present no difficulty but aeroplane application is obviously more suitable for open ranges where the caterpillars are feeding on grasses. In the case of cutworms application covers the soil surface, the crop plants and weeds with a fine layer of insecticide so the caterpillar comes in contact with the deposit as soon as it comes above ground.

*Bacillus thuringiensis* is evidently ineffective against *Laphygma* (Hall and Anders, 1959). Parasitism occurs but is not considered an important factor in control; more important are predators, especially birds.

REFERENCES

BROOKES, J. W. and ANDERSON, L. D., *J. Econ. Entomol.*, **40**, 220 (1947)

GANETT, P. and REED, J. P., *J. Econ. Entomol.*, **53**, 388 (1960)

HALL, I. M. and ANDERS, L. A., *J. Econ. Entomol.*, **52**, 877 (1959)

HAMBLYN, C. J., *New Zealand J. Agri.*, **98**, 329 (1959)
HARRISON, F. P., COAN, R. M. and DITMAN, L. P., *J. Econ. Entomol.*, **52**, 838 (1954)
HENDERSON, C. F., KINZER, H. G. and HATCHETT, J. H., *J. Econ. Entomol.*, **55**, 1005 (1962)
KULASH, W. M., *J. Econ. Entomol.*, **41**, 387 (1948)
KULASH, W. M., *J. Econ. Entomol.*, **42**, 705 (1949)
LOWE, A. D., *New Zealand J. Agri.*, **92**, 377 (1956)
NIRULA, K. K., *R.A.E.*, **51**, 256 (1954)
WHELLAN, J. A., *J. Agri. Rhodesia*, **51**, 415 (1961)
ZACK, E. H., *Agri. Gaz. N.S.W.*, **54**, 423 (1954)

## COLEOPTERA

### *Heteronychus sanctae-helenae* Blanch. *(Scarabaeidae)*

The Black Maize Beetle is a pest of maize in Australia. Related species occur in the southern parts of Africa, notably *H. lica* Klug, and *H. arator* F. There would appear to be no counterparts of these insects in other maize-growing districts of the world. The white grubs of the U.S.A. are similar entomologically, also belonging to the *Scarabaeidae* but their habits are quite different.

The Black Maize Beetle feeds on grasses and cereals including maize. It will attack vegetables but its favourite food would appear to be maize. Most of the damage to plants is caused by the adults, which feed below ground on the root-system of plants. Feeding can continue for many months. The larvae, which are characteristic Scarabaeid type, large fleshy and curved, also feed on the roots of plants but appear capable of surviving on the organic matter in the soil as their sole diet. The beetle passes through an annual cycle the adults surviving for at least nine months. Eggs are laid in the soil at the base of plants and the larvae live for about two to three months.

#### METHODS OF CONTROL

Cultural recommendations are usually made in connection with this pest. Ploughing and discing can destroy pupae and expose larvae to birds. Chemical measures were developed in 1945 which were much more realistic.

*Chemical Control.* Wallace (1945) in New South Wales, Australia, appears to have initiated trials with the newest synthetic insecticides, first DDT and then BHC. He found that DDT was toxic to adults in soil at 1 pt per 1,000 but in field tests only high rates of about 360 lb per acre were effective. Wallace (1946) also tried BHC first crude and later gamma BHC but his best progress was made with the idea of strip treatment. In this method only a narrow band of soil, where the maize seed was planted, was treated. By this method DDT 10% dust at 1 lb per 22 yd (approx. 200 lb per acre at yard rows) gave perfect protection, presumably by concentrating the dust at the position required. It could be also stirred into the soil with a cultivator or used in some fertilizer mixtures. Wallace also developed a base-of-plant treatment using a sort of drench. Gamma BHC at ·05% gave perfect control. Wallace (1948) suggested baits against the adults could also be used with gamma BHC insecticide, 3 lb of a 1·3% dust per cwt of bait. Seed-dressings are unlikely to be effective but no trials appear to have been carried out.

*Heteronychus* evidently prefers peaty soils, no doubt obtaining some nutrient from their content of organic matter. Peaty soils are drier whereas both adults and larvae are susceptible to wet conditions. In such circumstances the larvae suffer from 'Milky Disease' *Bacillus euloomarabae.*

### *Agriotes spp. (Elateridae)*

Wireworms are also pests of maize. Many species are concerned. In Europe *Agriotes spp.* with a four-year cycle are the most common but in the U.S.A. species of *Limonius* and *Melanotus* are more important.

*Agriotes lineatus* L.
*Agriotes obscurus* L.
*Melanotus communis* Gylk.
*Limonius canus* Lec.
*Limonius californicans* Mannh.
*Agriotes mancus* Say.

Injury is caused below ground by the larval stage which is a hard, stiff insect, bright yellow in colour. The larvae attack the stems of plants below the soil surface but they also attack seeds, especially large seeds such as maize.

Wireworms normally inhabit grassland and so injury is more likely in fields ploughed from grass. The usual sign of wireworm damage is patchy appearance in the field. As the larvae live for several years in the soil damage to crops after breaking up of grassland can continue at least two years but by the third year the number of wireworms in the soil has fallen so that it is too small to affect the crop. The adults prefer grassland into which to lay eggs but rotations including many cereal crops also allow the population of wireworms in the soil to build up.

### METHODS OF CONTROL

Various cultural measures are usually recommended against wireworms such as fallowing, sowing less susceptible crops after grass and so on, but control directly in relation to maize itself must be chemical.

*Chemical Control*. It is an established practise to control wireworms with modern synthetic insecticides, notably lindane, aldrin, dieldrin and heptachlor. Early trials also included DDT but this insecticide was found to be relatively ineffective as a soil insecticide against wireworms. Interest shifted to BHC and finally gamma BHC. At the rate of ½–2 lb of gamma BHC per acre good control of wireworm was obtained judged by increasing plant stand. Very many papers have been written about trials with soil insecticides against wireworms but for the protection of maize in particular have been almost entirely carried out in the U.S.A.

Soil application with gamma BHC, aldrin and heptachlor was effective as shown in repeated trials. Seed-dressing of maize with insecticidal dressings never gave satisfactory protection of seeds against wireworms and when gamma BHC was used at about 1% severe phytotoxicity often followed. Early trials with gamma BHC as a seed-dressing were carried out on cereals, especially wheat. The first trials on maize appear to have been carried out by Lange *et al.* (1949) and by Dogger and Lilley (1949). These trials and many later tests (Kulash and Monroe, 1954) were entirely in the laboratory in which germination was investigated and sometimes the effect of dressed maize seed on wireworms. There is a dearth of field tests with seed-dressing on maize against these insects. Kulash (1953) in North Carolina reported that seed-dressings of gamma BHC at 0·125% were ineffective in field tests although good in laboratory pot tests. Phytotoxicity of gamma BHC to maize at less than 1% by weight was reported by many observers (Dogger and Lilley, 1949). Duffield (1952) also reported phytotoxicity from gamma BHC, likewise Biggen and Blanchard (1955) and many other observers showed that even at 0·2% phytotoxicity can occur with gamma BHC.

The concensus of opinion would appear to be that seed-dressing is of little value on maize against wireworms, probably because each seed holds too little insecticide to protect it against vigorous attack from heavy infestations of wireworms. While maize is frequently dressed with a fungicide (usually TMTD) little use appears to be made of insecticidal dressings.

### *Diabrotica spp. (Chrysomelidae)*

Species *Diabrotica* are important pests of maize in the U.S.A. and Canada where they are the rootworms. The adults are small bronze or greenish beetles. Several species occur in certain parts of the U.S.A. corn belt, notably *Diabrotica longicornis* Say., and *D. duodecim-punctata,* Fab. The adults feed on foliage of many plants but evidently the larvae only feed on maize, attacking the larger roots. The cycle is annual, the insect overwintering as eggs. The larvae can become so numerous as to be often the most important pest of maize in certain regions of the U.S.A. Damage to the root system by the larvae usually causes the plants to fall over through lack of root-hold.

METHOD OF CONTROL

There seems to be little doubt that rootworm injury is intensified by continuous corn-growing. As these insects live principally on maize, the rotation of crops is in itself a method of control. Alternative crops, to break into rootworm build up, are clover and cereals, such as oats. Maize should be taken only once in three years.

*Chemical Control.* Early attempts to use soil insecticides (Hill *et al.*, 1948) found BHC superior to DDT. Application was made by spraying before and after planting. Kulash (1949) used dusts in the seed row and found BHC very effective and DDT of little value. Other investigations (Floyd and Smith, 1949) also confirmed the value of BHC. Different insecticides have also been used including aldrin and dieldrin. All are effective at recognised application rates. For gamma BHC this is 1–2 lb per acre, usually applied as dust before sowing. There is no evidence that seed-dressing can be used against *Diabrotica*.

## White Grubs *(Melolonthinae, Scarabaeidae)*

White Grubs are often pests of maize but this type of insect larva is more frequently a pest of grassland, especially in light and peaty soils. The beetles are usually large and feed on the foliage of trees but the larvae inhabit the soil as large white fleshy grubs, curved in a characteristic fashion. Many species occur as pests of maize. In the U.S.A. and Canada the species is mainly *Phyllophaga*. In Africa the species are *Adoretus, Schizonycha, Anomala,* etc. Some species spend three years of larval life in the soil, others only two. African species usually go through an annual cycle.

Populations in soil can become numerous but eggs are laid principally in grassland or fields covered in grasses or dense crops. These larvae can cause destruction of the roots of maize plants so that a patchy stand develops. *Schizonychus* and other African species behave differently in that they are not associated with grass land but can lay eggs in soil in cultivation.

METHODS OF CONTROL

The problem of control of Melolonthid larvae differs according to whether the insects inhabit grassland or arable land. On ploughed or arable land no difficulty should arise as crops can be rotated and time of sowing varied. Moreover chemicals can be easily introduced into the soil. If land contains many white grubs, it is best to crop with legumes or cereals and not with susceptible crops such as maize, potatoes, sugar beet and tobacco. In Africa, where the female beetle likes to oviposit in ploughed land, ploughing can sometimes be delayed until after the female beetles have finished egg-laying. In some countries where the larvae remain in the soil for 2–3 years, well recognized flight years are predictable. In such years the area under maize is reduced.

*Chemical Methods.* In ploughed land the number of larvae always tends to decline but if necessary land can be treated prior to sowing. Early work showed that BHC was superior to DDT for white grub control. Incorporation into the soil of BHC at 2 lb gamma BHC per acre was effective against Melolonthid larvae (Ehrenhardt 1957). Alternatively, aldrin at higher rates of 3–4 lb can be used.

In Africa, Tarr (1954) reported good control of *Schizonychus* larvae by seed dressings on sorghum. He used a dressing of TMTD 25% (against covered smut) with 20% gamma BHC at 1:450 (about 0·2%). There appears to be no evidence that seed-dressing will prevent injury to maize by other Melolonthid larvae.

## *Tanymecus abyssinicus* Hust. *(Curculionidae)*

This beetle has also been reported damaging maize in Abyssinia and Roumania. The adults feed on the young plants (Jannone, 1947).

## HEMIPTERA

Apart from the Chinch bug in the U.S.A. there are no important maize pests in this Order. Aphids, especially *Aphis maidis* Fitch are occasionally reported on maize but are of no importance. Likewise species of *Pyrilla* sometimes occur on maize in India and Pakistan.

### *Blissus leucopterus* Say. *(Lygaeidae)*

The Chinch Bug of the U.S.A. is a pest peculiar to America and appears to have no counterpart elsewhere. It occurs in Canada, Mexico and parts of Central America.

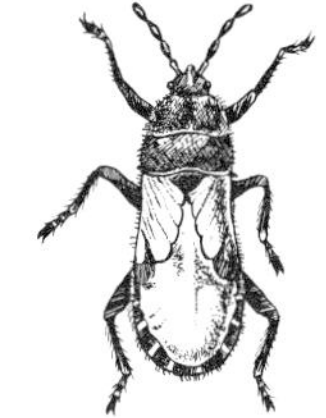

*Fig. 2.26.* Blissus leucopterus *(adult)*

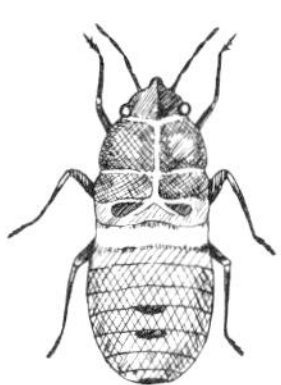

*Fig. 2.27.* Blissus leucopterus *(nymph)*

This insect lives on grasses and cereals, overwintering in the adult stage. It becomes a pest of maize when it moves on to this crop in July. It starts a new generation on maize and so the crop is invaded by many bugs. They leave the maize and return to grasses where they spend the winter.

The adult insect is small and black with white wing markings (Fig. 2.26). It is also a stink bug giving off a vile odour when crushed. Early nymphs (Fig. 2.27) are reddish but they become darker in later instars.

#### METHODS OF CONTROL

Chinch Bugs feed only on grasses, cereals and similar crops and do not feed on non-grass crops. Rotation of crops would tend to keep the numbers down, if cereals and maize were rotated with legumes.

Modern synthetic insecticides can be used against Chinch Bugs as necessary. Most insecticides are effective including DDT, gamma BHC, and parathion. More recently carbaryl has been shown to be effective.

## DIPTERA

### *Hylemyia cilicrura,* Rond. *(Anthomyidae)*

This is the only pest in this order and is called The Seed Corn Maggot. This insect is a true fly with a larval stage resembling a maggot. It attacks other plants beside maize, notably beans of the *phaseolus* type but probably the larvae are able to live successfully in decaying vegetable matter.

The fly deposits eggs in the soil, especially that in which there is decaying vegetable matter such as farmyard manure. The larvae moves through the soil and will attack seeds if present. Bean seeds are particularly susceptible but others including maize is also attacked. Several generations occur each year.

#### METHODS OF CONTROL

Cultural methods are hardly effective against this insect as its occurrence is seldom predictable. It is important to avoid planting susceptible crops in cold soil so that germination is delayed. Quick germination must be encouraged.

Soil application of insecticides such as gamma BHC, aldrin, and heptachlor will control the seed corn maggot easily. Such treatment is hardly justified unless crops are subject to attack. Seed dressing of maize is seldom undertaken to prevent attacks by this insect so no records of experiments of this kind exist. The insecticide gamma BHC should be used as a seed dressing at 0·3% of a 20% product.

REFERENCES

BIGGEN, J. H. and BLANCHARD, R. A., *J. Econ. Entomol.*, **48**, 255 (1955)

DOGGER, J. R. and LILLEY, J. H., *J. Econ. Entomol.*, **42**, 286 (1949)

DUFFIELD, P. C., *J. Econ. Entomol.*, **45**, 672 (1952)

EHRENHARDT, H., *R.A.E.*, **46**, 204 (1957)

FLOYD, E. H. and SMITH, C. E., *J. Econ. Entomol*, **42**, 908 (1949)

HILL, ROSCOE, E., HIXSON, E. and MUMA, M. H., *J. Econ. Entomol.*, **41**, 392 (1948)

JANNORE, G., *R.A.E.*, **38**, 131 (1947)

KULASH, W. M., *J. Econ. Entomol.*, **42**, 558 (1949)

KULASH, W. M. and MONROE, R. J., *J. Econ. Entomol.*, **47**, 341 (1954)

KULASH, W. M., *J. Econ. Entomol.*, **46**, 433 (1953)

LANGE, W. H., CARLSON, E. C. and LEACH, L. D., *J. Econ. Entomol.*, **42**, 942 (1949)

TARR, S. A. J., *Ann. Appl. Biol.*, **41**, 578 (1954)

WALLACE, C. R., *Agri. Gaz.*, **56**, 186 (1945); **57**, 200 (1946); **59**, 435 (1948)

## MAIZE RUSTS (*PUCCINIA* SPP.)

The two principal rusts attacking maize are caused by *P. sorghi* Schw. and *P. polysora* Under. Both have been of considerable importance during the post-war years. The story of their spread, their control and their effect is a good example of the importance of plant pathology to both primitive and advanced communities.

Maize rust due to *P. sorghi* produces circular to elongate cinnamon brown powdery pustules which arise on both surfaces of the leaf. Its life cycle is typical of those rusts which have an alternate host. The uredospores, or summer spores, serve to spread the disease from plant to plant. In the autumn, the teleutospores, which are black in colour, are produced. In the spring the teleutospores germinate producing sporidia, the small secondary spores which infect *Oxalis spp.* but cannot attack maize. The fungus goes through the sexual cycle on the alternate host and finally produces aecidiospores which start up the infection again on maize plants.

Maize rust is found in the U.S.A. and is common throughout Latin America and Africa. For many years it was regarded as of minor importance in the U.S.A., but it became increasingly prevalent during the 1950s (C.M.I., 1964a). It affected both dent and sweet corn hybrids particularly in the central States. The increased susceptibility of the maize plants would appear to be due to the replacement of the open pollinated maize by hybrids which lacked resistant genes. This necessitated the introduction of new genes which were provided by some of the maize varieties grown in Mexico.

The rust caused by *P. polysora* has smaller and more circular pustules than those of *P. sorghi*. It has a simple life history as it persists on maize throughout the year and no alternate host is known. It flourishes under tropical conditions with temperatures around 27°C and with high relative humidity. The rust due to *P. polysora* is of minor importance in the U.S.A. but is common in the tropical areas of South America. Prior to 1948 its known distribution was limited to the Americas (C.M.I., 1964b) but in 1949 it was found in Sierra Leone. The speed with which the disease spread was remarkable, in 1950 it reached the Ivory Coast, the Gold Coast and southern Nigeria. After a short pause, it moved on to the Cameroons, to East Africa as far as Zanzibar and down the east coast through Tanganyika as far as Zululand. A few months later it was spreading through the widely scattered islands of the Indian Ocean, and eventually reached Mauritius, Réunion, Madagascar and the Seychelles group. The securing of these bridgeheads finally resulted in its invasion of North Borneo, Siam and Malaya (Rhind, 1957).

The effect of the disease on the maize varieties grown in Africa was devastating, up to 70% of the crop being destroyed. It was thus a fearful threat to all those Africans and Asians who were dependent on maize for much of their food. The menace was met by the setting up in 1952 of a research unit at Ibadan, west Nigeria, and similar steps were taken at the same time in Kenya and Dahomey. What had to be done was obvious, namely the introduction of less susceptible varieties. Fortunately, the kinds of maize grown in Central America and Mexico were known to be resistant and although they were unsuitable for African conditions, they have proved to be excellent parents for the breeding of new varieties which are unaffected by the *polysora* rust.

The change was not immediately popular. The old standard West African maize varieties were white, soft and easy to pound, whereas the new ones were yellow and hard. Their introduction has, however, been doubly beneficial as not only has the crop yield been increased, but the dietetic value of the maize improved.

REFERENCES

C.M.I., *Descriptions of Pathogenic Fungi and Bacteria*, **3** and **4**, Commonwealth Mycological Institute, Kew (1964)

RHIND, D., *Plant Protection Conference 1956*, 23, Butterworths Scientific Publications, London (1957)

## LEAF DISEASES

Leaf blight and leaf spot commonly attack maize foliage, and if conditions favour the diseases, the damage to the leaves can cause serious crop losses.

### Leaf Blight (*Trichometasphaeria turcica* [Passerini] Luttrell *conidia Helminthosporium turcicum* Passerini)

Leaf blight has a wide distribution throughout the world and attacks not only maize but also Sudan grass and other sorghums. In the U.S.A. it is commonly found in the southern part of the Corn Belt, eastward to the Altantic coast and extending to Florida.

The lesions caused by the fungus first look water-soaked, before changing to light brown and finally as they dry out, dark brown to black. The disease starts on the lower leaves and then spreads to those above. The conidia, which are wind-borne, are produced abundantly on both surfaces of the leaves. The fungus overwinters on the maize trash and produces conidia in the spring to re-start the life cycle. The losses due to leaf blight vary from negligible amounts to as high as 50%.

#### METHODS OF CONTROL

In Florida in 1951 and 1952, the outbreaks of the diseases were sufficiently serious to justify the use of fungicides for its control. Sweet corn and hybrid maize seed growers sprayed or dusted their crops six to eight times with zineb fungicides. The use of fungicides is, however, only justified in special circumstances and most growers depend on the maize breeder to make use of the resistant inbred lines which are now known.

### Leaf Spot (*Cochliobolus heterostrophus* [Drechsl.] Drechsl.)

Leaf spot behaves in much the same way as leaf blight. In the field, there is a marked difference in the colour of the lesions, the leaf spot being light in colour, the other dark. The general life history of the two leaf diseases is similar, but leaf spot thrives in the warmer maize-growing areas of the U.S.A. Fortunately, most of the important commercial varieties of maize are relatively unaffected.

## SEED DECAY

This is caused by various fungi including:

Dry rot (*Diplodia zeae* [Schw.] Lév.)
Pink ear rot (*Gibberella zeae* [Schw.] Petch)
Seedling blight (*Gibberella fujikuroi* [Saw.] Ito ap. Ito and Kimura)

Maize seed when planted is vulnerable to infection by a number of fungi which may be either carried on the seed or present in the soil.

The seed-borne fungi include dry rot, pink ear rot and seedling blight. In the U.S.A. dry rot is rated as the most virulent member of the group and is particularly prevalent in the warmer and wetter maize-growing regions. Pink ear rot is more important in the cooler areas, but severe damage only occurs in cold soils. Although seedling blight is found throughout the U.S.A. maize-growing areas, it does not as a rule cause much loss as it is only weakly parasitic.

The soil-inhabiting fungi are, however, the predominant cause of decay of maize seed. Rots of this kind, as with many other seeds, are favoured by cold, wet soils which make for slow germination. Various species of *Pythium* are the main cause of seed rotting, and the optimum temperature for their activity lies between 48°F and 50°F which is rather too cold for maize. Other fungi, such as *Helminthosporium, Fusarium, Sclerotium* and *Corticium* occur, but they are all of minor importance compared with the *Pythium* species. If, however, the soil is warm, the maize seed germinates rapidly and losses are negligible.

## METHODS OF CONTROL

With all farming operations, the plant population per acre plays a most important part in the final crop yield and techniques to ensure this are quickly adopted. In common with other cereals, the use of sound seed combined with seed dressing is the best way of obtaining a full stand of maize. The first dressings used were the organo-mercurials but they have now been largely replaced by organic compounds such as thiram, dichlone and captan (U.S.D.A., 1953), because they are better protectants than the mercury compounds.

Maize is a difficult seed to coat with a dust because of its polished waxy skin and better adhesion has been obtained by treatment of the seed with a wet slurry dressing made by mixing a wettable powder with a small quantity of water. The slurry treatment has the further advantage of keeping the atmosphere round the treater dust-free, which is beneficial when either captan or thiram are being applied because although they are both relatively non-toxic they are unpleasant when inhaled.

For slurry application, captan and thiram are formulated as wettable powders which are used at the rate of 2–3 oz per 100 lb of seed. In the U.S.A. practically all the hybrid maize sold by the seed companies is treated in this way (Reed, 1965). In South Africa where dry rot is liable to be serious, the organo-mercurials were the preferred dressings, but captan and thiram slurries have now been introduced.

### REFERENCES

United States Department of Agriculture, *Plant Diseases, the Yearbook of Agriculture,* 337, The U.S. Government Printing Office, Washington, D.C. (1953)

REED, L. R., Personal communication (1965)

# SORGHUM

Sorghum is the outstanding cereal for growing in the drier parts of the tropical and subtropical regions of the world as it possesses remarkable powers of drought resistance. The world acreage under millet and sorghum is 256 million acres (F.A.O., 1964). It is very widely grown as a peasant crop in both Africa and Asia and is eaten mainly in porridge form as the grain is too low in gluten for making good bread. The fact that sorghum is grown in the less fertile agricultural areas and produces grain of medium palatability has tended to make it the Cinderella of the cereals. The growth in the world's population will force agriculturalists to make an increasing use of marginal land areas and sorghum appears to be the ideal crop for this purpose in the warmer and drier regions.

The peasant culture of sorghum makes it difficult to assess the relative importance of the different diseases attacking the crop. All parts of the plant can be affected by fungous diseases and their incidence varies with the climate and the variety grown. A survey of the grain losses in the British Commonwealth countries in Africa showed that smut was the most serious, responsible for an estimated 6·6% loss. The total loss due to all diseases was estimated as being at least 9·0% (Padwick, 1956). This figure may well be on the low side as diseases such as leaf blight, anthracnose and bacterial blights are very widely distributed and take their annual toll.

A very thorough survey of the diseases attacking sorghum has recently been written by Tarr (1962) and has been the main source of information for this section.

The pests which attack sorghum are, in most cases, the same as those which occur on maize, and accordingly do not require special consideration.

REFERENCES

*F.A.O. Production Yearbook 1963–1964,* **18,** F.A.O., Rome

PADWICK, G. WATTS, 'Losses caused by Plant Diseases in the Colonies', Phytopath., Paper No. 1, The Commonwealth Mycological Institute, Kew (1956)

TARR, S. A. J., *Diseases of Sorghum, Sudan Grass and Broom Corn,* Commonwealth Mycological Institute, Kew (1962)

Covered smut (*Sphacelotheca sorghi* [Link] Clinton)

In this disease, the grains in the seed head are filled with the dark brown spores of the fungus, which replace the normal food reserves of the seed. As the name indicates, the spores usually remain within the 'smut balls', and are released at threshing time. The fungus spores adhere to the surface of the grain and contaminate the healthy seed.

The disease has followed sorghum wherever it is grown, an almost inevitable result of the ease with which the fungus contaminates the seed. Losses vary greatly and although damage as high as 100% has been recorded, the overall figure would appear to be between 5% and 10%

As already indicated, the fungus is seed-borne. The spores germinate in the soil, but the actual mode of development is very variable. In essence, the process consists in the growth of a promycelium which bear sporidia. The sporidia then develop hyphae which penetrate into the young sorghum plant. The mycelium grows with the host without any apparent injury to it until it reaches the influorescence where it develops inside the grains. The general life history is very similar to that of bunt of wheat.

### METHODS OF CONTROL

The covered smut spores are susceptible to most of the fungicides used in seed dressings. Copper carbonate, the organo-mercurials, chloranil, dichlone and thiram, are all effective.

As there is no particular advantage in using the toxic organo-mercurials, the relatively safe organic materials are preferred. In the U.S.A. the sorghum seed is usually treated by the slurry method, similar to that used for maize. This involves the use of specialised seed treaters, which are only required when substantial tonnages of seed have to be dealt with.

The seed-dressing powders based on chloranil, dichlone or thiram are effective and are most suitable for use on a small scale. The treatment is very simple, 2–3 oz of the seed dressing are thoroughly mixed with a bushel of seed before sowing (Tarr, 1959).

Recent experience in northern Nigeria provides an excellent example of the very great difficulty of introducing a new technique to peasant cultivators. In this area there are approximately 8 million acres of sorghum. The Department of Agriculture realising the benefits to be obtained, arranged for the packaging of small quantities of seed dressing and their distribution to the local stores. This was supported by propaganda on the merits of dressing the seed with the result that many Africans dressed their seed, but the organisational difficulties were so great that the scheme was eventually dropped.

REFERENCE

TARR, S. A. J., *World Crops,* **11**, 442 (1959)

## OTHER DISEASES

Loose smut (*Sphacelotheca cruenta* [Kühn] Potter), a disease which is closely related to covered smut, is widely spread but is more localised in its incidence. It is easier to see in the field as it causes the plant to become stunted and at heading time the dark brown spores are exposed. The life-cycle is similar to covered smut, and is readily controlled by the seed-dressings described above.

Leaf blight (*Trichometasphaeria turcica* [Passerini] Luttrell [*conidia Helminthosporium turcicum* Passerini]) which has already been described as one of the diseases damaging maize, also attacks sorghum. Cross infection can occur, but some strains of the fungus are specific to each host.

The disease is easily seen on the older foliage where it causes elongated yellow-brown spots, often as much as one inch wide and several inches long. Light attacks do not cause much loss but when sorghum is grown in warm and humid climates, the disease quickly reaches epidemic proportions and causes severe crop losses.

Sorghum varieties resistant to leaf blight have been bred in the U.S.A. and this property can be transmitted by the appropriate breeding programme. The position is thus very similar to that with maize.

Anthracnose (*Colletotrichum graminicola* [Cesati] G. W. Wilson) causes spotting of the foliage of sorghum when it is grown under wet conditions, the progress of the disease being arrested by dry weather.

The fungus can also attack the stems, a phase of the disease known as red stalk rot. The infection weakens the stem with the result that it is easily blown over. Damage of this kind has caused very serious losses in the U.S.A. to broom corn, a sorghum whose dried panicle is used as a household broom.

Varietal resistance to both the leaf and stem phase of the disease has been demonstrated and the breeding of resistant varieties is therefore possible.

# III FIELD CROPS

## POTATO

To those living in temperate climates, the potato is a most important source of carbohydrate, but it does not flourish in the tropics. The climatic requirement for successful potato culture probably explains why the world acreage is only about 61 million acres (F.A.O., 1964).

The discovery of the potato in South America and its introduction into Europe is so well known that it need not be retold. Equally notorious is the outbreak of potato blight in Ireland in 1845, an epidemic which had the most devastating effect on a peasant population, dependent as it was on the potato for its main source of food. Never before, or mercifully since then, has a plant disease had such profound social and political effects. The Duke of Wellington summarised his feelings on the consequences of the epidemic with his comment 'Rotten potatoes have done it, they put Peel in his damned fright'.

To the plant pathologist, the potato blight story is one of outstanding interest, covering as it does much of the early history of plant pathology. On account of the importance of the crop, more work has probably been done on potato blight than on any other plant disease. In addition to blight, the virus disease leaf roll, wart disease, and black leg, have been chosen for more detailed discussion.

The history of the investigations into potato blight, wart disease and degeneration has been dramatically told by Large (1940). Textbooks on potato diseases have been written by Whitehead *et al.* (1953) and by McKay (1955). A world survey of potato blight epidemics and the control measures adopted has been made by Cox and Large (1960).

The main potato pest is the Colorado Beetle, which is widespread in Europe and the U.S.A. Soil pests, particularly wireworms, are also important pests in Europe. One of the principal problems in potato-growing is that of virus diseases, and a direct attack is now being attempted by insecticides employed to reduce the aphid vectors.

Potato root eelworm is still an unsolved problem and is widespread in Europe including the United Kingdom. It also occurs in the U.S.A. Other pests such as the tuber moth are of minor importance.

REFERENCES

COX, A. E. and LARGE, E. C., *Potato Blight Epidemics*, Agric. Handbook No. 174, U.S.D.A., Washington, D.C. (1960)

*F.A.O. Production Yearbook 1963–64*, **18**, F.A.O., Rome

LARGE, E. C., *The Advance of the Fungi*, Johnathan Cape, London (1940)

MCKAY, R., *Potato Diseases*, Irish Potato Marketing Co. Ltd., Dublin (1955)

WHITEHEAD, T., MCINTOSH, T. P. and FINDLAY, W. M., *The Potato in Health and Disease* (3rd Edn.), Oliver & Boyd, Edinburgh (1953)

## COLEOPTERA

### *Leptinotarsa decemlineata* Say. (*Chrysomelidae*)

This insect is the famous Colorado Beetle or Potato Beetle as it is known in the U.S.A., its country of origin. It is probably one of the best known insect pests in the U.S.A. where it turned its attention to the potato crop about 1860, forsaking its original food plant in the foothills of the Rocky Mountains. In the U.S.A., it quickly spread to the potato-growing states and by 1874 had reached the Atlantic Coast. About 1877, it appeared in Germany and, by 1914, had spread to the main potato growing regions of Lower Saxony. By 1922, it had reached France and Spain. It is now found more or less throughout the potato growing regions of the Continent but has so far not yet become established in the United Kingdom and the Scandinavian countries.

The beetle is a true leaf feeder; both adults and larvae feed on the foliage of potatoes. It is a large insect, the adult being about 20 mm in length, conspicuously marked in yellow with black stripes. The larvae are brick-red in colour about 15 mm long when fully grown. Larvae and adults together can quickly strip the foliage from any potato field so that the plants fail to grow and the tubers remain small. Each female can lay 500 eggs or even more. These are bright yellow and deposited in clusters of 20 to 30. Pupation takes place in the soil and sometimes two generations occur in a year. The insect can, but seldom does, feed on other plants.

Considerable interest attached to the occurrence of Colorado Beetle in England in 1945 and 1946. Obviously, the insect had been allowed to multiply unrestrictedly in France in the latter years of the war and many found their way over the Channel into England. In the same way, the Channel Islands, particularly Jersey, an important early potato growing island, were also invaded. Concerted effort, involving the spraying of all potato crops in Jersey, was necessary to secure the complete eradication of the beetle (Small, 1946). In England, the Ministry of Agriculture organised the spraying of all potato crops in Kent and other parts of southern England in an attempt to eradicate all possible infestations. As a result of these measures, the Colorado Beetle became the best known of all insect pests in England. Certainly, no insect could have been more conspicuous or easy to identify. By 1950, the interest had died down and now (1965) has largely been forgotten. It is doubtful if the Colorado Beetle would ever have succeeded in becoming established in this country.

#### METHODS OF CONTROL

In spite of its importance as a pest and capacity for survival the Colorado Beetle is easily controlled by insecticides. Formerly, arsenates were used to spray or dust the potato foliage including lead arsenate, calcium arsenate and Paris Green. One or two applications were usually necessary.

Modern insecticides are also effective. DDT was first used at 1 lb per acre as a 25% emulsion. Early trials showed that gamma BHC was in fact more effective both as a spray and dust (Kulash, 1947). Unfortunately, BHC in its crude form could cause off-flavour or taint in potato tubers. Even gamma BHC could cause taint if applied through the soil but sprays and dusts not exceeding $\frac{1}{2}$ lb per acre were satisfactory and could be used safely. Eventually a standard spray became a mixture of gamma BHC and DDT in the ratio of 1 to 4. Phosphorus compounds, such as parathion, were largely ineffective except a product known as Potasan (E.838) which was widely used in Germany. Other insecticides, such as dieldrin, were also effective. By 1960, the first indications of Colorado Beetle resistance to gamma BHC/DDT mixtures was reported from Germany (Heidenreich, 1960). As an alternative carbaryl (Sevin) was recommended but so far little resistance has been reported.

*Agriotes spp. (Elateridae)*

The soil living larvae of *Agriotes*, known as wireworms, attack many crops including temperate cereals, sugar beet and potatoes, especially in the more northern potato growing countries. The problem differs in potatoes as the tubers contain an enormous reserve of food compared with cereal seedlings but even a small population of wireworms in the soil can render the new tubers unfit for human consumption: quality of produce must be preserved and only a trace of damage from wireworms permitted. In sugar-beet injury to the fully grown roots is of no importance as these are processed but potato tubers are open to attack the whole time they remain in the soil from their formation until their harvest.

The life-cycle of the wireworm has been described under cereals, most species taking four years to complete it. It is the older and larger larvae which cause injury to potatoes as they make larger and deeper holes. Although feeding begins when the seed is planted, this attack seldom holds up the sprouting of the tubers, unless the shoots are attacked as sometimes happens. A second period of feeding occurs in late summer and autumn when the new tubers are attacked. Damage to the tubers can continue even after they are lifted and clamped, so that they can be sold only for pig food.

METHODS OF CONTROL

A crop like potatoes should never be taken on land known to harbour wireworms. They are so expensive to grow that a loss from wireworm damage is so much effort wasted. As potatoes are damaged by small numbers of wireworms, the grower is largely unaware of the risk until the crop is harvested. Rotations containing many cereals and forage crops engender wireworms and potatoes should not be grown in them. Potatoes taken on established arable land every third or fourth year should normally be safe from attack.

The advent of BHC made the direct control of wireworms possible for the first time in history. At A 2–6 lb per acre it gave excellent control when broadcast on to the soil (Greenwood, 1947). Unfortunately these rates caused off-flavour or taint to the new tubers. The purified gamma isomer of BHC instead of the mixed isomers, also tainted tubers when broadcast as dust at the rate of 12 oz per acre. Although it was impossible to recommend BHC or even gamma BHC on soils for potato growing, the wireworm problem was in fact solved. It was possible to avoid taint in the tubers by applying the insecticide at least eighteen months before the crop.

Aldrin was effective against wireworms and did not taint potatoes at normal rates of application. It was approved in the U.S.A., its country of origin, in 1953. In due course it was recommended in the United Kingdom and on the Continent at 3 lb per acre applied as a dust, a liquid or in mixture with a fertilizer (Bevan and Boyden, 1956). Eventually in the United Kingdom, aldrin was used for potatoes almost exclusively in fertilizer mixtures. About 20% of the total potato area was treated with aldrinated fertilizers.

REFERENCES

BEVAN, W. J. and BOYDEN, J. W., *Plant Pathol.*, **5**, 9 (1956)
GREENWOOD, D. M., *J. Econ. Entomol.*, **40**, 724 (1947)
HEIDENREICH, E., *Z. Angew. Entomol.*, **46**, 420 (1960)
KULASH, W. M., *J. Econ. Entomol.*, **40**, 640 (1947)
SMALL, T., *Agriculture*, **53**, 450 (1946)

LEPIDOPTERA

*Gnorimoschema (Phthorimaea) operculella* Zell. *(Gelechiidae)*

This little insect is the well known Potato Tuber Moth or Tuber Worm (Figs. 3.1 and

*Fig. 3.1.* Phthorimaea operculella *(adult)*

3.2). It is typical of the Tineiodae with narrow wings and occurs in the sub-tropics and tropics but not in the temperate regions as the insect ceases activity at 10°C. It occurs in the U.S.A. in the more southern states, in Central and South America, the Middle East, India and the Far East, Africa and the more southern European countries such as Spain, Italy and Bulgaria.

It is primarily a pest of potato tubers in store although it attacks the growing plant in the field. The adults emerge from the potato stores in April and May and the females deposit eggs on foliage of the potatoes in the fields. The caterpillar feeds on the foliage and bores down into the stems but this is an unimportant part of the attack. During later generations the number of moths increases and they turn their attention to the tubers. Eggs are deposited upon them if the tubers are exposed, especially during or after harvesting. The white caterpillars which

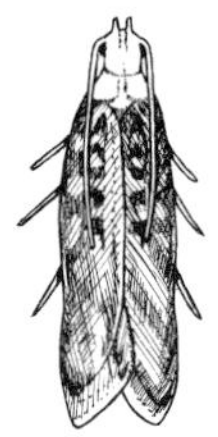

*Fig. 3.2.* Phthorimaea operculella *(adult)*

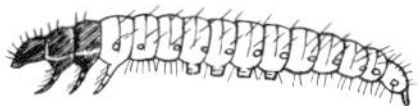

*Fig. 3.3.* Phthorimaea operculella *(larva)*

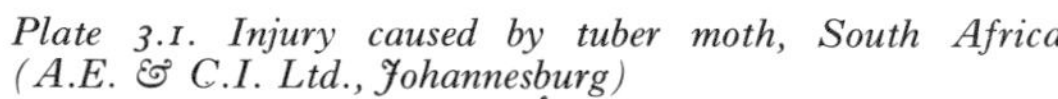

*Plate 3.1. Injury caused by tuber moth, South Africa (A.E. & C.I. Ltd., Johannesburg)*

are tinged with purple make shallow mines and tunnels in the tubers which tend to rot (Fig. 3.3). Pupation occurs in debris nearby (Plate 3.1).

The Potato Tuber Moth prefers potatoes but will also live on other plants, especially members of the *Solanaceae*. It also occurs as a pest on tobacco and egg plants.

#### METHODS OF CONTROL

Spraying against the Potato Tuber Moth during the growing season is possible but seldom undertaken. DDT applied several times at two-weekly intervals decreases the number of moths in the crop. This will decrease the amount of damage to the tubers but will not eliminate it entirely. Gamma BHC is also very effective and quick acting against the infestation on the foliage and stems.

Harvested tubers are usually protected and many insecticides have been tested for this purpose. DDT as a 5% dust sprinkled over the heaps of tubers gives good protection. Gamma BHC is also very effective as a 1% dust but may taint the tubers. Other insecticides can be used but those which are poisonous are best avoided. Carbaryl is ineffective against this insect (Bacon, 1960). For the disinfestation of tubers fumigation with methyl bromide at 2 lb per 1,000 cu ft is recommended.

REFERENCE

BACON, O. G., *J. Econ. Entomol.*, **53**, 868 (1960)

## HEMIPTERA

### *Empoasca fabae* Harris *(Jassidae)*

This is the Potato Leaf-Hopper of the U.S.A. It has no counterpart in other potato growing regions of the world. In the Middle East, where *Empoasca lybica* Berg. is common on cotton, the species on potato, namely *E. decipiens* Paoli. is of minor importance.

*Empoasca* is one of the most important pests of potatoes in the U.S.A. It invades the potato fields during the growing season from other plants, both crops and weeds and migrates northwards into areas where it cannot overwinter. On potatoes, injury is caused by the adults and immature stages sucking the cell sap from the undersides of the leaves. Attacked leaves become mottled and dry up, this damage being called 'hopper burn' which occurs when the numbers of nymphs exceeds two per leaf. In heavy attacks, the centre of the leaf area of the plant is destroyed, only the stems and mid-ribs remaining green.

The leaf-hoppers breed on the potato. The eggs are inserted into the mid-rib and the nymphs grow so quickly that sometimes two or three generations are completed on the crop. The leaf-hoppers are green and fly readily but can also hop for which the rear legs are specially adapted.

#### METHODS OF CONTROL

Leaf-hoppers are easily killed by insecticides. DDT at 1 lb per acre is effective on potato but more than one application may be necessary if the crop is invaded at different times during the season.

### Aphids *(Aphididae)*

Many species of aphids occur on potatoes, especially in the northern latitudes and are sometimes sufficiently numerous to cause damage to the foliage by sucking the cell sap. Attacked leaves tend to curl, usually downwards (Colour Plate 1). Where copper sprays are used to control potato blight, the presence of large numbers of aphids renders the foliage susceptible to copper injury which takes the form of hardening the growth. Aphids are also important vectors of virus diseases, notably of leaf-roll. Probably, they are more important as vectors than as pests in their own right as virus diseases constitute the main problem in potato growing. The following species are common on potato:

*Myzus persicae* Sulz.
*Macrosiphum solanifolii* Ashm.
*Aphis rhamni* Fons.

*Myzus persicae,* the peach and potato aphid, is green with slightly swollen cornicles. It is the principal vector of virus diseases of potatoes transmitting leaf roll and rugose mosaic (Virus Y). *Myzus* passes the winter in the egg stage on peach trees and other species of *Prunus.* After the winter eggs hatch, the aphid begins its development on peach. Some pass the entire season on this host plant but die out due to fungus diseases or being destroyed by predators.

Winged forms are eventually produced and the aphids fly away to live on numerous other plants including potato but also on various cultivated plants and weeds. At this stage, it freely migrates from one plant to another. In countries where the winter is mild, many aphids remain to reproduce on their summer food plants without the intervention of the egg stage at all. Where the winters are cold, the egg stage is essential for survival. In the United Kingdom, *Myzus* commonly overwinters in the active stage, usually as a wingless female. Even in countries lying to the south, such as Spain and Italy, eggs are freely deposited on fruit trees which are common at these latitudes. *Myzus* is a cool climate insect as it cannot survive high temperatures such as 80°F (28°C) which is fatal to them. *Myzus* is common in the Middle East, but only in the cooler months and disappears during the heat of the summer and for this reason is less important as a vector of virus disease there. At times when *Myzus* can build up numbers quickly, it becomes a more important pest on peaches than on its summer host plants. *Myzus persicae* occurs in most countries of the World.

*Macrosiphum solanifolii* occurs in Europe, the U.S.A. and South America as a potato aphid. It is ineffective as a vector of virus diseases although it can transmit them. It is a large aphid, either green or pink with long cornicles and a long cauda. It overwinters in the egg stage on *Rosa* spp. especially the Dog Rose *(Rosa carina).*

*Aphis rhamni* occurs in abundance on potato. It is an apple-green aphid, short and compact. It overwinters in the egg stage on Buckthorn *(Rhamnus cartharticus)* and can transmit virus diseases in the laboratory but is evidently an ineffective vector in the field. In epidemic years it causes direct injury to potato foliage.

*Virus transmission in potatoes.* Although virus diseases were recognised as maladies of potato many years ago, their virus nature became known only about 1914. The transmission of these diseases, particularly leaf-roll, was first established by Botjes in Holland in 1920. Confirmation came quickly from many sources. The problem of the degeneration of potato stocks grown in the same locality for several years had led to the importation of new 'seed' from special seed-growing areas. In the United Kingdom, the new potato seed came from Scotland and was used to plant about 50% of the entire potato area. By this means, the vigour of potato stocks was maintained. The traffic in seed potatoes and the recognition of virus diseases eventually led to the introduction of Certificates of Virus Status in the seed areas. Such schemes are now very elaborate and field inspection is backed up by laboratory testing for virus infection.

The importance of aphid transmission of virus diseases especially of *Myzus persicae* was also recognised but the problem why certain areas could produce seed potatoes with little virus infection took many years to solve. The fact that aphids were abundant at all places led to the puzzling conclusion that the absence of diseases was not due to the absence of aphids. The behaviour of *Myzus persicae* was investigated by Davies (1934) who showed that movement is governed by temperature, humidity and wind. Areas where little virus disease occurred, were those of low temperature, high humidity and much wind. Davies established an index of infection based on the number of aphids per leaf in mid-July. At a level of 20 aphids per leaf virus spread was at a minimum and such areas were found to be either mountainous or seaboard. Migration of aphids can occur over considerable distances.

Virus transmission by aphids in potatoes is brought about by winged aphids flying into the crop from outside. Frequently such aphids carry viruses which they have picked up from other crops of potatoes, self-sown potatoes after a previous crop and from some weeds. Within the crop itself, aphids can spread the diseases by constant movement both by winged aphids and by wingless forms also. Later in the season, the chances of infection are increased but its importance is lessened, as a late infection has little effect on the crop. *Myzus persicae* overwinters frequently in winter crops of brassicas from which an early movement into potatoes is possible.

*Spraying against aphids to control virus diseases.* In the 1950's many trials were carried out in the United Kingdom by spraying crops with DDT against aphids (Broadbent *et al.*, 1960). In due course, the new systemic insecticides such as schradan and demeton were tried. Whereas DDT at first gave disappointing results, the systemic insecticides were more successful but several applications were necessary starting as soon as the potatoes appeared above ground. It was found that aphids were killed slowly and it was established that the virus leaf-roll could be decreased by spraying but not rugose mosaic. The reason for this is that leaf-roll virus takes longer to be picked up by aphids and also a longer feeding period by the aphids to be transmitted. Rugose mosaic is, on the other hand, easily picked up and is transmitted soon afterwards. Fortunately, the ease of acquisition and transmission also means that the virus is very readily lost and, in a few hours, the aphids are no longer viruliferous, leaf-roll, however, is retained for several days. Good results in spraying were obtained in the United Kingdom and sprayed stocks were retained for several years without infection with leaf-roll increasing to more than 1–2%.

Spraying against aphids to minimise virus spread has not been generally adopted in many countries where it has been tried. In the U.S.A., aphid reduction did not lead to much lessening of disease (Klostermeyer *et al.*, 1956). In Holland, spraying was unsuccessful (Hille Ris Lambers *et al.*, 1953) and in general spraying potatoes against virus disease has not been worth while and is unlikely to do more than supplement existing practises.

Soil insecticides such as phorate (Thimet), disulphoton (Disyston) and menazon (Sayfos) are being tried. The object is to protect the foliage as soon as it appears above ground by placing the insecticide either in the furrow with the seed tuber or to coat the tuber with it. Later, if necessary, the foliage can be sprayed. Results at present indicate that 1 lb of insecticide per acre persists for 12 weeks which is adequate and suggests that increased yields would follow from the suppression of all aphids.

REFERENCES

BROADBENT, R., HEATHCOTE, G. R. and BURT, P. E., *Empire Potato J.*, **3**, 251 (1960)

KLOSTERMEYER, E. C., LANDIS, B. J., SCHOPP, R. and BUTLER, L., *J. Econ. Entomol.*, **49**, 164 (1956)

HILLE RIS LAMBERS, D., RIESTMAN, A. O. and SCHAPERS, A., *R.A.E.*, **44**, 282 (1953)

DAVIES, W. M., *Ann. Appl. Biol.*, **21**, 283 (1934)

## NEMATODA

### *Heterodera rostochiensis* Woll

This is the notorious Potato Cyst Eelworm or the Golden Nematode, as it is called in the U.S.A. It is found throughout the potato-growing countries of Europe including the U.S.S.R. In the U.S.A., it is limited to Long Island, New York State and in Canada, to Vancouver Island and Newfoundland. It is also found in India and Peru both at altitudes above 7,000 ft, in the Canaries and along the Mediterranean coast of North Africa. It is present in Eire and scattered in Northern Ireland. The complete list of countries in which the eelworm has been found is given by Southey (1959).

In England, the eelworm was first recognised in 1917 by Strachan and Taylor (1926) who state that there are indications of its presence in 1904. By 1920, it spread to the important potato-growing areas near Cambridge and was identified in most countries in northern Europe. It was first noted in Long Island, U.S.A. in 1941 (Chitwood, 1951) and confined to that area. It has now been found in Italy and Greece.

*Heterodera rostochiensis* is a cyst-forming nematode similar to the beet cyst eelworm, *Heterodera schachtii* Schmidt but differs from *H. schachtii* in many ways. *H. rostochiensis* possesses a spherical cyst (female nematode), it usually passes through only one generation annually on potato and the only crops it attacks are potato, tomato and egg plant. *H. rostochiensis* is a specialised parasite which has follows the potato in its distribution.

As a pest, it remains as one of the main unsolved problems of agriculture in Europe. As with sugarbeet, frequent cropping of the land with potatoes builds up the soil population until yield is affected. The tolerance level in fertile soils, is about 20 to 30 eggs per gram of dry soil. Above this level land is then said to be 'potato sick', the sickness occurring in patches. The plants wilt and lower leaves turn yellow (Plate 3.2). The root system is fibrous, bearing white and yellow cysts visibly adhering to it.

The life-cycle of *Heterodera rostochiensis* begins with the cysts, the swollen bodies of the female eelworms which persist in the soil. They contain eggs with unhatched larvae which remain within the cyst until potatoes are grown. Root exudates from the growing crop stimulate the eggs to hatch and the larvae escape from the cyst into the soil where they enter to roots of the plants. If the invasion of the roots is large, the roots fail to function properly and the plant remains stunted. After the young eelworms enter the roots, they enlarge and eventually burst through the root tissues and appear outside as swollen, flask-shaped bodies. The females enlarge, are white at first, but slowly turn yellow brown and then drop off into the soil. The male moults, regains its worm-like shape and soon escapes to move freely in the soil.

*Plate 3.2. Field infested with potato root eelworm*

When small numbers of eelworms attack the plants, little harm is caused. The time taken to complete the life-cycle varies with the soil temperature. The development is slow at first in spring, speeds up and is most rapid in July (Jones, 1950).

Potato eelworm is spread from place to place mechanically, that is, in infested soil. An important way in which this can happen is in soil sticking to seed potatoes when host and parasite are transported together. Local spread is by cultivations and by multiplication when potatoes are grown.

## METHODS OF CONTROL

'Potato sickness' arises from overcropping the land with potatoes, as when potatoes are taken every year, every other year or even if once in three years. A rotation in which potatoes are taken once every four years, is often insufficient but is safe for a time if the land is clean or only slightly infested to start with. A major factor in control by rotation is persistance of encysted eggs from year to year. The average rate of decline under fallow or non-susceptible crops is 33% per annum and so it takes from 4–6 years for numbers to fall to a safe level after potatoes are grown. In exceptional circumstances, potato sickness has appeared after a 10-year rest from potatoes.

Continual cropping of the land with potatoes inevitably leads to 'potato sickness' as was shown by Robertson (1939). He grew potatoes in clean soil from seed saved from year to year and produced 'potato sickness' in the eighth year. Early lifted crops support smaller populations and so escape attack, as in Jersey in the Channel Islands. Potatoes growing in soils with adequate moisture reserves yield more when attacked than crops suffering from water shortage.

There is no satisfactory chemical control which can be employed on a field scale. Innumerable substances have been tried. Many chemicals kill sufficient nematodes to give suitable yield but, on the improved root systems, the population numbers build up to levels higher than before. Dichloropropane-Dichloropropene (D-D) and chloropicrin are both effective but too expensive. Some dithiocarbamate and organo-chlorine compounds show promise but are also too expensive.

D-D is used mainly on tomato soils. It is a liquid product and is injected into the soil. D-D drops by gravity down pipes fitted behind the tines of a cultivator in rows about 9 in apart. The rate of application is about 20–25 gal per acre. About 6 weeks must be allowed after application for the fumes to escape from the soil before planting. On selected fields growing early varieties D-D can give economic returns. The eelworm content of glass house soils can be reduced by 98% (Stone, 1957) but in the open field growing potatoes always increases the cyst content of the soil even after the injection of D-D (Peters and Fenwick, 1948).

Metham-sodium (sodium N-methyl dithiocarbamate) another liquid is effective against *Heterodera* but is too expensive for field use. The rate for tomato soils is 100 gal per acre applied to the soil in water. The surface is sealed with water flooding for a time and later opened up to allow the escape of the gasses as the chemical is very toxic to all plant life. Mylone (tetrahydro-dimethyl-thiadiazine thione) is also effective applied as a 85% powder (Dazomet) (Peachey, 1963).

Control by resistant varieties has good prospects of success. Potatoes with a dominant gene for resistance have been bred and are now on the market. Tests have shown, however, that populations vary from place to place (Jones and Pawelska, 1963) so that the resistant varieties derived from this source cannot be used everywhere. More sources of resistance are known and from these further varieties with more genes for resistance are being bred. Some plant breeders' strains with two and three genes show promise of providing resistance to most of the field populations in the United Kingdom. Growing resistant varieties, however, induces genetic change in the eelworms.

REFERENCES

CHITWOOD, B. G., *Circ. U.S.D.A. No. 875* (1951)

JONES, F. G. W., *Ann. Appl. Biol.*, **37**, 407 (1950)

JONES, F. G. W. and PAWELSKA, K., *Ann. Appl. Biol.*, **56**, 27 (1965)

PEACHEY, J. E., *Chemistry and Industry*, 1736 (1963)

PETERS, B. G. and FENWICK, D. W., *Ann. Appl. Biol.*, **36**, 364 (1948)

ROBERTSON, D., *Scot. J. Agri.*, **22**, 172 (1939)

SOUTHEY, J. F., *Tech. Bull. No. 7, Mins. Agric., Fish and Food* (1959)

STONE, L. E. W., *Ann. Appl. Biol.*, **45**, 256 (1957)

STRACHAN, J. and TAYLOR, T. H., *J. Minist. Agr.*, **32**, 941 (1926)

## MOLLUSCA

Slugs and snails belong to the animal group which is composed principally of sea-living forms but the Class Gastropoda contains some land-living forms of which slugs and snails are the best known and are of some agricultural importance. Slugs are prominant pests of potatoes especially in districts of high rainfall. They attack the new tubers, making deep round holes. The commonest is the species *Agriolimax reticulatus* Mull. the Grey Field Slug which is common all over northern Europe. Sometimes species of *Milax*, or keeled slugs which carry a ridge of tissue along their backs, cause much damage and they feed below ground.

Slugs usually feed beneath the soil surface and only come to the top in moist warm weather. They also come out of shelter at night and return under cover during the daytime. The greatest enemy of the slug is dryness. Well-covered fields of grass and clover encourage slug breeding and low-lying fields often contain many slugs. Cultivated land harbours few slugs and is usually invaded from neighbouring land rough with grass and weeds. Farmyard manure applied before potato growing increases the risk of slug damage to the new tubers as slugs prefer to breed in pockets of manure.

Slugs are hermaphrodite, that is, each individual is both male and female. Eggs are deposited in soil at any time of the year but most are produced in the autumn. A newly-born slug takes about one year to become an adult.

### METHODS OF CONTROL

Slugs are extremely difficult to control in potatoes or in any field crop. The most effective chemical is metaldehyde which can be used in a bait with bran or similar attractive material. About 1 lb of metaldehyde is needed per acre for effective control but its high price make it uneconomic to use on a field scale. It can be made into a spray or a dust and applied to the soil surface which is a suitable method of application as with the bait on a small scale. Slug granules are now becoming popular which consist of pellets of farinaceous matter mixed with metaldehyde and which can easily be scattered over the surface of the soil. For prevention of injury to potatoes, treatment should be carried out before planting, chosing mild damp weather for the application of the granules, as slugs remain below ground if the weather is either frosty or dry.

## Potato Blight (*Phytophthora infestans* [Mont.] De Bary)

Potato blight is now almost universal, its distribution being practically the same as that of the potato. The disease is readily seen on the foliage, where the symptoms consist of dark brown spots which rapidly increase in size. If conditions favour the disease, the lesions quickly multiply, resulting in the destruction of the leaves (Coloured Plate 2) and finally the stems. Not only does the disease destroy the foliage, it also attacks the tubers. In the early stages the infected parts of the tuber turn reddish-brown (Plate 3.3), but in the later stages the tuber rots and becomes soft and useless. The double nature of the attack on the potato crop was obvious from the first outbreaks.

*Plate 3.3. Potato tuber infected with blight (A Plant Protection photograph)*

The destruction of the haulm prevents further growth of the tubers, whilst rotting in the clamp reduced the yield still further.

Looking back now, it is hard to remember that in the middle of the nineteenth century the cause of the potato disease was a subject of acrimonious dispute. The blight was held by some to be due to the plants becoming waterlogged, a state which permitted the fungus to grow on the unhealthy tissues. The other school of thought said that the fungus was the cause of the disease and not the consequence. The dispute was finally settled by de Bary who published two papers in 1861 and 1863 describing the life history of the fungus and the proof of its parasitic nature. The technique was the same as that which has already been mentioned in connection with black stem rust on wheat, 'sowing' the fungus spores on the host plant and observing the results. The parasitism of the

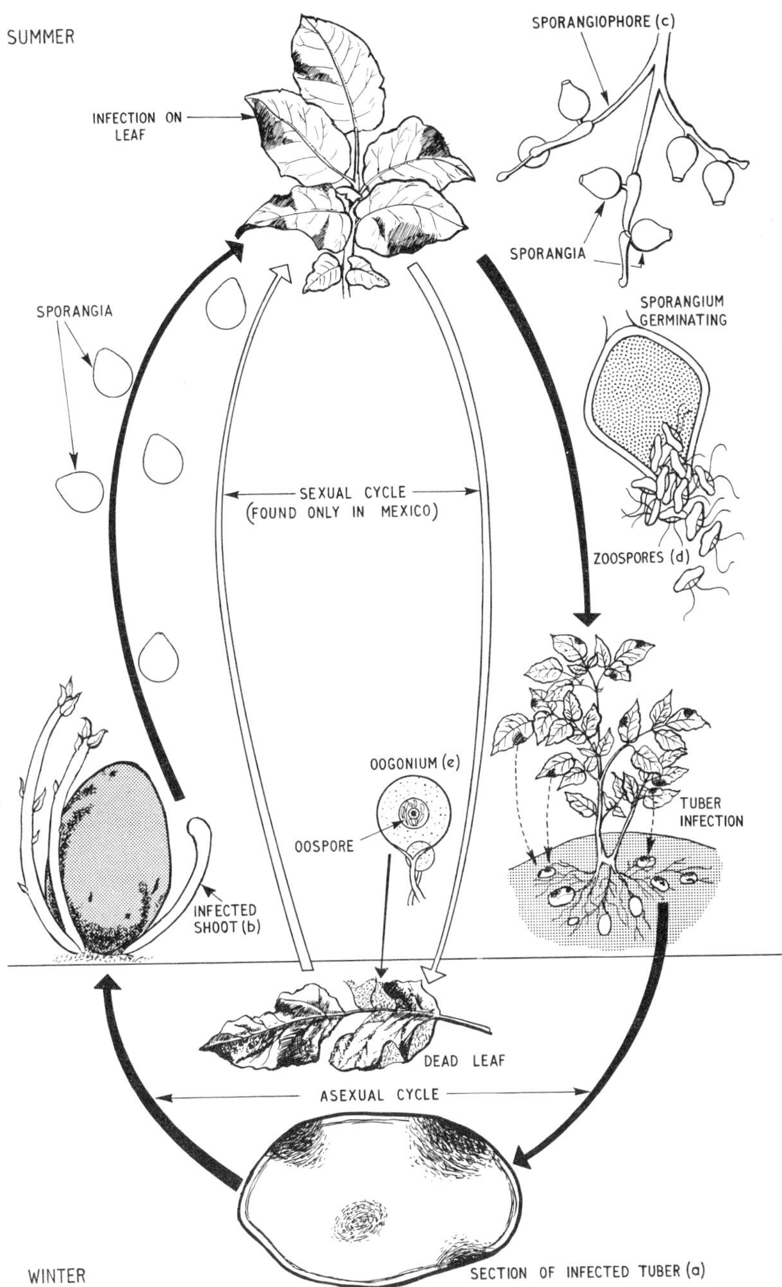


*Fig. 3.4. Life Cycle of Potato Blight. (a) Infected tuber. (b) Diseased shoot produced by infected tuber, (c) Sporangiophores bearing sporangia, (d) Zoospores released from the sporangium, (e) Oogonium and oospore*

potato blight fungus was unequivocally established when the treated potato plants showed the typical blight spots on the leaves, while the controls remained healthy.

Since then, many investigators have studied the fungus and although there is still one unsolved mystery, its life cycle is now well-known (Fig. 3.4). The fungus survives from one season to the next as a living mycelium in the tuber (a). In the spring a small proportion of the diseased tubers produce infected shoots (b) which bear the sporangiophores (c), the vegetative reproductive organs. The sporangia when ripe are carried either by wind or water drops on to the haulm. Provided that the leaves remain wet for a sufficient time, infection takes place.

The sporangia can behave in two ways. At high temperatures the spore puts out a germ tube which penetrates the leaf, but at lower temperatures the spore forms a number of smaller spores, called zoospores (d), which are mobile. The zoospores swim about in the drops of water on the leaf before settling down and developing a germ tube which starts off a new infection once it is inside the leaf.

Recent investigations have been aimed at tracking down the infected tubers which are the original sources of the potato blight outbreaks. The blighted tubers may be among the seed potatoes, or on the site of the previous season's clamps, or among dumps of discards, but the relative importance of these sources is not yet known.

It has been found that relatively few of the blighted tubers produce diseased stems, about 1 in 200 (Hirst *et al.*, 1960). Random sampling of the seed potato stocks on English farms showed that about 1% of the tubers were blighted. The two figures give a theoretical forecast of about one infector plant per acre.

This finding has been followed up by infra-red aerial photography of potato fields (Plate 3.4), which shows up blighted foliage (Brenchley *et al.*, 1962). In these photographs the initial foci of infection are scarce, the currently accepted estimate being about one infector plant in 250 acres (Brenchley, 1965). The reason for the discrepancy between the two estimates is not known.

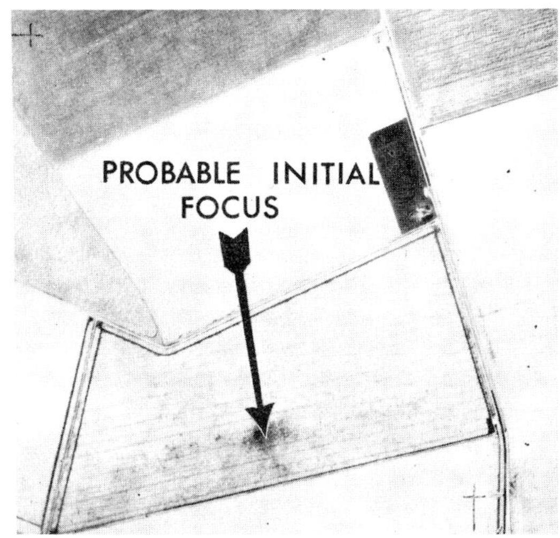


*Plate 3.4. Aerial photograph of potato blight focus (A Ministry of Agriculture photograph)*

The disease in the first phase spreads slowly from the initial foci, and the range is limited by the distance which water-borne sporangia travel. The next phase occurs when climatic conditions permit airborne sporangia to infect plants over a larger area, this type of distribution giving rise to daughter foci. When this stage has been reached the potential production of spores is large, so that continued wet weather can quickly result in the disease reaching epidemic proportions. If, however, the weather is dry, the progress of the disease is temporarily arrested.

Not only are the sporangia distributed on the foliage, but also on the ground, where most of them die, but a small proportion are washed down through the soil to reach the tubers, which become infected. The mycelium of the fungus penetrates the tuber, the infected area turning a foxy-red colour. Further infection can take place at lifting time from sporangia either in the soil, or from nearby diseased haulm. Obviously diseased tubers are discarded when the potatoes are picked up, but some inevitably get in the clamp. The fungus continues to develop inside the tuber during storage, a process which usually results in the tuber rotting.

It will be noted that the life-cycle of the fungus as described above is an asexual one, without the production of any sexually produced spores, a phase which occurs in many of the related fungi. Mycologists, from de Bary onwards, have devoted great efforts to the discovery of the missing link, the sexual or perfect stage fruits of the potato blight fungus. The oogonia, the sexually produced fruits, were first seen in artificial cultures of the fungus about 1908, but it was not until 1956 that they were found naturally occurring in blight spots on potato foliage in Mexico. The discovery was of importance, both scientifically and practically. From the scientific aspect it was the end of a search lasting one hundred years, from the practical viewpoint it meant that the raising of blight resistant potatoes was bound to be of great difficulty due to the ability of the fungus to produce new strains capable of attacking new varieties, a problem with which the wheat breeder has been familiar since the publication in 1916 of the discovery of a number of strains of the black stem rust fungus.

The unsolved mystery in the life cycle of the potato blight fungus is its apparent ability to produce new strains or races in the absence of the sexual stage (Cox *et al.*, 1960). The potato plant breeders were much encouraged in their endeavours to raise blight-resistant varieties by the absence of the sexual phase which is potentially capable of producing new races. But their hopes were crushed in 1932 when a new and virulent strain appeared in Pomerania. Since then in spite of much effort, all the potatoes bred for blight resistance have eventually succumbed to the disease. Fortunately the breeding work has made an important contribution by introducing new varieties with improved resistance to blight, but the likelihood of breeding a potato resistant to all blight races is now remote.

## BLIGHT CONTROL

Potato blight continued to damage the English and Irish potato crops for 45 years, but without the catastrophic results of the original outbreak in Ireland in 1845. The food shortage of the Irish peasant was alleviated by two changes which gradually took place—emigration, and the culture of more resistant varieties. At the time of the first attack, many of the varieties were very susceptible to blight, but in course of time they were replaced by others which, while not resistant, gave better yields in the blight years.

It was Millardet's discovery of Bordeaux Mixture, announced in 1885, which opened up a new era in the control of plant diseases. Although originally introduced for the control of vine downy mildew, Millardet realised that it would probably also be effective against potato blight. The first trials of the new fungicide against blight were carried out in France in 1885, but the United Kingdom was agriculturally asleep at that time, and five years passed before the first trials were carried out in Ireland (Craigie, 1892).

The original Irish trials were carried out with a mixture containing 20 lb of copper sulphate, 10 lb of unslaked lime and 100 gal of water, a concentration now referred to as 2% Bordeaux Mixture. It was recommended that the fungicide be applied at the rate of 100–120 gal per acre, putting on the first spray before the foliage met in the row, the second two to three weeks later, and in wet seasons, a third spray after the same interval.

The soundness of the original recommendations is demonstrated by their successful use with but few modifications for over 70 years. The main changes in Ireland have been the substitution of washing soda for lime to make Burgundy Mixture and a reduction of the copper sulphate concentration to 1% in areas where blight is not so severe as it is in the west. No changes have been made in the timing or the quantity of spray per acre.

In England it was found that the original Bordeaux Mixture was unnecessarily strong for the milder attacks of blight, enabling the copper sulphate to be reduced from 20 lb to 10 lb per 100 gal.

The great merits of Bordeaux Mixture, its effectiveness, its persistence on the foliage, and its low cost ensured its supremacy for 50 years. It had, however, two major disadvantages, it was troublesome to make up, and under certain conditions it could damage the crop.

During the 1930s various proprietary copper fungicides were put on the market which were very simple to mix. They consisted of various insoluble copper compounds mixed with wetting agents which dispersed readily in water to give suspensions ready for application. All the farmer had to do was to mix them with a little water in a bucket and pour it into the spray tank. These new copper fungicides were based on copper oxychloride, copper oxysulphate and cuprous oxide, and are generally used at the rate of $1\frac{1}{2}$–$2\frac{1}{2}$ lb of metallic copper per acre. Because of the ease of mixing, the fixed coppers made steady headway and by the 1950s they had largely supplanted Bordeaux Mixture in England and Holland.

The new copper fungicides did not, however, avoid phytotoxicity, the other major disadvantage of Bordeaux Mixture. All copper fungicides are liable to damage potato foliage, particularly in dry years when aphids have punctured the underside of the leaves. In such years in the absence of blight, copper spraying has caused reductions of yield varying from $\frac{1}{2}$–2 tons per acre (Cox *et al.*, 1960). In wet years the loss of yield is much smaller, and is more than counter-balanced by the gain in crop from blight control.

There was, therefore, a real need for safer fungicides, which could be used without any risk of crop reduction, a need which has been met by the introduction of the dithiocarbamate fungicides. Although these were discovered in the 1930s, their extensive use on potatoes did not take place until the post-war years. Two dithiocarbamates are now dominant, zineb and maneb, the standard rate of application being 1–2 lb per acre. They are particularly valuable in countries such as the U.S.A. where repeated applications have to be made to control insect pests and the addition of a fungicide is a simple precaution. As a result, the dithiocarbamates are now predominant on potatoes in the U.S.A. Their popularity is also increasing both in England and on the Continent. The number of fungicidal applications for blight control varies enormously in different parts of the world according to the incidence of the disease. For example, one spray is often adequate in parts of Western Germany, the usual programme in the English Fens requires two to three rounds, while in Maine, U.S.A., the average number of protective sprays is 6 to 7 but this may be increased to as many as 12 in a bad blight year.

Although spraying is the dominant method for the application of fungicides on potatoes, dusts can also be used for blight control. The two major advantages of dusts are that no water is required and the speed with which they can be applied, the disadvantage is that their adhesion to the foliage is only moderate so that the application has to be made frequently. It is the general experience that two dustings are the equivalent of one spray. Dusts tend to be used in areas where blight attacks are light, the growers often switching over to sprays should severe blight threaten, and in areas, as for example Peru, where water for spraying is difficult to obtain.

## BLIGHT IN TUBERS

In England the percentage annual loss of tubers due to potato blight is relatively small. The loss averaged 1·25% during the years 1953–56, varying from 0·1% in 1955 to 2·0% in the previous year. The relatively low loss appears to be associated with the extensive use of the variety Majestic which owes part of its popularity to the resistance of the tuber to blight infection.

Apart from the use of resistant varieties, the chief method of preventing tuber infection is by earthing up to provide a good cover of soil over them. It is also general practice to allow an interval of at least 10 days between the death of the haulm and lifting, in order to prevent the tubers coming into contact with live sporangia.

The effect of spraying on the amount of tuber infection is variable. In some cases, such as the sea clay soils of Holland, protective spraying of the foliage approximately halves the quantity of blighted tubers. But in other cases, spraying may postpone the onset of the disease until near the harvest, an occurrence which increases the percentage of blighted tubers.

The destruction of infected haulm, either mechanically or by chemical defoliants, was at one time thought to be a useful way of minimising tuber infection. In practice it has not proved very effective because of the conflict of purposes. To be successful, defoliation must be done before there is much blight present thereby reducing the yield. It is now generally accepted that the main purpose of defoliation is to make harvesting easier.

### METHODS OF APPLICATION

The original potato blight trials were carried out with knapsack sprayers, in which the operator carried the spray fluid in a tank on his back, held the spray lance in his right hand and operated the pump handle with his left. Although still most effective for the treatment of small areas, the use of such sprayers is arduous and unsuitable for large areas. Over the years the engineers have been active in producing spraying machines suitable for the treatment of many acres a day. In the post-war years, there has been a rapid development of aerial application using both fixed wing aeroplanes and helicopters. The aeroplane has the great advantage of low cost and simplicity of maintenance, assets which have made it dominant for aerial spraying, but the manoeuvrability of the helicopter makes it ideal for use on small fields.

### THE ECONOMICS OF BLIGHT CONTROL

The value of blight control has been studied intensively at the Ministry of Agriculture's Plant Pathology Laboratory at Harpenden during the past 20 years. The case for spraying during a bad blight year is straightforward. The growing period is prolonged for 2–3 weeks which allows the weight of tubers to increase by 2–3 tons an acre.

But the problem is, in fact, a very complex one for not all areas suffer from blight, and the annual frequency of blight attacks varies enormously. For example, in Mexico City, severe blight occurs every year, in the wetter parts of Europe about eight times in every ten years, but in the drier parts of Europe and the U.S.A., severe blight attacks are negligible (Cox *et al.,* 1960 c).

Intensive study in the United Kingdom has shown that routine spraying is undesirable except in the West Country and in the Fens particularly on susceptible varieties like King Edward, where blight attacks are sufficiently frequent to justify the practice.

The decision on whether to spray or not has been greatly simplified by Beaumont's work on the weather conditions which favour the outbreak of blight. He found that blight attacks were likely to occur following spells of not less than 48 consecutive hours during which the temperature does not fall below 50°F and the relative humidity of the air below 75%. When these conditions are fulfilled, the first signs of blight may be expected during the succeeding 7–14 days.

The investigations on the real losses caused by potato blight have been carried out in only a few countries. Its importance is such that it is likely to be the subject for further research for many years to come.

REFERENCES

BRENCHLEY, G. H. and DADD, C. V., *N.A.A.S. Quarterly Review,* **57,** 21 (1962)

BRENCHLEY, G. H., Personal communication (1965)

COX, A. E. and LARGE, E. C., *Potato Blight Epidemics,* Agric. Handbook No. 174, U.S. Dept. of Agriculture, Washington, D.C. (1960)

CRAIGIE, P. G., *Report on Recent Experiments in Checking Potato Disease in the United Kingdom and Abroad,* 6, H.M.S.O., London (1892)

HIRST, J. M. and STEDMAN, O. J., *Ann. appl. Biol.,* **48,** 489 (1960)

## POTATO DEGENERATION

English farmers during the eighteenth century recognised that their yields of potatoes were liable to decline. This change was particu-

*Plate 3.5. Leaf roll of potato, healthy plant and crop on the left, infected on the right (A Ministry of Agriculture photograph)*

larly obvious in the south of England where locally grown seed was used year after year. The deterioration in yield was called 'degeneration' and was ascribed to a reduction in vigour due to repeated vegetative propagation.

With this observation, there also went the knowledge that potatoes of the same variety when grown in isolated areas were as vigorous and productive as they were originally. This knowledge resulted in the gradual increase in the use of 'imported' seed and eventually to its becoming good cultural practice to plant fresh seed potatoes, particularly those grown in Scotland.

The idea that old varieties eventually became worn out also encouraged the raising of new varieties of potatoes. Farmers, by planting new varieties and Scottish seed potatoes avoided the losses caused by potato degeneration. More than one hundred years passed before a scientific explanation was given for the success of the empirical solution.

It was a Dutch scientist, Quanjer, who first started to look into the mysteries of degeneration, concentrating on leaf roll, a typical symptom of potatoes which had deteriorated. In the course of his experiments, potato shoots with leaf roll were grafted on to healthy plants. The disease spread into the previously healthy stock, infecting the whole plant. Transmission of disease by grafting was already known to occur with virus diseases and Quanjer therefore concluded that degeneration was due to a virus infection. His conclusion, which was published in 1913, has been confirmed by the many investigators who have worked on the subject since then. Another Dutch worker, Oortwyn Botjes, showed, a few years later that the leaf roll virus was transmitted by aphides. Thus, by 1920 two of the fundamental methods of investigating potato virus diseases had been developed and the basic facts about potato degeneration had been discovered.

In the years which followed the Dutch lead was enthusiastically followed up and the very complex story of the potato viruses unravelled. It has been summarised in the four concluding chapters of the book by Whitehead *et al.* (1953).

Twenty virus diseases are recorded as occurring in potatoes (Smith, 1957). Of these, it is generally accepted that leaf roll is responsible for the largest reductions in yield. It is found practically wherever potatoes are grown commercially. Its serious effect on yield and widespread distribution justify the selection of leaf roll as the most serious virus disease of potatoes.

Leaf roll is perpetuated by the planting of infected tubers which occur randomly throughout the field. The foliage on plants grown from such tubers usually shows the symptoms when the plants are about a month old, the first signs being seen on the lower leaves. When the virus is aphid-transmitted, it takes 10–15 days to reach the tubers and about 20 days elapse before the symptoms appear in the young growth in the top. Leaf roll infected plants are very obvious in the field as the upward curling of the leaf margins exposes the undersides of the leaves (Plate 3.5).

The way in which the virus affects the foliage and the yield has also been studied. The main physiological effect of the virus is to prevent the normal translocation of the carbohydrates manufactured in the leaves. In a normal leaf, the starch made during the day, is converted into sugar at night and moved to other parts of the plant and the tubers where it is reconverted to starch. In such a leaf practically all the starch is removed during the night, but in diseased leaves most of the starch remains. The accumulation of the starch in the spongy parenchyma cells causes the underside of the leaf to expand, with the result that the leaf curls.

The impeded carbohydrate translocation also explains the lower yields from leaf roll infected plants. The small supply of sugar from the leaves limits the number of tubers which develop and generally their size, and hence reduces the weight of the crop (Plate 3.5). Experiments have shown that the loss of yield depends on the particularly potato variety, varying from not less than 40% to as high as 90% (McKay, 1955).

The farming practice of using healthy seed potatoes is still the main method of preventing crop losses due to the virus diseases. The discovery of the part which aphids play in disseminating the disease has led to a wider choice of sites for growing seed potatoes. The areas which are particularly favourable are those which have low aphid populations, such as Scotland or the West of Ireland, where the wet and windy weather keeps the aphid numbers down. The same principle has been adopted in other countries such as Germany where seed potato production has flourished in areas with small aphid populations such as Lower Saxony, Schleswig-Holstein and Bavaria and Finisterre in France.

But in some countries, such as Holland, aphids are universal and consequently other methods have to be used to obtain virus-free seed potatoes. The Dutch research workers following up the lead given by Quanjer and Botjes came to the conclusion that it should be possible to do this by harvesting the seed potatoes before the virus has reached the tubers. To do this on a country-wide scale requires considerable scientific expertise and the closest collaboration between the official advisory service and the growers.

At the beginning of the season, the seed potato growers are given a forecast of the probable date when haulm destruction must be completed on the various groups of early, mid-season and main varieties. The crops are then inspected during the growing season for freedom from virus diseases. At the same time the entomologists are keeping a watch on the aphid population and when it reaches the stage when migration has begun, a warning is issued that haulm destruction must be completed in 14 days time. When this period has elapsed, the fields are inspected again, and if any foliage is present, the seed potatoes are down-graded.

The seed potato growers have a difficult problem to solve if the migration takes place early, for example the end of June, or early July. At this time the yield is still low, but increasing with every day that passes. Consequently, the grower must aim at destroying the haulm as late as possible but make sure that it is completed by the regulation date.

Haulm destruction has therefore been very thoroughly investigated on the Continent. In Holland, to obtain fast haulm kill, two chemical sprays are used, the first with sodium arsenite, and the second, 24 hr later, with DNOC. If there is less need for haste, mechanical destruction followed by a chemical spray may be preferred.

The procedure is similar in parts of Germany, but with a rather stronger preference for chemical defoliants than mechanical haulm destroyers. The wide range of defoliants available such as calcium cyanamide, arsenicals, sodium chlorate, DNOC, copper sulphate, pentachlorphenol and diquat all have their advantages and disadvantages. The most popular method is the use of calcium cyanamide on the freshly cut tops, but diquat has proved very effective, particularly on the early and mid-season varieties, and its use is rapidly expanding (Kabiersch, 1962).

Finally, a reminder that the alternative method of preventing virus transmission by direct control of aphids with insecticides has already been dealt with in the Entomological Section.

REFERENCES

KABIERSCH, W., *Outl. Agric.*, **6,** 268 (1962)

MCKAY, R., *Potato Diseases,* Irish Potato Marketing Co. Ltd., Dublin (1955)

SMITH, K. M., *A Textbook of Plant Virus Diseases* (2nd Edn.), J. and A. Churchill Ltd., London (1957).

WHITEHEAD, T., MCINTOSH, T. P. and FINDLAY, W. M., *The Potato in Health and Disease* (3rd Edn.), Oliver and Boyd, Edinburgh (1953)

## Wart Disease (*Synchytrium endobioticum* [Schilb.] Perc.)

The first official report of the presence of wart disease of potatoes was made in England in 1902, but subsequent investigation showed that it had been present in Cheshire as early as 1894. The disease appears as large, rough excrescences which develop both on the potato and the lower part of the stem (Fig. 3.5). Two properties of the disease emphasised the seriousness of the threat to England's potatoes, the very large percentage of the crop attacked and the long persistence of the disease in the soil.

Investigation of the disease was slow, mainly due to the absence of any organisation in the United Kingdom which was specifically charged with the duty of investigating plant diseases. Although its presence was recorded in 1902, a good description of its life history was not published until 1909 and a further twelve years elapsed before the publication of a detailed scientific account in 1921.

The study of the disease showed that it was due to a very primitive fungus, so primitive that it consisted of protoplasm without any cell wall. Although the life history took some time to unravel, it was not complicated. It overwintered by means of resting bodies called sporangia, which released zoospores when the soil warmed up in the spring. The zoospores swim about in the soil moisture and those which reach the eye of the potato settle down and penetrate inside the epidermal cells. The neighbouring cells are stimulated to grow, forming a swelling round the infected cell. The organism continues to develop inside the infected cell forming thin walled summer sporangia which gives rise to more zoospores. The continued release of zoospores and infection of new cells eventually results in the production of the warty excrescences from which the disease takes its name.

The overwintering sporangia are developed after the union of two zoospores forming a zygote which forms a thick walled covering and is thus protected during the winter.

## METHODS OF CONTROL

The practical measures for the control of wart disease owe much to G. Gough who was appointed in 1908 to study and report on it. He visited Lancashire and Cheshire where the disease was prevalent, and in the course of his inquiries found a gardener at Mouldsworth in Cheshire, who, in spite of heavily infected soil, was successfully growing a clean crop of potatoes of the variety 'Snowdrop'. This was a discovery of first-class importance and Gough in his report to the Board drew their attention to the existence of potato varieties resistant to wart disease.

Following the presentation of Gough's report, the vital step was taken of carrying out the systematic testing of potato varieties for resistance by planting them in heavily infected soil. Although most of the varieties then being grown were susceptible, five were resistant to the disease. Moreover, this was not a case of partial resistance with a small proportion of the tubers becoming infected, it was absolute.

In addition to this, legislation was passed making the disease a notifiable one and banning the sale of seed potatoes from the infected areas. Good use was made of these powers and the disease was thus prevented from spreading over the whole country.

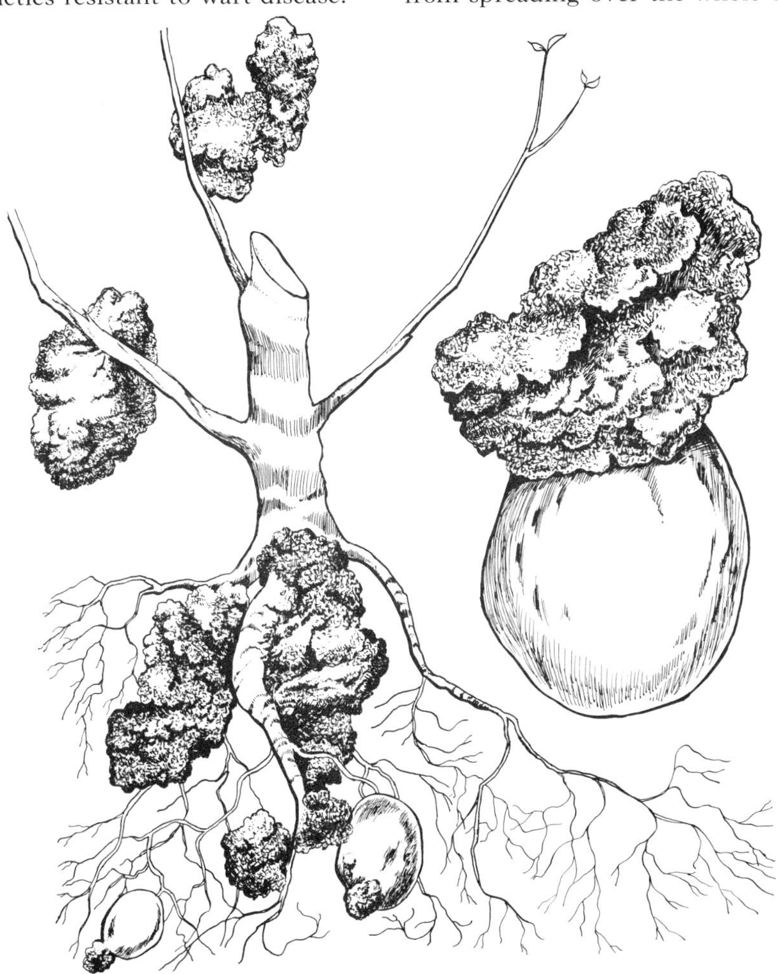

*Fig. 3.5. Wart Disease of potatoes*

It is interesting that the first disease map issued by the Commonwealth Mycological Institute in 1942 dealt with wart disease (C.M.I., 1942). The rigorous control exercised by governments throughout the world has successfully minimised its spread. The disease has been found in most of Europe, except Spain, in isolated sites in the U.S.A. and Canada, and in limited areas in South Africa, India and Japan.

Recent reports have shown that the fungus is capable of some variation, for races have been found in Germany which were able to attack previously immune varieties and evidence from Newfoundland would suggest that the race of wart disease present there differs from those in the United Kingdom and in the U.S.A. (Hanna, 1957).

Although the damage done by wart disease is now negligible, it remains an ever present threat to the potato crop. It is of great interest to plant pathologists for two reasons—an unusual example of complete resistance by some varieties of potato and a fine demonstration of the value of legislation in the control of a plant disease.

REFERENCES

C.M.I. *Distribution Maps of Plant Diseases,* No. 1, Commonwealth Mycological Institute, Kew (1942)

HANNA, W. F., 'Genetics in Relation to Crop Protection', *Plant Protection Conference 1956,* Butterworths Scientific Publications, London (1957)

### Black Leg (*Erwinia atroseptica* [van Hall] Jennison)

Black leg of potatoes is a well-known potato trouble and is found in most of the countries where potatoes are grown. The first symptoms of the disease appear on the foliage which is pale green in marked contrast to the darker green of healthy plants. When the affected haulm is pulled up, it parts easily from the seed potato as the disease causes the base of the stem to rot. On removing the haulm the characteristic black and slimy base of the stem is easily seen (Dowson, 1957).

Potato black leg is a bacterial disease whose development is closely linked with the amount of soil moisture. If the season is wet, or the site waterlogged, the disease may cause losses, but if the weather is dry, its progress is arrested.

The disease is mainly carried by infected tubers where the bacteria live in the vascular system and surrounding tissue at the heel end of the potato. As the potato grows, the bacteria reach the vascular system of the elongating shoots. If the attack is early, the shoot is usually killed, if late, the shoots become unhealthy but some tubers usually develop. In the very late infections, some of the bacteria invade the tubers and can overwinter in them.

#### METHODS OF CONTROL

The bacteria do not appear to overwinter in well drained soils, but they do so in waterlogged sites. It is thought that the soil-borne bacteria enter the potatoes through the lenticels. Control of the disease is difficult because it is not always possible to distinguish between infected and uninfected tubers. The typical sign of the presence of the bacteria in the tuber is heel-end browning, but it now appears that bacteria can be there without causing visible symptoms.

REFERENCE

DOWSON, W. J., *Plant Diseases due to Bacteria* (2nd Edn.), Cambridge University Press (1957)

### MINOR DISEASES

Dry rot (*Fusarium caeruleum* [Lib.] Sacc.)
Black scurf and stem canker (*Corticium solani* [Prill. and Delacr.] Bourd. and Galz.)
Skin spot (*Oospora pustulans* Owen and Wakef.)
Common scab (*Streptomyces scabies* [Thaxt.] Waks. and Henrici)
Powdery scab (*Spongospora subterranea* [Walln.] Lagerh. f. sp. subterranea)

The diseases which attack seed potatoes have received much attention and various treatments are used to protect them. The diseases in this group include dry rot, black scurf and stem canker and skin spot.

Potatoes suffering from dry rot shrink around the point of infection producing a series of wrinkles giving them a very typical appearance. Dry rot has not been so serious since some of the very susceptible varieties such as Doon Star declined in popularity. Stem canker is damaging in two ways, the overwintering sclerotia which look like small spots of tar adhere to the skin of the potato (Fig. 3.6) and spoil its appearance, while the active fungus can kill the young sprouts, particularly in the hot soils of sub-tropical areas. The lesions caused by the skin spot fungus are not easily seen at lifting time, but during storage they develop into superficial pimples about 2 mm in diameter.

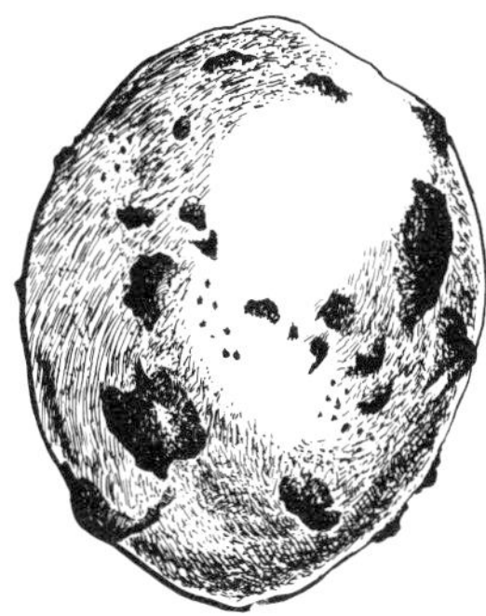

*Fig. 3.6. Sclerotia of Black Scurf and Stem Canker of potato*

Seed potato disinfection, which is best done immediately after lifting, is a three-stage process, thorough washing of the tubers to remove soil, immersion in the fungicidal bath and then drying. To do this on a commercial scale requires specialised machinery and consequently the treatment is usually limited to very large producers and co-operatives.

The most widely used fungicides for tuber disinfection are the organo-mercurial compounds, particularly methoxy ethyl mercury chloride (MEMC) and the ethoxy analogue EEMC. The concentration used varies with the dipping time. Good results have been obtained with 100 p.p.m. estimated as metallic mercury and immersion for 12 minutes.

Practical experience with seed potato disinfection has shown that the major benefits are the avoidance of storage losses and improved growth in the warmer parts of the world where stem canker is troublesome (Boyd *et al.*, 1967).

Specific treatments of seed potato diseases are also used. Stem canker can be controlled in the soil with quintozene. This is expensive but is used in Germany when seed potatoes have to be grown in infected soil (Kabiersch, 1962). Dry rot can be minimised by dusting the tubers with dusts containing 3% of tecnazene, a treatment which also has the advantage of suppressing sprout development.

Skin spot is not normally a serious problem, but it is of interest because it limited the use of propham as a sprout suppressor. Propham acts by inhibiting mitosis and thus not only checks the growth of the sprouts but also the formation of corky barriers which normally bar the skin spot fungus from penetrating deeply into the tuber. For this reason propham can only be used on potatoes free from skin spot.

Two diseases are particularly disfiguring to ware potatoes, common scab and powdery scab. In both cases the damage is mainly to

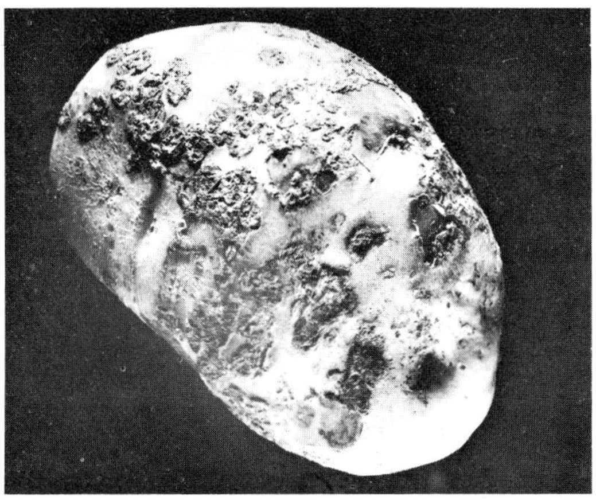

*Plate 3.6. Common Scab of potato (A Plant Protection photograph)*

the skin, but if the lesion is deep, it becomes ,necessary to peel rather thickly.

The typical symptoms of common scab are corky depressions (Plate 3.6). The disease is found in almost every potato-growing country in the world, and it is not easy to prevent. In practice, potato growers keep the disease within bounds by keeping the soil acid by using acid fertilizers such as sulphate of ammonia and superphosphate, by avoiding the use of lime, and by irrigating when the tubers are small.

Powdery scab occurs in the wetter parts of the British Isles, and on the eastern side of the U.S.A. and Canada. The symptoms consist of small pimples which rupture releasing quantities of powdery spores. The disease is minimised by cultural methods, particularly good drainage and crop rotation.

REFERENCES

BOYD, A. E. W. and PENNA, R. J., *Proc. 4th Brit. Insecticide Fungicide Conf.*, 294 (1967)

KABIERSCH, W., *Outl. Agric.*, **6,** 270 (1962)

The first commercial attempt to extract sugar from beet was made at the end of the eighteenth century, but the industry made little progress until Napoleon I in 1811 decided to encourage its development to free his country from dependence on the English monopoly of cane-sugar production. Since then, many other governments in the temperate areas of the world have thought it was wise to have a home-produced source of sugar and have therefore arranged for part of their supplies to be produced from sugar-beet.

Sugar-beet is mainly a northern European crop; large areas being found in France, Germany, Poland and United Kingdom. It is grown in all European countries to a greater or lesser extent. In southern Europe it is grown on a smaller scale. It is a less important crop in such countries as Spain, Italy and Bulgaria and limited areas are grown in Turkey and Egypt. In addition, large areas are grown in the U.S.A. and the U.S.S.R. Europe and the U.S.S.R. account for 16 million acres out of a world total of about 19 million (F.A.O., 1964).

Sugar-beet is attacked by many pests which may cause direct injury, or indirectly as virus transmitters. Generally speaking, the same pests occur wherever sugar-beet is grown, but those of Europe and neighbouring countries differ from those in America. *Aphis fabae* is an important pest in its own right. Formerly, soil insects were predominant, especially species of *Agriotes* (wireworms), but these pests have been overcome and have tended to attract less attention

In the south *Chaetocnema* and *Bothynoderes* are important pests and the problem of virus is of lesser magnitude. In America, soil pests are of importance. Sugar-beet pests in the United Kingdom have been described by Jones (1957).

In all countries, sugar-beet is grown under contract for the sugar-producing factories; the farmer does not, as a rule, grow sugar-beet on speculation of a sale. As a result, sugar-beet growing is well organised and supervised by factory representatives who advise the farmer on the problems of pests and diseases. New methods of control can therefore be introduced and will be taken up by all growers immediately.

The production of sugar-beet seed is an independent undertaking as sugar-beet is a biennial. Crops are especially grown for seed quite independently of the root crop.

Virus diseases appear to be the principal problem in sugar-beet culture in most parts of the world. In northern Europe virus yellows, which is aphid transmitted, is the predominant disease, but although present in North America, it is unimportant there. The reverse occurs with curly top, a controlling factor for sugar-beet cultivation in the western part of America, but although it is found in Turkey it has not been recorded in Europe. Much attention has also been paid to diseases affecting the seedlings as maximum plant populations per acre are important for the profitable production of the crop.

Hull's 'Sugar-beet Diseases' comprehensively reviews the subject from an English viewpoint, and also deals with diseases which are of greater importance abroad than in England. A review of the North American sugar-beet problems was published in the U.S. Department of Agriculture's yearbook on plant diseases (U.S.D.A., 1953).

REFERENCES

*F.A.O. Production Yearbook 1963–64,* **18,** F.A.O., Rome

HULL, R., *Sugar-Beet Diseases,* Bulletin No. 142 (2nd Edn.), H.M.S.O., London (1960)

JONES, F. G. W., *Sugar-beet Pests,* Bulletin No. 162, H.M.S.O., London (1957)

United States Department of Agriculture, *Plant Diseases, the Yearbook of Agriculture,* 509, The U.S. Government Printing Office, Washington, D.C. (1953)

## COLEOPTERA

### *Agriotes spp. (Elateridae)*

The larval stages or wireworms, occur throughout northern Europe and America but are absent from those countries with a warmer climate. They attack the roots of many plants just below soil level and were formerly important pests of sugar-beet destroying many acres. The sugar-beet seedling is particularly susceptible to wireworm injury to the hypocotyl (stem) just below soil level because, at that stage, the plant is small and has no power of recovery. Sugar-beet is grown in widely spaced rows and so few wireworms can destroy many plants. Sugar-beet is susceptible even after singling (i.e. selection of plants from the seedlings) until the root is about as thick as a pencil. The life-cycles of wireworms is given in the Cereals section.

### METHODS OF CONTROL

Land full of wireworm should not be cropped with sugar-beet which should never be grown on recently ploughed grassland until it has been cropped for at least two years. Likewise, land used predominantly for cereals should not be planted with sugar beet until a soil sample shows the wireworm population has decreased. In the 1930's, this kind of advice was all that could be given in the early days of sugar-beet growing, but now, soil insecticides can be employed against wireworms. The first was BHC which, broadcast as a $3\frac{1}{2}\%$ dust, gave perfect wireworm control. BHC upsets the mechanism of orientation in the wireworm which is unable to find plant food and tends to come to the surface. BHC as a broadcast dust, was quickly superseded by gamma BHC as a seed-dressing. This was used at the rate of 0·7% of a seed dressing containing 40% gamma BHC combined with mercury. Seed dressing was effective in the year of sowing and much cheaper than the broadcast application (Jones and Humphreys, 1954). Seed dressing of beet seed with gamma BHC, either in combination with mercury or applied as a seperate dressing, is the accepted method of wireworm control in all countries, the gamma BHC dressing being often applied by the farmer. Alternative insecticides, notably aldrin, can also be used. In England, whereas some thousands of acres were redrilled through losses from wireworm, nowadays the losses are negligible.

### *Atomaria linearis* Steph. *(Cryptophagidae)*

This little beetle, known as the Pygmy Beetle, was formerly of great importance as a pest of sugar-beet in northern Europe. It flourished in the 1930s when a good deal of sugar-beet was grown in the same land without rotation. The beetles overwinter in the soil and turn their attention to the sugar-beet when it is in the seedling stage. The beetles bite into the hypocotyl of the seedling just after it comes above ground. When the beetles are numerous, many seedlings can be destroyed but after the sugar-beet has passed this stage *Atomaria* is of no importance as it is incapable of injuring larger plants. The life-cycle occurs in the soil but the eggs and larvae are so small that they are seldom found.

### METHODS OF CONTROL

Sugar-beet in rotation is seldom seriously attacked. When beet is grown after beet or mangolds, the beetles become sufficiently numerous to damage the crop. Normally, the overwintering beetles disperse in April and May when suitable weather conditions for flight occur. In new fields, they are seldom present in sufficient numbers to cause appreciable injury. Sugar-beet and mangolds are the preferred food, the beetles sometimes feed on weeds but attack no other crops.

Direct action against *Atomaria* is now seldom necessary. Thompson and Edwards (1934) used a mixture of phenol and magnesium sulphate in which to soak the seed but their method was useless. Seed dressings containing gamma BHC are only partially effective against *Atomaria* but broadcast dressings of BHC as formerly used for wireworm control, are completely effective.

### *Chaetocnema concinna* Marsh. *(Chrysomelidae)*

The Beet Flea Beetle is similar to the turnip flea beetles in size and shape and, like them, possesses thickened femora on the rear legs for jumping. It occurs throughout northern

Europe but is only sporadically a sugar-beet pest. In the more southern beet growing regions such as Spain, Italy and Turkey, it is more important.

Flea beetles overwinter as adults and emerge to feed on foliage of plants in April and May, eating little holes in the seedling leaves. If the beetles are numerous, seedlings may be destroyed but normally the beetles are not very active except in hot dry weather when they fly readily and assemble in fields containing their food crops. *Chaetocnema* spp. also feeds on *Polygonaceae,* usually weeds.

METHODS OF CONTROL

When necessary, *Chaetocnema* is easily controlled with insecticides such as sprays or dust containing either DDT or gamma BHC. Application is made when the beet is still in the seedling stage and the holes in the leaves are becoming numerous. Sometimes, it is possible to control other beet pests at the same time such as the Beet Leaf Miner.

*Bothynoderes (Cleonus) punctiventris* Germ. *(Curculionidae)*

This insect is a large weevil about 1 in. long with a prominent proboscis (Fig. 3.7). It is an important pest on sugar-beet in central

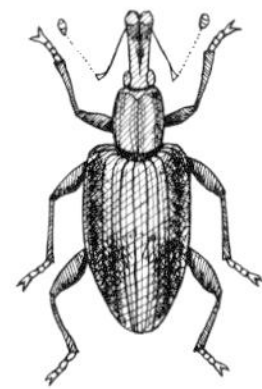

*Fig. 3.7.* Bothynoderes punctiventris *(adult)*

and southern Europe (Bogdanov, 1960) and occurs in Turkey. Like *Atomaria* and *Chaetocnema,* the adults overwinter and attack seedling plants at an early stage in April and May. The weevils are powerful but slow feeders and if numerous, can destroy the crop. The adults, on emerging from the winter, are attracted to open blooms and tend to migrate in large numbers across the soil. When the temperature reaches 70°F, they fly and disperse. The immature stages occur in the soil and feed on the roots of the beet. The females deposit about 100 eggs each near the food plants. A related species, *Cleonus mendicus* Gyll. occurs in Italy where *B. punctiventris* is absent.

METHODS OF CONTROL

As with *Atomaria,* the extent of the damage is dependent on the numbers of weevils, which in turn is dependent on the rotation pursued. Where beet is taken after beet, the weevil can accumulate in damaging numbers in the soil, but rotation normally keeps the numbers down. Injury is worse under hot and dry conditions which favour weevil activity, whereas cool wet weather makes them sluggish while the beet grows on freely (Eichler and Schrodter, 1951).

The insecticide commonly used against *Bothynoderes* is a dust containing 3% gamma BHC and 10% DDT at about 25 lb per acre, as the weevils are difficult to kill with normal insecticides. Dusts are preferred, probably because there is little field spraying equipment at present in countries where *Bothynoderes* occur.

*Blitophaga spp.* }
*Silpha obscura L.* } *(Dermestidae)*

These are known as Beet Carrion Beetles as the habit of the family is to feed on carrion. These species have developed a fondness for plant food. Both the larvae and adults feed on the foliage which they smear with a black exudation.

*Cassida spp. (Chrysomelidae)*

Several species of Tortoise Beetles and their larvae feed on beet. Both adults and larvae are green and make holes in the leaves but they are seldom numerous enough to cause much damage.

## Chafers *(Lamellicornia)*

The adults are well-known foliage feeders of woodland trees. The larvae live in soil and feed on the roots of many plants including sugar-beet. The life-cycle of some species takes three years to complete and some even four years. Damage to beet occurs in forest regions as the larvae near maturity. In many years the beetles are more numerous than in others and these are called 'flight' years. Damage to beet follows two or three years after a flight year but the problem is very local.

BOGDANOV, W., *R.A.E.*, **49**, 338 (1960)
EDWARDS, E. E. and THOMPSON, J. K., *Ann. Appl. Biol.*, **21**, 300 (1934)
EICHLER, W. and SCHRODTER, W., *Z. Angew. Entomol.*, **32**, 567 (1951)
JONES, F. G. W. and HUMPHREYS, K. P., *Ann. Appl. Biol.*, **41**, 562 (1954)

## DIPTERA

### *Pegomyia betae* Curtis *(Anthomyidae)*

The Beet Leaf Miner or Beet Fly is a common pest of sugar-beet in northern Europe but disappears in the more southern beet-growing countries. The injury consists of blisters in the leaves caused by the larvae or maggots which feed on the leaf tissues between the upper and lower surfaces (Plate 3.7). When many eggs are deposited, the mines may destroy the entire assimilating tissues of seedling beet and decrease yields by 30–40%. Later generations occur and the leaves of the larger beet are also attacked but, at this stage, the injury is more apparent than real.

Flies occur in late April or early May in northern latitudes and the females deposit white, elongated eggs on the undersides of the leaves in twos and threes. The early mines are narrow and winding but later, as the larvae increase in size, large patches are eaten and several mines in one leaf often join up. The second generation occurs in July. The fly itself resembles a house fly and is seldom seen. The larvae when they have completed their development drop out of the leaf into the soil where they pupate.

*Plate 3.7. Sugar-beet leaf showing damage from beet leaf miner (I.W. Callan)*

#### METHODS OF CONTROL

When beet fields are concentrated in one area, the Beet Fly can build up large numbers as the flies emerging from the old beet fields can easily find the new crop. Normally, the attack starts before or during 'singling' when the single plants are selected to stand the season. Attacked plants at this stage, can be removed and the sound ones left.

Beet fly can be controlled by insecticides and the beet grower should be prepared to spray from mid-May onwards when the first mines are seen and the eggs numerous. Probably, the most effective insecticide is parathion which is very rapid in action and kills the larvae in the leaf (Dunning, 1956). It is very easily applied in 20 gal per acre of water using 16 fl oz of a 20% product. Other insecticides are also effective notably trichlorphon (Dipterex) but probably the best insecticide is dimethoate (Rogor) as this is a systemic insecticide also effective against aphids. DDT, aldrin and similar insecticides are also effective but, as spraying against aphids is often necessary at the same time, should not be chosen as they are liable to kill the insects predatory on aphids without effectively killing the aphids. Spraying against the second generation is not usually necessary.

REFERENCE

DUNNING, R. A., *Brit. Sugar Beet Rev.*, **24**, 131 (1956)

## HEMIPTERA

### *Aphis fabae* Scop. *(Aphididae)*

The Black Bean Aphid or Beet Aphid occurs throughout Europe south to Turkey. It is an important pest of beans *(Vicia fabae)* and occurs on many plants including weeds. It is one of the most important pests of sugar-beet as it attacks both the root and seed crops. The attacks occur in June and July and can lower the yield of beet by several tons per acre and ruin the seed crop entirely. It transmits virus diseases of beet, notably mosaic and the yellows viruses but as it forms large colonies and moves less than *Myzus persicae* it is less important as a vector.

*Aphis fabae* overwinters as an egg on *Euonymus europeus,* a tree common in Europe especially on chalky soils. This is the main plant on which eggs occur but they can also be deposited on a few other shrubs. The eggs hatch in February, and, after two generations of wingless females, winged forms appear which leave *Euonymus* and fly to summer food plants, especially beans and sugar-beet. In Britain, aphids usually leave *Euonymus* in late April and can be found on beet in the second half of May. In the more southern countries, the aphids may reach the beet earlier and when they are smaller. In many, the aphids can survive the winter outdoors without going through the egg stage.

Reproduction on the summer food plants is continuous as the aphids are all females and produce living young. The population builds up quickly and further spread by winged forms takes place in the summer months. Return migrants colonise *Euonymus* in September and there produce sexual females. Males from the summer hosts mate with them. Winter eggs are again deposited.

As a vector of the yellows virus, *Aphis fabae* spreads the disease mainly within the crop as the first arriving aphids are non-viruliferous. Later migrations from summer food plants are too late to be of importance in the spread of the diseases.

#### METHODS OF CONTROL

The destruction of the winter egg-bearing plants is not a practical control method for two reasons. Firstly, aphids can travel over long distances in air currents and secondly, insecticides can now be used on the beet crop whereas formerly the aphids could not be reached as they inhabited the underside of the beet leaves. Parathion gave the first practical control of *Aphis fabae* on beet because when it was applied from above it penetrated the leaf lamina and killed the aphids beneath. The most reliable insecticides are those of the systemic type which enter freely into the leaf tissues and remain effective for 10–20 days. The most widely used in northern Europe is methyl-demeton (Metasystox) applied at 12–16 fl oz per acre. Other systemic insecticides are equally effective. Application is made in mid-June and again if necessary in mid-July (Plate 3.8).

*Plate 3.8. Sugar-beet attacked by Aphis fabae. Left: untreated. Right: sprayed with insecticide*

Special attention should be paid to the seed crop which is usually treated earlier because it becomes infested with the first migration of aphids from the *Euonymus*. Spraying is difficult because the crop is tall but it can be sprayed by aeroplane or helicopter with complete success at 3–4 gal per acre.

*Myzus persicae* Sulz. *(Aphididae)*

Unlike *Aphis fabae, Myzus persicae* is seldom a pest in its own right on sugar-beet but as a vector of virus diseases it is much more important. *Myzus* transmits the yellows virus complex and its importance as a vector arises from its ability to transmit very many such diseases, its omnivorous habits and its restlessness on plants. *Myzus* can be found in many countries in which sugar-beet is grown but is less prevalent in the more southern regions.

*Myzus persicae* is known as the Peach and Potato Aphid because it lays eggs on peach and other related *Prunus* spp. It feeds on many summer food plants and spends the winter as an aphid in those countries where the winter is less severe, notably in the United Kingdom where it overwinters on perennial or winter crops and on many weeds. It migrates as soon as the temperature is about 70°F and winged forms are usually present at all times. It is a green species and readily distinguished from *Aphis fabae*.

### VIRUS YELLOWS

The yellows viruses occur throughout northern Europe and although present are less important in the more southern and warmer countries such as Spain, Italy and Turkey. Yellows viruses also occur in the U.S.A. (Hills *et al.* 1963). In the United Kingdom, the early approach to virus control was an attempt to break the continuity of the virus cycle from one season to the next by the seed crop. Sugar-beet is a biennial and so the seed crop carries the infection, collected in one year, into the next when it is transmitted again by aphids to the root crop. In consequence sugar-beet seedlings (stecklings) for the seed crop were raised in areas away from the main beet growing centres. Furthermore, stecklings were inspected and certified and stocks showing more than 10% virus infection were classified as infected. These measures decreased the degree of virus in the seed crop but had less effect on the root crop.

There are many sources of yellows viruses other than sugar-beet seed, notably mangold clamps which harbour both virus-carrying plants and *Myzus* which therefore can emerge fully infected. Certain weeds also carry the virus and another source is the rooted beet tops from a previous crop which may begin to grow in old fields previously beet. Frequently, such rooted tops are in cereals and are of little importance as a source of virus. Ribbans (1963) argues that the main source of virus infection is still the seed crop and in the United Kingdom, the levels of yellows infection early in the season are related to the average temperatures in February. Seed crops are relatively free from virus plants so that many other hosts in the shelter of gardens may also be an important source of infection. In Spain, it is not uncommon for the root crop to remain in the ground all the winter and is still in position when the new crop is sown. In these circumstances both *Myzus* and *Aphis fabae* can survive.

*Spraying for virus control.* Spraying with systemic insecticides against *Myzus persicae* to minimise virus infection and spread began about 1948. The first experiments were made on the seed crop with the insecticide nicotine. In due course, schradan was tried and decreased the yellows in the seed crop by half with a corresponding increase in the yield of seed (Hull and Gates, 1953).

Spraying the root crop to decrease yellows was first attempted in 1951 in western Germany (Steudel, 1952). The systemic insecticide demeton (Systox) was used with good results (Linke, 1952). In the United Kingdom, similar experiments began in 1954 firstly with demeton and later with methyl-demeton (Metasystox) both of which were successful. In 1957, spraying on a commercial scale began and has continued every year since then (Hull, 1958).

Spraying usually begins in early June with methyl-demeton used at 12 fl oz per acre. Other systemic insecticides are also suitable such as dimethoate (Rogor). Early infection greatly decreases yield but in the United

Kingdom, *Myzus* seldom reaches the beet before late May. Sugar losses have been calculated from virus infection at $2\frac{1}{2}$ cwt for every 10% of infection by the end of August (Hull, 1958).

The latest idea is to use systemic insecticides as a seed or soil treatment. Menazon is being tested as a seed dressing at $2\frac{1}{2}$–5% and can also be used in the soil as a 5% granule at 20 lb per acre. Disulphoton (DiSyston) is also being tested but at present it is doubtful if these treatments will be economic.

*Eutettix tenellus* Bak. *(Jassidae)*

This little insect is the Beet Leaf-Hopper of the U.S.A. It is an important pest of beet there because it transmits the virus disease called 'Curly Top'. The virus can infect many other plants including tomato and is especially common in the south-western part of the country. *Eutettix* lives and breeds on many plants including beet, on which two to three generations occur. If the beet is invaded by leaf-hoppers carrying the virus, the yield suffers especially that of the seed crop if attacked in the autumn when the plants are small. Threatened crops are sprayed with DDT (Douglas, 1948, Hills *et al.*, 1963).

*Lygus pabulinus* L. *(Miridae)*

This is a capsid bug which occurs commonly on weeds around field edges before moving into the sugar beet. It possesses toxic saliva which causes distortion of the young leaves of the plant when the bugs feed on them. It is easily controlled by spraying the field edge and the weeds with DDT.

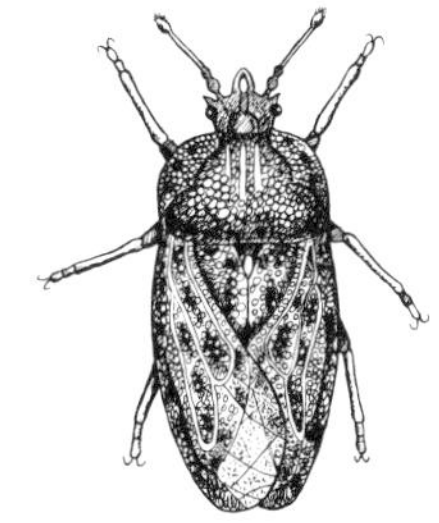

*Fig. 3.8.* Piesma quadrata *(adult)*

*Piesma quadrata* Fieb. *(Tingidae)*

This insect is easily recognised as it has reticulated wings (Fig. 3.8). In Europe particularly in Germany and Poland, it can transmit the virus causing 'Curly Top' (Krauselkrankheit). This disease is of little importance and action is seldom necessary except in local beet growing regions.

REFERENCES

DOUGLASS, J. R., GUTSON, K. E. and HALLOCK, H. C., *J. Econ. Entomol.*, **41,** 814 (1948)

HILLS, O. A., CONDRIET, D. L. and JEWELL, H. C., *J. Econ. Entomol.*, **56,** 690 (1963)

HULL, R. and GATES, L. F., *Ann. Appl. Biol.*, **40,** 60 (1953)

HULL, R., *Agriculture,* **65,** 62 (1958)

LINKE, W., unpublished (1952)

RIBBANS, C. R., *Nature,* **197,** 4867 (1963)

STEUDAL, W., *Z. Pflanzkrank.*, **59,** 418 (1952)

## LEPIDOPTERA

*Plusia gamma* L. *(Noctuidae)*

This is the Silver Y Moth. The caterpillar is a semi-looper and is common throughout Europe as the moths are migratory and can fly many hundreds of miles. Caterpillars appear on the beet in July and August and make holes in the foliage. Leaf-feeding caterpillars are rare on sugar-beet but epidemics do occur sometimes more especially in the warm climates.

*Caradrina exigua* Hubn. *(Noctuidae)*

This moth is probably the same as *Laphygma exigua* known as the Beet Armyworm which occurs in the U.S.A. *Caradrina* is found in warm countries such as Turkey and can occur in large numbers when it attacks beet at soil level. The moths deposit large numbers of eggs in the soil which hatch and give rise to tiny caterpillars. These rapidly grow up and attack the crop, sugar-beet being particularly susceptible to injury when the plants are in the seedling stage.

### METHODS OF CONTROL

Action against these insects is difficult as they live in the soil but DDT is often used either as a 10% dust or as a spray. The object of the application is to coat the soil surface, plants and weeds with a thin layer of insecticide over which the caterpillar must walk when it rises to the surface of the soil. The old method of using a poison bait of bran and sodium arsenite is still effective but a safer insecticide such as DDT is now used. Treatment of a similar insect, *Agrotis segetum* L. in the United Kingdom, is recorded by Petherbridge and Stapley (1937).

### *Loxostege sticticalis* L. *(Pyralidae)*

This is the Beet Webworm which is common in the U.S.A. and is one of the group of Pyralid foliage-feeding caterpillars which spin the leaves of their food plant into tubes. In the U.S.A., about three generations occur. The caterpillars are green with a black stripe down the dorsum and are easily controlled with DDT or an insecticide of this type. Several other species occur but their food plants overlap.

REFERENCES
PETHERBRIDGE, F. R. and STAPLEY, J. H., *J. Minist., Agric,* **44**, 43 (1937)

## NEMATODA

### *Heterodera schachtii* Sch.

This is the Beet Cyst Eelworm or Beet Eelworm, an important pest of sugar-beet. Often, its presence is more a threat than as a cause of actual crop losses. It is controllable by rotation and its presence in land is usually an indication of overcropping with sugar-beet.

The Beet Eelworm is present in Great Britain, northern Europe, the U.S.A. and all established beet-growing countries. In Great Britain, it is well distributed throughout beet-growing areas but especially in intensive areas such as the black fens. In the U.S.A. and Germany, it is widely distributed in the beet-growing regions. An account of this nematode has been given by Southey (1959).

*Heterodera schachtii* was discovered in Europe about 1859 and was soon recognised in the beet-growing soils of Europe. In Great Britain, it was first found on mangolds near Bristol in 1928 and first on beet in 1934 (Petherbridge, 1934). It appears to have been known in the U.S.A. since 1906 (Thorne, 1941). *H. schachtii* belong to the cyst-forming nematodes (c.f. *H. rostochiensis* on potato) in which the female eelworm is a lemon-shaped chitinous sac in which 200 to 300 eggs can remain protected for several years. A few eggs hatch spontaneously every year for several years and the young eelworms escape from the cysts, by the root exudates from the growing crop.

The larvae or second stage nematodes enter into the rootlets, become sedentary and enlarge. The females continue to enlarge, remain attached by their heads but rupture the root cortex and appear outside the root. They become lemon-shaped, are white at first but slowly turn brown when they die. At first they remain attached to the root by a neck but eventually drop off into the soil where the cycle starts again in the same season. The males, after bursting out of the root tissues, become worm-like again, seek out and fertilize the females.

The fact that the swollen females remain attached to the roots for a time enables the observer to detect the presence of the nematode by pulling plants out of the soil. The nematodes injure the root system of the plant as its function is impaired by the presence of nematodes in the tissues, and the plant fails to make progress. Typical nematode-attacked plants are stunted, with an exceedingly branched root system. When soil is full of cysts and the beet grows badly, the land is said to be 'beet sick'.

METHODS OF CONTROL

The chief cause of land becoming 'beet sick' is over cropping with sugar-beet which increases the numbers of cysts in the soil to a level where the crop is affected. Alternative crops, when taken after beet, allow the numbers to decline. Unfortunately, many other crops can be attacked by *Heterodera schachtii* and, when grown, maintain the nematode status of the soil. Furthermore, certain weeds are also susceptible and help to perpetuate the pest (Jones, 1956).

*Heterodera schachtii* will attack almost all *Cruciferae,* including weeds, as well as a number of non-cruciferae. It also attacks many *Chenopodiacae* which is the same family as sugar-beet. On the other hand *Graminae* and most *Leguminosae* are immune, so that cereals and legumes can safely be grown (Winslow, 1954).

Rotation is the usual method of control. In some countries, notably the United Kingdom, sugar-beet is not permitted to be grown after sugar-beet or mangolds or any other crop which is susceptible to *Heterodera schachtii.* An interval of four years must elapse after sugar-beet and the growing of any such crop. Legislation to this effect is in force and applies to certain scheduled areas (Sugar-Beet Eelworm Order, 1952). Similar recommendations have also been made in many other countries. The best practice with land already infested is to grow grass and clover or a similar forage crop and leave it down for several years.

In the U.S.A., soil injection with the nematocide dichloropropane-dichloropropene (D-D) is practised at 30–40 gal per acre using a special tool drawn by a tractor. The nematocide flows in to the soil in lines about 9–12 in apart. This method is expensive and only gives temporary relief—by no means eradicating the nematode from the soil. Injection is used in conjunction with the rotation of crops.

Eelworm can easily spread from one field to another in infested soil. The growing of seed potatoes is prohibited in field heavily infested with Beet Eelworm, as the soil adhering to them will be infested with eelworm cysts. Spread, however, is difficulty to prevent but is of minor importance in comparison with crop rotation as a means of control.

In Holland and in the United Kingdom, in light alkaline soils, severe stunting of beet appears to be caused by certain migratory nematodes namely

*Longidorus attennatus* the Needle Nematode and *Trichodorus flevensis* the Stubby Root Nematode.

The first attacks seedlings, feeds on root tips and prevents the development of laterals so that a small plant with a normal tap root and no laterals appear. The second, in great numbers, entirely prevents roots from penetrating deeply so that a stunted plant develops with many horizontal fangs. In the United Kingdom, these disorders are grouped under the term 'Docking Disorders'. These nematodes are also found on the eastern coastal plain of the U.S.A. In warmer climates, the Root Knot Nematode (*Meloidogyne* spp.) and the False Root Knot Nematode *(Nacobbus)* are becoming important beet pests especially where irrigation is practised.

REFERENCES

JONES, F. G. W., *Ann. Appl. Biol.,* **44,** 25 (1956)
PETHERBRIDGE, F. R., *J. Min. Agr.,* **41,** 825 (1934)
SOUTHEY, J. F., *Min. Agr. and Fish Tech. Bull.* No. 7 (1959)
THORNE, G., *Farmers Bull. U.S.D.A.,* No. 1514 (1941)
WINSLOW, R. D., *Ann. Appl. Biol.,* **41,** 591 (1954)

## VIRUS YELLOWS

A beet field severely infected by virus yellows is easily recognised in late summer as the general appearance of the field is golden yellow instead of the normal bright green of a healthy one. Closer inspection will show that it is the older leaves which show the symptoms, the younger leaves usually remaining green (Coloured Plate 3). If the plants have been infected early in the growing season the older leaves all turn yellow and later slowly die off, but if the infection is late in the year only scattered plants have the bright yellow leaves caused by the virus.

The importance of the disease has only been recognised during the past thirty years, but the losses caused by it are now clearly established. For example, the average annual loss in England for the years 1949–60 was estimated to be 340,000 tons, varying from negligible amounts to as much as one million tons of beet in 1957 (Hull, 1961).

The investigations on the disease carried out in the 1940s made the cycle clear. The virus survives the winter in infected plants, particularly seed crops of sugar-beet, mangolds and red beet, and in clamped mangolds and red beet. There are also other minor sources such as wild beet which grows abundantly on the shore in parts of East Anglia, small unharvested beet plants on the farm and garden, crops of spinach beet and sea-kale beet, and a few weeds such as goosefoot, groundsel, and chickweed.

The virus is carried from the overwintering source to the crop by aphids, the peach-potato aphid being easily the most important vector. The overwintering aphis population varies greatly in numbers, depending on the severity or otherwise of the winter. In a mild winter, large numbers survive on brassica crops, and in the course of their spring movement some feed on virus yellows infected plants before alighting on sugar-beet seedlings. In a hard winter few aphides survive as adults but the egg stage on peach trees ensures the continuance of the species. When the population is small, it takes time to build up in the spring with the result that the onset of virus yellows is slow and small in amount.

## METHODS OF CONTROL

This brief description of the virus yellows problem shows that there are two theoretical ways to control the disease, namely by reducing the sources of infection, and by killing the vectors. In either case the problem was a formidable one.

The first approach was to reduce the amount of overwintering inoculum in the seed crops, the major source of the disease. Healthy stecklings, the young plants grown for transplanting, and then for the production of seed, can be grown by ensuring their isolation from sources of infection. This is done in three ways, by growing the stecklings in areas with no beet or mangold crops, by ensuring adequate separation between the stecklings and other beet fields and by growing the stecklings under a cereal cover crop.

The phyto-sanitary approach played an important part in cutting down the incidence of virus yellows, but the introduction of persistent systemic insecticides which killed aphides feeding on the beet provided the major weapon for the defence of the crop. This aspect is dealt with in greater detail in the Entomological Section.

The possibility of breeding varieties which are immune to virus yellows has not been overlooked, but immunity to the virus has not been found. However, lines have been selected for development which are not as seriously affected as the existing commercial varieties (Hull, 1961).

REFERENCE
HULL, R., *J. Roy. agric. Soc. Engl.*, **122,** 101 (1961)

## CURLY TOP

The curly top virus is prevalent in North and South America, but although it is present in Turkey, it is absent in Europe. Affected plants are dwarfed, with yellow leaves which curl inwards.

The virus is an economically important one because of its effect on the yield of sugar-beet. In the U.S.A., a bad attack can reduce the normal average of 15 tons of beet per acre to 5 tons or less. The effects of the disease were particularly felt in the irrigated areas to the west of the Rocky Mountains where severe outbreaks forced the farmers to give up sugar-beet growing.

The virus is present in many of the indigenous plants which grow near the sugar-beet fields. It is carried by a leaf hopper *(Eutettix tenellus)* which feeds on the wild plants during the winter. Some of the infected leaf hoppers migrate to the sugar-beet in the spring and transmit the disease while feeding on them.

### METHODS OF CONTROL

Attempts have been made to check curly top both by destroying the infected wild plants and by killing the vectors. Although these steps were of some value, the most effective answer came from the plant breeder. The damage done by curly top was so serious that a special research programme was started by the United States Department of Agriculture in 1929. This led to the introduction of a tolerant variety in 1934, and improvements have been made in the succeeding years. The sugar-beet varieties now available in the U.S.A. ensure that the crop will be an adequate one, even in years when virus infection is very prevalent.

## BLACK LEG

(Caused by various pathogens, particularly *Pleospora bjoerlingi* Byford syn. Phoma betae Frank, *Corticium solani* [Prill. and Delacr.] Bourd. and Galz., Pythium ultimum Trow, *P. intermedium* de Bary, and *Aphanomyces cochlioides* Drechsler)

When good natural seed is sown at the usual rate of 10–15 lb per acre, abundant seedlings are produced which give a full final stand after the usual small percentage of losses due to seedling diseases. The tendency in the industry is to use lower seeding rates, and it follows that the smaller the amount of seed

*Plate 3.9. Four stages in the destruction of sugar-beet seedlings by black leg (R. Hull of Broom's Barn Experimental Station)*

sown, the higher must be the survival rate to ensure the optimum plant population. The introduction of rubbed and graded seed sown with precision drills has been an important advance in growing an evenly spaced braird, this simplifying singling. Should monogerm seed and mechanical singling be adopted, it will be even more essential to avoid seedling losses (Hull, 1961).

Two groups of fungi attack the seedlings, those which are present in the soil, and one which is carried by the seed. The effect on the seedlings is very similar, the stem at about soil level shrinks and turns black (Plate 3.9), hence the general name of black leg for this group of diseases.

Four different soil fungi can cause black leg. In eastern England two species of *Pythium* are common, *P. ultimum,* and *P. intermedium.* In North America the beet water mould *(Aphanomyces cochlioides)* is liable to be serious in wet soils. *Corticium solani* attacks a small percentage of the seedlings in England, but in the U.S.A. a more virulent strain is responsible for serious losses.

The predominant cause of black leg is the seed-borne fungus *Pleospora bjoerlingi,* better known under its old name of *Phoma betae.* The fungus is very common on the leaves and stems of the seed crop and produces spores which may be splashed on to the seed cluster. If this occurs, the fungus penetrates the seed coat and then becomes dormant until the seed germinates. The amount of seed infection varies with the season, roughly speaking the wetter the harvest season, the greater the amount.

### METHODS OF CONTROL

Methods of controlling the seed-borne phase of black leg have received much attention from plant pathologists. Organomercurial seed-dressings have been used for this purpose for many years. For sugar-beet seed the standard rate was 12 oz of a powder dressing containing 1–2% of organically combined mercury per 100 lb of seed. The seed dressing was usually applied in a seed dressing machine which ensure thorough mixing of the fungicide with the seed. The treatment effectively reduced the amount of black leg infection and all seed distributed by the British sugar factories between 1945 and 1960 was so treated (Byford, 1961).

The introduction of precision drills sowing rubbed and graded seed at the rate of approximately 6 lb per acre called for still more effective methods of disinfecting the seed. The problem was solved by introducing an ethyl mercury phosphate (EMP) steep. The rubber and graded seed is soaked in an EMP solution at a concentration of 40 p.p.m. for 20 minutes. The practical problems of ensuring freedom from mercury toxicity, the handling of large quantities of wet seed which have to be dried, and the disposal of the toxic effluent were all serious difficulties which had to be overcome (Ridge, 1962). Work is therefore being continued on the development of a short wet treatment which would avoid the difficulties of the steep method.

Although emphasis in this Section has been on the fungicidal aspects of seed treatment, insecticidal seed-dressings are of equal importance. Frequently the two materials are combined to give a dual-purpose product. The use of insecticides in this way is dealt with in the Entomological Section.

#### REFERENCES

BYFORD, W. J., *Brit. Sug. Beet Rev.,* **29,** 119 (1961)
HULL, R., *J. Roy. agric. Soc. Engl.,* **122,** 103 (1961)
RIDGE, J. D., *Brit. Sug. Beet Rev.,* **30,** 181 (1962)

### *Cercospora* Leaf Spot (*Cercospora beticola* Sacc.)

*Cercospora* leaf spot is a common disease of sugar-beet which is liable to become a dominant factor in growing the crop wherever the climate is hot and humid, but which usually does little damage in countries with more clement weather, as in England. It is thus one of the serious obstacles to sugar-beet growing in central and southern Europe and the middle-west of the U.S.A.

The symptoms, when present, are easily seen on the older leaves, small roundish spots, grey in the centre and surrounded by a reddish-brown ring. Examination under a hand lens of the necrotic centre of the spot will show small black dots which are the fruiting bodies. The fungus can multiply rapidly during warm wet weather and the spots become so numerous that they coalesce and eventually kill the leaf. A badly diseased plant is so checked that both the root weight and the sucrose content are severely reduced.

The life cycle of the *Cercospora* leaf spot pathogen is straightforward. Infected seed is the main source of inoculum in the spring, but the fungus can also survive on diseased foliage in the soil, one of the reasons for the inadvisability of planting sugar-beet after sugar-beet. Lesions on the seed coat produce airborne spores which can infect the cotyledons of the seedlings and thus provide the nucleus from which the disease can build up later on if conditions favour it.

### METHODS OF CONTROL

Dry seed dressings containing organomercurial compounds have not proved very effective in reducing the amount of primary infection, but steeps with the same active ingredient are more efficient. Field spraying or dusting with copper fungicides have also been used to control the disease and have given useful increases in yield when the leaf spot outbreak has been severe. The economic justification for spraying has, however, disappeared in the U.S.A. with the introduction of resistant varieties. Although these varieties are not entirely immune in bad leaf spot years, the number of lesions is sufficiently small to allow good crops to be harvested.

## COTTON

Cotton, in spite of competition from synthetic fibres, holds a basic place in the world's textile industry. Its magnitude as an agricultural crop is clearly demonstrated by the large area of 84 million acres (F.A.O., 1964) which is required for its cultivation. It is grown in many countries, in some such as Egypt it is the dominant crop and provides the country with its greatest source of revenue.

Cotton requires a warm climate in which to grow, the minimum average summer temperature in the American cotton belt is 77°F. Cotton cannot tolerate frost and requires a minimum of 200 frost-free days. Its culture is therefore concentrated in the sub-tropical and tropical areas of the world such as the southern regions of the U.S.A., India, China, Brazil, southern Russia, and many parts of Africa.

Until the introduction of mechanical harvesting of cotton in the U.S.A. in the 1940s, cotton could only be grown in areas where there was abundant labour for picking. For this reason it tended to be a peasant crop harvested by family labour. Except in the U.S.A., this is still the pattern.

Cotton, moreover, is a plant which attracts large numbers of insect pests. While there are few diseases of importance, pests constitute the greater problem on cotton; some pests have in fact threatened the whole cotton industry. This is true for the Cotton Boll Weevil in the U.S.A. and the leafworm in Egypt. Pests are frequently the limiting factor in cotton production.

The pattern of the pest species is also interesting, each region possesses its own dominant pest as shown in Table 3.1.

The Pink Bollworm is generally distributed in all cotton-growing countries but is the dominant pest only in some. Many pests such as *Heliothis, Prodenia, Earias, Bemisia, Lygus,* and red spider occur on many other plants and are not specific to cotton as is *Anthonomus* and the Pink Bollworm.

Pests of cotton in Africa are well documented by Pearson (1958), and in India by the Indian Central Cotton Committee (1960). There are many books on cotton in the U.S.A. The cotton story in Egypt is given by Brown (1953). Much information on pests of cotton, mainly in Africa, are to be found in the Empire Cotton Growing Review.

Although pests are the predominant problem on cotton there are several cotton diseases of considerable economic importance, particularly bacterial blight, sore-shin and *Fusarium* wilt.

In the U.S.A., the Cotton Disease Council makes an annual estimate of the losses caused by different diseases. This is valuable to

**Table 3.1.** DISTRIBUTION OF THE PRINCIPAL PESTS OF COTTON IN THE WORLD

| *Country* | *Pest* |
|---|---|
| India | Earias, Heliothis, Empoasca |
| U.S.A. | Anthonomus, Heliothis, Alabama, Red Spider |
| Brazil | Alabama, Aphids |
| Turkey | Empoasca, Earias, Prodenia |
| Spain | Heliothis, Earias, Red Spider |
| Uganda | Lygus |
| Sudan | Empoasca, Bemisia |
| Egypt | Prodenia, Earias, Platyhedra |
| East Africa | Dysdercus |

research workers as pin-pointing the most profitable field for further investigation and to cotton-growers as an indication of the most useful disease precautions. For the five years 1957–61 the total loss caused by pathogenic fungi and bacteria was estimated at 14·49%, representing 575,000 tons of cotton. The three diseases at the top of the list were seedling diseases responsible for 2·7% loss of the total crop, *Verticillium* wilt with 2·2% and boll rots with 2·1% (Cotton Disease Council, 1962).

Information on cotton diseases will be found in Brown and Ware's (1958) comprehensive survey of the industry and also in books dealing with cotton in particular countries such as the Monograph on Cotton in India (Ind. Cent. Cott. Comm. 1960) and Egyptian Cotton (Brown, 1953).

REFERENCES

BROWN, C. H., *Egyptian Cotton,* Leonard Hill Ltd., London (1953)

BROWN, H. B. and WARE, J. O., *Cotton* (3rd Edn.), McGraw-Hill Book Co. Inc., New York (1958)

Cotton Disease Council, U.S.A., *Plant Disease Reptr.*, **46,** 8, 609 (1962)

*F.A.O. Production Year Book 1963–64,* **18,** F.A.O., Rome

KHAN, Q. and RAO, V. P., *Cotton in India,* Indian Central Cotton Committee, Bombay (1960)

PEARSON, E. O., *The Insect Pests of Cotton in Tropical Africa,* Comm. Inst. of Ent., London (1958)

## COLEOPTERA

### *Anthonomus grandis* Boh. *(Curculionidae)*

The Cotton Boll Weevil is a pest in Mexico and Central America. It is said to have originated in Mexico and first entered the U.S.A. in 1892 in the State of Texas. It has now spread to the central cotton-growing areas of the U.S.A. except the extreme northern border. Probably no insect, except perhaps Codling Moth, has made such an impact on the agricultural world and no insect has been so well documented.

In the natural state no doubt, the weevils lived on wild cotton plants but now there appears to be no alternative host plant.

The adult weevils overwinter in the cotton fields and emerge in the early summer. The adults begin to feed on the terminal growth. They are true weevils with a long, slender, curved rostrum. They are capable of flight under suitable conditions of temperature. Their real interest lies in the flowerbuds (squares) and bolls (seed capsules) which they attack and in which the females deposit eggs, usually one egg per flower or boll. Each flower may be punctured several times as the weevil seeks pollen on which it feeds. Each female can lay up to 300 eggs. The larva, which lives inside the flower or boll is small, curved, legless and white. It feeds on the floral parts or developing fibre. The larva pupates within the boll. Many generations of the weevil can be completed in a season.

The feeding of the adult weevils causes the bracts of the flowers to open (flare) and often dry up or drop off. The weevil-feeding prevents the flowers from setting and, in the boll, reduces the production of fibre. Losses of up to 1,000 lb per acre of seed-cotton are possible with an average loss of 300 lb.

#### METHODS OF CONTROL

Cultural methods have been of little value against the Cotton Boll Weevil and only direct action with insecticides has made it possible to minimise the depredations of this insect. Formerly, the widely used insecticide was calcium arsenate powder which the weevil picked up as it tested the surface of the plants with its rostrum. The powder was eventually taken into the stomach of the insect. It was necessary to apply calcium arsenate dust (40%) every 4–5 days using about 10 lb per acre per application. Some risk attached to this use of the compound which could cause arsenic burn.

Modern insecticides have now entirely superceded calcium arsenate. First came the era of BHC which was used in combination with DDT (for *Heliothis*) as a 20% dust. This phase endured from 1947–54. The next phase was toxaphene and finally methyl parathion.

The control of *Anthonomus* is bound up with the control of other insects on cotton, especially *Heliothis* and the subject is dealt with under 'The Development of Cotton Insecticides', which occurs later in the chapter.

## LEPIDOPTERA

### BOLLWORMS

#### *Heliothis spp. (Noctuidae)*

The Cotton Bollworm of U.S.A. or the American Bollworm as it is called outside the Western Hemisphere is *Heliothis zea* Boddie. This is undoubtedly a different insect from *H. armigera* Hb. of other countries (Fig. 3.9).

*Fig. 3.9.* Heliothis armigera *(adult)*

This latter species attacks cotton in southern Europe, the Middle East, India and the Far East, the whole of Africa and Australia.

*Heliothis* is found in all the principal cotton-growing countries of the world but it is not always the dominant pest. In the U.S.A., *Anthonomus* takes precedence and *Heliothis* is probably of greater importance than the leafworm, *Alabama*. In the Middle East, *Earias* is of greater importance than *Heliothis* although both these species are present, except in Egypt where *Heliothis* is absent. *Heliothis* occurs in India and Africa where it is known as the America Bollworm but in these countries *Diparopsis, Empoasca, Earias* and *Dysdercus* are more important. In Egypt, *Prodenia* is of greater importance as it is also in Turkey.

The importance of *Heliothis* on cotton in different countries is bound up with the type of cropping practised especially the proximity of maize and other preferred crops and the interchange of insects between them. In some countries, *Heliothis* attacks occur at the beginning of the cotton crop, in others, it is only later generations which attack cotton. Attacks are also associated with the intervention of a diapause in the pupal stage. This has the effect of prolonging this stage, producing a peak of emergence from pupae of different ages.

*Heliothis* is a migrant moth, meaning that the adults are capable of flying or travelling over considerable distances themselves. The life-cycle of *Heliothis* is much the same in all parts of the world including *H. armigera* and *H. zea* in U.S.A. These Noctuid moths are capable of laying vast numbers of eggs, up to and over 1,000. The females deposit the eggs, which are flattened and yellow, on the leaves and squares, egg-laying beginning at flower-bud formation. The caterpillars feed on the shoots, leaves and buds but only the older larvae attack the bolls. The caterpillars attack several bolls, and do not enter entirely, within as do the larvae of *Earias,* but remain partly outside. The fully grown larva is green and large. Pupation occurs in the soil. There are several generations a year.

*Heliothis* feeds on many different host plants, in fact maize is probably the most preferred of the crop plants. It can also survive on wild plants. The damage caused to cotton is associated with the destruction of the flower buds, flowers and frequently the bolls. Eating into the boll is often followed by bacteria or fungi which spoil the fibre.

### METHOD OF CONTROL

Parasitism of *Heliothis* has never been high enough to prevent damage. Attempts to supplement the number of parasites by artificial breeding have not been successful. Trap cropping with maize in cotton has been practised with some success and is still a recognised method of minimising damage from *Heliothis*. Such a practice can however, often serve to intensify the attack if not carefully watched.

Insecticides are now in general use against *Heliothis* and at present the best insecticide is DDT. Several applications as a dust or spray are necessary. Other insecticides are also effective notably endrin, carbaryl (Sevin) and, more recently, azinphosethyl. As explained under *Anthonomus,* cotton insecticides are employed against the insect complex and seldom against individual pests.

### *Earias insulana* Boisd. *(Noctuidae)*

This is the Spiny Bollworm of the Middle East (Fig. 3.10). It is a major pest in all the countries of this region, including Turkey. *Earias fabae* Stoll. is widely distributed in India, but *E. insulana* is the principal pest species, especially in the drier cotton regions of the Punjab. *E. fabae* is also found in Africa but is not considered important in the Sudan, where it is occasionally seen. *Earias* is reported from the Far East but this is not a cotton-growing region and from Australia. *Earias* will feed on many different plants but always has the habit of boring usually into the terminal growth. It is however, seldom a pest of other crops. Other hosts are *Malvaceae*, especially *Hibiscus* and *Abultilon*.

The moth is small for a Noctuid and distinguished by its apple-green forewings. Eggs are flattened and bluish-green. The larva is predominantly brown with yellow markings. The segments of the body bear four long noticeable papillae giving the insect its name (Fig. 3.11). Pupation occurs on the soil surface and in trash.

The eggs are laid singly on the plants. The larva usually bores firstly into the terminal growth which withers as a result, causing the plant to side-shoot. Flower buds are attacked on appearance and finally the bolls, which may drop off after attack, especially if they are young. Bigger bolls are often invaded by several larvae which themselves may wander from one boll to another. The fibre in the boll is thereby ruined. Several generations occur in the course of a year but *Earias* breeds continually, there being no diapause. The duration of the cycle is reduced by lower temperatures. On cotton, breeding often leads to 5 or 6 generations each one more numerous than the preceding, except in countries where cotton is taken in the cooler season, e.g. Uganda and Sudan. In countries where conditions of climate, alternative food crops and a favourable cotton season occur *Earias* becomes a pest. In Iraq over 50% of the bolls can be attacked.

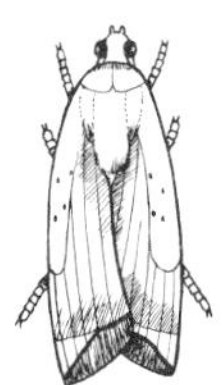

*Fig. 3.10.* Earias insulana *(adult)*

*Fig. 3.11.* Earias insulana *(caterpillar)*

### METHODS OF CONTROL

Cotton farmers have been forced to take some precautionary measures where *Earias* is a serious pest and the destruction of free-growing cotton is of the greatest importance. Coupled with this precaution, the growing of early maturing varieties of cotton is also a valuable means of reducing the numbers of *Earias*.

Formerly, control of the *Earias* caterpillar was attempted with calcium arsenate, a stomach poison as for *Anthonomus*. Cryolite, a contact and stomach insecticide was also used in the Middle East. This is a naturally occurring sodium fluoaluminate and is used as a dust. Modern insecticides have also been used as dusts against *Earias* especially DDT and gamma BHC. No insecticide gave a satisfactory control of heavy attacks until the introduction of endrin, which, however, had to be used as a low volume spray. Early trials in Iraq showed that this insecticide was superior to others (Walker 1954).

Recent trials with carbaryl (Sevin) and azinphosethyl have shown these insecticides also to be effective against *Earias* (Ahmed 1961). Several applications are necessary to protect plants against *Earias*, starting at flowering and continuing until the early bolls are formed. Up to 10 applications may be necessary.

### *Platyhedra gossypiella* Saund. *(Tineidae)*

This is the notorious Pink Bollworm which occurs in all the principal cotton-growing areas of the world, except at present Rhodesia and South Africa. The reason for its wide distribution is almost certainly due to its ability to attach itself to cotton seed and become distributed with it. Even so, its status as a pest is lower than that of many other insects but its threat is ever present. Considerable research for its control was initiated many years ago in the U.S.A. at Brownsville but no completely effective measure has been developed against it. As a rule the infestation starts slowly but builds up later in the season often to 100% (Plate 3.10).

The moth itself is undistinguished, belonging to the *Tineidae* and as such, it is small and greyish-brown, with fringed wings. (Fig. 3.12). The egg is difficult to find in the field because it is green in colour. Moths emerge in spring and the females deposit eggs on the buds and bolls, always at night. Eggs are usually hidden either singly or in groups. The larvae enter directly into the flower or boll and attacked flowers drop off.

*Plate 3.10. Bottom: normal cotton. Top: heavily attacked by pink bollworm, Egypt*

*Fig. 3.12.* Platyhedra gossypiella *(adult)*

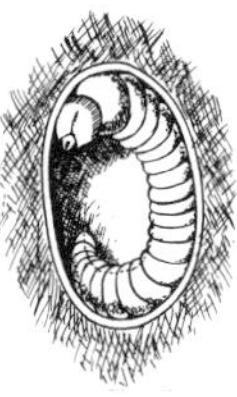

*Fig. 3.13.* Platyhedra gossypiella *(larva in cotton seed)*

Bolls may be attacked by several larvae but usually one section of the boll is sufficient for one larvae to complete its development. Pink Bollworm larvae, on entering a boll, make their way to the seeds. Early maturing larvae quit the bolls, drop to the ground and pupate. In older bolls, only the seeds are attacked, the larva making a cocoon within the attacked seed or by spinning two seeds together (Fig. 3.13). This type of larva enters a diapause evidently determined by climatic conditions and remains within the seed until it is sown the following year.

The number of generations in countries with a well-defined cold season, is about seven, but where cotton continues to grow plants become continually infested. In order to break the life-cycle cotton plants are collected from the field and must be destroyed according to the law in some countries before spring—this is a 'Close Season'.

.Losses from Pink Bollworm vary from country to country. In Egypt, before measures against were instituted, losses were estimated at 50% but nowadays losses are much less and doubtfully exceed 10%

## METHODS OF CONTROL

*Cultural Method.* In Egypt and in India measures against the Pink Bollworm have consisted of:

1. Treatment of the seed to prevent the carry-over of larvae from one season to the next.
2. Removal of cotton stalks from the fields and their destruction by March 31st.
3. Cultivation of early maturing varieties to prevent early infestation of the bolls to avoid a build-up.

Treatment of cotton seed has been practised in many countries usually by heat, either from steam or from heating chambers. A temperature of 140°F is necessary for 5–10 minutes to kill the larvae. More recently, fumigation of batches of seed with methyl bromide serves the same purpose. Formerly, this could be accomplished with either carbon bisulphide or hydrogen cyanide.

Early maturing varieties of cotton produce and ripen bolls before the bollworm has had time to multiply. In Egypt, Menufi was the variety developed for this purpose. The older later maturing varieties would no doubt give higher yields but would be overwhelmed by the Pink Bollworm before the crop gathering could be completed.

Campaigns for cotton-stalk collection have been very successful in reducing infestation. The Pink Bollworm, unlike *Earias* appears to have very few alternative food plants. The carry-over of the generations from year to year is in no way supported by alternative hosts and the insect relies entirely on cotton which is frequently unavailable to the first emerging adults.

*Chemical Method.* Chemical control of the Pink Bollworm has met with limited success. Probably the insecticide DDT has given the most consistant results but insecticides are seldom employed solely against Pink Bollworm. There is evidence that some of the newer insecticides such as carbaryl, azinphosethyl or fenthion (Lebaycid) are better.

### *Diparopsis watersi* Roths. *(Noctuidae)*

This is the Sudan Bollworm of Africa. It occurs in countries north of the Equator except Egypt, but including West Africa and Aden. *Diparopsis castanea* Hamps. the Red Bollworm occurs south of the Equator in South Africa, the Rhodesias and in Nyasaland.

*Plate 3.11. Cotton boll showing the Sudan bollworm (Agricultural Research Institute Samaru, Northern Nigeria)*

*Diparopsis* adults are light brown to yellow, with well-defined wing markings. The eggs are light blue, the larvae are a reddish colour. The eggs are deposited on the leaves and not on the flowers and bolls. The larvae seek out the flowers and bolls and enter them. Unlike *Heliothis,* the larva, once it has entered the boll, disappears completely and rarely emerges to enter another (Plate 3.11). Pupation occurs in the soil. There are several generations each year.

*Diparopsis* in Africa tends to replace *Earias* and *Heliothis* of other cotton-growing countries. It is particularly important in Nyasaland where a good deal of work has been carried out upon its life-cycle and behaviour. It is an important pest where cotton is rain fed or irrigated, emergence is initiated by water.

METHOD OF CONTROL

Insecticides have been employed against *Diparopsis* in those countries where it occurs as a pest. DDT used alone or in combination with gamma BHC has proved effective when applied as a routine programme beginning at first flowering. DDT is used at 1·5 lb per acre either as a spray or dust, sprays generally have given superior results. Endrin at 0·5 lb per acre as a spray has also been effective.

## LEAFWORMS

### *Prodenia litura* F. *(Noctuidae)*

This is the Egyptian Leafworm and the dominant pest of cotton in Egypt. It also occurs in other countries of the Middle East notably Israel, Iraq and Turkey and in many other countries including India and the Far East, Australia, all Africa but not in the Western Hemisphere. Its dominance as a pest seems to be confined to the Eastern Mediterranean. *Prodenia* is omnivorous, feeding on many different plants including clover (Berseem), tobacco, and some fruit trees.

The moth is brownish-grey (Fig. 3.14). The eggs are creamy. The caterpillar is variable in colour but with dark markings along each side of the dorsal surface. The earlier larval stages are green but this colour changes and becomes darker, almost brown to black at later instars. The pupae occur in the soil.

*Prodenia* larvae are leaf-feeders. The devastating leaf damage which can be caused by *Prodenia* is associated with very large numbers of over 1,000 eggs laid by each female moth in clusters of 50–100. The larvae tend to remain together on the same leaf at first but after a few days they leave the plant in the day and lie concealed in the soil. The larvae ascend the plants after sunset, and scatter through the crop. The larval development is completed in two weeks. In Egypt, about seven generations occur in a year but not all on cotton.

*Fig. 3.14.* Prodenia litura *(adult)*

The early instars of *Prodenia* can grow without notice but later instars can quickly strip the leaves from the plants. Bishara (1934), the Egyptian entomologist, states that attacks always occur just after irrigation; the peak population in Egypt occurring in June. Previously, the moth has survived on berseem and transferred to cotton when the berseem dried out.

METHODS OF CONTROL

In Egypt, the standard method of reducing the attack on cotton by *Prodenia* was by hand-collection of the egg masses. This was carried out by groups of boys and girls. In years when the attack has been light, this method has been successful in keeping the insect in control but in other years, the insects abundance usually outstrips the ability of the pickers to keep it in check. It is then necessary to resort to insecticides. 1949, 1950 and 1951 were years of exceptional abundance of *Prodenia* but 1952 and 1953 were years of slight attack.

*Chemical Control.* In Egypt, this began in 1950 when the so-called Cotton Dust was introduced. This consisted of 3% gamma BHC, 10% DDT and 40% sulphur plus filler. The object of the sulphur was to suppress aphids, a recommendation derived from the days when calcium arsenate was used against *Prodenia* and sulphur was included. Formulations of Cotton Dust were also available without sulphur styled 3:10:0 as distinct from 3:10:40 with sulphur. Sulphur also proved useful in keeping down red spider.

Experiments by the entomologists of the Royal Agricultural Society and by the

Ministry of Agriculture from 1946 onwards with insecticides showed that 10% DDT did in fact give a good kill of *Prodenia* caterpillars, except where they were half-grown, but the insecticide tended to depress the crop. On the other hand, BHC appeared to stimulate the cotton as well as suppressing aphids. Various combinations were tried, 5% DDT was too little as was 1% gamma BHC and so the combination of 3% gamma BHC plus 10% DDT was found to be the best. Sprays were not satisfactory at that time, and so Cotton Dust, applied several times at about 8–12 Kg per feddan (acre) depending on the size of the cotton, became established. Very large quantities were used in 1951.

The experience of the 1951 season showed that there was a build-up of red spider on cotton, especially in the Northern Delta. Likewise the bollworm, *Earias insulana* increased in numbers. Experiments with other insecticides led to the development of toxaphene and toxaphene/sulphur dusts. Toxaphene itself is toxic to red spider and at 20% is effective against *Prodenia*. Sprays of toxaphene emulsion were also introduced.

The next development in Egypt in 1952 and 1953 was the use of low volume sprays as formulations of DDT and gamma BHC were now available in emulsion form. Application was made with knapsack sprayers using 60–90 litres wash per acre.

Toxaphene has continued to be used in Egypt until recently. Endrin and more lately carbaryl (Sevin) have also been used on a big scale although there is still a considerable usage of 9% gamma BHC and 30% DDT emulsion (Hassan 1960).

The *Prodenia* problem is still not completely solved, owing to the abundance of moths and the wide variety of alternate foods. No insecticide can eradicate the insect completely as the larger caterpillars frequently escape destruction.

### *Alabama argillacea* Hubn. *(Noctuidae)*

This is the leafworm of U.S.A., Central and South American corresponding to *Prodenia* in the Old World. It is an important pest in the cotton-growing regions of the Western Hemisphere.

The adults are dull coloured, greenish. Eggs are usually deposited singly. The caterpillars feed on all parts of the cotton plants and are sometimes to be classed as armyworms. Pupation occurs on the plant. There may be several generations in a year.

*Alabama* is essentially a cotton insect, the larvae feed exclusively on cotton. The adults possess a barbed proboscis and attack fruit especially citrus and peaches. The caterpillar is basically green with longitudinal stripes of black and white.

### METHODS OF CONTROL

*Alabama* is not a difficult insect to control as it is susceptible to modern insecticides. Measures carried out against *Anthonomus* and *Heliothis* are usually sufficient. Probably the most effective insecticides are methyl parathion and endrin, the former being widely used in the U.S.A.

## HEMIPTERA

### *Empoasca lybica* de Berg. (Jassidae)

This is the Cotton Jassid of the Sudan. According to Pearson (1958), *Empoasca facialis* Jacobi also occurs but only in regions of equatorial South and West Africa. Other species of *Empoasca* occur notably E. *devastans* Dist. of India also on cotton. *Empoasca* on cotton occurs throughout the Near East and is found in Turkey, Greece and the cotton-growing countries of eastern Europe. Species also occur in South America.

The adults are small, green, wedge-shaped insects which scatter quickly when disturbed. Eggs are deposited in the leaf veins or mid-rib on the under surface where the nymphs usually remain, coming to the upper surface at night. Several generations occur in the course of a year. The population of Jassids can increase rapidly with detrimental effects on the foliage on which they feed exclusively.

The jassid population declines rapidly in the absence of cotton but the insect survives on alternative plants and some weeds. Jassids are pests in regions of low rainfall where there is hot dry weather for most of the cotton season.

### METHODS OF CONTROL

It was observed about 1920 in South Africa, that cotton possessing hairs resisted Jassids. This property of the cotton plant was successfully utilized in Africa in regions subject to attack by Jassids. There was some doubt as to the mechanism of resistance but it was thought that the hairs prevented egg-laying by adults. Unfortunately hairy cotton did not always possess other desirable characteristics of quality and yield. Sometimes hairy types were more susceptible to bollworm injury.

Jassids are susceptible to modern insecticides especially to DDT. Spraying with DDT against *Empoasca* has been practised in the Sudan since 1945, usually one application is all that is necessary using 1 lb per acre. Originally, application was made by ground machines but subsequently aerial application at 2 gal per acre became more popular. Various experiments showed that 1 lb of DDT per feddan (acre) was the optimum although $\frac{3}{4}$ lb could give satisfactory results. The amount of wash could be reduced to the lowest possible limit of 3 pt per acre with satisfactory results.

In other countries notably Turkey and India, cotton dusts based on DDT and gamma BHC are usually preferred owing to water shortage. Jassid control is usually part of a cotton insect complex and in the Sudan treatment with DDT usually resulted in an increase in the population of Whitefly *(Bemisia tabaci)*.

### *Bemisia tabaci* Genn. *(Aleyrodidae)*

This is the Cotton Whitefly which is principally a pest of cotton in the Sudan. It occurs in other parts of Africa and in India but is of limited importance elsewhere. It also occurs on tobacco.

The name of Whitefly is taken from the characteristic appearance of the small moth-like adults. The nymphs are generally immobile except in the first instars and resemble scale insects. The eggs are stalked and attached to the undersides of the leaves. Several generations occur in a season.

Injury to cotton leaves is caused by constant feeding of the nymphs which build up during the season, exceeding a hundred per square inch. In the absence of cotton, the Whiteflies survive on alternate plants notably vegetables and on many weeds. The adult is also capable of transmitting leaf-curl virus, but most varieties cultivated are resistant to this disease. Whitefly does not seem to have appeared in Egypt.

### METHOD OF CONTROL

As already mentioned Whitefly build up followed DDT spraying against Jassids in the Sudan. Although DDT kills the adult Whitefly and the nymph, Jassids and Whitefly undoubtedly compete for leaf area so that removal of the jassid competition enables the Whitefly to increase in numbers. Other insecticides are effective against Whitefly notably parathion and endrin. Both have been used to a limited extent in the Sudan.

### *Psallus seriatus* Reut. *(Miridae)*

The Cotton Flea Hopper appears to be the most likely insect in U.S.A. corresponding to the Hemipterous pests of African cotton. *Psallus,* however, feeds on other parts of the cotton plant than the leaves and perhaps should be more likened to the *Miridae* below.

### *Lygus vosseleri* Popp. *(Miridae)*

This is an African insect and of particular importance in Uganda where it has assumed the status of a pest over the last 25 years. *Lygus* is a relatively small insect, dull coloured and elliptical in shape typical of this family.

*Lygus* possesses, common in this type of insect, toxic saliva which kills cells when injected into them. *Lygus* feeds on vegetative buds, flower buds and young bolls. Flower buds, if attacked, tend to drop off but leaf buds do not, the leaf itself showing a tattered appearance when it unfolds due to the killing of cells. As the terminal buds drop off, other growths take their place tending to give the plant an appearance of a forest of shoots. *Lygus* continues to attack cotton while it continues to produce new growth but quits the plant when it matures and new growth ceases to be produced.

Eggs are inserted into the tissue of the plant. Nymphs are extremely active and go through five instars. *Lygus* occurs principally in Uganda but is found in other regions of similar climate, i.e. hot and moist. It moves on to cotton from alternate food plants of which there are many and on which it maintains itself in the absence of cotton. Probably the most important alternative food plants are cereals and grasses.

### METHOD OF CONTROL

Many trials have shown that DDT is an effective insecticide against *Lygus* when used at 1 lb per acre either as a dust or spray. The use of DDT as a 25% miscible liquid at 3 pt per acre four times at weekly intervals is now an established practise. Early trials were carried out to prove the value of spraying and bringing about an increase in crop. It was found that the benefit from spraying was on the late-sown crop. Early-sown cotton sprayed with DDT matured early but unprotected cotton continued to grow and eventually produced a similar yield. Late-sown cotton if unsprayed failed to produce bolls which matured (MacKinley and Geering, 1957).

In some regions of Uganda, *Lygus* is attacked by a parasite of the *Braconidae* which, at times, totally overtakes and wipes out the *Lygus* population.

### *Dysdercus spp. (Pyrrhocoridae)*

These are the Cotton Stainers of Africa (Fig. 3.15). Several species occur as pests of cotton of which according to Pearson (1958) three are common—D. *fasciatus* Sign., D. *nigrofasciatus* Stal. and D. *superstitiosus* F. Some species occur as pests of cotton in India, notably D. *cingulatus* Fabr. The name Cotton Stainer arises from the habit of the insect of feeding on the boll and injecting saliva which causes a discoloration of the lint. In India, *Dysdercus* is called the Red Cotton Bug due to the dominant colour red

*Fig. 3.15.* Dysdercus fasciatus *(adult)*

on the forewings (hemi-elytra) of the species there. Species of *Dysdercus* also occur in South America on cotton.

Eggs are deposited in batches in the soil or on any debris. The second instar nymphs disperse to seek out food plants. The nymphs tend to retain their habit of clustering together during feeding. On cotton, the preferred food is the ripening boll as the bugs attempt to reach the seeds which are the main food of these insects, in fact seeds of many plants especially cotton and related *Malvaceae.* Cotton is invaded by adult *Dysdercus* which fly into the crop but breeding within the crop can only occur if open bolls are present as early instars can only reach the seeds in open bolls. The occurrence of *Dysdercus* on cotton is influenced by the abundance of alternate hosts and the population of *Dysdercus* achieved upon it.

Damage to the cotton crop is largely caused to the bolls and seeds, but the piercing of the bolls by the adult bugs causes a discoloration of the lint which is stained a rusty red. The staining organism is fungoid and is injected with the saliva of the bug. Seeds pierced by the bugs develop abnormally and the germ is frequently killed and the lint spoiled.

METHODS OF CONTROL

Before the advent of modern insecticides, methods of control practised against *Dysdercus* consisted of collection of the bugs by hand and trapping by means of heaps of seeds. A combination of hand-picking the bugs daily and trapping was thought to be worth while but direct evidence of this appears to be lacking.

While the insecticides gamma BHC and DDT are both highly toxic to *Dysdercus* they are seldom employed solely against these insects. *Dysdercus* control is usually taken in with action against *Heliothis* and other bollworms.

*Nezara viridula* L. *(Pentatomidae)*

This is an insect widely distributed through the world occurring in Africa, southern Europe, India, U.S.A., Central and South America and Australasia. It is a large green shield bug although the immature stages are variously coloured, black, white and red.

Eggs are laid in large batches of 40–100 eggs stuck together. The adults prefer the green bolls of cotton. Injury is similar to that caused by *Dysdercus* and *Nezara* can also introduce fungus disease into the boll.

*Oxycarenus spp. (Lygaeidae)*

These are small bugs very active on the plants (Fig. 3.16). They occur as different species in all regions of Africa. *Oxycarenus laetus* Kirby occurs in India where it is known as the Dusky Cotton Bug. These bugs are all seed-feeders and occur on cotton as the bolls open. The bugs are frequently included in the cotton when it is picked.

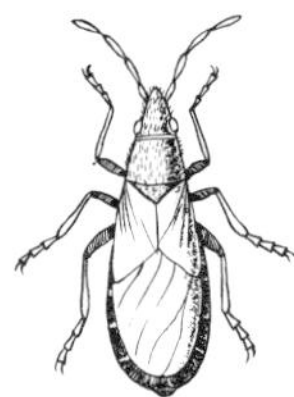

*Fig. 3.16.* Oxycarenus laetus *(adult)*

*Campylomma spp. (Miridae)*

*C. nicolase* Piet. and Reut. occurs in the Sudan and Egypt and a similar species occurs in Nigeria. *Campylomma* is a small insect and is similar to *Lygus* in its habits and effect on cotton. The principal damage is a tattering of foliage.

*Creontiades pallidus* Ramb. *(Miridae)*

This is another small bug found principally in Egypt and the Sudan. It causes bud shedding but it is not regarded as an important pest.

*Aphis gossypii* Glover *(Aphididae)*

The Cotton Aphid is widely distributed in the cotton-growing countries of the world being found in Central and South America, U.S.A., Africa, the Near and Middle East, India and the Far East. It also occurs in Europe where it is more important as a pest of *Cucurbitacaea.*

On cotton, this green aphid is found at all stages of growth. It is mainly important as a pest on seedling cotton but sometimes it builds up later on bigger plants. The damage it causes consists of loss of cell sap, twisting and puckering of growing foliage and the deposit of a sticky sugary substance on the foliage.

Aphids have developed as pests, following the use of insecticides on cotton. In U.S.A., the use of calcium arsenate against the Boll Weevil and in Egypt against *Prodenia* led often to outbreaks of aphids. In Egypt, sulphur was included with calcium arsenate to suppress aphids. Insecticides in common use against aphids are BHC (in Cotton Dust), parathion (mainly in the Americas) and certain systemic insecticides notably methyl-demeton.

## THYSANOPTERA

### Thrips *(Thysanoptera)*

Certain species of thrips attack cotton especially in the early stages of growth. These species are:

*Scirtothrips dorsalis* Hood in India.

*Thrips tabaci* Lind. in Africa and the U.S.A.

*Caliothrips* spp. in the U.S.A.

More damage by thrips to cotton is caused in dry regions. Thrips, in all stages of development, feed on the undersides of leaves. Normally, species of thrips breed on weeds and other crop plants and transfer to cotton when the other plants dry up.

## ACARINA

### *Tetranychus telarius* L.

This is the Red Spider Mite. It occurs on cotton as well as many other plants, including deciduous fruit trees. Many species of *Tetranychus* are said to be pests of cotton but probably the variants of *T. telarius* are the most important. This species occur all over the world, but appears to be of the greatest importance as a pest of cotton in the U.S.A. probably because of the great usage of insecticides there. Occasionally red spider out-breaks occur in Egypt following heavy usage of sprays and dusts against *Prodenia*.

Red spider causes a drying-up of the foliage in cotton. The leaves turn red at first, finally brown and are then shed. Heavy infestations show the foliage of the plant to be covered with innumerable mites in all stages of development.

#### METHOD OF CONTROL

In the U.S.A., routine red spider control is undertaken especially in Texas. Systemic insecticides are used, mostly demeton often applied as a spray by air. In Egypt, sulphur is included in Cotton Dust to prevent the rise of red spider populations but action by special compounds is seldom taken. For several years Toxaphene was preferred to DDT against *Prodenia* solely because it possessed some action against red spider.

## THE DEVELOPMENT OF INSECTICIDES ON COTTON

Cotton is a crop which has created a greater demand for modern insecticides than any other. One of the reasons for this is the fact that cotton is a cash crop for which the grower is almost certain to obtain a monetary return commensurate with the yield and quality of the crop he grows. Secondly, insect pests are of the greatest importance on cotton and often the limiting factor in cotton production.

In the U.S.A., the largest cotton-growing country in the world, insecticides are widely used and each cotton-growing state publishes its own recommendations every year. Any insecticide is recommended if it is of any use on cotton. In other countries, such as Egypt and Turkey large quantities of insecticides are also used although application is by hand.

Early insecticides, such as calcium arsenate dust, were quickly replaced post-war by modern synthetic chemicals especially DDT and BHC. Insecticide combinations became customary about 1948 (Ewing *et al.,* 1947) when mixed BHC/DDT dust was used. The object of the mixture, first used in the U.S.A., was to control the insect complex with one treatment. This mixture was employed against the Boll Weevil and Bollworm; BHC being effective against the weevil and DDT against the bollworm. Other insects were also susceptible to the mixture such as *Empoasca, Dysdercus,* leafworms and thrips (McKinley, 1956). In Egypt, Cotton Dust continued to be used against *Prodenia litura* until recent times (Hassan *et al.,* 1960). Some formulations included sulphur to prevent the increase of red spider. Cotton Dust is widely used in many cotton growing countries and is effective against all the common cotton insects except the Spiny

Bollworm and the Pink Bollworm. Against these insects new insecticides were introduced notably endrin against the Spiny Bollworm but no effective insecticide has so far been found against the Pink Bollworm.

Other developments were the introduction of liquid insecticide formulations instead of dusts. This occurred early in the U.S.A. and later in Egypt when the liquid version of the cotton dust mixture was introduced about 1951. Application was made at about 10 gal per acre. This is a low volume application; high volume of 100 gal per acre would have been quite impractical.

In the Sudan, straight DDT has been widely used since 1945 principally against the Cotton Jassid. After early application with ground-spraying equipment, aerial application over the cotton area of the northern Gezira became standard practice from 1954 onwards; Maxwell-Darling (see under Pearson, 1958) comments that records in the Sudan over 30 years show the average yield to have been 4·1 kantars up to 1948 and thereafter up to 1955 4·5 kantars—an increase due partly to nitrogenous manuring and partly to DDT spraying against Jassids. The general opinion given is that response to spraying increased the crop by 1 kantar (316 lb) but DDT spraying increased white-fly as already stated and, in the southern Gezira, Joyce (1955) stated that this nullified the response to spraying against Jassid.

Other insecticides have also been developed on cotton, notably toxaphene which was used for many years in Egypt. Methyl parathion found wide use in the U.S.A., Central and South America because it was effective against the Boll Weevil, various leaf-bugs, including aphids, as well as some leafworms. Methyl parathion was of little use against the bollworms. Ethyl parathion was evidently insufficiently active against Boll Weevil and never became a cotton insecticide.

At the moment DDT is still widely used on cotton but may give way to carbaryl and azinphos-ethyl (Gusathion). Carbaryl is probably the most effective insecticide yet tried against the Pink Bollworm. Systemic insecticides are in use against red spiders.

REFERENCES

AHMED, D. and NAOUM, A. N. W., *Hoefchen Briefe*, **2,** 94 (1961)
BISHARA, I., *Bull. Soc. Entomol. Egypt.*, **18,** 223 (1934)
EWING, K. P., PARENCIA, C. R. and IVY, E. E., *J. Econ. Entomol.*, **40,** 374 (1947)
HASSAN, A. A., SOLIMAN, A. A. and HOSNY, M. M., *Bull. Soc. Entomol. Egypt.*, **44,** 393 (1960)
JOYCE, R. V., *F.A.O. Bull.*, **3,** 86 (1955)
MACKINLEY, K. S., *Empire Cotton Growing Rev.*, **33,** 282 (1956)
MACKINLEY, K. S. and GEERING, Q. A., *Bull. Entomol. Res.*, **48,** 383 (1957)
WALKER, R. L. and HAIDARI, H. S., *J. Econ. Entomol.*, **47,** 367 (1954)

## Bacterial Blight (*Xanthomonas malvacearum* [E. F. Smith] Dowson)

Bacterial blight of cotton has received a number of names which emphasise the main symptoms in the part concerned. Hence it has been named angular leaf spot from the symptoms shown on the leaves, blackarm disease when the branches are attacked, and gummosis from the gum exuded by infected bolls. There are various biologic races of the bacteria, a factor which has to be taken into account by the cotton plant breeder.

Infected plants produce bacterial slime which is distributed by wind and rain. The bacteria can infect all the above-ground parts of the plant (Plate 3.12), giving rise to lesions on the leaves, petioles, stems and bolls. Systemic infection from the leaves down the petiole and into the stem can occur, but it is the exception rather than the rule. Seed contamination is the main source of infection for the succeeding crop, but some bacteria may survive in foliage débris left behind after the crop has been harvested.

Bacterial blight occurs in most of the cotton-growing countries of the world. It usually does little damage to those crops which are grown under irrigation, but it is liable to be serious on crops grown under natural rainfall. Severe losses from this disease have been recorded in the U.S.A., and it is of major importance in Uganda and the Sudan. Although present in Egypt, it does not do much damage as the very low rainfall prevents its spread. In India, the outbreaks

*Plate 3.12. Bacterial blight of cotton. Infection has spread from the coyledons into the stem and upper leaves (Cotton Research Station, Namulonge, Uganda)*

are sporadic, probably due to the natural resistance of the indigenous cottons.

METHODS OF CONTROL

Much research has been done on controlling bacterial blight. In many areas natural selection has operated over the centuries. In West Africa, for example, during the course of 200 years, the punctatum cottons have become nearly immune to the disease. The plant breeder has thus been able to find genes for resistance to bacterial blight, and eventually incorporate them into varieties meeting today's demands (Knight, 1957).

Plant breeding is a slow process and occasions may arise when more rapid methods have to be adopted. This was exemplified in the Gezira in the Sudan where the long-term yield of about 400 lb of lint cotton per acre was reduced in 1930–31 to 130 lb by bacterial blight attacks. It was therefore necessary to introduce seed treatment to disinfect the seed before sowing. The use of seed dressings and plant hygiene quickly arrested the disease.

In Africa, the bacteria responsible for bacterial blight mainly survive on the cotton seed. It has been shown that internal infection is relatively unimportant, so much effort has been put into seed disinfection. It has long been known that this can be done by delinting the seed with strong sulphuric acid, but this treatment is unsuited to African conditions.

As already indicated, the use of mercurial seed dressings in Africa was first put into practice in the Sudan. Over the years numerous trials have been carried out to determine both the value of the treatment and the optimum dosage rate for the seed dressing. It was shown that a mercuric chloride-iodide seed dressing at a rate of 0·057% mercury on the seed reduced the number of diseased seedlings per acre from 50,000 to 150. There was therefore excellent justification for the policy of treating all the cotton seed sown in the Sudan (Tarr, 1959).

Mercury seed dressings although so effective suffer from the disadvantage that they are highly toxic and can only be used where there is thorough control and supervision. The rather different conditions under which cotton is grown in Uganda, Kenya and Tanganyika made it advisable to use less toxic materials. The problem was solved by adopting cuprous oxide for the treatment of seed. Although many comparative trials have shown that copper fungicides are less effective than those based on mercury compounds for the control of bacterial blight, their safety has made them the choice for the treatment of bacterial blight of cotton in East Africa.

Cuprous oxide seed dressings are used at the rate of 1:150 to 1:300, the stronger rate being used where the disease is serious.

The East African cotton seed after ginning is still fuzzy so that the seeds adhere together. The seed is therefore difficult to disinfect as it is not easy to ensure that each seed is coated with the seed dressing. It has consequently been necessary to use either rotary drum mixers in which the seed and disinfectant are treated in batches, or specially designed auger-type mixers which are continuous in operation. It says much for the enthusiasm of those concerned that in Uganda alone some 21,000 tons of cotton seed are treated each year (Wickens, 1957 and 1958).

The future control methods for bacterial blight have been given much thought in East Africa and the present plan is not to depend solely on the plant breeder for raising resistant varieties but to continue using seed dressings in order to keep the bacterial population at a low level.

REFERENCES

KNIGHT, R. L., 'Blackarm Disease of Cotton and its Control'. *Plant Protect. Conf. 1956*, 53 (1957)

TARR, S. A. J., *World Crops*, II, 401 (1959)

WICKENS, G. M., *Empire Cotton Growing Rev.*, **35**, 170 (1957)

WICKENS, G. M., *Empire Cotton Growing Rev.*, **35**, 9 (1958)

## Sore-shin (*Corticium solani* (Prill. and Delacr.) Bourd. and Galz.)

There are a number of soil fungi which can attack cotton in the seedling stage. These include *Pythium spp.*, *Fusarium spp.* and *Corticium solani,* but *Corticium* is often the most serious of the complex. Sore-shin-affected seedlings are attacked in the stem, which turns dark to reddish brown. Seedlings are frequently killed.

*Corticium solani* is found throughout the U.S.A., and is particularly serious in Oklahoma (Brown *et al.* 1958).

### METHOD OF CONTROL

The disease has been difficult to control because of its natural occurrence in the soil, but recent work has shown that quintozene is helpful provided that *Corticium* is the main fungus as this fungicide has no effect on either *Pythium* or *Fusarium.* Quintozene is applied at the rate of 4–5 lb active ingredient per acre, either in the form of a dust or a spray. The cost of the treatment can be reduced by strip application (Hartzfeld, 1957).

## Stem canker (*Macrophomina phaseoli* [Maubl.] Ashby syn. *Rhizoctonia bataticola* [Taub.] Butler)

In India stem canker is one of the most serious pathogens. It is frequently associated with *C. solani*. Stem canker is responsible for a sudden wilting of the cotton plant, followed by its death. The optimum soil temperature at which the two fungi kill the cotton plants differs slightly, 35°C for *C. solani,* and 39°C for *M. phaseoli*.

### METHOD OF CONTROL

The control of stem canker is based on lowering the soil temperature, thereby making conditions less favourable for the fungus. In India this is down by sowing a cover crop of the moth bean *(Phaseolus aconitifolius)* at the same time as the cotton. The bean does not interfere with the growth of the cotton, but shades the soil and thus reduces the temperature below the optimum level for attack. The method is said to be most effective (Vasudeva, 1960).

REFERENCES

BROWN, H. B., and WARE, J. O., *Cotton* (3rd Edn.), 185, McGraw-Hill Book Co. Inc., New York (1958)

HARTZFELD, E. G., *Agr. Chem.*, **12,** 7 (1957)

VASUDEVA, R. S., 'Diseases', *Cotton in India,* Indian Central Cotton Committee (1960)

## *Fusarium* Wilt (*Fusarium oxysporum Schl. f. vasinfectum* [Atk.] Sny. and Hans.)

*Fusarium* wilt of cotton occupies an important place in the history of plant pathology as it was the first important crop disease which was defeated by the introduction of resistant varieties (Large, 1940).

The fungus, which lives in the soil, enters the cotton plant through the roots and rapidly develops inside the water-conducting vessels of the wood. This interference with the water supply causes a variety of symptoms. In some cases, the older leaves first turn yellow and then brown, and finally drop off after shrivelling, leaving the plant defoliated. In other cases, cotton plants, which are apparently healthy, suddenly wilt and finally die.

The disease was first recognised in Carolina in the U.S.A. in the 1890s, but it is now widespread in the States, particularly in the south-east. It has also been recorded from Egypt, Africa, Brazil and India.

The fungus, after it has killed the cotton plant, continues to live saprophytically within it, so that ploughing in the trash increases the amount of disease present in the soil. The fungus also produces two kinds of spores, conidia which are short-lived, and are the main means of spread during the growing season, and chlamydospores which are the resting stage and enable the fungus to survive from one season to the next.

There is good evidence that root-knot nematodes facilitate the entry of the fungus into the roots of the cotton plant, so that the incidence of the disease is likely to be higher in soils with large nematode populations than in those with but few.

It has also been found that there is an interrelation between *Fusarium* wilt and potash deficiency in some of the American cotton belt soils. The use of a balanced fertilizer containing an adequate quantity of potash has been effective in reducing the incidence of wilt symptoms.

W. A. Orton, who was appointed by the U.S. Department of Agriculture to study the disease, soon observed that there were marked differences in the susceptibility of the cotton plants to the disease, for even in badly affected fields there were usually some survivors. The first stage in the campaign against the wilt disease was to encourage the farmers to keep the seed from the more resistant plants and thus build up their own stock of a less susceptible variety. This was followed up by variety trials of American and introduced cottons. One of the Egyptian varieties, Jannovitch, was outstandingly resistant and was almost unaffected compared with the susceptible varieties where 95% of the plants were killed. The quality of the cotton of the resistant varieties was not quite up to standard, but it was not long before the cotton breeder had succeeded in marrying quality with *Fusarium* resistance, and by 1909 this threat to the American cotton growing industry had been repulsed. During the succeeding years, plant breeders have been able to incorporate wilt resistance into their new varieties, so that *Fusarium* wilt is now of minor importance.

REFERENCES

LARGE, E. C., *The Advance of the Fungi*, 311, Jonathan Cape, London (1940)

### *Other Cotton Diseases*

The importance of *Verticillium* wilt (*Verticillium albo-atrum* Reinke and Berth.) in the U.S.A. has been mentioned previously. The fungus can attack the cotton plant at any stage from seedling to maturity. The seedlings are usually killed, while the effect on older plants is that of stunting accompanied by chlorosis of the leaves. The chlorosis pattern is frequently distinctive, occurring on the leaf margins and between the veins. When the attack is severe, partial defoliation takes place, while most of the bolls drop off.

The disease is not a universal one. It is found throughout the U.S.A. cotton belt, particularly in the Mississippi Valley and also in Peru and Uganda. It does not occur in Egypt, and its presence in India is doubtful (C.M.I., 1959).

The fungus is mainly soil-borne, but it can also survive in the trash from an infected plant. It is not present in the seed. Control is difficult, but while the use of resistant varieties is the main defence, various cultural methods such as crop rotation have been advocated.

Boll rots, which are found in most of the cotton-growing countries, are due to various fungi. Insect feeding punctures may also assist fungal infection. A survey of the common cause of boll rot carried out in the U.S.A. recorded various species of the following fungi: *Alternaria, Fusarium, Aspergillus, Rhizopus* and *Penicillium.*

There is no one simple method of reducing losses due to boll rots. The main emphasis is on adequate aeration of the lower part of the plant by choosing suitable varieties, by not using excessive quantities of nitrogenous fertilizer, and avoid over-irrigating. In addition, the use of insecticides is sometimes necessary to get rid of the insects whose feeding indirectly increases boll rotting.

Virus diseases of cotton are unimportant except in the Sudan and Nigeria where certain varieties of cotton can be seriously damaged by the leaf curl disease (Tarr, 1951). Plants affected by the virus have a spindly appearance with twisting of the leaves and petioles. It is thought that the virus can reduce the crop by as much as 50%.

The Egyptian-type cottons, which are the dominant ones in the Sudan, are highly susceptible, while the American types which are grown on a smaller scale are practically unaffected.

The virus survives between crops in infected cotton and is carried by a white fly *(Bemisia tabaci)* which not only lives on cotton, but on a variety of other host plants.

Various methods of controlling leaf curl virus have been investigated, such as the application of insecticides to kill the vector, the use of resistant varieties, and the prevention of virus carry-over from one season to the next. In practice, the most effective method has been found to be the elimination of the virus reservoir by grubbing all the cotton plants after the crop has been harvested. This is no mean task when it is appreciated that there are 20,000 to 30,000 plants per acre. The introduction of the technique provided an effective answer to the menace of cotton leaf curl, and helped to safeguard the production of the Sudan's most important export.

REFERENCES

C.M.I., *Distribution Maps of Plant Diseases,* No. 365, Commonwealth Mycological Institute (1959)

TARR, S. A. J., *Leaf Curl Disease of Cotton,* Commonwealth Mycological Institute (1951)

Sugar-cane is grown in the tropics and subtropics and produces about half the world's sugar requirements, the balance being mainly derived from sugar-beet.

The indigenous sugar-canes are found in Asia and extend as far as the South Pacific. From early times the crop was carried abroad and it had reached Africa and Europe by the fifteenth century. It was introduced into the New World soon after it was discovered and since then has spread into favourable areas throughout the tropics.

Although the industry had simple beginnings, the efficient milling of the cane and the extraction of the sugar from the juice now requires large and expensive factories. Consequently, sugar-cane can only be grown on an extensive scale where mills have been built to process the cane.

The principal cane-growing areas are in Central and South America and the Caribbean Islands. Together with the U.S.A. and Mexico this region produces nearly two-thirds of the world's sugar from cane. The biggest single producing country is Cuba, with a figure of over 7 million tons. Other large producers are Brazil, Puerto Rico, Mexico, Argentina and the Dominican Republic. All the countries in this region produce some sugar from cane, and some islands such as Jamaica, Barbados and Trinidad, produce little else.

In the Old World, sugar is produced on a large scale in India, Pakistan, Taiwan, the Philippines and Java. The total Asian production, however, is little more than that of Cuba. Very little sugar-cane by comparison is grown in Africa, the biggest area being in Natal. Australia remains the only other large sugar-producing area in the world, but the islands of Fiji and Mauritius also produce a notable quantity of cane sugar. Finally, a little sugar from cane is produced in Europe in the south of Spain.

The main sugar-cane areas of the world appear to have their own groups of pests which do not occur elsewhere. For example, the two principal pests in the Western Hemisphere are the shoot borer *Diatraea* and the sugar-cane froghopper *Aeneolamia*. These do not exist in other sugar-cane-growing areas but their counterparts occur as the Pyralid shoot and top borers of India and *Pyrilla,* a Fulgorid not found elsewhere. In the Australian sugar-cane areas of Queensland, the cane beetle is the most important pest, an insect not found elsewhere.

Sugar-cane pests do not appear to have followed cane growing round the world but local pests seem to have become adapted since the introduction of the crop. There is no collected account of sugar-cane pests at present.

The history of sugar-cane varieties demonstrates the continual search for those which are resistant to disease. Earle (1946) gives an illustration of this in his description of the variety Otaheite which was accepted as the best sugar-cane for much of the nineteenth century. The first signs of trouble occurred in 1840 in Mauritius, probably due to root diseases; about 1860 it was attacked by gummosis in Brazil; in 1872 it was infected by a new disease in Porto Rico which made it unproductive. In Cuba and in the West Indies it gradually became less productive. In all the cases mentioned variety trials were carried out to find replacements which would resist the dominant disease. Thus, two factors have been at work in sugar-cane culture for many centuries, namely the survival of the fittest and the unwitting dispersal of diseases which often occurred before their importance was recognised.

The deliberate breeding of new resistant varieties was not possible until the technique of cross-pollination and the production of fertile seeds was worked out in 1888 in Java and independently in the following year in Barbados. Since then the plant breeders have raised enormous numbers of seedlings for testing and selection, a more difficult task than might be supposed. It has been stated that only one out of approximately one hundred thousand seedlings will be good enough for distribution to planters. The process of screening for the many qualities required is so rigorous that ten years will probably elapse between the raising of the seedling and its ultimate selection (Wiehe, 1963).

The importance of making information available on sugar-cane diseases has been recognised by the International Society of Sugar-Cane Technologists, who have set up a Standing Committee to co-ordinate reports on the subject. A list of the sugar-cane diseases, their causes and their distribution, is published at the Society's triennial congress (Martin *et al.*, 1963). The Society has also been instrumental in the production of two volumes entitled *Sugar Cane Diseases of the World* (Martin *et al.*, 1961; Hughes *et al.*, 1964). In addition to the above, two earlier works, one by Edgerton (1955) and the other by Earle (1946) have been consulted in the preparation of this Section.

REFERENCES

EARLE, F. S., *Sugar Cane and its Culture,* John Wiley & Sons Inc., New York (1946)

EDGERTON, C. W., *Sugarcane and its Diseases,* Louisiana State University Press, Baton Rouge (1955)

HUGHES, C. G., ABBOTT, E. V. and WISMER, C. A., *Sugar Cane Diseases of the World,* **2,** Elsevier Publishing Co., Amsterdam (1964)

MARTIN, J. P., ABBOTT, E. V. and HUGHES, C. G., *Sugar Cane Diseases of the World,* Elsevier Publishing Co., Amsterdam (1961)

MARTIN, J. P., 'Sugar Cane Diseases and their World Distribution', *Proc. Intern. Soc. Sugar-Cane Technologists, Mauritius 1962,* 815 (1963)

WIEHE, P. O., 'The Role of the I.S.S.C.T. in promoting our Knowledge of the Sugar Cane Plant', *Proc. Intern. Soc. Sugar-Cane Technologists, Mauritius 1962,* 10 (1963)

## LEPIDOPTERA

## SHOOT BORERS

### *Diatraea saccharalis* Fab. *(Pyralidae)*

The most famous of the sugar-cane borers is this species, known as the Moth Borer or Small Moth Borer. It is the most important pest in the Caribbean region, especially in Jamaica, but it also occurs in Venezuela, St. Kitts, Barbados, the Dominican Republic, the U.S.A. in Louisiana and Trinidad.

Straw-coloured adults deposit clusters of flat eggs on the undersides of leaves. The spotted caterpillars feed on the leaves but later enter the stalk and bore into the pith. The cycle lasts 30–40 days and pupation occurs in the stalks. Several generations can occur in the course of the season.

The damage caused by these borers takes many forms. First is the killing of the central growing shoot after germination of the cane sett. This is called the 'dead heart'. This damage is not as a rule particularly important as tillers can fill up the gaps. Later generations are more numerous and the larval tunnels in the stems cause side-shooting instead of the cane stalk growing to its full height. The

*Plate 3.13. Top : shoot borer damage to ratoon cane. Bottom : normal cane*

*Plate 3.14. Close-up of borer damage, Jamaica (J. R. Metcalf)*

mechanical injury to the stalk causes it to break under strain as well as reducing the weight of the stalk at harvest (Plate 3.13). Bored canes tend to mature early and produce a low weight. There is also a reduction in the amount and quality of juice extracted from bored stalks (Plate 3.14). Bored stalks also make poor planting material, especially if the top of the shoot is attacked. In general it is stated that loss in sucrose from bored cane is from 10–20% annually. Bates (1956) gives the percentage of bored stalks in British Guiana as 54·3 as an average from 2,000 fields surveyed and refers to *Diatraea canella* Hamps which is a similar borer to *D. saccharalis*. Other species of *Diatraea* also occur in sugar-cane in neighbouring countries.

### *Scirpophaga nivella* Fab. *(Pyralidae)*

This is the Top Borer of sugar-cane in India. This insect is similar to *Diatraea* in most particulars. The moth is silvery white with a tuft of orange yellow scales at the end of the abdomen. Clusters of eggs are laid on the underside of leaves covered with scales from this tuft. The caterpillar enters the central shoot of the plants by boring down the mid-rib of the leaf. Pupation occurs in the cane and several generations occur in the season. It also occurs in the Phillippines.

This insect causes 'dead hearts' in young cane but also goes on to bore in the older cane. The insect remains active throughout the year.

### *Chilo tumidicostalis* Hamp. *(Pyralidae)*

This insect occurs in Bihar, India, where it bores in the upper part of the sugar-cane stem. Two or three generations occur a year.

### *Chilotraea infuscatella* Snell *(Pyralidae)*

This insect is similar to *Scirpophaga,* and occurs in India and the Philippines (Fig. 3.17). It was formerly *Argyria stricticrapsis* Hamp. It is an early borer and said to prefer dry conditions. The egg clusters are silvery,

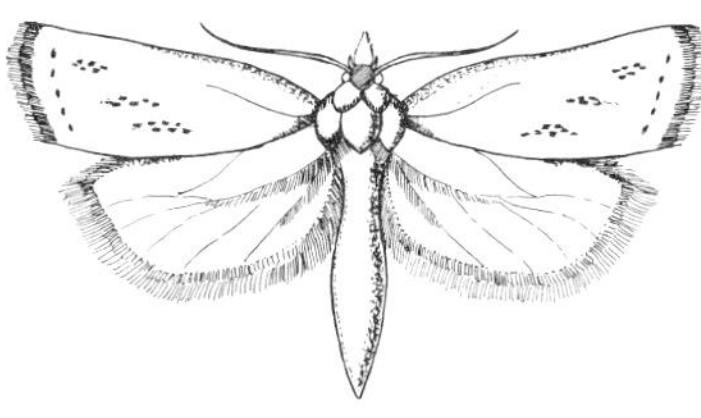

*Fig. 3.17.* Chilotraea infuscatella *(adult)*

overlapping but uncovered. The caterpillar is striped in purple (Agarwala, Haque, 1955). There are five generations annually. In India, Agarwala (1955) gives the loss in cane yield due to *Chilotraea* as 0·55% but sugar as 6·69% in Bihar. In all India, losses from borers are given as 8·17% of yield and 2·26% of sugar from 1945–52 (Agarwala and Prasad, 1954). Khanna *et al.* (1957) gives 8·2–12·6% as loss in yield.

### *Chilotraea auricilia* Dolgan *(Pyralidae)*

This insect is again similar but more localised in India. It is favoured by dry conditions. It also occurs in Java. It tends to remain active in India in the winter months, especially infesting unharvested shoots which have developed late.

*Emmalocera depressella* Swinh. *(Pyralidae)*

The borer is known as the Root Borer in India as it tends to feed low down on the plant cutting across the base of the shoot. Eggs are also laid low down on the plant. Early generations can cause complete death of the cane but later generations have little effect and only tend to attack side shoots. Several generations occur in a year (Cheema, 1953).

*Bissetia steniellus* Hamp. *(Pyralidae)*

This insect was formerly known as *Chilotrypetes* Bisset. The moth lays clusters of eggs on the upper surface of the leaves, there being 2–3 broods a year. The caterpillars which have violet stripes and spots, attack the top part of the cane usually after the monsoon and is too late to cause 'dead hearts'. It hibernates during the winter.

*Proceras sacchariphagus* Boj. *(Pyralidae)*

This insect is the shoot borer attacking cane in Mauritius. It is similar in habits and damage to the Top Borer in India. It causes 'dead hearts' in young cane but also bores into large cane.

Other borers of lesser importance occur in Mauritius.

*Sesamia inferens* Wlk. *(Noctuidae)*

In Mauritius there are at least 5 overlapping generations and 20–60% 'dead hearts' may be found (Montia, 1954). This insect is really a pest of maize (see page 50) but attacks sugar-cane in Mauritius in the early stage of growth.

*Agyroploce schistaceana* Sn. *(Tortricidae)*

This insect also attacks early cane and occurs in sugar-cane in Java. There are six generations in a year.

*Crambus melacellas* Dinf. *(Pyralidae)*

This borer occurs in Mauritius and attacks the young sugar-cane below soil level (Williams, 1959).

METHOD OF CONTROL

*Cultured Methods.* Many recommendations have been made of this type to reduce the losses from borers. The earlier cane is planted the less it is attacked. Summer planted cane tends to be heavily attacked and also carries borers through the winter whereas autumn planted cane does not.

The treatment of cane stubble and trash also bears on the abundance of borers. Both harbour borers, especially when trash includes a high proportion of millable cane. It should be removed, but the removal of stubble is difficult and seldom, if ever, carried out. Trash should be burnt or raked into the centre of the row and ploughed under about February. 'Water shoots' developing on harvested cane are attacked by borers and serve to carry them through the winter. 'Water shoots' are usually left to encourage ratooning later. These shoots should also be removed. Flooding of the stubble also kills overwintering larvae and is sometimes followed.

*Hand Methods.* Collection of egg masses by hand, usually by children, was formerly practised both for *Diatraea* in British Guiana and in India for *Chilotraea*. Eggs, when collected, are kept in order to allow parasites to emerge unharmed. A reduction in early attack is claimed but egg collection is only possible for the first generation.

At this stage the removal of 'dead hearts' is also practised. The 'dead heart' is pulled out and the larvae left behind is killed by means of a stab with a bicycle spoke. Alternatively the shoot is cut off below the larval level. Basheer (1958) gives some information on removal of 'dead hearts' in India. Removal once only, reduced the infection by about half, i.e. from 35% bored in the untreated to 20%.

*Resistant Varieties.* Everywhere varietal susceptibility has been investigated by recording the number of canes bored. Recommendations are always available locally concerning which varieties are best grown in borer areas. Thick stemmed varieties like POJ 2878 are heavily attacked.

*Chemical Control.* The use of insecticides against sugar-cane borers is on the whole not promising. In India, BHC has been used as a spray or dust with variable results. Both BHC and DDT as 2·5% dusts and sprays of 0·25% of 50% wettable powders applied at monthly intervals reduced infestation but had little effect on yields (Basheer, Krishnamurthy and Nagarajan, 1955). In the U.S.A., DDT and other insecticides have been tried without much success. DDT has in fact tended to increase the population of borers, but DDT coupled with 'dead heart' removal gave a good reduction of *Chilotraea* in India (Basheer, 1958). Application can only be made against early attack while the field is still sprayable by ground equipment. In the U.S.A., a successful dust widely used in Louisiana was cryolite (Ingram, Bynam, Charpentier, 1947) at weekly intervals against first generation borers. BHC 2% dust also gave control but tended to lead to an increase in borer population as with DDT mentioned above.

Later experiments claimed that toxaphene dust was promising. Endrin began to be used in the 1950's by Dugas (1952) who achieved 50% control with four-weekly and eight-weekly applications. In further work by Long and others (1959) good control was also achieved with 2% granules at 12 lb per acre applied four times twice weekly by aeroplane. Increase in yield of 20–100% of sugar was also recorded after treatment with insecticides but DDT granules caused an increase in borer damage and an actual loss in yield in the 1958 experiments.

The case for insecticides for the control of sugar-cane borers is not strong. While insecticides may be used in more highly organised countries such as the U.S.A. their adoption elsewhere has not followed. In India, considerable efforts have been made to use insecticides but these have by no means been accepted generally. Insecticides are seldom used against borers in Central and South America.

*Parasite Control.* Attempts have been made to use the natural enemies of sugar-cane pests. Against *Diatraea,* the Tachinid Fly (*Lixophaga diatraea* Tomms.) has proved of some value in Louisiana (Charpentier, 1958) and of considerable value in Cuba where it was artificially bred and released in 1949 (Scaramuzza, 1951). Most attempts have been made with the egg parasite, *Trichogramma minuta* Riley., but normal parasitism of borer eggs is too low to be of any value. Attempts to increase the degree of natural parasitism by artificial breeding of *Trichogramma* on flour moths have failed in the U.S.A., in Trinidad, in Barbados (Metcalf, 1959) and in India (Box, 1960). De Souza (1947) concluded that in Brazil there was little chance of increasing parasitism by the Tachinid *Theresia braziliensis* Tns., because of hyperparasitism. Box (1953) states that *Paratheresia claripalpis* Wlk. and *Metagonistylum minense* Tns. were effective parasites of *Diatraea* in parts of Venezuela during 1951–53 and in British Guiana. In India, natural parasitism of *Bissetia* ranged from 2–15% depending on the month (Kapoor, 1957).

REFERENCES

AGARWALA, S. D. D. and PRASAD, S. N., *India Sugar,* **4,** 445 (1954)

AGARWALA, S. B. D. and HAQUE, M. W., *Indian J. Entomol.,* **17,** 307 (1955)

BASHEER, M., *Indian J. Entomol.,* **20,** 164 (1958)

BASHER, M., KRISHNAMURTHY, C. and NAGARAJAN, K., *Indian J. Entomol.,* **16,** 350 (1955)

BATES, J. E., *R.A.E.*, **46**, 356 (1956)
BOX, H. E., *R.A.E.*, **43**, 220 (1953)
BOX, H. E., *Sugar*, **55**, 51 (1960)
CHARPENTIER, L. J., *J. Econ. Entomol.*, **51**, 163 (1958)
CHEEMA, D. S., *Indian J. Entomol.*, **15**, 134 (1953)
DE SOUZA, D., *R.A.E.*, **35**, 189 (1947)
DUGAS, A. C., *Louisiana Agr. Expt. Sta. Tech. Bull.* (1951)
INGRAM, J. G., BYNAM, E. K. and CHARPENTIER, L. J., *J. Econ. Entomol.*, **40**, 779, **41**, 914 (1947)
KAPOOR, M. S., *Indian J. Entomol.*, **19**, 132 (1957)
KHANNA, K. L., NIGAM, L. N. and PURI, V. D., *R.A.E.*, **47**, 290 (1957)
LONG, W. H., CONCIENNE, E. J., HENSLEY, S. D., MCCORMICK, W. J. and NEWSON, L. D , *J. Econ. Entomol.*, **52**, 821 (1959)
METCALFE, J. R., *Trop. Agric. (Trin.)*, **36**, 199 (1959)
MONTIA, L. A., *R.A.E.*, **44**, 317 (1954)
SCARAMUZZA, L. C., *R.A.E.*, **42**, 271 (1951)
WILLIAMS, J. R., *R.A.E.*, **48**, 447 (1959)

## HEMIPTERA

### *Aeneolamia varia saccharina* Dist. *(Cercopidae)*

This insect is the Sugar-cane Froghopper. It occurs in Trinidad and to a lesser extent in Venezuela, Mexico and Brazil. There is no similar insect in the Old World. In British Guiana, the species is *A. flavilatera* Wlk.

The insect flies readily and both immature and adult stages feed on the cane. When numerous, as later on in the season, the cane can be stripped of leaf tissue and dry up, so that whole fields appear brown, as if burnt. The life-cycle is of the greatest importance as control measures make use of the fact that eggs are deposited in the soil at the base of the cane. The nymphs arising from the eggs are covered with 'spittle' and feed on the cane roots. They develop through five instars into adults, which move higher up the cane. There are several generations in a year.

#### METHODS OF CONTROL

Early attempts in 1946 to control the froghopper with insecticides made use of drift dusting with BHC, using a 5% dust at 20 lb per acre and fogging with a TIFA machine. These methods gave good results within reason but while the dust carry was about 120 yd the TIFA fog was only about 10 yd.

A much better result was achieved when BHC was used against the nymphs in the spittle masses by a soil application round the base of the cane. This system was begun by Mr. H. C. Jones in Jamaica and taken up in Trinidad by Blackburn (1949) and Potter and Carrington (1949). The cane stool was taken as a sampling unit. In Trinidad, if the froghopper population exceeded 12 per stool BHC 4% dust was used at 1 cwt per acre applied by a hand duster. The normal time for treatment was May/June. Fewkes (1961) states that more nymphs are found in multi-stemmed stools and suggests an improvement in sampling.

Resistance to BHC dusts developed in 1957–58 after about ten years of successful treatment. Other insecticides are now being tried. Vlitos and Merry (1961) report good results with carbaryl (Sevin) and isobenzan (Telodrin) and a long residual effect is claimed. Carbaryl is particularly useful as it is not a chlorinated hydrocarbon. Phosphates have also been successful, particularly carbofenthion (Trithion) as a 2% dust.

### *Perkinsiella saccharicida* Kirk. *(Fulgoridae)*
### *Saccharosydne saccharivora* Westw.

The economic importance of this family is entirely in its association with sugar-cane. In the West Indies these two species are often pests. *Perkinsiella* also occurs in Mauritius where it breeds on young cane. The nymphs are active in the damper part of the cane especially at its base. Adults occur on the foliage. Eggs are laid in the leaf blade, development taking 4–5 weeks, breeding being continuous. In Mauritius, *Perkinsiella* transmits Figi disease (Frappe, 1955).

*Saccharosydne* occurs in the U.S.A., Central and South America. It causes sooty mould to grow on the cane because of copious exudation of a sugary liquid. Eggs are laid in the leaves and are covered with wax. The insect sometimes becomes a pest but the invasion of the tissues by fungi seems more important (Guagliumi, 1953; Box, 1950). Both species occur on grasses.

*Pyrilla perpusilla* Wlk. *(Fulgoridae)*

This insect is an important pest of sugar-cane in India especially in the North (Fig. 3.18). It overwinters in cane stubble and develops on the sprouts. Later it migrates to the new cane plantings. It continues to breed throughout the summer and autumn building up large numbers by September (Gupta and Avesthy, 1954). The damage to the cane results from the sucking of the insects which reduces the sugar content. The foliage is also soiled by the insect when they are present in large numbers by the exudation of a sticky substance common to this group of insects. *Pyrilla* can also live on grasses.

METHODS OF CONTROL

Action against *Pyrilla* is often necessary in India. The insect is not difficult to kill with insecticides and BHC was first used both as a

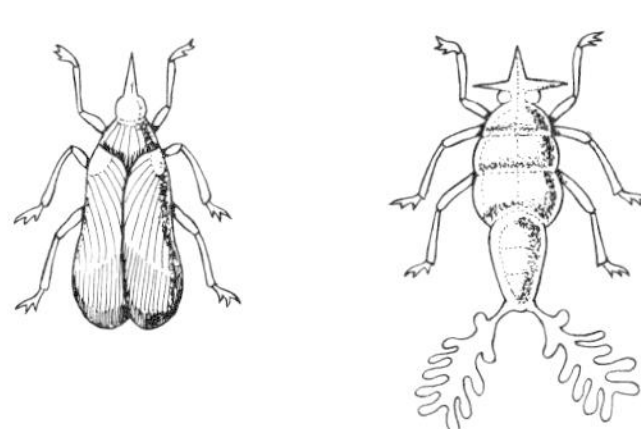

*Fig. 3.18.* Pyrilla perpusilla *(adult and nymph)*

dust and as a spray. BHC 5% dust at 60 lb per acre was needed in summer and autumn but 20–30 lb was sufficient earlier in the season. BHC spray can also be used at 25–50 gal of wash for the early season and 100 gallons or more for later sprays.

Other insecticides have also been tested and recently endrin has given complete mortality in four days. Endrin 20% has been applied by aircraft using 4 pt per acre (Singh *et al.* 1956 Gupta and Avesthy, 1955; Butani, 1958).

Action is seldom necessary against *Perkinsiella* but the insect is susceptible to BHC. Normally it is kept in check by predators such as the Mirid *Cyrtorhinus mundulus* Bredd. an egg predator from Hawaii. Predators also keep the insect in control in Mauritius. *Saccharosydne* is controlled when necessary in the West Indies with malathion.

*Aleurolopus barodensis* Mask. *(Aleyrodidae)*

This species of white fly is reported as causing serious damage to ratoon cane in India (Fig. 3.19) (Gupta and Avesthy,

*Fig. 3.19.* Aleurolopus barodensis *(nymph on leaf)*

1954). The insect breeds within the leaf sheath, especially of the lower leaves. Fungal growth often follows leading to a reduction in sugar content (Singh, Kalra and Sandhu, 1956). Continuous breeding occurs from March to September building up to a peak.

*Saccharicoccus sacchari* Ckll *(Pseudococcidae)*

Mealybugs are reported in India as occurring commonly on sugar-cane in a similar manner to white fly. Mealybugs are also reported occurring in Florida and Louisiana. These insects occur where cane is allowed to sprout during the winter.

*Macropes excavatus* Dist. *(Lygaeidae)*

This species is reported damaging cane in India (Gupta and Avasthy, 1954). The nymphs are red but the bugs are black and the insect is called the sugar-cane blackfly. No such species occur in the Western Hemisphere. Again the presence of these insects is associated with winter trash and sprouting. The insects can be very damaging to ratoon cane which turns white under severe attack.

*Silpha flava* Forbes. *(Aphididae)*

The yellow sugar-cane aphid is reported from U.S.A., Jamaica, Trinidad, British Guiana and Venezuela. It feeds on the undersides of the leaves. It is doubtfully of economic importance.

Other species of aphids also occur from time to time on sugar-cane, notably *Aphis maidis* Fitch, the cane leaf aphid which occurs in U.S.A. No aphid species has been noted on sugar-cane in the Old World.

REFERENCES

BLACKBURN, F. H. B., *Trop. Agr. (Trinidad)*, **26**, 93 (1949)
BOX, H. E., *R.A.E.*, **40**, 389 (1950)
BUTANI, D. K., *R.A.E.*, **48**, 497 (1958)
FEWEKES, D. W., *J. Econ. Entomol.*, **54**, 771 (1961)
FRAPPE, C., *R.A.E.*, **45**, 171 (1955)
GUAGLIUMI, P., *R.A.E.*, **43**, 222 (1953)
GUPTA, B. D. and AVESTHY, P. N., *Indian Sugar*, **4**, 387 (1954); **4**, 557 (1955)
POTTER, T. E. R. and CARRINGTON, A. J., *Trop. Agr. (Trinidad)*, **26**, 113 (1949)
SINGH, H., KULRA, A. N. and SANDHU, J. S., *Indian Sugar*, **5**, 689 (1956)
VLITOS, A. J. and MERRY, C. A. F., *World Crops*, **13**, 470 (1961)

## ISOPTERA

Termites or White Ants have proved to be among the greatest nuisances to sugar-cane cultivation. This is especially true of India. White ants also attack cane in Australia, but do not occur as pests in the Western Hemisphere.

The species which are responsible for cane injury in India are:

*Odontotermes assmuthi* Holmgr.
*Microtermes obesi* Holmgr.
*O. assmuthi* Holmgr.
*Coptotermes heiris* Wasm.

In Australia, the Giant White Ant is responsible but other species occur in freshly broken soil.

Termites attack the cane sett immediately after planting and destroy the eye-buds. Sometimes over 80% of the setts are attacked. Eventually the termites spread into the interior of the sett, totally destroying it.

All termites live in nests as they are social insects (Figs. 3.20, 3.21). The damage to the cane is caused by the worker cast. The nests of the species causing damage to cane setts are underground, not in the large dome-shaped mounds seen above ground. The underground nests cannot easily be located and often exist a long way from the site of the damage.

The wood-boring species also attack sugar-cane but only, as a rule, when this is planted

*Fig. 3.20. Termite (winged adult)*

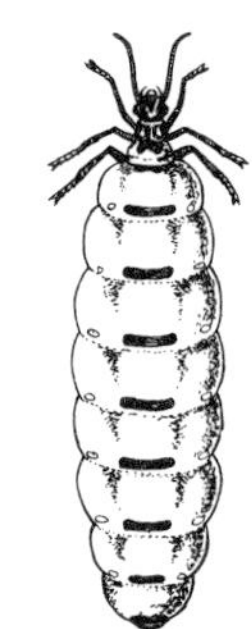

*Fig. 3.21. Termite queen*

on recently cleared land. While pieces of wood still remain in the soil crops, especially sugar-cane, are open to attack. These species, however, eventually quit the field entirely.

### METHODS OF CONTROL

Destruction of the termite nests is the obvious method of eradication. Nests can also be fumigated with carbon bisulphide or baited with arsenic. These methods are not suitable for the cane sett attacking species as the nests can seldom be located. Control therefore has been directed to protecting the cane sett in the soil.

Early methods used a steep of 2% phenol in water in which the setts were soaked. This gave good protection and an increase in germination of the buds. Modern insecticides have also been tried, especially BHC used as a 5% dust applied to the setts in the open furrow at 20 lb per acre (Gupta, 1950; Rao, 1953). Attempts have been made to use BHC as a sett dip at 0·25%. Dipping setts is cheaper than the application of dust but not always as effective. BHC dips are also liable to be phytotoxic.

Other insecticides have also been used against termites, both as sett dips and as dust, notably aldrin and dieldrin. Aldrin has proved very effective as a 2·5% dust at 20 lb per acre furrow treatment and at 0·25% suspension. This amounts to a very low rate of 0·5 lb per acre of aldrin. Agrawala (1955) claims that against *Microtermes,* aldrin and dieldrin are superior to BHC, giving better termite control and a greater germination. Increased yield followed control.

## COLEOPTERA

Beetle pests are most important in sugar-cane in Australia where many *Lamellicornia* assume the status of pests. The damage is caused by the grubs feeding below soil. The different species are all very similar in appearance and habit. The grubs are white fleshy larvae and curved in appearance. The difference between them can be established by either an examination of the spines on the ventral surface of the body or of the mandibles. The life-cycle normally occupies one or two years. The adults seldom feed on the sugar-cane foliage but some species feed on special trees. The adults emergence usually takes place from October to December, after the rains.

In Australia the following types are recorded as pests. Local names only are given for most species.

Greyback beetle *(Dermolepida alborhirtum* Waterh)

French's cane beetle *(Lepidiota frenchi* Blkb.)

Consotrina beetle *(L. Consotrina* Gir.)

Childers Cane Beetle *(Pseudolophylla furacea* Burns.)

Bundaberg cane beetle *(L. trichosterna* Lea.)

*Clemora smithi* Arr. Occurs in Mauritius and attacks the roots of cane. It occurs also in Barbados but so far has not been recorded elsewhere.

### *Cochliotis melolonthoides* Gerst.
### *Anomala exitialis* Pér.

Both species attack sugar-cane in Tanganyika (Jepson, 1956). Both ratoon and plant cane are attacked by the larvae causing stunted growth. *Cochliotis* has one generation a year. Jepson stated that 8,000 grubs per acre are needed before damage becomes visible.

### METHODS OF CONTROL

This has been worked out in detail in Australia where the insecticide BHC has been in common use in the soil since 1949, superceding the older method of using carbon bisulphide. The present accepted method is to apply 75 lb per acre of 20% BHC (2·6% gamma BHC) in the furrows, as for termites. This treatment protects the crop for three years. Only 50 lb per acre need be used if protection for one year only is needed.

Post-emergence (after shooting) application can also be made with the dust in bands along each side of the cane row. The dust is then stirred into the surface soil. Such an application can be used on ratoon cane if an attack develops (Toohey, 1960; Mungomery, 1947; Buzacott, 1947).

The use of insecticides applied to the soil against cane grub of this type have been successful in countries other than Australia. BHC has been used in Tanganyika against *Cochliotis* and *Anomala* and aldrin against

*Clemora* in Mauritius (Williams, 1958). It would appear that aldrin is tending to supersede BHC as for termites on the grounds of stability in the soil, less phytotoxicity and equal killing power.

Hand method of control in collecting of either beetles or of grubs has never been very successful although these measures had been practised for many years in some countries.

Biological control by making use of natural enemies has been advocated particularly with the Scoliid wasps. The level of parasitism, however, has never been particularly high under natural conditions.

### *Agriotes spp. (Elateridae)*

Wireworm are the larval stage of *Agriotes* and related species. Wireworms are well known pests in northern regions both of Europe and America, principally of cereals and sugar-beet. In Queensland, Australia, the wireworm species *Lacon variabilis* Cand. is often of economic importance attacking the cane setts and the new shoots. Sometimes wireworms are pests in the U.S.A. The life-cycle of the wireworm is long, taking four years to become completed. In Australia, species completing an annual cycle are said to be more important.

#### METHODS OF CONTROL

Fortunately wireworm are very susceptible to BHC and the treatment recommended against the Lamellicorn grubs is also effective against wireworms. Less gamma BHC per acre is in fact needed, $\frac{3}{4}$ lb of gamma BHC being sufficient applied in the furrow at planting time (McDougall, 1947).

## ORTHOPTERA

Locusts and grashoppers are often pests of sugar-cane and, if numerous, where the cane is weedy, can destroy a good deal of the green foliage of the plants leaving only the mid-rib. Probably it is true to say that certain species of grasshoppers are more important as regular pests rather than the recognised true locusts although *Locusta migratoria* L. has been recorded feeding on sugar-cane in Australia. In India, Gupta and Avestley (1954) record the following species as damaging sugar-cane:

*Colemania sphenaroides* Bol. (the Deccan wingless grasshopper)
*Hieroglyphus banian* Fb. (the rice grasshopper)
*H. nigrorepletus* Bol.

In Australia the following species sometimes attack sugar-cane (Swan, 1955; Mungomery, 1947):

*Chortoicetes terminifera* Wlk. (Australia plague locust)
*Austroicetes cruciata* Sans (Little plague grasshopper)
*Gastrimargus musicus* F.

#### METHODS OF CONTROL

Where action is necessary grasshoppers are easily killed with insecticides. In sugar-cane, it is usual to recommend either a bait with bran and BHC or a dust of BHC. Bran baits with molasses consist of 100 lb bran, $2\frac{1}{2}$ lb of 20% BHC, with water and molasses to moisten it. The bait is scattered in the fields at 20 lb per acre. Dusts of BHC 20% can also be used. The methods of locust and grasshopper control with other insecticides and techniques are described elsewhere, sugar-cane being a relatively unimportant crop in which control measures have developed.

REFERENCES

AGAWALA, S. D. B., *J. Econ. Entomol.*, **48,** 533 (1955)
BUZACOTT, J. H., *R.A.E.*, **38,** 137 (1947)
GUPTA, B. D., *Current Sci. (India)*, **19,** 344 (1950)
JEPSON, W. F., *Bull. Entomol. Res.*, **47,** 377 (1956)
MCDOUGALL, W. A., *R.A.E.*, **37,** 281 (1947)
MUNGOMERY, R. W., *R.A.E.*, **38,** 89 (1947)
RAO, G. N., *Indian Sugar*, **3,** 339 (1953)
SWAN, D. C., *J. Dept. Agr. S. Australia*, **59,** 85 (1955)
TOOHEY, C., *Cane Growers Quart.*, **23,** 86 (1960)
WILLIAMS, J. R., *R.A.E.*, **47,** 196 (1958)

## VIRUS DISEASES

All commercial sugar-cane varieties are vegetatively propagated by laying lengths of cane in a furrow and covering them with soil. Clonal propagation on such a vast scale provides ideal conditions for the dissemination of virus diseases, and it is therefore not surprising that they are the most important ones affecting the crop.

The first disorder of this kind to be recognised was sereh disease, but although it is now ascribed to a virus, its exact nature has not been determined. Five other virus diseases—mosaic, Fiji disease, streak, chlorotic streak and ratoon stunting—have at one time and another threatened the industry.

Sereh disease appeared in Java in the 1880s infecting the popular variety Black Cheribon. Affected plants were severely dwarfed, so much so that infected stools looked like big tufts of grass. The threat to the industry was so serious that many scientists set to work investigating the problem, but in spite of their efforts the cause of the disease, and its mode of transmission, other than the planting of infected cane, remained a mystery. The danger from sereh disease was at first circumvented by establishing high altitude nurseries for the production of plant cane (seed cane) as it was found that the disease did not spread under these conditions. This method, which saved the Javanese sugar-cane industry, was continued until 1926 when the introduction of the resistant variety P.O.J.2878 made the use of mountain nurseries superfluous.

Of the recognised virus diseases, mosaic is rated as one of the world's most important sugar-cane diseases and potentially the most destructive. It produces chlorotic stripes on the foliage. On susceptible varieties its effect is devastating, for example in Porto Rico it was responsible for reducing the yield of cane from 25 tons per acre to about 12 tons.

Mosaic was first observed in Java about 1892, but since then it has spread to practically every cane-growing country in the world, the only exceptions being British Guiana, Mauritius and Thailand.

The answer to mosaic has been the introduction of resistant varieties, either by selection of existing varieties, or by deliberate breeding. For example, in Louisiana, U.S.A., where mosaic had become a major problem, breeding for resistance started in 1923. The programme was highly successful, and by 1955 95% of the acreage was planted with the new varieties. In 1956, however, a new strain of the virus occurred which was capable of infecting the hitherto resistant canes. This challenge was met by roguing seed cane nurseries to ensure the elimination of all mosaic-infected cane (Abbott, 1963).

The next three viruses on the list above do not call for more than a brief description. Fiji disease, as the name indicates, was first recognised in the island, and by 1908 was becoming so destructive that it was thought that it would destroy the sugar industry there. The disease causes severe stunting, but the characteristic feature is the rib-like galls on the underside of the leaf. The next virus to cause anxiety was streak, which spread through the Natal cane fields in the 1920s. The symptoms on Uba, the main variety involved, were short pale streaks on the leaves. From 1928 onwards another virus, chlorotic streak, occurred in many cane-growing countries. The stripes are often long and have irregular margins, a character which distinguishes it from other diseases. Chlorotic streak is not thought to cause severe crop reductions except in fields with poor drainage. As with mosaic, all three viruses were eventually mastered by the introduction of resistant varieties.

The latest in the series of virus diseases first appeared in Queensland in 1944. It was found that the first crop of a cane variety, Q.28, grew normally but on ratooning many plants showed retarded growth, hence the name, ratoon stunting. The virus was found to reduce the yield of ratoon crops of Q.28 by as much as 12 tons per acre, thus making its control essential.

The discovery of the virus in Australia led to a search for it in other countries, and it has now been recorded from South Africa, Hawaii, Mexico, the British West Indies, Porto Rico, and the U.S.A. Ratoon stunting has aroused great interest as it is suspected of being the undetected cause of the decline in vigour and productiveness of many varieties which have had to be discarded for these reasons.

The virus does not appear to be carried by insects, but it is known that it is transmitted mechanically. This can be done in the laboratory by injecting juice from an infected cane into a healthy one. In the field, it is transmitted by the cane knife and the cutter planter.

### METHODS OF CONTROL

The discovery that the ratoon stunting virus can be inactivated by heat treatment has introduced a new approach to the control of virus disease in sugar-cane, as this then enables growers to continue growing existing varieties instead of having to introduce new ones.

The hot water treatment is widely used in Queensland. With this method the cane is steeped in hot water at 50°C for 3 hr and then immediately protected by dipping into a bath containing an organo-mercurial fungicide. The only adverse effect is that the germination of the treated cane is liable to be variable (Robinson, 1963). Hot air treatment is preferred for immature seed cane as it is less damaging. In Louisiana where it is widely practised, the cane is treated at 58°C for 8 hr. Both the first cane and also the first ratoon crop from the treated cane are suitable for planting for the production of commercial crops (Abbott, 1963).

REFERENCES

ABBOTT, E. V., 'Problems in Sugar Cane Disease Control in Louisiana', *Proc. Intern. Soc. Sugar-Cane Technologists., Mauritius, 1962,* 739 (1963)

ROBINSON, P. E., 'Appraisal of some Cane Disease Control Measures', *Proc. Intern. Soc. Sugar-Cane Technologists., Mauritius,* 1962 (1963)

## Smut (*Ustilago scitaminea* Syd.)

Sugar-cane smut is indigenous in the Asiatic cane-growing countries, and also occurs in South Africa, Mauritius and Queensland. The smut was introduced into the Argentine with disastrous consequences as P.O.J.36, the main variety at the time, was very susceptible. The damage caused by the smut was so serious that by 1945, five years after its recognition, the variety P.O.J.36 had practically disappeared.

The disease is very easily seen as infected canes produce whiplike growth 2–3 ft long at the top of the stalks. It is probably a modified inflorescence. The 'whip' when it first emerges is covered by a white membrane, which eventually ruptures exposing the dusty black spores. Infected canes are usually also severely stunted.

The spores are carried by the wind and are thus widely distributed. Although the spores may land on any part of the cane, the only susceptible point is the bud. The fungus enters the bud behind the scales, and after penetrating to the meristem becomes dormant. When a cane with infected buds is planted, the fungus grows within the new shoots and is responsible for the symptoms already described.

### METHODS OF CONTROL

In India, cutting off the 'whips' and destroying them has been claimed as an effective method, but such a treatment is only possible in areas with abundant labour. In most countries the answer is to plant varieties which are immune, or relatively immune, to smut.

## Pineapple disease (*Ceratocystis paradoxa* [Dade] Moreau)

Fungicides have not played much part in sugar-cane culture but investigations in South Africa on the control of sett-rot demonstrated the value of disinfecting the cane before planting.

The research work was carried out at the Mount Edgecombe Experimental Station in Natal, where irregular germination of the plant cane was often a problem, particularly if the cane was planted during dry weather. Examination of diseased setts showed that a variety of fungi and bacteria were liable to cause fermentation of the tissues of the cutting, pineapple disease being one of the most frequent. Numerous fungicides were screened, and the organo-mercurials were found to be easily the most effective. During the course of the work it was noticed that some of the fungicides, in addition to controlling the diseases, also improved the germination and hence the final stand of cane.

### METHODS OF CONTROL

The treatment is relatively simple. The organo-mercurial solution is made up at a concentration of 0·015% mercury. The solution is then poured into a large container to a depth of about 3 in. Bundles of sugar-cane setts are then dipped into the solution, each end being treated in turn. If desired, a dye can be added to the dipping bath to mark the setts which have been dipped. In Australia cutter-planters have a spray attachment which treats pieces of cane before planting, while in some other parts of the world bulk dipping is practised (Plate 3.15).

The idea of having to disinfect cane setts was not at first greeted with enthusiasm, but the merits of the technique gradually ensured its acceptance. Although developed in South Africa, sett disinfection is now extensively used in both Mauritius and Queensland, Australia.

*Plate 3.15. Bulk disinfection of sugar-cane setts, Sudan (A Plant Protection photograph)*

The introduction of the disinfectant treatment was of considerable practical importance in South Africa, where drought sometimes occurs at planting time. Under these conditions untreated cane is particularly liable to rot, but disinfected cane remains unimpaired until the soil becomes moist enough for germination. Disinfection thus made it possible to plant the cane at the normal time, even if the ground was too dry for immediate germination, instead of having to wait until the rains came (Anon. 1953).

REFERENCE

Anon., *World Crops,* **5**, 497 (1953)

## OTHER DISEASES

In addition to the diseases already described, there are others which can damage the roots, the stem and the foliage.

Numerous fungi have been isolated from diseased sugar-cane roots. The first to be identified was *Marasmius* root rot (*Marasmius sacchari* Wakker), which was in Java in 1895 but has since been recorded practically wherever cane is grown. Affected plants appear to be severely injured and at the appropriate time the small toadstools of the fungus develop on the basal leaf sheaths. For many years *Marasmius* was accepted as an important cause of root rots, but it was subsequently shown that it was mainly saprophytic and that it could not attack vigorously growing cane.

The next fungi to be placed in the dock were various species of *Pythium,* particularly *P. arrhenomanes* Drechsler, which was responsible for root rots in Hawaii. The fungus attacks the tips of young roots and kills them, laterals are then developed and these attacked in turn with the result the root system is a very poor one. It was also shown that there were various strains of *Pythium,* some of them highly pathogenic. For some years plant pathologists believed that *Pythium* root rot was one of the major causes of root injury, but it is now realised that there are various other factors which have an important bearing on the reaction of the cane to the fungus.

There are two bacterial diseases which were at one time of considerable economic importance to the sugar-cane industry, gummosis or gumming disease (*Xanthomonas vasculorum* [Cobb] Dowson) and leaf scald (*X. albilineans* [Ashby] Dowson), but their ravages have now been curtailed by the use of resistant varieties.

Gummosis, as the scientific name indicates, is found in the vascular bundles of the cane and the bacteria also live in the leaves. The presence of the disease is easily seen when the cane is cut, as infected canes exude a gum which stains the end of the cane orange as it dries out. The pathogen is spread through the cane-fields by wind-driven rain drops containing the bacteria which enter the leaves through wounds.

The disease can cause considerable reductions in the yield of sugar when it attacks susceptible varieties. As previously described, it had a very serious effect on the Brazilian sugar-cane industry and was responsible for heavy losses in Queensland until it was eventually eradicated. It is still of current interest in Mauritius and Réunion where it is suspected that new strains of the bacterium have arisen because cane varieties such as R.397 and M.147/44 which were previously regarded as resistant have in recent years broken down.

The symptoms of leaf scald are variable, but typically there are narrow white lines which run from the end of the leaf to the base of the sheath. As the leaf ages, the white strips gradually turn brown and finally wither. A longtitudinal cut through the cane will usually show that the vascular bundles are light red in colour, particularly near the nodes, but no gum oozes from the cut stem. Leaf scald is mainly spread by planting infected sets but contaminated cutting knives also help to disseminate it.

Although leaf scald is no longer a major problem in sugar-cane culture, there was a serious outbreak in British Guiana about 1950. This was due to the dominant variety B.34104 being susceptible and its replacement by resistant varieties has banished leaf scald.

Downy mildew (*Sclerospora sacchari* Miy.) is a foliage disease which is rated as of major importance in Australia, Fiji and Formosa. It does not occur in the New World.

Leaves infected by the fungus bear long pale green stripes which turn yellowish with age. The abundant conidia develop on the stripes during the summer months and spread the infection through the field. The fungus has a curious effect on canes infected in the field stimulating them to grow more rapidly. Infected canes are thus speedily seen. When infected canes are used for planting, the converse occurs as the growth from them is poor.

Downy mildew has been of particular importance in Australia where the disease appears to have been present since 1901. The planting of two very susceptible varieties in the Mackay district during the years 1934 to 1938 allowed the disease to build up seriously. In 1940 a campaign was begun to eradicate it. Two steps were taken, the introduction of resistant varieties and the rigorous removal of any infected plants. These were so successful that the disease was completely eliminated from the district by 1944 and this has permitted the reintroduction of the more popular susceptible varieties. There has been no recurrence of the outbreak in the area (Steindl, 1963).

REFERENCE

STEINDL, D. R. L., 'The Role of Roguing in the Control of Sugar Cane Diseases in Queensland', *Proc. Intern. Soc. Sugar-CaneTechnologists., Mauritius, 1962,* 737 (1963)

# TOBACCO

Tobacco, which for centuries was regarded as a harmless solace for mankind, has recently come under a cloud on account of the statistical correlation between cigarette smoking and lung cancer. The warning has not yet had much effect on tobacco consumption so that the production and manufacture of tobacco products remains a major industry. Taxation of tobacco forms a considerable part of the revenue of most countries, and no other agricultural product bears such heavy taxes.

The world production of tobacco in 1955 was estimated at more than 4 million short tons, occupying 9 million acres for its production. The tobacco plant is remarkably tolerant and can be grown in soils varying in texture from light sands to clays, and in climates from the tropics to the temperate regions.

The U.S.A. grows about 25% of the world's tobacco and is the leading producer and exporter. Home production largely supplies the needs of those countries which can grow tobacco, but Southern Rhodesia, Brazil, Cuba, Greece, Indonesia, the Philippine Islands and Turkey are all major exporters (Lucas, 1958).

Tobacco cultivation is on a different level from one country to another. Likewise, the quality varies as well as the type. In many countries it is a very specialised and highly organised industry, the manufacturing often being in the hands of state monopolies. In other countries such as India it is grown in a less organised fashion and is largely locally consumed.

In the U.S.A., India and the Far East the main pests are lepidopterous, large caterpillars feeding on the foliage or buds. In Europe, the main pest is *Thrips tabaci,* while in Africa, white fly and aphids are important. Tobacco is among the few crops in which soil-living nematodes are important pests and sometimes a limiting factor in production. Most pests of tobacco are also pests of other crops. The only exclusive pest appears to be *Thrips tabaci*.

Although the tobacco plant is undemanding in its basic cultural requirements, the most valuable leaves are those which are large and bright in colour. This combination of qualities is not easy to obtain because large leaves are linked with high fertility and good colour with low fertility. Such a sequence is best obtained on light sandy soils which are heavily fertilised at the beginning of the season and then lose nitrogen by leaching during the summer; conditions which are found in the great tobacco-growing areas of North and South Carolina and in Southern Rhodesia.

The need for plenty of nitrogen in the early stages of the growth of the tobacco plant undoubtedly increases its susceptibility to various diseases whose relative importance shows great variation from country to country. As a generalisation it can be said that root rots are the predominant diseases in the U.S.A., whereas foliage diseases are the main trouble in Southern Rhodesia and Australia. Although there is a tendency for all diseases to become universal, strict quarantine regulations have helped to limit the incidence of such major diseases as blue mould, wildfire and some virus diseases.

The tobacco plant is liable to be attacked by disease at any stage from seed to maturity, but the main interest of the plant pathologist is in the seed-bed where crowded plants grown under moist conditions provide ideal conditions for fungi and bacteria. For this reason, seed-bed hygiene is described before dealing with each disease.

Both Lucas (1958) and Wolf (1957) have described the tobacco diseases of the world, with emphasis on those present in the U.S.A., whilst Hopkins (1956) has dealt with the same subject with particular reference to African problems.

REFERENCES

HOPKINS, J. C. F., *Tobacco Diseases with Specific Reference to Africa,* Commonwealth Mycological Institute (1956)

LUCAS, G. B., *Diseases of Tobacco,* The Scarecrow Press Inc., New York (1958)

WOLF, F. A., *Tobacco Diseases and Decays* (2nd Edn.), Duke University Press, Durham, North Carolina (1957)

## LEPIDOPTERA

### *Heliothis armigera* Hb. *(Noctuidae)*

Several species of *Heliothis* are listed as attacking tobacco but it is doubtful if they are true species as *H. armigera* appears to occur in all the different tobacco-growing countries including Europe and the Far East, where it is known as a budworm. In the U.S.A., *H. virsecens* Fab. is the species on tobacco.

The moths are dull-coloured of the noctuid type and deposit large numbers of eggs on the foliage. The greenish larvae tend to eat the buds rather than feeding on the leaves, hence the name budworm. Pupation occurs in the soil. The damage to tobacco is caused by the caterpillars entering into the buds at an early stage of growth and they bore through the tightly folded leaves. The holes so made become magnified when the leaves open and expand. This damage reduces the market value of the leaf. The caterpillars are also serious pests of the seed crop, entering the seed pods and destroying the seed.

#### METHODS OF CONTROL

Probably the most widely used insecticide against *Heliothis* is DDT. It can be used as a spray or dust applied to the centres of the plants. Probably the best formulation of DDT for use on tobacco is the wettable powder applied at 3 lb per 100 gal of a 75% product. The object of the application is to prevent the caterpillars from eating the buds. Regular sprays every 7–10 days are necessary and these are directed into the tops of the plant, after they are set out in the field. Endrin is also very effective but certain exporting countries do not recommend it. The bacterial insecticide *Bacillus thuringiensis* has proved satisfactory in the U.S.A. but is slow in action.

### *Prodenia litura* Fab. *(Noctuidae)*

The caterpillars of this moth are voracious feeders and are extremely important pests of tobacco. It is an insect of the Old World, being found in the Middle East, India and Australia. The moths are dull brown in colour and the females deposit egg masses of 100 or more on the foliage, leaving them covered with scales from the female body. The caterpillars tend to remain together in their young stages but spread out later. This insect is also an extremely important pest of cotton.

### *Protoparce sexta* John. *(Sphingidae)*
### *Protoparce quinquemaculata* Haw.

These insects are hornworms, large caterpillars of the Hawk Moth family, known by the conspicuous spine at the end of the body

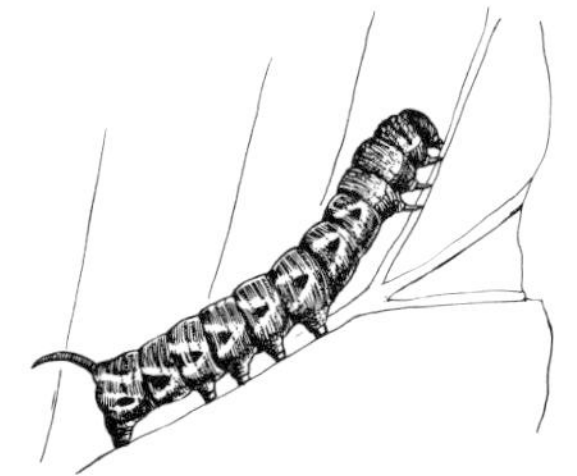

*Fig. 3.22.* Protoparce sexta *(caterpillar)*

(Fig. 3.22). They are well-known tobacco pests in the U.S.A. where they occur. The moths fly at dusk and the females deposit single eggs on the lower side of the leaves. The caterpillars grow to 3–4 in in length and can eat large quantities of foliage. The winter is passed as a pupa and a partial second generation occurs. Species of *Polistes (Vespidae)* prey heavily on the caterpillars.

### *Euoxa spp. (Agrotis) (Noctuidae)*

These caterpillars are known as cutworms and feed in the soil. They are not particularly important pests of tobacco but in some years can cause much damage. The newly set out plants are cut off at soil level but some feeding on the leaves also takes place.

Other foliage feeding caterpillars can also be found on tobacco notably *Crambus* spp. in U.S.A. and *Plusia spp.* in Australia. *Gnori-*

Plate 1

*Potatoes showing leaf-curling following aphid attack. Untreated plot mid-right, remainder treated with insecticide*

Plate 2

*Potato foliage destroyed by potato blight (A Shell photograph)*

Plate 3

*Virus yellows of sugar-beet. Plant on the left side infected, on the right side healthy (A Shell photograph)*

Plate 4

*Leaf bronzing caused by the fruit tree red spider*

Plate 5

*Air-blast fruit spraying machine*

Plate 6

*Oranges attacked by black scale, Lebanon*

Plate 7

*Orange tree affected by Tristeza virus, Spain*

Plate 8

*Coffee leaf rust, Kenya (A Shell photograph)*

Plate 9

*Coffee berry disease, healthy berries red, diseased berries black, Kenya (A Plant Protection photograph)*

Plate 10

*Pile of cocoa pods affected with black pod (A Plant Protection photograph)*

Plate 11

*Tea bushes showing bronzing caused by mites, Indonesia*

Plate 12

*Damage to banana stool by banana weevil, Uganda*

*moschema opercullela* Zell. and *G. heliopa* Lower. *(Tineidae)* both attack tobacco and other plants, the former insect being known as the Potato Tuber Moth. Eggs are laid both on the plant and in the soil. The larvae, which are quite small, feed within the leaf and often enter into the mid-rib as well as boring into the growing point and stems. They occur in the seed-bed and are frequently planted out in infested seedlings. The larvae pupate in cocoons either in the leaf mine or in the soil.

### METHODS OF CONTROL

DDT can be recommended against all the above caterpillars as for *Heliothis*. For the control of cutworms the insecticide must be applied to the base of the plants either as a spray or as a dust so that the soil is contaminated. Aldrin can also be used in this way. The older method of cutworm control made use of a bran bait containing DDT at 2 lb per 25 lb bran. Gamma BHC and aldrin can also be used in baits but the insecticides must not come in contact with the foliage.

For the very large Sphingid caterpillars, hand-picking can be carried out but many insecticides can be used against them. It is important to ascertain that there are no residues to affect the taste of the tobacco as residues on tobacco leaf can be as high as 50 ppm but these are often reduced by processing. The bacterial insecticide *Bacillus thuringiensis* was suggested to overcome this problem. It was particularly effective against species of *Protoparce* but not others.

## COLEOPTERA

### *Epitrix spp. (Chrysomelidae)*

Several species of this type of flea beetle occur on tobacco usually in the U.S.A. and South America. These insects are called Tobacco Flea Beetles. Attacks occur in the seed-bed and the seedlings can be badly damaged, checked and often destroyed. The beetles are brown in colour and are characterised by jumping. The larval stages are passed in the soil where the beetles hibernate during the winter. They feed on many other plants beside tobacco.

### METHODS OF CONTROL

Insecticidal sprays and dusts are effective against all flea beetles. The most commonly used insecticide is DDT.

## HEMIPTERA

Insect species of the families *Aphididae* and *Aleyrodidae* can be very important pests of tobacco for three reasons. First, they suck the cell sap of the leaves and shoots causing a weakening of the plant. Second, they spoil the foliage with honey dew, a sugary substance thrown off by the insects. Third, they transmit certain virus diseases.

### *Myzus persicae* Sulz. *(Aphididae)*

This is the principal species of aphid found on tobacco. In Rhodesia, *Myzus persicae* can transmit the very damaging virus diseases known as Rosette and Bushy Top (Plate 3.16). It also occurs in the Far East but evidently does not transmit viruses there and is not a pest of great importance (Smith, 1946). *Myzus persicae* also occurs on European tobacco, and in the U.S.A. where it has threatened the whole tobacco industry in Georgia and Florida. It appears to be of only minor importance in South America and no virus diseases are transmitted.

*Myzus persicae* overwinters as an egg on peach trees and certain other *Prunus* species. It has an infinite capacity for overwintering as an aphid on many plants and weeds in countries where the winters are less severe. The winged forms begin to arrive on the food plants when the weather becomes warm and they move rapidly from plant to plant as the species is very active and restless. Ultimately,

*Plate 3.16. Tobacco plants showing effect of bushy top virus, Rhodesia (J. W. Drummond)*

colonies of aphids are produced, usually in the growing point and copious quantities of honey dew are discharged to fall on the leaves below. The transmission of the virus diseases in Southern Rhodesia are caused by the movement of the winged aphids.

METHODS OF CONTROL

Aphid control is very fortunately easy and many chemicals are recommended. Particularly valuable is parathion used at ·05% of a 20% product. Malathion has been preferred in some countries and is used at 0·1% of a 50% product. More recently, systemic insecticides have come into use such as methyl-demeton (Metasystox) and dimethoate (Rogor) which are more effective but also more expensive. In Rhodesia, where the protection of the plants is vital to prevent the spread of virus diseases dimethoate (40%) is recommended as a soil drench to seed-beds at 16 fl oz in 40 gal or spraying at 32 fl oz in 25 gal at weekly intervals (Legge, 1960). Menazon (Sayfos 70) can also be recommended at 9 oz in 40 gal as a seed-bed drench or for weekly spraying. Attempts are now being made to add systemic insecticides to the soil to give greater persistence.

*Bemisia tabaci* Genn. *(Aleyrodidae)*

This insect is a white fly common in Africa and the Far East. *Bemisia* overwinters as an adult usually on brassicas and begins to reproduce when the weather becomes warmer. It also occurs on many weeds, notably *Convolvulus, Hibiscus* and *Ipomea.* From these weeds it moves on to tobacco. The females lay eggs on the undersides of the leaves, the eggs being pointed and stalked. The first larva is mobile but the second and third are not, remaining fixed to one spot on the foliage. The fourth stage is sessile and is often called the 'pupa'. Many generations occur in the course of a year until reproduction ceases at the advent of the cold weather.

*Bemisia tabaci* transmits leaf-curl of tobacco (Storey, 1935), a disease which can also be transmitted by other species.

METHODS OF CONTROL

White flies are difficult to control because very large numbers occur as the population builds up; constant spraying is necessary. Probably the most effective insecticide is parathion used at ·05% of a 20% concentrate which kills the adults and immature stages. Malathion is also effective but both this insecticide and parathion are of too short duration. DDT, especially in miscible liquid form, is effective against the adult and some immature stages. It remains for a much longer time. Endrin can also be used.

Fortunately, white flies are not of widespread occurrence and probably the best way to reduce them on tobacco is by the destruction of weed hosts which should be carried out by herbicides over an area around field edges. Many weeds also harbour the leaf-curl virus but probably the main source is from self-sown tobacco on waste land or old stalks carrying the disease from one season to another.

## THYSANOPTERA

### *Thrips tabaci* Lind.

This is the most important pest of tobacco and occurs in near-eastern and south-eastern European areas. It is not considered important in other countries but it also occurs in South Africa where with other thrip species

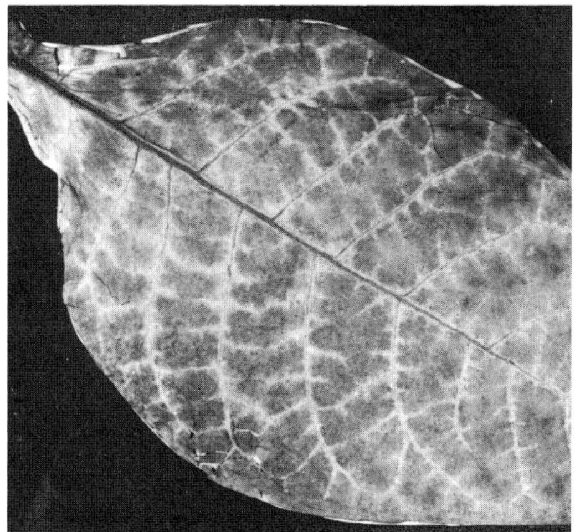

*Plate 3.17. Thrips injury to tobacco leaf, Turkey (A Soydan, Tobacco Research Institute, Istanbul)*

it can transmit some virus disease complexes. Thrips cause leaf injury making a silvery patch and reduce the quality of the leaf and its value (Plate 3.17). Thrips transmit the virus disease Spotted Wilt which occurs in many cultivated and wild plants (Hopkins, 1956). *Thrips tabaci* spends the winter in the soil as a nymph but quickly becomes active in warm weather. All stages occur on the tobacco leaf, feeding until it is picked.

#### METHODS OF CONTROL

Many insecticides can be used against thrips and probably the best and most effective is parathion at ·05% of a 20% product. This is used once in the seed-bed and twice after planting out. Parathion also controls other tobacco insects at the same time.

## NEMATODA

### *Meloidogyne spp.*

This nematode is known as the Root Knot Eelworm which lives in pieces of plant root in the soil. It occurs in all the major tobacco producing areas to a greater or lesser extent. Action must be taken against it. When a susceptible plant is introduced into the soil, eggs of the nematode are induced to escape from the female cyst and enter the root hairs of the plant. Here they increase in size and those destined to become females take on a globula appearance and are pearly white. When heavily invaded, the plants wilt and make poor growth, the root systems are continually renewed to replace those blocked. The species also causes galls to form on the roots which become knotted and twisted. The tissues eventually break away and drop into the soil carrying the nematodes with them. The normal practice of growing plants in seed-beds and transplanting them enables the nematodes to spread as the infection is carried on the roots of the transplants. Constant re-cropping of the land with tobacco also builds up populations in the soil. The Root Knot Eelworm has many plants on which it can live so there is little chance of starving it out. The female can remain in the soil unchanged with viable eggs for several years.

#### METHODS OF CONTROL

The rotation of crops and fallowing will tend to reduce the number of nematodes in the soil but so many plants are attacked by the species that only direct action by using chemicals is really satisfactory. Those chemicals which are suitable for application to the soil are usually expensive so that only the treatment of seed-beds is economic. One acre of seed-bed will plant about 100 acres of flue-cured tobacco. Several soil fumigants are available, notably EDB (ethylene dibromide) and D-D (dichloropropane-dichloropropylene). These can be injected into the soil by means of a special injector either by hand or by tractor-mounted equipment. Probably the product in most general use today against Root Knot Eelworm in tobacco is methyl bromide which also has the advantage of killing weeds. The application is made from sealed containers each carrying about 1 pt which is led into the soil through a polythene tube. The soil, at this time, must be completely covered with a sheet until the fumigation is completed. About 1 lb of methyl bromide is needed per 100 sq ft of soil surface and the operation takes 24 hr.

REFERENCES

HOPKINS, J. C. F., *Tobacco Diseases,* Commonwealth Institute (1956)

LEGGE, J. B. B., *Tobacco Res. Bd. of Rhodesia & Nyasaland, Leaflet No. 1* (1960)

SMITH, K. M., *Parasitology,* **37,** 21 (1946)

STOREY, H. M., *E. Afr. Agr. J.,* **1,** 148 (1935)

## METHODS OF CONTROLLING DISEASES IN TOBACCO SEED-BEDS

The raising of clean, healthy seedlings is an essential part of successful tobacco growing. From the pathological viewpoint there are three vital steps, namely, soil sterilisation of the seed-bed, seed disinfection, and protection of the seedlings with fungicides.

The original method of sterilising the soil was by fire. Shortly before sowing time the seed-beds are covered with brushwood or other combustible material such as maize cobs or stalks. The bed is best fired on a still day to ensure that the soil is heated to a depth of 4 in. The ash is then removed and the surface raked in preparation for seed sowing. The heat not only kills disease organisms in the soil but also weed seeds.

The open-fire method is still used in the U.S.A. on sites where suitable fuel is available. It is well suited to Rhodesia where the clearing of virgin land yields abundant brushwood, but the more sophisticated methods of soil sterilisation used by glasshouse growers are also suitable for use out of doors.

Steam sterilisation has been used by tobacco growers in the northern tobacco areas of the U.S.A. Steam from a boiler is led into the soil by either a grid or by an inverted pan. Steaming continues for 20–30 min, and to be effective, the temperature 6 in below the surface should reach 60°C. Although the technique is sound, it is going out of use on account of the cost and shortage of boilers.

In the U.S.A., chemical soil sterilisers have become increasingly popular, particularly because they enable the grower to use the same site for his seed-beds year after year. The best all-purpose material is methyl bromide as it is a combined fungicide, nematocide and weed seed killer. It is used at the rate of 9 lb per 100 sq yd and applied under a gas-proof cover to ensure that the gas penetrates the soil. The cover is left on for 24 hr, and after removal, the vapour disperses so quickly that seed can be sown 48 hr after the cover has been taken off. The disadvantage of methyl bromide is that the gas is highly toxic if inhaled, and it must therefore be used with great care.

Chloropicrin is also a good soil steriliser as it deals with nematodes, soil fungi and bacteria, but it does not kill weeds. Chloropicrin is unpleasant to handle because of its lacrimatory properties.

Formaldehyde and acetic acid can also be used but their employment has declined on account of their limited fungicidal spectrum and their ineffective control of either nematodes or weeds.

The seed in all tobacco growing countries is normally cleaned with care in order to remove debris which may carry disease. After cleaning, seed disinfection is carried out if necessary. It is not widely practised in the U.S.A., but is strongly advocated in southern Africa where the seed is very liable to carry pathogenic bacteria and fungi. The most suitable disinfectant for tobacco seed is silver nitrate which is used at a w/v concentration of 1 in 1,000 water. The seed is steeped in the solution for 15 min and after spreading thinly on cheesecloth trays, put into a warm cabinet to dry.

The treatment if correctly carried out has no effect on germination. It is more effective than dusting with the organomercurial seed

*Plate 3.18. Top: effect of blue mould on tobacco seedlings, Turkey (A Soydaṇ, Tobacco Research Institute, Istanbul). Bottom: healthy tobacco seedlings (J. W. Drummond)*

*Plate 3.19. Blue mould on mature tobacco-leaf, France (Institut Technique du Tabac, Bergerac)*

dressings and safer than formalin or corrosive sublimate.

Finally, the plants in the seed-bed have to be protected from the various bacteria and fungi which can damage, or in some cases destroy all the plants in the seed-bed. This is done with either fungicidal dusts or sprays, the latter being the most popular method. The particular fungicide used will depend on the group of diseases to be controlled, but the programme is a thorough one requiring up to twelve applications.

## Blue Mould (*Peronospora tabacina* Adam)

To this disease must be awarded the doubtful honour of being the most serious world disease of tobacco. Seedlings are particularly vulnerable and are killed if the disease is unchecked (Plate 3.18). It is not so serious after the seedlings have been transplanted, except in Australia and Europe, where it causes severe damage in the field (Plate 3.19).

The first obvious symptom of blue mould on small seedlings is that the leaves become erect instead of lying flat close to the ground. With older plants the disease causes round, yellow patches on the upper side of the leaves. Examination of the underside of the leaf will show the bluish, downy growth, composed of conidiophores and conidia, from which the disease gets its name. The abundant production of conidia encourages the rapid spread of the disease which can quickly kill all the plants in the seed-bed.

Blue mould was first recognised as a disease of cultivated tobacco in Australia in 1891, and it has been a serious disease there since then. The fungus was identified in the U.S.A. as early as 1885, but it did not cause much loss until 1931, when there were serious epidemics in Georgia, North and South Carolina, Virginia and Maryland. The reason for the interval between the discovery of the fungus and its attack on cultivated tobacco is not known for certain, but it has been suggested that the expansion of tobacco growing in Georgia–Florida area after the First World War enabled the disease to spread from indigenous tobacco in Texas to cultivated tobacco grown in the south-eastern states.

Its appearance in Europe is of very recent origin. It was found in the United Kingdom in 1958 and later was seen in Holland, Belgium, Germany and Switzerland. In 1960, it reached south-west Europe and was reported as having reduced tobacco production in the U.S.S.R. By 1961, its conquest of Europe was completed and it had also spread to North Africa.

The severity of the attack and its effect on yield is demonstrated by the European production figure for 1961 of 371,000 tons of tobacco: 100,000 tons less than the previous year (Critopoulos, 1962).

Blue mould does not occur in South Africa and it is to be hoped that the quarantine laws will enable it to be excluded.

The life history of blue mould is very similar to that of other members of the same genus. The pathogen survives the winter in two ways, on living plants and as dormant oospores. In the spring the main source of inoculum comes from diseased foliage on overwintering plants. Destruction of all tobacco plants during the winter is therefore an important step in controlling blue mould. The oospores play a smaller part as they only infect tobacco seedlings planted in soil containing the previous season's diseased leaves. Once infection has taken place, the fungus grows rapidly inside the leaf and produces conidiophores and conidia 6–10 days later. This is the explanation of the speed with which the disease can build up to epidemic proportions.

### METHODS OF CONTROL

In the U.S.A. the dithiocarbamate fungicides, used either as dusts or sprays, have given excellent control of blue mould. For spraying, 65% zineb is used at 3·6 lb per 100 Imp gal, and 76% ferbam at 4·8 lb per 100 Imp. gal. Both the older materials have been partially superseded by maneb which is effective at the low dilution of 0·6 lb per 100 Imp. gal.

Due to the rapid expansion of the seedling leaves, it is necessary to spray frequently to keep them covered with a fungicide. The usual recommendation is two sprays a week, which means 8 to 12 applications in the seed-bed.

In Europe, the campaign against blue mould has been co-ordinated by the Centre de Coopération pour les Recherches Scientifiques Relatives au Tabac (Coresta) in Paris. Their programme advocates both crop hygiene and fungicidal treatment of the plants at all stages of growth.

Dusting is preferred for the seed-bed using either 6·5–7·0% zineb or 3·5–4·0% maneb dusts. Dusting about twice a week is recommended, a frequency which usually requires about 20 applications. The quantity of dust applied varies with the size of the seedlings, light at first and then gradually increasing it, averaging about ¼ oz per sq yd.

In the field, maneb is the chosen fungicide either as a 3·5–4·0% dust, or as a spray containing 0·15% active ingredient. The dusts should be applied every five days, increasing the quantity as the plants grow. About 17 applications are made at an average rate of 27 lb. per acre (Coresta, 1965).

REFERENCE

CORESTA, Personal Communication (1965)

CRITOPOULOS, P., *Common. Phytopath. News,* **8**, Pt. 3, 33 (1962)

## Wildfire *(Pseudomonas tabaci* [Wolf and Foster] Stevens) and Angular Spot *(Pseudomonas angulata* [Fromme and Murray] Stapp)

Two bacterial diseases, wildfire and angular spot, plague tobacco-growers in most parts of the world. They are closely related but with sufficient difference to justify their separation. Wildfire makes its first appearance in the seed-bed as a pale, greenish-yellow spot on the leaves. As the spot ages the centre turns brown, surrounded by a characteristic halo of pale yellow tissue. Angular spot is usually inconspicuous in the seed-bed for, if present, it only forms small brown spots with no halo, but on older leaves in the field, the spots increase in size becoming noticeably angular in shape.

Both diseases are widespread throughout the tobacco-growing areas of the world, with the exception of Australia which is still free from wildfire and did not have angular spot until 1952.

The bacteria enter the leaves through the stomata, but the disease does not become epidemic unless the leaves become water-soaked. Tobacco varieties differ in their susceptibility to water-soaking and hence in their resistance to the disease. In general, it is the thin-leaved varieties which are most readily soaked with water.

### METHODS OF CONTROL

In the older tobacco growing countries, the bacteria are present in the soil, so that the emphasis in control is placed on the treatment of the seed-beds with the bactericides, particularly drenching with copper fungicides. In areas such as Rhodesia where much of the tobacco land is virgin soil, the bacteria can only occur if brought in on contaminated tobacco débris, on tools, or on the seed. Hence, in Rhodesia the importance of hygiene is stressed and seed disinfection is regarded as essential. This is supplemented by the regular spraying of the seed-beds with copper fungicides.

## Granville Wilt *(Pseudomonas solanacearum* [E. F. Smith] E. F. Smith)

Granville wilt is a bacterial disease which mainly affects the vascular system of the plant. It takes its name from a county in North Carolina, U.S.A., where it was first noticed. Since then it has been found in most tobacco-growing countries, with the exception of South and East Africa. It is a serious problem in North America and Indonesia.

The first signs of the disease are seen on the lower leaves, which wilt, followed by the same symptoms on the younger leaves. Sometimes only one side of the leaf wilts, while the other side remains turgid, a very characteristic symptom of Granville wilt. As the disease progresses, the older leaves turn yellow and then brown when they are dead. The destruction of the foliage makes it useless for the manufacture of tobacco and has caused heavy financial loss to growers, particularly in North Carolina and Indonesia.

The bacteria which cause the wilt live in the soil and enter the tobacco plant through the roots. Experiments have demonstrated that the entry is facilitated by the presence of wounds such as those made in the field by root-knot nematodes (*Meloidogyne spp.*). The bacteria are very persistent, and cases are known where they have survived in the soil for ten years.

The long period of sixty years during which the disease went unchecked was due to the absence of any resistant genes in the recognised commercial varieties. The wanted genes were eventually found in tobacco varieties obtained during a collecting expedition to Central and South America in 1934–35. It took the plant breeders ten years to incorporate resistance into tobacco plants acceptable on the U.S.A. market. The first introduction was called Oxford 26 and it has been followed by even better varieties which have helped to restore prosperity to the stricken areas. Soil fumigation is a useful additional check where the wilt problem is aggravated by the presence of soil nematodes.

## VIRUS DISEASES

The tobacco plant is susceptible to numerous virus diseases. Three of these have been chosen for discussion, part of their interest being the methods used to control them.

### *Tobacco Mosaic*

Tobacco mosaic is the most important of the three economically, for it is estimated to cause a 1% annual loss of tobacco in the U.S.A.

It is also of historical and practical concern to virologists.

The symptoms of tobacco mosaic are easily seen, as infected plants have a yellow and green mottle of the leaves. The cause of the disease was, for many years, a great mystery. The first contributor to its elucidation was Mayer, who in 1886 published a paper describing his investigations. He had found that the injection of filtered sap from a diseased plant into a healthy one transmitted the disease. Some six years later, it was shown that sap filtered through a porcelain filter through which no bacteria could pass would also transmit the disease. It was thus made clear that the infective principle belonged to a new group of pathogenic organisms to which the name virus was given. Since then, tobacco mosaic virus has proved to be an excellent laboratory subject. It is easily transmitted, for it is only necessary to rub a tobacco leaf with a little virus to obtain infection. It can be purified chemically and photographed by an electron microscope.

#### METHODS OF CONTROL

The control of tobacco mosaic disease is dependent on hygiene and crop rotation as there are as yet no commercial antiviral spray materials, nor are there any completely satisfactory mosaic immune varieties.

The first step is the production of virus-free plants for transplanting. All workers who handle the plants must have clean hands and avoid smoking while working. In the field any diseased plants should be removed before the first cultivation in order to avoid the risk of transmission during the operation. Fields which have grown a heavily infected crop should be rested from tobacco for a year as there is some evidence of carry-over of the virus in the soil.

### *Leaf curl*

Leaf curl, in marked contrast to tobacco mosaic, is not sap-transmissable, but is carried from diseased to healthy plants by white flies *(Bemisia spp.)*. The virus causes the leaves to pucker and the margins to turn down. If infection takes place at an early stage, the leaves are useless. The virus survives from one season to the next in infected plants and is then carried by the white flies either to the seed-beds or to the plants in the field.

#### METHODS OF CONTROL

Leaf curl has been very successfully controlled in Southern Rhodesia by the introduction of a two-month break between the end of the old crop and the seed-sowing for the new. The 'close season' ensures that the infected white flies are eliminated as there is no infected growing tobacco. This scheme has been a great success and the only serious outbreaks since its introduction have been traced to tobacco plants which have not been destroyed. This is regarded as one of the outstanding examples of disease control in the tropics by legislation (Hopkins, 1956).

### *Spotted Wilt*

Spotted wilt, known as kromnek in South Africa, is a widely occurring tobacco disease but is not found in the U.S.A. It mainly affects older plants, the symptoms being dwarfed stems with buckled leaves.

The virus has many hosts including tomato, zinnia, petunia, nasturtium, potato and dahlia. It is carried by various species of thrips *(Frankliniella* spp. and *Thrips tabaci)*. The numerous hosts and vectors make it a difficult disease to control.

#### METHODS OF CONTROL

Tobacco plants when young are not very attractive to thrips so that the early infestation is light and the wilt transmission small. A mathematical approach suggested that planting two seedlings instead of one at each site would provide one healthy one when they were singled. This was borne out in practice as it was exceptional for both seedlings to be infected (Van der Plank *et al.*, 1944).

REFERENCES

HOPKINS, J. C. F., *Tobacco Diseases with Special Reference to Africa*, 125, Commonwealth Mycological Institute (1956)

VAN DER PLANK, J. E. and ANDERSSEN, E. E., *Farming S. Africa*, **19**, 391 (1944)

## Frog-eye (*Cercospora nicotianae* Ell. and Ev.)

Frog-eye has a wide distribution, but although of minor importance in the U.S.A., can be a problem in Rhodesia and is very serious in cigar tobacco in the East Indies.

The typical frog-eye spot is a roughly circular brown spot with a white or pale brown centre. Occasionally the white centre is absent, with the result that the spots may resemble those caused by angular spot, but the presence of tufts of conidiophores, seen with a hand lens, provides confirmation that the spots are due to frog-eye.

The disease overwinters on infected tobacco débris and in the spring produces conidia which spread the disease to the seedlings. If the disease is present on the seedlings at planting-out time, it will inevitably increase and although visible spots may not be obvious, it is certain to give rise to brown spot when the leaf is cured.

### METHODS OF CONTROL

The frog-eye fungus is controlled by regular spraying of the seed-beds with copper fungicides at five-day intervals. The usual concentration is 3 lb of a 50% copper oxychloride wettable powder per 100 gal of water, using rather stronger mixtures in the wet weather. In areas where frog-eye is serious, it is essential to keep the seedlings completely protected against it in order to ensure that they are absolutely clean at the time of planting out.

## OTHER DISEASES

Two root diseases, black shank *(Phytophthora nicotianae* Breda de Haan var. *nicotianae)* and black root rot *(Thielaviopsis basicola* [Berk. and Br.] Ferraris) caused serious losses until means were found of checking them.

Black shank has steadily spread throughout the U.S.A. tobacco-growing areas during the last 30 years, and is a major disease in Java. The fungus, which lives in the soil, can attack plants of all ages and eventually kills them. As the name indicates, the base of the stem turns black and the roots die.

Black root rot was rated as the most serious tobacco disease in the U.S.A. in the 1920s. The typical symptoms are blackened roots accompanied by stunting in the field. The disease is at its worst when the soil temperature is low, but at higher temperatures recovery can take place.

Fortunately, tobacco varieties resistant to the attacks of the two fungi were available. This has enabled the plant breeder to incorporate resistance into new varieties.

A powdery mildew (*Erysiphe cichoracearum* DC.) attacks tobacco in many parts of the world with the surprising exception of the U.S.A., where it does not occur. Typical mildew attacks start on the lower leaves as the tobacco plant reaches maturity. The earliest signs of the disease are small, powdery patches on the underside of the leaves. They quickly multiply until both sides of the leaf are covered with a white coating.

The fungus is susceptible to sulphur dusts or sprays, but while it is safe to use sulphur in the seed-bed, it cannot be used on plants in the field because it would taint the leaf. Recently, dinocap has been found both effective and non-tainting, provided that an interval of 7–10 days is left between the last spray and reaping. For mild attacks, $\frac{1}{2}$ lb of 25% dinocap wettable powder per 100 gals of water is sufficient, but the rate should be doubled if the mould is serious. As a rule, four or five sprays are sufficient (Cole, 1963).

REFERENCE

COLE, J. S., *Rhodesian J. Agr. Res.*, **1**, No. 2, 65 (1963)

# IV FRUIT

## DECIDUOUS FRUIT

Deciduous fruit is grown principally in Europe. The only other parts of the world with areas of any magnitude are the U.S.A. and, to a lesser extent, Japan. The situation in China is unknown.

The main types of deciduous fruit are apples, pears, plums, cherries and peaches. Apples predominate in area—Europe accounting for about 22 million acres out of a world total of 37 million. The principal apple-growing countries are Italy, the U.S.A., Japan, France, the United Kingdom and West Germany. Large numbers of cider apples are also grown in some countries. Roumania and Yugoslavia grow more plums than any other country. Pears are grown mainly in Italy, and so are cherries. Peaches occupy about 11 million acres, about equal to pears, but exceeding the area under plums. The principal peach country is the U.S.A. with about 40% of the world's total and equal to the whole of Europe. Italy is the main peach-growing country in Europe, and is in fact the premier deciduous fruit-growing country in Europe.

Fruit-growers early recognised the contribution which science could make to their industry. The experiment stations in the U.S.A. led the way in testing the new insecticides and fungicides for orchard use, and as a result of their recommendations, the application of pesticides was introduced into American orchards during the 1890s. In the United Kingdom, The National Fruit and Cider Institute was started at Long Ashton in 1903, while the Wye College Fruit Experiment Station was founded in 1913 at East Malling. Since then the labours of the plant pathologists have enabled a peaceful revolution to take place in the apple and pear orchards of the world, transforming them during the past seventy years from jungles infested with pests and diseases into very efficient plantations from which the insects and fungi have been nearly banished.

The number of recorded insects and allied pests of fruit in the different parts of the world are legion. Even in the United Kingdom there are so many insects living on fruit trees that their study is a subject in itself, but they are exceedingly well described by Massee (1954).

It is impossible to deal adequately with this vast subject of fruit and allied pests but, fortunately, many of the most important pests are common to all the main fruit-growing countries of the world.

Apples appear to suffer more from pests than other kinds of fruit. The main apple pest is the Codling Moth which occurs wherever apples are grown. The Fruit Tree Red Spider

Mite and related species of mites have risen to become among the most serious of apple pests over the last 30 years, a problem created by the increasingly high standard of fruit production. In the warmer parts of Europe, the San José scale ranks as a pest of first importance.

Pears have similar problems to apples, but usually in a milder form. The Mediterranean Fruit Fly is the most important pest of pears as it is also of peaches.

It is on deciduous fruit that the part played by beneficial insects has been studied. Likewise, it is also on fruit that the growers and research workers have been confronted with the problem of insect resistance to insecticides. While the value of beneficial insects in fruit-growing has never been established the problem of resistance has still to be faced in its full intensity.

While many fungi can attack both apples and pears, two diseases are of outstanding importance on apples, apple scab and powdery mildew. In recent years, great advances have been made in the control of apple scab, leaving apple mildew as the most serious disease with which apple-growers have to contend.

On pears, pear scab is a major disease, while powdery mildew is rare. Fire-blight however, is serious, particularly in parts of the U.S.A.

The most important disease of peaches is leaf curl, which occurs wherever the crop is grown. The fruit is also susceptible to attack by the brown rot fungi which invade the fruit as it begins to ripen and are sometimes responsible for serious losses.

The literature on the diseases of deciduous fruits is abundant, but has been conveniently summarised by Wormald (1955) and by Anderson (1956).

REFERENCES

ANDERSON, H. W., *Diseases of Fruit Crops,* McGraw-Hill Book Co. Inc. New York (1956)

MASSEE, A. M., *The Pests of Fruits and Hops* (3rd Edn.), Crosly Lockwood & Son Ltd., London (1954)

WORMALD, H., *Diseases of Fruits and Hops* (3rd Edn.), Crosly Lockwood & Son Ltd., London (1955)

## LEPIDOPTERA

### *Carpocapsa pomonella* L. (*Tortricidae*)

This insect is the Codling Moth—an insect which causes maggoty apples. Apples attacked by the Codling Moth are also said to be 'wormy'. Presumably, as much has been written about this insect as any other, it is reasonable to suppose that Codling Moth had something to do with the recognition of entomologists as people who could be useful to the agricultural industry.

Codling Moth (Fig. 4.1) occurs in all the main apple-growing countries of the World except possibly Japan and the Far East. It

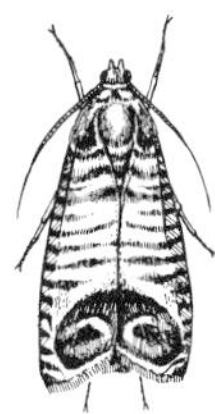

*Fig. 4.1.* Carpocapsa pomonella *(adult)*

prefers warmer climates and so is found in greater abundance in the South of France, Italy, South Africa, California, Oregon and such places. In northern Europe and in the United Kingdom, it is only occasionally damaging as a pest.

The life-cycle starts with the emergence of the adults in June, in early summer. The moths are small and grey with a dark brown patch at the wing tip. They fly at night and require a warm atmosphere of about 15° C for pairing and subsequent egg-laying. Eggs are deposited on the fruit, usually singly, but sometimes in groups of two or three. Sometimes eggs are placed on leaves or stalks. They are typical of the family *Tortricidae,* being flattened in shape. The tiny caterpillar which comes out of the egg is very restless and tends to wander about before entering the apple. A favourite place of entry is the 'eye', probably because of the roughened surface of the skin at that point. Within the apple, the caterpillar turns to the centre and attacks the seeds or 'pips'. The caterpillar

(Fig. 4.2) as it grows up, becomes pinkish in colour and finally quits the apple, which remains on the tree, and descends the trunk. It makes a cocoon on the tree usually under rough bark where it remains until the following season. Pupation then takes place and the moths emerge.

Sometimes, the caterpillars leave the fruit after it has been picked so that cocoons are made in the apple-boxes in the store. On emergence the moths make their way back to the orchard, frequently depositing eggs on the trees nearest to hand.

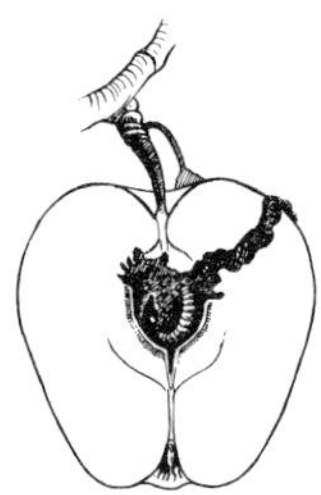

*Fig. 4.2.* Carpocapsa pomonella *(caterpillar in apple)*

As already said, the Codling Moth likes a warmer climate to that in the United Kingdom where only one generation occurs each year. In years when the weather is exceptionally warm, as in 1959, a partial second generation develops, some caterpillars pupating immediately after cocoon spinning and emerge as new moths the same year. In South Africa a second generation normally occurs and in the Middle East and the South of France sometimes a third as well (Plate 4.1).

The amount of fruit damaged varies enormously. In countries where two generations occur, a successful first generation can lead to considerable damage from the second, often amounting to 90% of the fruit.

## METHODS OF CONTROL

The control of Codling Moth has always presented difficulties until the advent of modern insecticides. Formerly, methods of orchard hygiene were advocated in which fallen fruit was collected and destroyed. Loose bark from trees was removed to prevent over-wintering. Tree-banding either with sacking or specially prepared bands was used to trap caterpillars seeking a place to spin a cocoon for hibernation. Some bands were introduced which were chemically treated in order to fumigate the larvae which found shelter in them. Such methods could be used but were much more suitable for small scale operations.

On a large scale, spraying was recommended usually with lead arsenate which acted as a stomach poison to the caterpillar as it attempted to bite its way into the fruit. Lead arsenate certainly gave some measure of protection if a good cover was kept on the fruit skin but it was necessary to spray several times in a season, beginning at petal fall, Unfortunately, routine applications of this kind led to undesirable residues on the fruit. Such an occurrence was notable in 1958 when £100,000 value of apples from the Lebanon were imported into England and were found to carry 31 ppm of lead and 16 ppm of arsenic both above the permitted

*Plate 4.1. Codling Moth entry holes in apples*

level. Such a deposit could not be removed by wiping, rubbing or even washing in water. Only washing in dilute hydrochloric acid removed the lead arsenate effectively.

More recently DDT has come into use as a spray against Codling Moth. This insecticide is used at 2 lb per acre and gives a much more certain control than lead arsenate, as it acts immediately on the young caterpillar, as it crawls over the treated surface of the apple. Against the first generation, two or three sprays are needed at an interval of 10 days beginning at 80% petal-fall. If the first generation larvae escape, further sprays will be needed against the second generation. A six spray programme is usually necessary which can be reduced to four, where the insect is already under good control.

Other insecticides can be used with success notably parathion at about 1½ lb per acre. More recently carbaryl (Sevin) at 3–4 lb of 50% and azinphosmethyl (Gusathion) at 2 lb of 25% product have also proved successful.

*Compatibility.* Fruit sprays are usually applied as mixtures of insecticides and fungicides, the latter being usually routine. The suitability of such mixtures has always presented some problem in compatibility. One of the worst products of this type is lime-sulphur—a widely used fungicide against apple scab and apple mildew. Unfortunately, none of the commonly used insecticides can be used with safety with it, as lime-sulphur is strongly alkaline. Modern organic fungicides are now being widely used on fruit and do not present difficulties in compatibility.

*Resistance.* The problem of insect resistance to insecticides is becoming of the greatest importance in crop protection both to growers and advisers. The control of Codling Moth with lead arsenate was pursued for very many years, notably in the U.S.A. and in South Africa. Both these countries reported Codling Moth resistance to lead arsenate, evidently a strain developed which was unaffected. The introduction of DDT solved the problem, at least temporarily, as DDT resistance was reported from the U.S.A. in 1955 (Glass and Fiori, 1955). Resistance to DDT was also reported from Canada in 1960 only eleven years after the start of DDT spraying (Fisher, 1960). In 1957 resistance was reported from Australia after 10 years of spraying (Morris and Baer, 1959). So far resistance has yet to be reported from South Africa and Europe.

The obvious answer to resistance is to find another chemical. From DDT, the growers turned to parathion and to malathion, both organo-phosphates. The only other group of chemicals at present available as alternatives to the above two types is the organo-carbamate group of which carbaryl (Sevin) is the best known. Resistance to DDT is by no means universal and is often present in only a few orchards in the country reporting the occurrence of resistance.

Attempts to use natural insecticides such as Ryania, which is a product without contact action on insects, has been unsuccessful as the degree of control is too poor. Furthermore, Ryania is unsuitable as a spray material, as it is bulky being the ground bark of a tree, wets out poorly and is far too difficult to handle.

*Biological control.* This method of reducing losses from Codling Moth has also proved unsuccessful. Nel (1942) gives an account of attempts to use biological methods in South Africa. During the war, lead arsenate was unobtainable in South Africa, so that there was an admirable opportunity to try biological methods. The parasites available were *Pimpla heliophila* Cam. which attacked the larvae and pupae and *Trichogramma luteum* Gir. which attacked the eggs. Various introduced parasites were brought in but were unable to be established. Natural parasites are normally scarce in sprayed orchards so that mass liberation of *Trichogramma* was necessary to build up the numbers.

Unfortunately, too many Codling Moths from the first generation escaped the attention of the parasites so that the second generation greatly increased in numbers, and outstripped the parasites. Another difficulty was in the maintenance of the parasites when the population of Codling Moth fell off. South Africa returned to spraying at the end of the war when DDT became available.

### *Laspeyresia molesta* Busch. *(Tortricidae)*

This insect is known as the Oriental Fruit Moth (Fig. 4.3). It originated in the Far East, either in China or Japan. It spread outwards, reaching Australia and the U.S.A. in the early years of the twentieth century and was discovered in Europe about 1920. It is now common in Italy and France where it is known as 'La Tordeuse Oriental'. It attacks many kinds of fruit especially peach and is found in all peach-growing countries except South Africa. As a pest, it is similar to the Codling Moth, belonging to the same family but it has slightly different habits. The Oriental Fruit Moth attacks first the twigs and afterwards the fruit. It is probably more important as a pest of peaches.

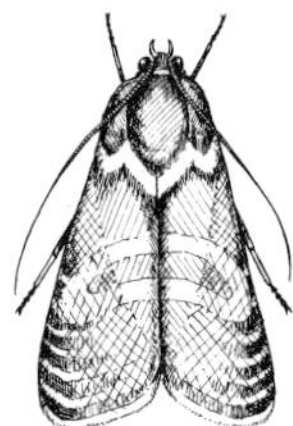

*Fig. 4.3.* Laspeyresia molesta *(adult)*

The moths, which resemble Codling Moths, emerge about the end of the blossom period and deposit many eggs on the undersides of leaves. The young caterpillars bore into the young new growth on the tree which, as a result, dies back (Fig. 4.4). Several shoots may be so bored by the same caterpillar which is pink in appearance. The caterpillars quickly grow up, spin cocoons on the tree, sometimes at the stalk end of the fruit, and pupate. The second generation of moths deposit eggs on the twigs and leaves but the caterpillar attacks the fruit, entering it usually through the stem end (Fig. 4.5).

*Fig. 4.4.* Laspeyresia molesta *(damage to peach shoot)*

Sometimes it is only the third generation which attacks the fruit, a favourite point of entry being where two touch together. At a later stage, the attack increases so the peaches may suffer a total loss. Further generations may even occur, up to four or five, depending on the temperature. Besides peach, pears, plums and quince may be attacked especially if they are grown near to peaches.

#### METHODS OF CONTROL

There is really no satisfactory method of controlling Oriental Fruit Moth. Several old established practices must be mentioned, among them is the cutting out of growth attacked by the first generation. This will remove many caterpillars and reduce the strength of the second generation. The use of sack bands around the tree trunk, as for Codling Moth, can also be practised.

Many investigations have been carried out in an attempt to control the Oriental Fruit

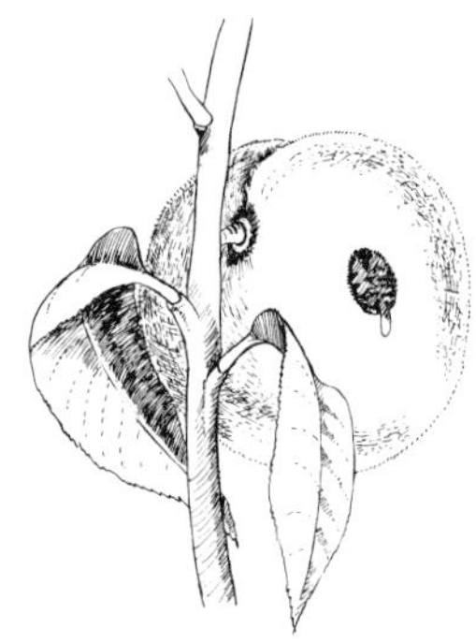

*Fig. 4.5.* Laspeyresia molesta *(damage to peach)*

Moth by means of insecticides. Very little success has been achieved, probably because of the number of overlapping generations make timing difficult. DDT at 0·1% has been successfully used but at least five and often more applications are required during June, July and August.

The emergence of the adults after the winter can be ascertained by means of bait traps as for Codling Moth. Parasites are of little importance although often supplement the DDT treatment.

*Other Tortricidae*

The following are the principal fruit eating species usually found in northern Europe, North America and Australia.

*Laspeyresia funebrana* Tr. This occurs on plum, and is often known as the Red Plum Maggot.

*Pammene rhediella* Clerck. On apple and is similar but earlier than the Codling Moth. Spraying at petalfall is a successful method of control.

*Argyroploce variegana* Hb. This is an apple species. It feeds on the leaves which it spins together into a clump. It has one or two generations in the year overwintering as a half-grown larve.

*Spilonota ocellana* Schiff. This is also a foliage feeder, mainly on apple. It overwinters as a half-grown larva so that some feeding takes place in the late summer and some in the spring. Considerable feeding of a nuisance type is caused by the caterpillar biting into the skin of the ripening apple, especially where two fruits touch together (Plate 4.2).

*Adoxaphese orana* F. and R. This species also occurs on apple and is notorious for the shallow damaging depressions made in the ripening fruit.

*Cacoecia oporana* L. This is the commonest Tortricid in the United Kingdom. It is a foliage feeder and also feeds on the fruit in August and September.

*Cacoecia rosana* L. This is a very common species on apple. In this species, the eggs overwinter and hatch out in April at pink-bud.

*Acrolita neavana* Hb. This species also feeds on the leaves and sometimes on the fruit.

*Argyrotaenia velutinana* Wlk. This is the Red-Banded Leaf Roller which occurs in the U.S.A. It has two generations in the year and feeds on the foliage but it also causes much damage to the ripening fruit. It is heavily parasitised.

*Austrotortrix postvittana* Wlk. This is the Light Brown Apple Moth of Australia. It established itself as a pest of importance about 1947–48 when DDT became a principal part of the spray programme against Codling Moth.

METHODS OF CONTROL

These leaf eating and fruit eating *Tortricidae* are becoming increasingly important as pests of fruit, especially when they attack the apple itself towards the picking period as such damage, although little in amount, lowers the market value of the crop. The species which actually enter the fruit are equally important especially if numerous. Normally, DDT as a spray against Codling Moth frequently controls the other species of the leave-eating type but those which overwinter as a caterpillar require a special spray at bud-burst.

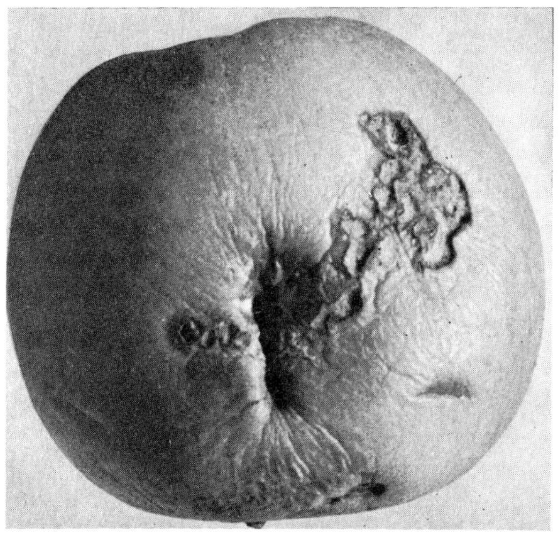

*Plate 4.2. Damage to surface of apple by Tortrix caterpillar*

The Red-Banded Leaf Roller is not controllable with DDT which is relatively ineffective against it. Parathion has been used at ·01% applied after blossom. In Australia, the Light Brown Apple Moth is also not affected by DDT and another similar insecticide must be used, known as DDD applied twice at 0·1%.

## LEAF MINERS IN FRUIT

The following species feed on the leaves between the upper and lower surfaces. They are all members of the family *Tineoidea*, which contains species of minute moths and tiny caterpillars. Several generations occur annually, usually four. The following are the most important European species, which are found in the more southern countries notably in Italy and Austria. Similar species are to be found in Japan. The numbers and balance between the species varies from year to year. Severe winters eliminate those which hibernate as an adult (Kremer, 1963).

*Lyonetia clerkella* L. This is a common and well-known species. It hibernates as an adult and lives principally on apple.

*Lithocolletis blancardella* Fabr. This species makes winding galleries in the apple leaves as does *Lyonetia* but it differs in hibernating in a cocoon in fallen leaves.

*Leucoptera (Cemiostoma) scitella* Zell. This species makes leaf blisters, that is round patches, in the leaves. It hibernates as a pupa on the tree.

*Stigmella (Nepticula) malella* Stut. This species is similar and makes blisters.

## METHODS OF CONTROL

Both *Leucoptera* and *Stigmella* are susceptible to insecticides especially to parathion used at 0·2%, as this material penetrates freely into the leaf tissues. Other phosphorus insecticides are also effective. *Lyonetia* and *Lithocolletis* are very resistant to insecticides especially when they are fully grown. For these species, it is essential that the application of insecticide is made at the very beginning of the attack that is at the first appearance of the mines. Parathion and related insecticides are also effective.

### *Hyponomeuta spp. (Tineoidea)*

There are several species of these little insects known as Small Ermine Moths. They are characteristic in making tents in the apple trees, the caterpillars being strongly gregarious (Plate 4.3). The adults of the different species also resemble each other, being white winged with black spots, hence the name ermine (Fig. 4.6). The species on apple is *H. padellus malinellus* Zell. and on plum *H. padellus padellus* L. but there appears some confusion as to the exact identity of those living on different food plants.

*Hyponomeuta* is an insect cauing damage to fruit trees throughout Europe also extending

*Plate 4.3. Tented nest of caterpillars of small ermine moth*

into Asia Minor and further eastwards. They are not found outside these regions. The moths appear in summer and deposit eggs on the twigs of trees in groups of 20 or so. They soon hatch but the young caterpillars remain under the cover of the egg-mass until the following year. Then they come out and feed on the young foliage on the tree, at first consuming only the upper epidermis of the leaf. Sometimes they mine into leaf tissues.

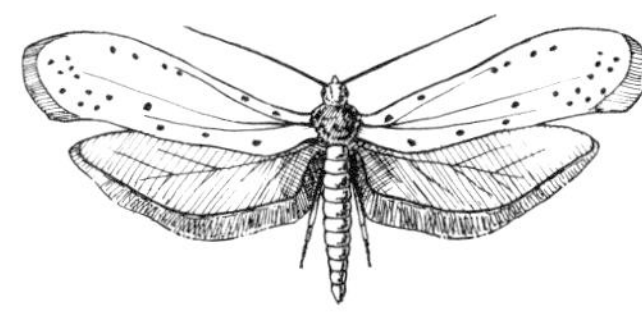

*Fig. 4.6.* Hyponomeuta padellus *(adult)*

Eventually they make a web among the branches within which the caterpillars finish feeding and spin cocoons. The fully-grown caterpillar is grey with a row of black spots along each side.

When the insects are numerous they cause great damage to the tree which is full of huge conspicuous nests.

### METHODS OF CONTROL

The old method of dealing with an infestation of Small Ermine Moth was to collect the nests in summer and destroy them by burning. Insecticides are now available and two methods are practised, either a dormant spray or a spring spray. The dormant spray consists of oil to penetrate the covering under which the young caterpillars are sheltering. The normal DNC/oil winter spray is quite satisfactory if used at 5% strength.

For the spring spray, parathion is the most effective and should be used soon after bud-burst. If the caterpillars have reached the nest forming stage, it is necessary to employ high pressure sprays applied by means of a hand-lance. It is vitally necessary to break up the nest and for this purpose ordinary cover sprays applied by automatic sprayers are usually too gentle.

## Leaf-eating *Geometridae*

Several species of this family are general foliage feeders, living on the leaves of many kinds of tree including fruit trees. The caterpillars are distinguished by progressing by 'looping' the body caused by the absence of the first three pairs of sucker feet. Most caterpillars are variously coloured greens and browns but some have grown to resemble twigs and often take up a twig-like position on the tree. The three comon species are as follows:

*Operophtera brumata* L. The Winter Moth
*Erannis defolaria* Clerck. The Mottled Umber
*Alsophila aescularia* Schiff. The March Moth

All three species are common in northern Europe. The females possess tiny vestigial wings and, after fertilisation, as they cannot fly, ascend the trunks of the trees by climbing up. Eggs, green at first, are deposited in cracks in the twigs or in crevices on the branches. The eggs, which turn orange in colour, hatch at bud burst and the young caterpillars move on to the newly opened buds, where they feed. On apples, the caterpillars are fully grown by the blossom period and feed in the opening flowers which they destroy in large numbers. Later, they attack the newly formed fruitlets eating large pieces from them. Finally, the caterpillars drop to the ground and hibernate in the soil in a cocoon, pupation taking place in late May or early June.

### METHODS OF CONTROL

Foliage feeding caterpillars of this type are easily controlled by means of a DDT spray applied at bud-burst. This should be a routine spray in northern Europe in any fruit-spraying programme. If allowed to develop, the caterpillars can easily spread to neighbouring trees.

On a small scale in gardens, the practise of surrounding the tree trunk with a sticky band, specially prepared for the purpose, has some merit and is very cheap. The object is to prevent the wingless females from gaining the upper branches of the tree.

REFERENCES

FISHER, R. W., *Can. J. Plant Sci.*, **40,** 580 (1960)

GLASS, E. H. and FIORI, B., *New Yk. Stat. Agric. Expt. Stat. No. 999* (1955)

KREMER, J., *Pflz Nachr.*, **16,** 1 (1963)

MORRIS, D. S. and BAER, R., *J. Agr. Victoria*, **57,** 619 (1959)

NEL, R. I., *J. Entomol. Soc. S. Africa*, **5,** 118 (1942)

## HEMIPTERA

### *Aspidiotus perniciosus* Comst. *(Coccidae)*

This insect is known as the San José Scale and is probably one of the most important pests of apple and other deciduous fruit in the world. The scale originated in China and appeared in Europe in the 1930s in the countries in central and southern Europe, making its appearance first in Austria and soon afterwards in adjoining countries. It can now be found in all countries, including Russia, in the region of the Black Sea. It appeared in the last quarter of the nineteenth century in the U.S.A., where it caused great damage. The name originated in the San José valley of California where the insect became established as a serious pest. It was found in the south of France for the first time in 1935 and is known there as 'Le Pou de San José'.

The entire tree can become infested with San José Scale. In such circumstances the tree may die—the infested twigs dying first. The scale also attacks the apple itself at the stem end and, where one settles, a small red spot occurs so that attacked fruit has a mottled appearance (Plate 4.4). Such an appearance reduces its market value. Even so, the San José Scale is primarily a pest of the wood of the tree. In appearance, it is circular, about 0·1 in across with a raised centre, grey in colour.

The life-cycle of the San José Scale is as follows. The insects prefer warmer regions and overwinter there as a partly grown scale, usually as the 1st or 2nd instar. As the trees come into growth in the spring, the scales feed and become mature. The males, which are winged, seek out and fertilise the females which produce large numbers of young. These leave the shelter of the scale parent and move freely over the tree as 'crawlers'. They soon settle down and start to suck out the cell sap from the wood or leaves. They mature, become true scales but totally immobile and secret a waxy covering over their bodies. The male scale is slightly more elongated than the female and is in great abundance in the early generations. A single scale can produce 400 eggs so that with succeeding generations enormous numbers of insects can invade the tree in a season.

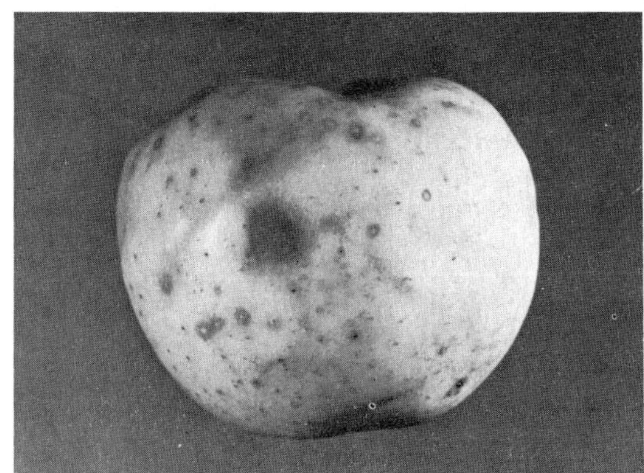

*Plate 4.4. Apple showing marking caused by San José scale (A Shell photograph)*

The San José Scale can be spread by the wind from tree to tree. It can also be taken on the bodies of insects and birds from orchard to orchard. The scale has many other food plants on which it can live besides apple and is found on other fruits and many ornamental trees and shrubs.

#### METHODS OF CONTROL

Before the advent of spraying machines, the San José Scale was impossible to eradicate but with the introduction of oil sprays in the early part of the twentieth century it became possible to take action against it. Oil spraying is still the standard method of scale control practised. Mineral type oils are used either for dormant spraying or for semi-dormant both at an equal rate of $3\frac{1}{2}\%$. The DNC/oil preparations can also be used applied in the period just prior to bud-burst, the action of the oil destroys the scale. Alternatively, summer oils can be used at $1\frac{1}{2}\%$: this is the white oil type highly refined to avoid injury to the foliage. The summer application is most effective if applied after the appearance of the first young scales after the hatching of the eggs.

Lime-sulphur, a standard fruit-tree spray, can also be used in the dormant period at 12%. Parathion is also effective against San José Scale and is often used in mixture with white oil. Other phosphorus insecticides are also effective and are best applied to apple at petal-fall.

*Other Scale Insects*

Many other *Coccidae* occur on fruit trees and vary in their importance as pests.

*Lepidosaphes ulmi* L.

This is the Mussel Shell Scale, the name being taken from the mussel-shell-like appearance of the mature scale. In France, it is known as La Cochinille Virgule which is also descriptive. It is chiefly a pest of old apple trees and also occurs on pears, plums and many other trees. It is a bark-inhibiting scale and is not found on the fruit or leaves. Against the Mussel Shell Scale, dormant sprays are preferable particularly the tar oil type, as the insect does not occur on the leaves.

*Lecanium corni* Bché.
*Lecanium persicae* F.

These scale insects occur principally on peaches and plums. The females are relatively large being about 0·2 in across, slightly elongated and brown in colour. Each female is capable of producing about 2,000 eggs and lives on the underside of the foliage along the leaf mid-rib. The winter is passed on the trunk and branches of the tree as a half-grown scale, which migrates back to the leaves in the spring.

*Aphididae*

Many species of aphids occur on fruit trees, some being specific to apples, others to pears, cherries and so on. Generally speaking these insects are important pests because, left unchecked, they can multiply rapidly. Each aphid is a female capable of giving birth to living young (viviparity).

Aphids occur in all deciduous fruit-growing countries in the world especially those with a well-defined cold season, as aphids cannot survive in countries where there is a high summer temperature. In Europe, the U.S.A., Canada, Japan, South Africa and Australia aphids are ranked as pests but not in the sub-tropical regions where they are replaced in importance by scale insects. The principal species on apple are as follows.

*Aphis pomi* De G. The Green Apple Aphid. This species remains on apple and has no alternate summer food plant.

*Anuraphis roseus* Bak. The Rosy Apple Aphid. This is purple in colour and leaves the apple in summer to go to plantains.

*Rhopalosiphum insertum* Wlk. The Oat Apple Aphid, green in colour, leaves the apple in summer and goes to cereals and grasses.

*Eriosoma lanigerum* Haus. The Woolly Aphid of Apple. In England this species remains on apple.

*Brachycaudus helichrysi* Kalt. The leaf-curling Plum Aphid lives on plum, is green in colour and goes to *Myosotis* and certain *Compositae* in the summer.

*Hyalopterus pruni* Geoff. The Mealy Plum Aphid which lives on the underside of the plum leaves without causing them to curl. It migrates to *Phragmites arundo* the common reed.

*Anuraphis pyri* Fonsc. The Pear-Bedstraw

Aphid is green in colour and migrates to bedstraw in the summer.

*Myzus persicae* Sulz. The Peach Potato Aphid lives on peaches but migrates to potatoes and many other plants in the summer.

*Anuraphis persicae* Fonsc. A brown species which occurs on peach where it spends its whole life, overwintering on the roots.

*A. persica nigra* Smith is a similar species found in Italy and the Rhone Valley in France.

Many other species occur on the various kinds of fruit, but a long list would serve little purpose here. All the species overwinter on the fruit tree of their choice in the egg stage, except the Woolly Aphid, *A. persicae* and *A. persica nigra*. The tree is the primary host plant of the insects. The eggs are shiny and black, deposited in the autumn by oviparous (egg-laying) females. The eggs hatch the following year—some very early—and the aphids move to the buds as soon as these open. The first aphids reproduce viviparously, that is to give rise to young aphids already living, and further generations are reproduced in this way. After two or three generations winged forms are produced (alatae) which fly off to find the summer food plant which is the secondary host plant. Much later in the year a return migration to the fruit tree occurs but this migration is made by males and females which give rise after pairing to oviparous females, which lay the overwintering eggs. The oviparous females are always wingless.

Aphids are leaf and shoot feeding insects. Their ability to cause injury to the tree depends on the powers of multiplication possessed by these little insects. Large numbers can be built up quickly and all suck sap from the tree. The withdrawal of sap from the different parts attacked stunts the growth and inhibits the proper functioning of the leaves which usually curl up. The fruit fails to set and reach a worthwhile size. Furthermore, the aphids frequently become oversupplied with sap and they must therefore throw off the excess in the form of honey-dew, a sugary substance which falls on to the fruit and leaves. The fruit is thereby soiled especially as moulds often grow on the surface. This adds to the overall effect on the insect on the tree.

The Woolly Aphid of apple is an exception to the general behaviour outlined above for fruit aphids. The life-cycle differs in that the egg stage does not occur on apple at all. The apple appears to be the summer food plant or secondary host plant. In the U.S.A., eggs are deposited on the elm tree which is the true winter host plant. This phase of the life-cycle does not occur in Europe, where the aphid remains in the active stage on apple all the year. In some countries, such as South Africa migration to the roots occurs and galls on the root system follow. This movement does not occur in England. Winged forms are produced and serve to spread the insect to other apple trees.

The Woolly Aphid is a true gall-forming insect. Where it feeds the growth proliferates and a gall or swelling is formed. On the apple tree, the Woolly Aphid lives mainly on the wood, moving on to the new growth in the summer months. Where the aphids settle, the wood tends to split open often allowing the disease Canker *(Nectria)* to enter.

The Woolly Aphid secretes large quantities of wax so the colonies of the insect are always covered with white curling wax very wool-like, hence the name. This wax makes the insect difficult to wet with insecticides.

*Myzus persicae* also modifies its life-cycle slightly in that it is capable of living on peach all through the summer without the need to migrate to other food plants. Only aphids, which have spent the summer on alternate food plants can give rise to sexual forms which lead to the return migration to the peach for the deposition of the overwintering egg.

## METHODS OF CONTROL

Fortunately, since the development of insecticides, aphids have proved among the easiest of insects to kill. Before the time of insecticides and spraying machines to apply them effectively, no control was possible. Aphids were at that time often the limiting factor in fruit production, a fact particularly true of plums.

The first insecticide used against aphids was nicotine but this required efficient spraying. Probably the era of effective aphid control on fruit can be dated from the appearance of the tar oil winter-wash. This began in the 1920s when tar washes were used in the dormant period of the tree against aphid eggs. While very successful as a method of control, tar oil was laborious and unpleasant to apply. At a dilution rate of 5% applied at 250 gal per acre large amounts of wash were needed. Later, DNC/oil winter-wash was designed to deal with two insects at once—the DNC component killed the eggs of aphids and the oil killed the eggs of the Apple Capsid Bug which was, at that time, a very severe apple pest. In recent years, the DNC/oil winter-wash has been modified for use against the eggs of the Fruit Tree Red Spider for which less oil is needed.

Spraying against aphids in the spring became popular when synthetic insecticides were developed and proved to be more effective than the older spring wash of nicotine. Tar oil was replaced, partly because of the labour involved, and partly because aphid control could now be added to the routine fungicidal spray programme. The first insecticide used in this way was gamma BHC applied at bud burst on apples and it could also be used on plums, cherries and pears. More recently, systemic insecticides have found favours as spring washes. Many insecticides are available to the fruit grower for spraying against aphids even in the summer against *Aphis pomi* and *Hyalopterus*. Likewise summer spraying is often necessary against *Myzus persicae* on peach. Woolly aphid always requires spring treatment as there is no winter egg. Sprays of gamma-BHC are very effective if applied at the pink bud stage when the aphids begin to leave the cracks in the bark where they have passed the winter. This insecticide cannot be used later in the summer and must be replaced by malathion or a systemic insecticide of which type Vamidothion is the most effective. Menazon, a new systemic insecticide, is also effective when applied before the blossom period.

Aphids are heavily attacked by parasites but their reproductive rate often outstrips that of the parasite and damage is frequently caused before it can gain effective control. Many predators feed on aphids, particularly the larvae of the *Syrphidae*. The most well-known of the aphid parasites is *Aphelinus mali* Hald., a tiny Chalcid wasp, which was brought to England especially to prey on the Woolly Aphid. It inserts an egg into the body of the aphid. The maggot-like larva destroys it, turns into an adult and escapes from the aphid skin through a hole, clearly visible to the naked eye. Aphids parasitised by *Aphelinus* also lose their 'wool'. *Aphelinus* is particularly effective in warm countries, such as South Africa, where it can pass through several generations in the course of a season but it has not been effective in England as it cannot survive the damp winters. The parasite sheltering in the aphid's skin, is not killed by winter washes but is readily destroyed by DDT when applied in the summer. It is said to have originated in North America, was introduced into France and finally into England.

## ACARINA

### The Red Spider Mites

These little mites, which feed on the foliage of fruit trees are not insects but Acarina which, in turn, belong to the larger group of spiders, the Arachnida. They possess four pairs of walking legs and the body is divided into two regions as distinct from three, as in the insects. They have no antennae.

Three species are important pests of deciduous fruit but the differences in nomenclature adopted makes the identity of each species difficult to establish. The three species are as follows:

*Panonychus ulmi* Koch
*Tetranychus telarius* L.
*Bryobia praetiosa* Koch.

*Panonychus ulmi* Koch

This species is known as the Fruit Tree Red Spider or the European Red Mite (Fig. 4.7). It occurs throughout Europe and North America. It is found on many plants but is especially important as a pest of apples and plums. In appearance, the mite is minute and generally similar to related species. It is usually red in colour and bears heavy spines on the dorsum.

The life-cycle of the Fruit Tree Red Spider is distinct and serves as a difference in the species. It over-winters as an egg on the tree. The eggs are brick red in colour and, if numerous upon the tree, are so thickly placed, that the undersides of twigs and branches appear to have been smeared with red paint. The winter eggs remain unhatched until the following spring. Hatching begins in England about pink-bud on apples—about a month later than the eggs of aphids. The first stages possess three pairs of legs but in the 2nd and 3rd stages gain another pair. Adults of both sexes occur but the female is much more numerous than the male.

On reaching maturity, the females deposit summer eggs on the foliage usually on the underside of the leaves. These eggs are a paler red than the winter eggs and are deposited continuously during the season. In England, according to Colyer (1954) there are 5 generations before the winter eggs are laid. A female can in fact lay summer eggs and winter eggs at will.

The mites attack the foliage by .feeding on the cells, which they puncture and suck out the sap. If they are numerous, this causes the leaves to assume a bronzed appearance, eventually becoming brown and, at this stage, the tree may quickly defoliate (Colour Plate 4). Further, the failure of the leaves on the tree leads to the fruit being undersized and of poor colour. Apples, when heavily attacked, show the stalk cavity to be filled with red spider eggs.

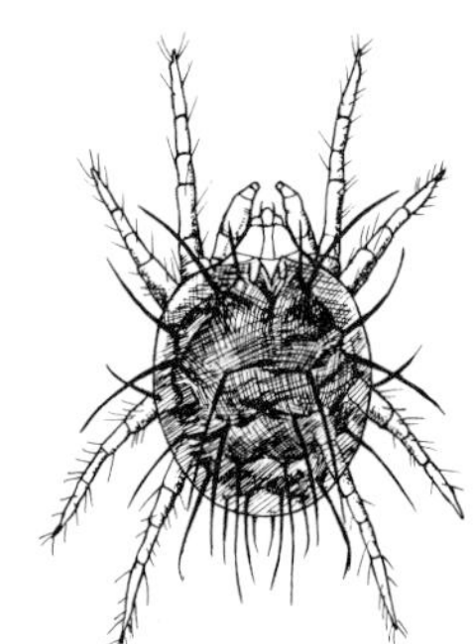

*Fig. 4.7.* Panonychus ulmi *(adult)*

*Tetranychus telarius* L.

This species is known as the Red Spider Mite and is probably identical with the Two-Spotted Mite, *T,. bimaculatus* Harvey in the U.S.A. and with *T. althaeae* v. Haust. and *T. urticae* Oud. ·in Europe (Fig. 4.8). The species is exceedingly common and is found on innumerable kinds of plants, including trees, shrubs, flowers, vegetables and weeds. It can be found in all countries with a moderate climate, warm in summer and mild in winter. In England, it is found both outdoors and under glass. It is the principal mite on cotton and occurs in the cotton-growing regions of South Africa, Spain, Italy, California and Australia. It is a severe pest of peaches, which suffer little from *Panonychus.*

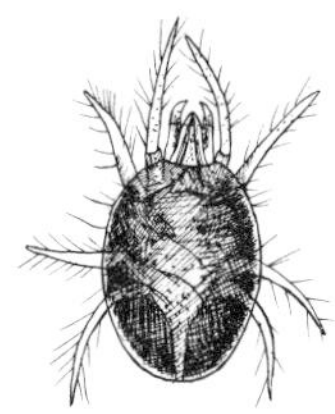

*Fig. 4.8.* Tetranychus telarius *(adult)*

*T. telarius* differs from *P. ulmi* in several respects. Primarily, it over-winters as a mite usually on weeds, often as a brick red female, as there is no winter egg. It is normally paler in colour than *P. ulmi* but can change according to its food. It carries dark markings on each side of the body and the spines are much thinner than those of *P. ulmi.* On apples, it behaves in a similar way to *P. ulmi* but usually passes through more generations and builds up a huge population in the course of a season. The fine web spun by *T. telarius* on all leaves attacked by it is also characteristic of the species.

*Bryobia spp.*

The species of *Bryobia* mites on fruit were formerly grouped under *B. praetiosa* Koch. This species has now been split up and *Bryobia* is now known variously as *B. rubrioculus* Scheut. on apples and pears in the United Kingdom, *B. arborea* M. & A. for the same species on apples and pears in the U.S.A., *B. praetiosa* Koch. on apples and

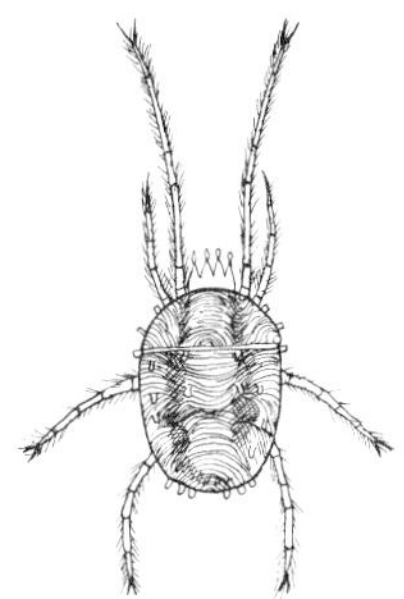

*Fig. 4.9.* Bryobia praetiosa *(adult)*

pears in South Africa and *B. ribis* Thomas on currant and gooseberry. Another species, also living on apples and pears as well as grasses and which also invades houses, is *B. graminum* Schr. *Bryobia* can become an important pest if it is allowed to build up large numbers, as it does on peaches and pears sometimes in South Africa.

*Bryobia* is distinguished from *Panonychus* and *Tetranychus* in its broad body which carries spoon-shaped bristles (Fig. 4.9). In colour, it is dull red and carries its first pair of legs, which are much longer than the others, out in front of the body. *Bryobia* overwinters as eggs, deposited on the trunk and main branches of the tree but they are larger than those of the other two species. There appear to be no males. Infestations usually die out in summer after causing similar injury to the tree as that of the other species. Attacked leaves are covered with brown spots of excreta.

METHODS OF CONTROL

*Pre-war situation.* Probably more effort has been applied to the control of the plant-feeding red spider mites on deciduous fruit in recent years than to any other pest problem. Certainly, since the advent of synthetic insecticides the problem has assumed even greater importance than ever before.

Formerly, the Fruit Tree Red Spider in the United Kingdom on apples and plums was kept in check by lime-sulphur, a fungicide applied against the disease apple scab *(Venturia inequalis)*. This method was partially successful but the control was greatly improved by the introduction of mineral oil sprays applied in the dormant season against the winter eggs. The oil sprays were of a semi-refined type and were used at 3% oil. They gave a very high degree of winter egg mortality and the combination of the two sprays, one in winter and the other in summer, gave a good control. The position was not entirely satisfactory as the red spider, with its enormous powers of reproduction, could build up during the season from a very small number of surviving winter eggs.

*Post-war situation.* The method of control in England changed dramatically for several reasons during the post-war period. The discovery of DDT and its use on fruit against caterpillars began to bring about an increase in the red spider populations on fruit trees. Growers were urged not to use DDT in the post-blossom period because the insecticide eliminated from the orchard the predatory insects which helped to keep the red spider in check. Fruit-growing itself had also changed in so far that growers were concentrating on growing varieties of apples which would store well, such as Cox's Orange Pippin and Worcester Pearmain, both highly susceptible to red spider injury. The problem, therefore, became more real than it had formerly appeared to be in the older type of mixed orchard.

Fruit-growers began to use an increasing number of sprays, brought about by the ease of application following the introduction of sprayers powered from the tractor and fully automatic in action. This led to a general improvement in orchard hygiene, with the complete elimination of competing pests such as aphids, capsids, leaf-feeding caterpillars and others. More fertilizers were used so that the trees became more vigorous and the leaves more succulent. It has been shown that leaves with a high nitrogen content lead to greater populations of red spider mites (Post, 1964.)

All these factors brought the problem of the Fruit Tree Red Spider into greater prominence. The introduction of parathion as a fruit-tree spray in 1950, gave the fruit grower his first opportunity of testing a really efficient acaricide. Early application of parathion at 0·01% applied twice gave remarkable kills of red spider. Parathion, being highly poisonous to man, was not liked by officials but shortly after its introduction, red spider resistance to parathion was reported from the U.S.A. and soon became common in other parts of the world. A new group of compounds called summer ovicides began to attract attention. The first of these was chlorfenson (CPCBS) reported in the U.S.A. during 1950 under the Code No. K.6451 (Barnes 1951). This compound was non-poisonous, non-insecticidal and killed, not only the summer eggs of the red spider, but also all active stages except the fully-grown adult. It proved remarkably effective and began to be used in various fruit-growing countries including South Africa, Australia, Canada and in England. Other compounds of this type were also under investigation (Kirby and Read, 1954) including diphenyl sulphone and fenson (CPBS) which proved phytotoxic on apples.

Unfortunately, the red spider mites developed resistance to this type of compound in the U.S.A. (Hoyt and Harries, 1961) and later in England (Collyer and Kirby, 1958). Other similar compounds were also introduced notably chlorocide (Brooks, 1957) and tetradifon (Tedion) a Dutch product but resistance to this group has now been reported from the U.S.A. Other compounds were also under examination for activity against the phosphate-resistant mites, notably dicofol (Kelthane) and Aramite which killed the active stages. Dicofol was also ovicidal.

The discovery of the systemic insecticides gave the fruit grower yet another chemical against the Fruit Tree Red Spider and many of these, such as methyl-demeton and dimethoate, are in use today.

The position regarding *Tetranychus telarius* is much the same although no winter sprays can be used against it as there is no winter egg and the opportunity to spray occurs only in spring and summer. *Bryobia* is very susceptible to lime sulphur and the adoption of organic fungicides in its place led to *Bryobia* appearing in enormous numbers. Fortunately, *Bryobia* is susceptible to acaricides, more so than the other species, and its control presents no problem.

*The parasite/predator complex and the effect of DDT.* DDT was not the first chemical thought to kill the insects feeding on the Fruit Tree Red Spider as Massee (1929) showed that tar oil winter wash reduced the predator *Anthocoris nemorum* L., a Cimicid bug feeding on the winter eggs of red spider but the effect of DDT was more pronounced due to the elimination of the principal red spider predator *Blepharidopterus angulatus* Fall. (Collyer, 1952). This insect was known as the Black-kneed Capsid, a name which had instant appeal to all fruit growers who attempted to preserve it in their orchards.

While there is little doubt that the introduction of DDT led to a build up of the red spider population in apple orchards other factors play a part (Clancy and McAlister, 1956). The predator theory fits the facts very well, particularly the fact that in unsprayed orchards, where there are abundant predators, the red spider population is at a low level. Predators alone cannot be relied upon to control red spider unaided and it is only in derelict orchards that predators keep the red spider in check (Clancy and Pollard, 1952). The predator status of different orchards is unknown and sprays must in any case be used against other pests, notably the Codling Moth. Unsprayed orchards frequently possess poor leaf and lack nutrition, factors tending to keep red spider at a low level. The grower uses sprays to improve the quality of his fruit and must accept red spider as part of the problem. Some observers suggest that DDT stimulates the reproduction (Davis, 1952).

The use of acaricides frequently leads to a build up of red spider, particularly parathion, which kills the predators but acaricides also preserve the leaf surface enabling the red spider to live longer into the autumn and deposit a large number of winter eggs. Where acaricides are omitted the leaf is destroyed by the mites and the population dies out prematurely and only a few winter eggs are laid.

Red spider predators have been investigated many times and some observers claim that the *Typhlodromid* mites have the greatest influence on the red spider population. These little mites are even smaller than the red spiders themselves and are extremely susceptible to sprays of all kinds, especially sulphur. Attempts have been made to employ the mildest fungicides and to eliminate all injurious sprays to preserve these mites and other beneficial insects. An attempt of this kind has been made in Nova Scotia (Pickett, 1960) where the orchards are small and scattered and there is a large reservoir of beneficial insects. It is unlikely that the average fruit grower will be able to make use of these ideas and he is more likely to rely on chemicals over which he has some control.

*Red Spider Resistance to Chemicals.* The phenomenon of insect resistance to chemicals is now well-known and has become prominent following the wide use of synthetic insecticides. The red spider mites have become among the most notorious as pests capable of developing resistance and the succession of chemicals introduced for their control during the 1950s has already been mentioned.

Resistance to parathion was reported in 1952 both in the U.S.A. and the United Kingdom after only three years of usage. Summer ovicides were first commercially used in 1954 and resistance to chlorfenson followed after five years of use. In the early 1960s, resistance to both dicofol and tetradifon was reported from the U.S.A. (Asquith, 1962) so that it appeared that mite resistance could develop to any chemical after a period of time. The nature of resistance is probably that of mutations, occurring in the very large numbers of forms which arise during a season, those possessing resistance quickly dominating the population. Even so, resistance is by no means wholesale in that it is often restricted to a few orchards.

Unfortunately, there are only a few chemical groups which are acaricidal and the wide use of organo-phosphates as fruit sprays against other pests quickly leads to mites becoming resistant to them. At present, the use of alternating fruit-spraying programmes with different chemicals year by year is about the only solution to the problem which can be advised.

REFERENCES

ASQUITH, D., *J. Econ. Entomol.*, **55,** 780 (1962)

BARNES, M. M., *J. Econ. Entomol.*, **44,** 672 (1951)

BROOKS, R. F., *J. Sci. Food Agr.*, **8,** 38 (1957)

CLANCY, D. W. and MCALISTER, H. J., *J. Econ. Entomol.*, **49,** 196 (1956)

CLANCY, D. W. and POLLARD, H. N., *J. Econ. Entomol*, **45,** 108 (1952)

COLLYER, E. and KIRBY, A. H. M., *Ann. Rep. East Malling Res. Sta.*, 131 (1958)

COLLYER, E., *J. Hort. Sci.*, **28,** 246 (1954)

COLLYER, E., *Ann. Rep. East Malling Res. Sta.*, 141 (1952)

DAVIS, D. W., *J. Econ. Entomol.*, **45,** 1011 (1952)

HOYT, S. C. and HARRIES, F. H., *J. Econ. Entomol.*, **54,** 12 (1961)

KIRBY, A. H. M. and READ, W. H., *J. Sci. Food Agr.*, **5,** 323 (1954)

MASSEE, A. M., *J. Min. Agr.*, **36,** 253 (1929)

PICKETT, A. D., *J. Econ. Entomol.*, **52,** 1103 (1960)

POST, A., *R.A.E.*, **52,** 326 (1964)

## DIPTERA

### *Ceratitis capitata* Wied. *(Trypetidae)*

This is the notorious Mediterranean Fruit Fly or Med Fly, an insect pest of the greatest importance on the deciduous and many other tropical and sub-tropical fruits, including wild varieties. It is one of several fruit-feeding flies but is the most destructive species on account of its distribution and wide range of fruits attacked. It occurs principally in those countries bordering the Mediterranean but is also found in Central and South Africa, Western Australia and the west coast of South America but is absent from India, the Far East and the U.S.A. It appeared in Flordia in 1929, where a campaign of eradication was started and concluded fourteen months later with the complete elimination of the fly.

The fruit suffering most loss is peach. Pears and apricots are also attacked but apples, while susceptible, are not heavily attacked. All citrus fruit is attacked but vines are grown too far north for the grapes to be an important host. In Hawaii, bananas are attacked. The Med Fly is said to have spread from Equatorial Africa, reaching Europe about 100 years ago. It prefers countries with a mild climate and where the winter has an average temperature of 50°F. Although the fly can occur in countries with a much colder winter than above, such as Spain, it remains quiescent for a much longer period. Where winter temperatures are above 60°F as in Florida, it becomes active much earlier in the year. The multiplication of the fly requires a succession of ripening fruits, such as loquats, peaches, pears and citrus on which it can breed as it only attacks ripe fruit. In hot countries, deciduous fruits are not so commonly grown and are replaced by citrus but here the development of the fly is restricted by the absence of suitable fruit before the citrus becomes ripe.

The Med Fly has enormous powers of multiplication. For a few days after emergence, it feeds on fruit juices and then the female inserts a batch of eggs beneath the surface of the fruit by means of a hard, pointed ovipositer. Many eggs are placed in each spot and each female is capable of depositing several hundred eggs. These are typical, being white and spindle shaped. They hatch in a few days and the larvae, which are headless and legless maggots, enter into the flesh of the fruit. Attacked fruit (Plate 4.5) often drops off and may be attacked by moulds at the oviposition punctures. The larvae are fully grown in about fourteen days and then drop into the soil for pupation. The winter is passed in the puparium or sometimes as hibernating adults. Many generations can occur in a season depending on the availability of ripe fruits and of a favourable temperature when 10–15 may occur in a season. The fly itself is slightly smaller than a house-fly but is easily distinguished by its colour which is predominantly yellow and brown with black markings and the wings carry black areas along the veins. At rest, the wings are held wide, not folded over the dorsum.

*Plate 4.5. Pear showing damage from larvae of fruit flies (Fruit and Food Technology Research Institute, Stellenbosch, South Africa)*

## METHODS OF CONTROL

The standard method of Fruit Fly control is by means of a poisoned bait. The origin of this method must be credited to C. W. Mally in South Africa who is said to have derived the idea from observing house-flies feeding on drops of water running down a window-pane (Whitnall, 1953). Mally's bait consisted of

arsenate of lead—4 oz
sugar —3 lb
water —5 gal

Mally first used this bait in 1904 and a similar bait was used in the eradication of the Med Fly from Florida in 1929. The method of baiting is to place the bait solution in glass containers in the trees. A mixture known as 'Clensel' was also widely used, based on bran which was allowed to ferment before adding the sugar and poison. Bottles, containing this mixture were hung in trees and known as 'Clensels', the bait mixture being replenished every week.

The next important step was the introduction of prepared baits using yeast which acts as the attractant similar to fermenting bran. This idea is due to Steiner (1952, 1955) who introduced the attractant called protein hydrolysate. Using this material, Steiner made up a bait as follows:

| | | |
|---|---|---|
| Malathion 25% w.p. | — | 2 lb |
| Protein hydrolysate | — | $\frac{1}{2}$ lb |
| Water | — | 150 gal |

This type of bait was applied weekly as a coarse spray to the trees, using about $\frac{1}{2}$ pt to the tree, during the ripening period of the fruit. Many baits of this type can be made up but those to which yeast or a similar material is added are the best (Myburgh, 1957). Various insecticides can be used as the poison. Parathion is too dangerous and children have been known to eat the bait in bottles for the sugar it contained and malathion is obviously safer. Lead arsenate has been entirely dropped being too slow in action. The poison must give a rapid knock down so that flies, feeding on the droplets of bait, are killed before they become satiated and leave to begin oviposition.

Attempts have been made to use cover sprays to leave a residue of toxic insecticide over the tree. DDT, BHC, parathion and later dieldrin were all tried with varying success but treatment must embrace a wide area to be successful and high rates of insecticide are necessary. Lebaycid, a new, long lasting insecticide, has proved very effective on peaches in South Africa where two sprays at 0·025% gave effective control and persisted for several weeks (Steiner and Hinman, 1952; Myburgh, 1961).

REFERENCES

MYBURGH, A. C., *S. African J. Agr. Sci.*, **4**, 615 (1961)
MYBURGH, A. C., *J. Entomol. Soc. S. Africa*, **24**, 345 (1957)
STEINER, L. F., *J. Econ. Entomol.*, **45**, 838 (1952)
STEINER, L. F., *Proc. Hawaii Entomol. Soc.*, **15**, 601 (1955)
STEINER, L. F. and HINMAN, F. G., *J. Econ. Ent.*, **45**, 388 (1952)
WHITNALL, A. B. M., *J. Entomol. Soc. S. Africa*, **16**, 230 (1953)

## APPLE AND PEAR DISEASES

### Apple Scab (*Venturia inaequalis* [Cooke] Wint.) and Pear Scab (*Venturia pirina* Aderh.)

Apple scab and pear scab are closely related fungi and from the fruit-grower's viewpoint behave in a similar way. They occur wherever these fruits are grown. Owing to the larger size of the apple industry, much more attention has been paid to apple scab than to pear scab and most of this section is therefore devoted to apple scab. The basic facts of the life history of this fungus and the principles underlying its control will be found in an article by Moore (1939).

*Plate 4.6. Apple scab on fruit and foliage (A Plant Protection photograph)*

The apple scab fungus damages the tree in many ways, most of them obvious, a few more obscure. The fungus attack on the fruit is easily seen, particularly in the later stages. The young infections appear as slightly irregular small black spots. As the fungus develops, the central area dies out leaving a light brown corky area in the centre with a blackish margin where the fungus is still active (Plate 4.6). The infected area of the apple does not grow as rapidly as the healthy part with the result that diseased apples are lop-sided and the scabbed area cracked. Not only does the apple scab make the fruit unsightly, but scabbed apples are liable to rot from the entry of other fungi, and also to shrivel during storage due to increased moisture loss.

In addition to attacking the fruit, the fungus also lives on the leaves and shoots. The early stages of the growth of the fungus on the leaf are difficult to see as the spot is small and olive green in colour, but as it gets older, it gets bigger in size and darker in colour and is only too obvious. Severe scab infection of the leaves causes premature leaf drop with the consequence of reduced fruit size and possibly a smaller crop in the succeeding year.

On the shoot the fungus forms pustules which erupt through the rind. The fungus pad on the shoot remains alive during the winter, but is gradually sloughed off during the following summer leaving corky scars in its place. Shoot infection is serious as a source of infection in spring and wounds provide suitable sites in which cankers can develop, eventually killing the shoot.

The less obvious damage occurs when the fungus attacks the young fruitlets. Careful investigation has shown that such attacks severely reduce the amount of fruit which sets, thereby causing a serious reduction in yield of fruit. Owing to the variety of ways in which the apple scab fungus damages the tree and the severity of the attacks, apple scab has long been regarded as the most serious disease of apples.

The life history of the apple scab fungus (Fig. 4.10) had been worked out by 1897 (Large, 1940). It had been shown that the fungus overwinters in two ways, the sexual stage on the dead scabbed leaves, and vegetatively in the pustules on the young shoots. The phase on the dead leaves is particularly interesting as the fungus forms many small perithecia (a) about the size of a pinhead, which contain numerous small sacs called asci (b). The ascospores (winter spores) (c) develop inside these sacs and are ejected into the air during the spring. The fungus gun shoots the spores about one centimetre into the air and those that are caught by air currents float away.

The pustules on the wood produce spores of a different type, conidia (summer spores) (d) which are mainly water-borne. These are released from the fungus pad only when it is wet, and are then splashed around by rain and wind.

It will be apparent from their different methods of dissemination that the winter spores can cause very widespread infection throughout an orchard, whereas the summer spores are localized in their effects. Furthermore, the winter spore discharge lasts for about 10 weeks, whereas summer spores are produced throughout the growing season. Both types of spore germinate under moist conditions on either leaves or fruitlets, giving rise to the vegetative phase of the fungus. The developing fungus becomes visible in about 10 days producing the scab spots previously described. The fungus soon starts to produce summer spores, which under favourable conditions quickly build up a serious attack.

At the end of the season, the fungus on the shoots becomes dormant, while on the dead leaves it forms the perithecia previously described.

Inadequate scab control in the Wisbech area during the early 1950s led to a thorough study of certain details of its life history which bore directly on the incidence in the orchard. The conditions under which the spores are ejected from the dead leaves, the number of spores present in the atmosphere of various orchards, and the conditions necessary for spore germination have been investigated in great detail (Hirst *et al.*, 1961

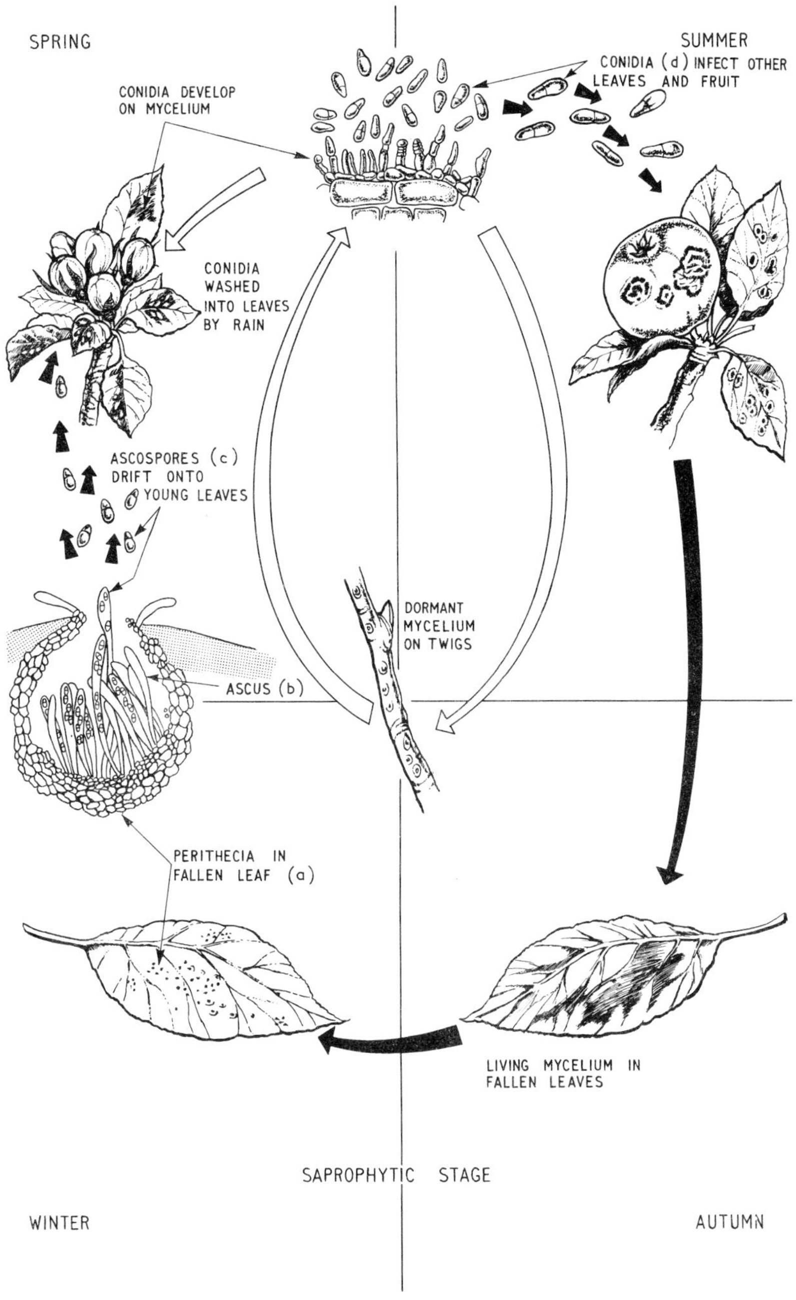


*Fig. 4.10. Life Cycle of Apple Scab. (a) Perithecia, (b) Ascus, (c) Ascospores, (d) Conidia*

and 1962), while foliage infection in relation to wet and dry periods has been studied at East Malling (Moore, 1964).

It is now known that the infected dead leaves must be wetted by rain for large ascospore flights to take place; dew results in the release of relatively few spores into the air. The spore content of the air has been measured by means of an ingenious spore trap (Plate 4·7) which sucks in air and passes it over a sticky glass plate to which the spores adhere. Subsequently, the spores are counted, and the numbers are assessed in relation to rainfall and temperature. Great variation in the numbers of spores was observed, varying from a negligible amount in the cleanest orchard to as many as 4,000 per cubic metre per hour in the most heavily infected. As might be expected, the variation in spore count was related to the quantity of dead leaves present in the orchard and their degree of infection.

It was also found that the quantity of dead leaves surviving the winter was related to the number of earthworms in the soil, the larger the earthworm population, the smaller the amount of leaves. It was a surprising discovery that earthworms can play a part in keeping down apple scab.

*Plate 4.7. Spore trap in an orchard (Rothamsted Experimental Station)*

## METHODS OF CONTROL

The first spray trials with Bordeaux Mixture to control this disease were carried out in the U.S.A. in 1891. By 1895 American orchardists were being recommended to put on four sprays, at bud burst, pink bud, petal fall and fruitlet. There were snags as certain varieties of apple were russeted by the spray, but those which were tolerant of copper were scab-free; a great advance in the art of fruit-growing. However, there was an obvious need of another fungicide to use on the copper-sensitive varieties. This milder fungicide was discovered in the U.S.A. in 1907 and was made by reacting sulphur with quicklime. It was tested more fully during the next three years and was found to be very effective for scab control, particularly on the varieties which were damaged by copper, and also on those which were not. The new technique was followed in England where it began to be used in 1911.

The use of four sprays per season was only effective when very persistent fungicides such as Bordeaux Misture were used. With the introduction of lime-sulphur, more frequent spraying was necessary, and growers were advised to time their sprays according to the stage of development of a tree. A typical lime-sulphur programme would be 3% at bud burst, 2% at green cluster and pink bud, 1% at petal fall and fruitlet, and one or two succeeding sprays at ¾%, a total of six to seven sprays.

The gradual replacement of Bordeaux Mixture by lime-sulphur was mainly due to the reduced risk of damage. The search for even less phytotoxic compounds was continued and was eventually rewarded by the discovery of various organic compounds which were as effective as copper, but which did no damage to the tree.

The progress made and the many contributors to it is illustrated in Table 4.1.

**Table 4.1.** ORGANIC FUNGICIDES USED FOR APPLE SCAB CONTROL

| *Fungicide* | *Date of Introduction* | *Original Developer* |
|---|---|---|
| Thiram | 1931 | E.I. Du Pont de Nemours & Co., U.S.A. |
| DRB (Nirit) | 1942 | Farbwerke Hoechst A.G., Germany |
| Zineb | 1943 | Rohm & Haas Co., U.S.A. |
| Dichlone | 1943 | U.S. Rubber Co., U.S.A. |
| Ziram | 1943 | E.I. Du Pont de Nemours & Co., U.S.A. |
| Phenyl mercury compounds | 1945 | Numerous developments after experiments at the East Malling Research Station, United Kingdom |
| Glyodin | 1946 | Union Carbide Chemical Co., U.S.A. |
| Captan | 1949 | Standard Oil Development Co., U.S.A. |
| Dodine | 1956 | American Cyanamid Co., U.S.A. |
| Dithianon | 1961 | E. Merck A.G., Germany |

These compounds have varied in popularity in different parts of the world, but the most successful of them all has undoubtedly been captan. In Holland a powerful fungicide such as DRB (Nirit) or a phenyl mercury compound or dodine is used pre-blossom followed by captan or thiram post-blossom. In Italy zineb is the preferred fungicide, probably due to its manufacture on a very large scale for use on vines. In the U.S.A., where the majority of these new compounds were discovered, captan has to share the market with its numerous competitors.

Prior to about 1950 the spray programmes for apple scab control were intended to maintain a fungicide film on the surface of the foliage and fruit to kill alighting spores before infection took place. To do this efficiently required spraying at regular intervals not exceeding 14 days, a difficult schedule to achieve when hand-spraying was the only method of application. Protectant spraying has been simplified by the introduction of the improved machinery described below and by the use of the new organic fungicides which can safely be applied more frequently as they are normally harmless to the foliage and fruit skin.

The discovery that the organo-mercury fungicides could kill scab infections up to five days old led to a new approach to scab control. Sprays could be put on after a scab infection period to kill the fungus which was already present in the leaf. This new technique had the merit that the application was made at the time when it would be most effective and also of sometimes permitting a small reduction in the average number of sprays required, especially in dry seasons. Its limitation was that some varieties of apples were too sensitive to allow the use of mercury on them. It is now known that some other fungicides, such as dodine and captan, also have limited 'curative' properties, so that growers can combine the protective and 'curative' methods when desirable.

Although scab control has been based from the beginning on breaking the life cycle in the spring at the ascospore stage, research workers have been aware of another possible approach, namely the killing of the fungus on the dead leaves, and hence the prevention of spore discharge in the spring. Attempts to do this were made by spraying DNOC on to the floor of the orchard. Perithecia formation was inhibited on the leaves which were hit by the spray, but the technique was not used commercially on account of the number of leaves that escaped the spray and the cost of the materials. Hutton (Anon., 1956) in New South Wales, made a notable advance by spraying the foliage with high concentrations of phenyl mercury chloride as soon as possible after the fruit had been picked, when the leaves are all accessible. In one trial carried out in an isolated orchard, the results were remarkable, one autumn spray in 1955 cut down the overwintering inoculum to such low levels that no spring or summer scab sprays were necessary. At the end of the season a very small number of scab spots were found on the leaves so that it was necessary to use the 0·05% PMC autumn spray.

It is now clear that scab control with one autumn spray is possible only with isolated orchards, but this new approach will undoubtedly assist growers even in the most densely planted areas by reducing the inoculum and thus making scab control easier and more effective in the spring.

The chronicle of the advances in fungicides can also be paralleled in the machinery world, where the spraying machines have advanced from mobile hand-operated pumps to mechanical pumps, and finally to automatic sprayers with powerful fans which blow the spray through the tree (Colour Plate 5). Improved spraying methods have facilitated an increase in the number of sprays applied. Starting from the original four rounds, the typical anti-scab programme now requires 6 to 8 sprays per season, but in areas where the scab attack is intense, as in northern Italy, it may be as many as 20.

It will thus be seen that the status of apple scab has changed during the last seventy years from a scourge to a minor, but nevertheless, ever-present threat. The advance in the knowledge of the disease, improved fungicides and spraying machines make it readily controllable, and its presence is a signal that better management is called for.

REFERENCES

Anon., *Agr. Gaz. N.S. Wales,* **67,** 425 (1956)

HIRST, J. M. and STEDMAN, O. J., *Ann. Appl. Biol.,* **49,** 290 (1961)

HIRST, J. M. and STEDMAN, O. J., *Ann. Appl. Biol.,* **50,** 525, 551 (1962)

LARGE, E. C., *The Advance of the Fungi,* 288, Jonathan Cape, London (1940)

MOORE, M. H., *Ann. Rep. East Malling Res. Sta. 1938,* 265 (1939)

MOORE, M. H., *Ann. Appl. Biol.,* **53,** 423 (1964)

## Apple Mildew (*Podosphaera leucotricha* [Ell. and Everh.] Salm.)

The conquest of apple scab opens the field to other contenders for the doubtful honour of being the most important disease of apples. Most fruit-growers would agree that apple mildew is now at the head of the list.

Apple mildew is a typical powdery mildew and gives the affected parts a floury white appearance (Plate 4.8). It is first seen in the spring on flower trusses, on the leaves growing from terminal buds and less frequently on the lateral leaves of one-year old shoots. The presence of the fungus makes the flowers pallid and the leaves are somewhat strap-shaped. During the summer the disease spreads to some of the young foliage and shoots.

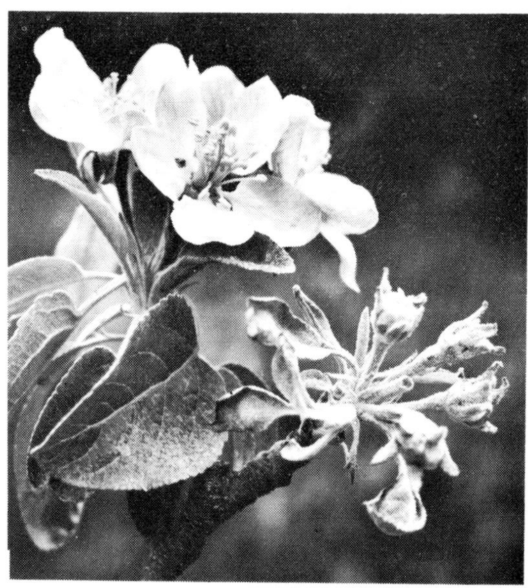

*Plate 4.8. Apple mildew, healthy flower truss on left, infected on the right (A Plant Protection photograph)*

The main damage done by the fungus is the injury to the shoots, which makes them useless. The attacked shoots, which have a grey-silvery appearance during the winter, have to be cut out during pruning, thus reducing tree size and also sometimes making it difficult to shape the tree. The injury to the leaves must reduce their efficiency and in severe attacks the fungus may grow on the skin of the fruit causing russeting.

The fungus is found wherever apples are grown. It flourishes in a dry climate and is liable to be particularly troublesome where apples are grown under irrigation. The fungus overwinters in infected flower and leaf buds and can only survive on living tissue, but it does not persist on the mildewed shoots because the exposed mycelium on the outside dies during the winter.

In the spring the infected tissues form the primary phase of the disease. At this time the fungus covers both surfaces of the diseased leaves, a sign that the growing point was infected. The white appearance associated with apple mildew is due to the presence of a thin superficial felt on the surface and the quantities of conidia which are borne in chains (Fig. 4.11). The conidia are blown about by the wind, and in suitable conditions start up fresh infections on the new growth, thus initiating the secondary phase. The secondary infection usually takes place on the underside of the leaf and often causes slight crinkling, and upturning of the margin, which may become discoloured, an obvious symptom. The susceptibility of the foliage is related to its age, the resistance increasing as it gets older.

Apple mildew was not generally serious when lime-sulphur was the main scab fungicide but it began to build up from 1954 onwards for reasons which are discussed below. The changed status of the disease has been responsible for a very thorough re-examination of the life history of the fungus and a search for improved methods of control (Aerts *et al.*, 1957).

The conditions governing the germination of the spores have been investigated. This can best be studied by placing the spores on an apple leaf as they do not readily germinate

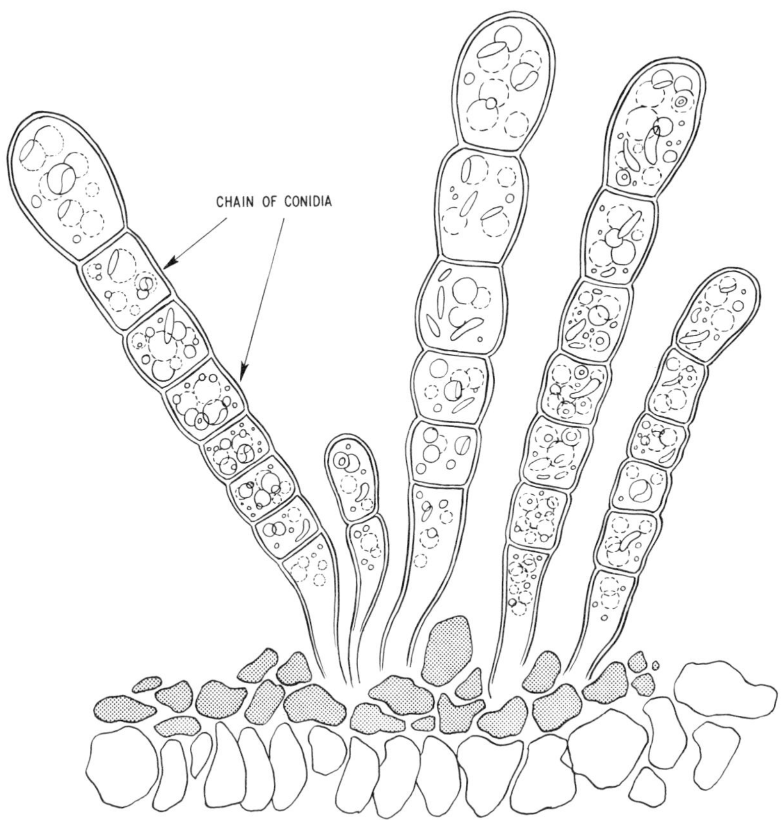


*Fig. 4.11. Apple Mildew. Formation of conidia*

on a glass slide. Their germination is controlled by two factors, temperature and humidity. The higher the humidity the better the germination, but the presence of a water film is limiting. It is now known that some germination of the spores can take place even at quite low temperatures, the optimum is 20°C and 33°C is lethal.

The concentration of mildew spores in the air has been measured at East Malling by the Hirst spore trap. No spores were caught until the pink bud stage was reached and the maximum output of spores occurred in June with minor peaks in July and August. There was also evidence that the peak of secondary infections was reached about 14 days after the maximum spore release.

The way in which apple mildew survives from one season to the next has already been briefly mentioned. The fungus penetrates the buds by means of hyphae which grow down the leaf petioles and get inside them before the scales become tightly shut. It is thought that direct conidial infection also takes place. The flower buds appear to be susceptible for about one month, but for the terminal buds on the extension shoots it is about two months, which may be the reason for their frequent infection.

Various suggestions have been put forward in explanation of the increased severity of apple mildew attacks from 1954 onwards. The change was probably due chiefly to the replacement of lime-sulphur by organic fungicides, particularly captan. This fungicide is specific for apple scab and does not control apple mildew which multiplied unchecked until it was realised what had happened. Changes in pruning techniques are also thought to have been partly responsible.

## METHODS OF CONTROL

Apple mildew has proved to be a difficult disease to control, particularly on susceptible varieties such as Jonathan and Cox's Orange Pippin. Two factors appear to contribute to this, the high susceptibility of the young leaves and the enormous spore production. Both factors make it difficult to protect the young foliage because new leaves are constantly growing and the abundance of spores ensures that some reach the leaves.

In controlling apple mildew there are two objectives, to check the build-up of secondary infections and to keep the buds healthy. This is difficult but experience has shown that particular attention to mildew control in the month following petal fall reduces flower bud infection and hence reduces the amount of inoculum produced in the succeeding spring.

Sulphur has long been known as an efficient fungicide for the control of the powdery mildews. Thus the spray programmes which used lime-sulphur against apple scab also kept apple mildew down. It has already been mentioned that the introduction of the organic fungicides allowed mildew to flourish, but in spite of this growers continued to use them in preference to lime-sulphur because they gave marked increases in yield and enhanced fruit finish. The first step was to use milder forms of sulphur, such as the dispersible formulations, but these are sometimes unsatisfactory on sensitive varieties such as Cox's Orange Pippin. There was therefore a real need for another milder fungicide, a want which was met by dinocap.

Initially, the 25% dinocap formulation was used at a concentration of 1 lb per 100 gal of water applied at fortnightly intervals. This gave fair control, but gradually it was realised that so long an interval between sprays did not protect the new young leaves. Much better control has been obtained by spraying at weekly intervals with half the standard strength, particularly when maximum protection is needed (Moore *et al.*, 1964).

The search for better anti-mildew fungicides has been pursued by many spray chemical manufacturers. This has resulted in the introduction of binapacryl, and others are on trial. They are welcome additions to the fruit-grower's armoury against mildew.

It is of interest that all the fungicides mentioned as active against apple mildew also have some acaricidal properties. Sulphur, except at high temperatures, does not have much effect, but dinocap is of real assistance in keeping red spider down. Binapacryl is a good acaricide and obviates the need for specific red spider control measures.

The build-up in apple mildew also coincided with intense interest in techniques for reducing the volume of spray required per acre, generally described as low volume spraying. With this technique the quantity of wash is reduced to 50 gal, or as low as 20 gal per acre. It is now generally accepted that the lower volumes are adequate for mild mildew attacks, but volumes of 100 gal or more per acre are advisable when the attack is heavy. If weekly spraying is being done, there does not seem to be the same necessity to use high volume sprays.

At the height of the mildew attacks, fruit-growers were forced to use every possible way of overcoming the disease, and attention was paid to ways of reducing the amount of inoculum in the spring. This was mainly done by cutting out the mildewed trusses and shoots from pink bud onwards; or where this was not possible on account of the size of the tree, spraying during the dormant season with a DNOC-petroleum oil at a concentration of 0·1% DNOC (Moore *et al.*, 1962). Both measures are expensive and were helpful at a time of crisis, but now that the more skilful use of the mildew fungicides has checked the disease the supplementary treatments are not as vital as they were.

REFERENCES

AERTS, R. and SOENEN, A., *Hoefchen Briefe,* **10,** 109 (1957)

MOORE, M. H., BENNETT, M. and BURCHILL, R. T., *Ann. Rep. East Malling Res. Sta. 1961,* 97 (1962)

MOORE, M. H., KIRBY, A. H. M. and BENNETT, M., *Ann. Rep. East Malling Res. Sta. 1963,* 123 (1964)

## Apple Canker (*Nectria galligena* Bres.)

While apple canker does not qualify as a major apple disease, it is very widely distributed and is most troublesome in the wetter fruit-growing areas. The fungus is a wood parasite and damages trees by killing both young shoots and older branches. The fungus is mainly spread by conidia which are produced in enormous numbers in pustules, present on the cankers, and by ascospores in autumn and winter.

The conidia, which are water-borne, can infect older branches, particularly in the crotch, but leaf scars are the main sites of entry. The scars are most susceptible for about one hour after the leaves have fallen, as at this time, the spores can be sucked inside the vessels, a site which provides ideal conditions for germination. The bud-scale scars can also be infected but are less important than the leaf scars. The autumn is thus the main period of infection (Crowdy, 1952).

### METHODS OF CONTROL

Once apple canker becomes well established in an orchard, it is difficult to control. It is therefore most important to deal with it as soon as it appears. Infected shoots must be cut out, while cankers on branches must be cleaned and treated with organo-mercury fungicides. Should the disease show signs of getting out of hand, it may be necessary to put on both autumn and spring sprays of Bordeaux Mixture, or other copper fungicides (Moore, 1960). Spraying by itself is unlikely to control the disease completely, and the first step must be individual treatment of the established cankers.

## Bitter Rot (*Pezicula alba* Guthrie [syn. *Gloeosporium album* Osterw.]) Perennial Canker and Fruit Rot (*Pezicula malicorticis* [Jacks] Nannf. [syn. *Gloeosporium perennans* Zeller and Childs])

The two diseases, bitter rot and perennial canker, better known to fruit-growers as *Gloeosporium,* have caused serious losses of fruit in storage in recent years. The responsible fungi normally live on dead wood in the tree such as old spurs and pruning stubs (Corke, 1959), but the spores can also infect the fruit. An unusual feature is that the fruit infection takes place during the growing season and remains latent until the fruit begins to ripen. The fruit is thus apparently sound when put into store, but when taken out four months later, losses as high as 50% have been recorded. The disease is difficult to control, but tree hygiene, coupled with later summer protective captan sprays, have helped to keep the disease within bounds (Hamer, 1962).

### Fire-Blight Disease (*Erwinia amylovora* [Burrill] Winslow *et al.*)

A bacterial disease is a serious problem for apple and pear growers throughout the U.S.A. Although known as fire-blight disease of pear, the casual organism can also attack apples. The disease was found in New Zealand in 1919 and in England for the first time in 1958.

The bacteria overwinter in cankers on the branches and in the spring appear on the surface in droplets. They are carried to the flowers which are the main entry points by insects and by rain. The bacteria multiply rapidly and spread down the spur into the branch, killing the invaded parts as they travel down the branch during the summer. In the early stages the typical symptoms are scattered dead spurs and small shoots, but during the summer, whole branches can be seen with brown dead leaves.

#### METHODS OF CONTROL

In the U.S.A. there are two essential steps to control the disease, the cutting out of cankers, followed by three weak Bordeaux Mixture sprays at seven-day intervals during the blossom period. The antibiotic streptomycin has also been used, but it is only effective when the temperatures exceed 70°F. Fortunately for English fruit-growers, only one variety of pear, Laxton's Superb, has proved to be particularly susceptible, and the official policy of destroying all infected trees has minimised its spread (Crosse *et al.*, 1959).

### Brown Rot (*Sclerotinia fructigena* Aderh. and Ruhl)

To the older generation of fruit-growers, brown rot was a source of annual loss. The fungus is a wound parasite and enters fruits whose skin has been broken by hail, birds, apple scab, or insects. The great advances which have been made in controlling fruit-eating larvae, particularly codling moth and tortricids, and the improvements in the control of apple scab have practically banished brown rot from the orchard.

#### VIRUS DISEASES

The virus diseases of apples and pears have been intensively studied during the past fifteen years, and no less than twenty have been identified in apples, and nine in pears. With one exception they all appear to be propagated by man, so the use of virus-free scions and rootstocks will do much to keep this serious potential threat out of the world's orchards of the future (Posnette, 1963).

REFERENCES

CORKE, A. T. K., *J. Hort. Sci.*, **34,** 85 (1959)

CROSSE, J. E., BENNETT, M. and GARRETT, C. M. E., *Ann. Rep. East Malling Res. Sta. 1958*, 151 (1959)

CROWDY, S. H., *Ann. Appl. Biol.*, **39,** 569 (1952)

HAMER, P. S., *Grower*, **58,** 734, 738, 782 (1962)

MOORE, M. H. and BENNETT, M., *Ann. Rep. East Malling Res. Sta. 1959*, 85 (1960)

POSNETTE, A. F., *Virus Diseases of Apples and Pears*, Commonwealth Agricultural Bureaux, Farnham Royal (1963)

### Leaf Curl (*Taphrina deformans* [Berk.] Tul.)

Leaf curl is a very easily recognisable disease of peaches, and, if present, can be seen soon after the young foliage has expanded. The disease usually attacks the whole leaf, but sometimes only part of it is affected, causing it at first to turn pale green with a velvety bloom on the upper surface. The fungus also causes the leaf to thicken, and as the upper surface becomes slightly more enlarged than

*Plate 4.9. Peach leaf curl (A Shell photograph)*

the lower one, the leaf puckers (Plate 4.9). The diseased leaves soon change colour, turning red or purplish-red and finally brown, before falling off some months later. More rarely the fungus attacks the young shoots and it can also affect the blossoms and fruit.

Light attacks have little effect on the crop, but severe ones causing defoliation not only reduce the crop during the current season, but also lower the vigour in the following year. A survey in the U.S.A. showed that failure to control the disease was responsible for annual losses of about 15% of the crop.

The leaf-curl fungus has accompanied the peach tree on its migrations to different parts of the world, but its incidence is closely related to the weather at the time when the leaves are emerging from the bud. If the weather is dry as in the irrigated areas of southern California, the disease is rarely seen; in the typical commercial peach-growing areas of the world, the disease is moderate, but in places such as England when there is a mild, wet spring, it can be very severe.

Although the general life-cycle of the fungus is well-known, some of the details of the overwintering phase are uncertain (Caporali, 1964). The dispersal of the fungus is ensured by the abundant production on the infected leaves of ascospores which are borne on air currents through the orchards. Some of these spores lodge on the branches and shoots and appear to initiate a vegetative phase which is followed by the formation of thick-walled spores before the coldest part of the winter. In the spring these hibernating spores give rise to new conidia which may be re-distributed by rain and some may land on to the opening leaf buds. These spores germinate and infect the young leaves under moist conditions. The fungus then proliferates inside the leaf and quickly reaches the reproductive stage forming an hymenium below the cuticle. The development of the hymenium soon causes the cuticle to rupture exposing the layer of asci from which the ascospores are discharged. The presence of the layer of asci gives the surface a whitish bloom, previously mentioned in the description of the symptoms.

### METHODS OF CONTROL

The principle on which control is based is to kill the spores by applying a fungicide before infection has taken place. This is essential because once the fungus has penetrated the leaves, it cannot be eradicated. To be effective the sprays must be put on in good time, in some cases both an autumn and a spring spray are used, but in most areas a single spray in the spring before bud movement begins is sufficient.

The leaf curl spores can be killed by many different fungicides. The older fungicides based on copper and sulphur in the form of lime-sulphur are those most commonly used but some of the dithiocarbamates are claimed as being even more effective. Trials in France have shown that ziram with thiram in second place both gave better control than a copper fungicide. The organic fungicides were used at the rate of 2 lb per 100 gal, the copper fungicide at 5 lb (Debeau, 1960). In the U.S.A., ferbam is one of the recommended fungicides for leaf curl control (Anon., 1962).

A variety of spray programmes are used in the different peach-growing areas of the world. On the Atlantic side of the U.S.A. two applications are advised, the first in the autumn after leaf drop and the second in the spring before bud swell. The fungicide can be either ferbam at 1¾ lb per 100 gal, or Bordeaux Mixture at 10–10–100 for the first spray followed by a weaker one at 6–6–100 in the spring.

In Australia, excellent control is obtained with a single Bordeaux Mixture spray at a concentration of 10–10–100 plus ½ gal of white oil. Copper oxychloride at 5 lb per 100 gal, together with the white oil, is also effective. Good control can also be obtained with a 5% lime-sulphur spray, but its use involves the risk of bud injury to some of the early varieties (Anon., 1956). Lime-sulphur is the preferred fungicide in South Africa as it is less expensive than products based on copper. Peach growers in France may put on as many as three fungicidal applications. The first at leaf fall can be either thiram or ziram, the second in January using copper oxychloride, and the third in February or March with a choice of thiram or ziram (Sopra, 1965).

REFERENCES

Anon., *Agr. Gaz. N.S. Wales,* **67,** 649 (1956)

Anon., *New York State Insecticide and Fungicide Conference 1962,* Cornell University, New York (1962)

CAPORALI, L., *Rev. Appl. Mycol.,* **43,** 591 (1964)

DEBEAU, M., *Phytoma,* **114,** 19 (1960)

Sopra, Personal communication (1965)

### Brown Rot (*Schlerotinia fructicola* [Wint.] Rehm., *S. Laxa* Aderh. and Ruhl. and *S. fructigena* Aderh. and Ruhl.)

As peaches reach the ripening stage, another risk faces the grower, the rotting of the fruit due to the brown rot fungi. As the name indicates, the fruit turns brown and shortly afterwards the small powdery cushions bearing the spores appear on the surface of the fruit. The mycologist recognises three distinct species of *Sclerotinia* as being responsible. The most damaging is *S. fructicola* which is the dominant species in North America, Australia and New Zealand. *S. laxa* occurs in Europe but is uncommon in North America. The third species *S. fructigena* is only found in Europe.

The losses due to brown rot vary with the season. When the weather is wet, orchard losses may be as high as 50% to 75% with the remainder of the fruit often rotting before it gets to market. Such devastating losses have pointed to the need for a thorough investigation of the life history of the fungus and for ways of checking it. Although the three species of *Sclerotinia* possess somewhat similar life cycles, the description which follows deals with *S. fructicola* as it is the destructive species in North America and Australia.

The fungus is capable of surviving from one season to the next in two main ways, either in mummified fruit, or in wood cankers. The mummified fruit may persist on the tree in which case they produce conidia in the spring, or if they fall on the ground, apothecia are formed which discharge ascospores in the spring. The wood cankers are also a source of conidia. The first phase of infection takes place during blossom time, when the flowers are liable to be attacked in wet weather. If they succumb, the fungus may penetrate into the spur on which the flower was borne, and form a canker which can produce spores during the summer. There are thus a number of sources of inoculum which are responsible for the second phase, the invasion of the fruit as it begins to ripen.

*S. fructicola* is mainly a wound parasite as it usually enters the peach through a break in the skin. Mechanical injury such as twig punctures or hail damage provide suitable sites for fungal entry, but insect damage is usually more important. In the U.S.A., plum curculio *(Conotrachelus nenuphar)* and oriental fruit moth *(Laspeyresia molesta)* are the most important insects damaging the skin. In Australia the main insects concerned are the oriental fruit moth and light brown apple moth *(Tortrix postvittana)*.

When the weather is very favourable to the fungus, it is probable that it can attack sound fruit, thus leading to the almost complete loss of the crop.

### METHODS OF CONTROL

From the description which has been given, there are certain obvious steps which must be taken to keep the fungus at bay, namely orchard hygiene, and insecticidal and fungicidal spray programmes. The inoculum must be kept down by cutting out brown rot cankers after the fruit has been picked, and by the removal of all mummified fruit. Insecticides must be used to kill those insects which can damage the skin, while the fungicides are required to protect the blossoms, and later the fruit, from fungal attack.

In the U.S.A., captan at $2\frac{1}{2}$ lb or dichlone at 10 oz per 100 gal is used pre-blossom. Post-blossom, the choice lies between captan or thiram at $2\frac{1}{2}$ lb, or wettable sulphur at 6 lb per 100 gal. About five post-blossom sprays are advised, at cot split, cot fall, 7–10 days later, and then an interval until two weeks before picking, with the last spray just before the fruit is harvested (Anon., 1962).

In Australia the spray programme follows a similar pattern, starting with Bordeaux Mixture at 10–10–100 plus $\frac{1}{2}$ gal of white oil per 100 gal applied when the flower buds are pink. The effective post-blossom fungicides are thiram, ziram, captan and dispersible sulphur used at their standard concentrations. Four to five sprays are necessary, at petal fall, at cot fall, followed by two or three pre-harvest sprays as required (Hutton *et al.*, 1960).

REFERENCES

Anon., *New York State Insecticide and Fungicide Conference 1962*, Cornell University, New York (1962)

HUTTON, K. E. and KABLE, P. F., *Agr. Gaz. N.S. Wales*, **71**, 236 (1960)

## MISCELLANEOUS PEACH DISEASES

### Peach Yellows

The peach tree and its fruit are liable to be attacked by many other disease organisms, but two of them call for mention—peach yellows and peach mildrew.

Peach yellows is the name given to a disease which was recognised in the Delaware Valley as early as 1791. Its importance is due to the fact that it is a lethal disease causing the rapid decline and death of the tree. It was named, however, from the yellowing of the foliage on the infected shoots. Other symptoms are premature ripening of the fruit with which is associated abnormally bright colouring, and the production of willowy bunches of shoots, especially near the crutch.

Peach yellows is of particular interest to plant pathologists on account of the pioneer work on it which was undertaken by Erwin F. Smith of the U.S. Department of Agriculture. His investigations from 1888–95 showed that the disease was not caused by either a fungus or bacterium. He discovered that a bud from a peach yellows tree grafted on to a healthy one transmitted the disease. Erwin Smith recognised that he was dealing with a new kind of casual agent and called it a contagium, but it was not long before it was classified as a virus. It is also worth recording that Erwin Smith suspected that the peach yellows might also be transmitted by an insect, a suspicion which was not confirmed until 1933 when it was shown that the plum leaf hopper *(Macropsis trimaculata)* was a vector.

It is now known that plum trees, both wild and cultivated, can be symptomless carriers of the peach yellows virus. The plum leaf hopper, as the name indicates, feeds on plum foliage and should it migrate to a peach orchard, can carry the virus with it. It has thus taken many years to unravel the story of peach yellows, to track down the indigenous plum trees as the original source of the virus, and to identify the insect vector.

Until Smith's work was undertaken, the incidence of the disease was increased by the propagation of infected material. Since then, the eradication of infected peach trees and the use of virus-free budwood has nearly banished peach yellows from America.

## Peach Mildew (*Sphaerotheca pannosa* (Fr.) Lév. ver *persicae* Woronich)

Powdery mildew of peach is liable to be a serious problem in areas with a dry summer climate. It is rated as one of the most serious peach diseases in Egypt, and has proved troublesome in the Cape Province of South Africa. The youngest foliage is the most susceptible, but the fungus can also attack the shoots and more rarely the fruits.

### METHOD OF CONTROL

The fungus spores are as readily killed by sulphur fungicides as are those of the other species of powdery mildew, but the disease is hard to control on peaches because of the difficulty of maintaining a fungicide on the new foliage which is being produced during the growing season.

# CITRUS FRUIT

Citrus fruits must be high on the list of the many gifts which Asia has given to mankind. Over the centuries the sweet orange has become the most widely cultivated variety but the acid fruits such as the sour orange and the lemon were the first to arrive in Europe, probably during the eleventh century. The somewhat scanty records suggest that the sweet orange arrived in Europe early in the fifteenth century and it was clearly well-known a hundred years later. The citrus fruits were obviously greatly valued as Colombus took them to Haiti on his second expedition in 1493. They were introduced into Florida about 1565, but it was not until 1769 that citrus trees were planted in California.

The citrus tree will tolerate light frosts, prolonged exposure to temperatures below 28°F is fatal. It is grown commercially in the sub-tropical regions of the world between the latitudes of 35° north and 35° south. Many parts of the world with a suitable climate for citrus have low rainfall so that much of the world's citrus is grown under irrigation. Such climatic conditions favour insect pests rather than diseases, and for the majority of citrus-growers it is a continual battle to keep their trees in good health.

Citrus is one of the most important kinds of commercial fruit grown in the world. The principal producing areas are the Mediterranean region and the U.S.A. Out of a total estimated world area of 2,700,000 acres nearly 1,000,000 are grown in the U.S.A., especially in Florida and California. The Mediterranean region includes Spain, Italy, Morocco, Algeria, Greece, Tunisia, Turkey, Egypt, Portugal, Syria, Lebanon and Israel, all being exporting countries. Eleswhere in the world, citrus is grown on a large scale, notably in Japan, India, Brazil, Mexico, Argentina, Ecuador and some other South American countries. The production is on a lower scale and the fruit is largely home consumed. South Africa remains the only other exporting country.

The predominant pests of citrus are *Hemiptera,* especially scale insects and mealy-bugs. It is interesting to reflect that this perennial sub-tropical crop is the host plant of these sedentary immobile insects, which rely on mechanical transportation for their dispersal. Citrus provides the ideal host for such insects which would find survival impossible on a rotational crop. The most important scale insect species are the red scale and the black scale. Other scales are also notable pests as are also mealybugs and white flies. Red spider is generally regarded as also serious both in the U.S.A. and South Africa. In the Mediterranean region its place is taken by the rust mites. The Mediterranean Fruit Fly is also of the greatest importance There are, in fact, innumerable pests found on citrus and these have been well described by Quayle (1938), Ebeling (1959) for the U.S.A. and Bodenheimer (1951) for the Mediterranean region.

Nearly all the experimental work and development trials on citrus pests and diseases has been carried out in California preceding investigations in other citrus areas by at least thirty years. California is still the premier place for citrus research carried out at the Citrus Experiment Station, Riverside.

With most world crops, it is fairly obvious which are the diseases of major importance, but this is more difficult with citrus as although many of the pathogens are wide-spread, their relative importance may vary from region to region. For example, melanose, which is probably the most damaging fungus disease in Florida, is of minor importance in California. There are also diseases such as black spot which have a limited distribution but which may be the most serious one in the area in which they occur.

Accordingly, there are no very clear leads as to which diseases should be considered as the major ones affecting the crop. The choice has therefore fallen on some of the most widely distributed pathogens such as the brown rot gummosis, and foot rot due to various species of *Phytophthora,* melanose, the fruit storage rots due to *Penicillium* species, and a virus disease, Citrus Tristeza or quick decline. An account is also given of black spot as it is of considerable current interest.

All those in search of information on citrus diseases turn to Fawcett's (1936) textbook on the subject and his chapter on the same topic in *The Citrus Industry* edited by Batchelor and Webber (1948). The *Color Handbook of Citrus Disease* (Klotz *et al.*, 1948) assists in their identification. A concise account of the citrus diseases in Florida and recommendations for their control has been written by Knorr and his colleagues (1957).

REFERENCES

BATCHELOR, L. D. and WEBBER, H. J., *The Citrus Industry*, Chap. XI, University of California Press, Berkeley and Los Angeles (1948)

BODENHEIMER, F. S., *Citrus Entomology in the Middle East*, W. Junk, S-Gravenhage (1951)

EBELING, W., *Sub-tropical Fruit Pests*, University of California (1959)

FAWCETT, H. S., *Citrus Diseases and their Control* (2nd Edn.), McGraw-Hill Book Co. Inc., New York (1936)

KLOTZ, L. J. and FAWCETT, H. S., *Color Handbook of Citrus Diseases* (2nd Edn.), University of California Press, Berkeley and Los Angeles (1948)

KNORR, L. C., SUIT, R. F. and DU CHARME, E. P., *Handbook of Citrus Diseases in Florida*, Bull. 587, Univ. of Florida Agr. Expt. Sta. Gainesville (1957)

QUAYLE, H. J., *Insect Pests of Citrus*, Comstock Publishing Co. Inc. (1938)

## HEMIPTERA SCALE INSECTS

### Fam. 1. *Diaspididae*

This type of scale is known as an armoured scale. They are the dominant species and are difficult to control because they are covered with a permanent waxy shield. They remain entirely sessile.

### *Aonidiella aurantii* Mask.

The red scale is probably the most important pest of citrus in California, South Africa and the Mediterranean region. It also occurs in Australia and Japan where it probably originated. It appears to favour a dry climate.

Red scale invades the entire tree, attacking the wood, the foliage and the fruit, particularly that of orange which can be heavily infested, so heavily, in fact, on the fruit that there is no space between individual scales. Such an infestation can reduce the size

*Plate 4.10. Top: red scale injury to orange tree. Bottom: healthy orange tree, Cyprus*

of the fruit as well as rendering it without market value. Heavily attacked trees shed their leaves and the branches die back (Plate 4.10).

The life-cycle of the red scale is straightforward. The eggs occur under the female scale and hatch there. Eventually the young scales emerge and move over the tree for a day or two before finally inserting their mouth-parts into the tissues and thereafter remaining immobile for the rest of their lives. The young scale is the 'crawler' stage but it soon produces a waxy covering over itself while the legs and antennae slowly atrophy. The scale eventually becomes adult but the actual passage to the adult stage is complicated with many moultings and changes of colour. Predominently the female scale is circular, slightly reddish in colour, with a white raised centre and a greyish margin; in all about 2 mm in diameter. The scale destined to become a male is slightly elongated.

The life-cycle is not particularly rapid—its duration depending on the temperature. At 90°F the cycle is completed in about two months. The female produces about 150 'crawlers'.

*Aonidiella citrina* Coq.

This is the yellow scale of California. It also occurs in Florida and Central America. It is not important in the Old World. For all practical purposes it is identical with the red scale.

*Chrysomphalus aonidium* L.

This is the black scale of the Mediterranean region but is also known as the Florida Red Scale where it replaces the red scale of California. It is one of the main scale pests in Florida and appears to prefer a higher humidity than the Californian Red Scale. It occurs in all the main citrus-growing regions including South America. In appearance it is similar to the red scale and is in fact reddish in colour but distinctly darker (Colour Plate 6).

The life-cycle of the black scale is very similar to that described for the red scale. The eggs are produced and hatch under the scale as described for the red scale. The duration of the life-cycle and other details are similar. The male inhabits a slightly elongated scale.

*Chrysomphalus dictyospermum* Morg.

This scale is also distributed in all the main citrus-growing areas of the world but is of lesser importance than the foregoing. It is very similar to the Californian Red Scale in all particulars and is, in fact, known as the Spanish Red Scale, being the most important species in Spain. It is also a pest in Italy and Sicily but not in the Eastern Mediterranean.

*Lepidosaphes beckii* Newn. (= *pinaeformis* Bché)

This is the purple scale of the Mediterranean. It is very widely distributed occurring in Florida, California, Mexico and South America. It is absent from South Africa. It is probably the most important scale in South America, Florida and in those countries not dominated by the red scales.

In shape the purple scale is curved and elongated or mussel-shaped. The eggs are protected by the female scale as in other species and, after hatching, the crawlers move out over the tree. The crawlers produce long entangling threads which loosely envelope the body until the first moult when the waxy covering begins to appear. The threads remain for a time until the insect is about half-grown. The scale covering the male is much smaller than that of the female.

Several generations occur in a year, each lasting about two months. The purple scale attacks all parts of the tree including the fruit.

Fam. 2. *Coccidae*

This group of scales are unarmoured or soft that is they have no permanent waxy covering but possess a waxy dorsum. All soft scales produce quantities of honey-dew.

*Saissetia oleae* Bern.

This is the black scale of Olives and is more fully dealt with in that section. It also occurs on citrus and is a serious pest in California and the western Mediterranean but is evidently of no importance in South Africa. The scale lives principally on the foliage and twigs of the tree but produces a copious quantity of honey-dew which showers down on the developing fruit. Sooty moulds grow on this substance so that the fruit is soiled and must be washed at harvest. The female scale is larger than those just described, it is black, dome-shaped, with an H-mark on the dorsum. It is found in all citrus-growing areas.

The productive capacity of the black scale of Olives is enormous. Often 2,000 eggs are produced by a female over a period of many months. The crawlers disperse over the tree but are also freely transported by mechanical means and by the wind. The scale nymph grows up to maturity slowly and can still move freely over the tree until approaching maturity, when the legs become functionless. There is usually only one generation each year.

Males also occur and are distinguished by being a different colour from the female.

*Coccus hesperidum* L.

This is known as the Soft Brown Scale. It is a very common scale and widely distributed, occurring in all citrus-growing countries. It is very common in the U.S.A., the Middle East and South Africa. The adult female is smooth, convex and light brown in colour. In length it is about 4 mm and lives on very many plants even in the northern latitudes, where it can be found under glass. As a pest, it is of little importance on citrus in the U.S.A. but it is much more damaging in the Middle East and also in South Africa.

The insect produces copious quantities of honey-dew which is the main reason for its importance as a pest. As far as is known there is no male and the young are produced by the female without the occurrence of an egg stage. The scale is also mobile and can move if necessary from its original feeding place. One or two generations occur in a year. This scale is also extremely attractive to ants.

*Coccus pseudomagnoliacum* Knw.

This is the Citricola Scale of California, where it is an important pest in the San Joaquin Valley. It occurs in no other country except Japan.

Although there is only one generation a year, large numbers of over 1,000 eggs are deposited by each female in the spring. The scale grows during the whole of the year. The immature scales are flat and transparent but as they migrate to the branches in the autumn and winter they become darker. They mature in the following year. The male is rare.

*Ceroplastes spp.*

These are wax scales of which there are several species occurring in different citrus-growing countries of the world. *Ceroplastes sinensis* Del G. is common in the Mediterranean citrus areas. It is a large scale 4–5 mm in diameter, creamy white and divided into several segments. These species are seldom of importance except in some districts, such as Australia where *C. destructor* Newst. is said to be a pest.

Fam. 3. *Margarodidae*

This family is more closely related to the Pseudococci or Mealybugs. Scales are covered with quantities of wax.

*Icerya purchasi* Mask.

This is the notorious Cottony Cushion Scale of California, probably historically the most well-known scale. It is a native of Australia and appears to have been introduced into California in 1868 or 1869 by accident. It caused considerable damage to the citrus orchards there although citrus is not the only host plant. As a result of the serious depredations by the scale, a natural predator was introduced into California from its native Australia to overcome the scale pest. This predator was the lady-bird beetle *Rhodolia (Vedalia) cardinalis* Muls. known as the Vedalia Beetle. This insect, which fed upon the scale, was successful in reducing the numbers to negligible proportions.

The female Cottony Cushion Scale is large, coloured red or brown and partially covered by wax. The scale produces an egg sac which is like cotton in appearance and fluted. This sac may contain over 1,000 eggs. The eggs hatch and the young scales, which are red, scatter over the tree, usually preferring the twigs. Males are rare.

## METHODS OF CONTROL

The control of citrus scales insects affords examples of many methods of insect control. Firstly, the insecticidal method which includes fumigation—unique for an outdoor crop—spraying with oils and spraying with modern insecticides. Secondly, biological methods including one of the best known and successful parasite introductions. Finally, it is in citrus that the problem of insect resistance first became evident, so that the need of alternative spray programmes was recognised.

*Fumigation.* The fumigation of citrus trees, according to Essig (1931), began in 1885 in California against *Icerya purchasi*. The object of the operation was to envelop the tree with hydrogen cyanic acid gas (HCN) retained in a tent (Plate 4.11). The gas was generated outside the tent and introduced into it through pipes. This method was successful in spite of the evident crudity of the procedure. The introduction of the predator, *Vedalia cardinalis* against the scale, made fumigation no longer necessary but it was continued against other species notably *Aonidiella* and *Chrysomphalus*. At this stage, about 1889, the 'pot' method of generating HCN was invented. This method made use of sodium cyanide and sulphuric acid which were reacted together in a pot under the tent. This gave to the operator a much better control of dosage. During the following thirty years the fumigation of citrus continued to be practised with gradual improvements in the technique, especially in the control of dosage. The use of the marked tent, proposed by R. S. Woglum, entomologist to the Californian Citrus Exchange, was such a step forward. This tent enabled the dosage to be assessed immediately after erection of the tent according to the size of the tree.

*Plate 4.11. Citrus tree under tent ready for fumigation, Egypt*

The generation of the gas outside the tent was again attempted with better equipment leading finally to the use of liquid HCN located and pumped in from outside. This method was first used by C. W. Mally in South Africa in 1914 (Mally, 1915) and was in use in the U.S.A. and the Middle East in the 1920s. Fumigation was usually carried out in July but sometimes repeated later about October. The standard dose was 1 cc HCN gas per 100 cu ft of tent space.

The idea of generating HCN gas from powders, such as calcium cyanide, were never successfully developed and liquid HCN continued to be preferred. It was supplied in cylinders and so made application easy.

Many hazards attended the use of HCN gas, as it is fatally toxic to man. Fumigation was also dependent on stillness in the atmosphere. Overdosing, a common occurrence in the earlier years, could cause the tree to drop its leaves and fruit. HCN fumigation, by modern criteria, is full of pit-falls both for the operator and for the trees. It is interesting to reflect that this method of insect control endured for at least 60 years, taking a steady toll of operators, in order to keep the citrus tree free from destructive insects. The public conscience is now so prickly that almost any insecticide is suspect as a potential hazard to the operators and to the general public.

The problem of red scale resistance to HCN must be mentioned. This phenomenon occurred in certain districts in California about 1914 when it was found that both the California Red Scale and Florida Red Scale were difficult to kill. Much investigation followed these observations and many explanations put forward to account for the comparative failure of HCN after so many years of success. In spite of all the various ideas then current about the distribution of the gas in the tent, predisposing scale condition, protective stupefaction and so on, the true nature of resistance was elucidated only by Quayle (1938) who found the existence of resistant strains of *Aonidiella* and *Saissetia*. Evidently mutant forms occur which were selected by recurrent fumigation and gradually spread throughout the citrus area. Scale resistance did not occur in the Middle East and appears to have been recorded only in California, probably due to its long history of 30 years of fumigation.

*Oil Spraying*. Spraying with mineral oil came to the rescue of the citrus industry in California threatened by scale forms no longer susceptible to fumigation. Spraying began about 1914 in California but it is largely a post-1914-war development. A good deal of trial and experiment was necessary before the specification of the spray oils was properly understood. The classification of oils based on physical characteristics of boiling point and viscosity enabled research workers to distinguish one oil from another and abandon such loose terms of 'light', 'medium' and 'heavy', hitherto used.

Oils are normally used at 1–2%, applied in high volume of 4–5 gal per tree. Application is normally made in July but can be repeated if necessary later in October. The recommendation for spraying can only be made in the light of local experience.

Spray oils are not without their hazards also and they can cause leaf and fruit fall. It was shown by de Ong and others (1927) that the phytotoxic properties of oils can be removed by treatment with sulphuric acid which reacted with the aromatic hydrocarbons of the benzene type. The remaining saturated paraffinic type oils are not phytotoxic so that the degree of purification is determined by the residue unsulphonated. Citrus spray-oils are based on those of at least an unsulphonated residue (UR) of 90%—white oils in fact. Heavier oils required an UR of 95% but they can be used at lower rates.

Even so, oil is liable to lead to some leaf fall but oil spraying is especially dangerous when the tree is suffering from drought; oil also causes a burn of the surface of the fruit and leaves. Oil sprays can delay the ripening of the fruit and furthermore can reduce the sugar content so that the juice from oil-sprayed fruit is more acid. Climatic conditions also affect the susceptibility of citrus to oil sprays as mentioned above—heavy rain is also adverse following oil as causing a condition known as 'water spot'. In general it can be said that oil sprays tend to reduce the quality and yield of fruit but have the advantage of being very effective against nearly all citrus pests, certainly the most important ones, as well as being quite safe to handle and apply.

*Synthetic Insecticides*. The discovery of DDT and its potency against so many insect species was followed by attempts to use it against all pests. Among them were scale insects on citrus. It was soon clear that DDT in fact possessed no toxic effect against scales and, moreover, tended to aggravate the position. DDT added to oil sprays, far from increasing their effect, caused the reverse—there were more scales after spraying than with oil alone. It was also observed that the Citrus Red Mite increased wherever DDT was used.

DDT was soon followed by other synthetic insecticides including those of the phosphate group. Parathion, the first of these, became available in 1947 and was soon found to be highly toxic to scale insects of all kinds by direct contact. Citrus growers soon adopted the parathion technique and research stations issued spray programmes such as that given by Carman (1953) who recommended 1½ lb of parathion 25% wp for the control of red, yellow and purple scales in California. Application was normally given once in July, but sometimes a second spray was needed. The South African citrus growers soon switched from oil to parathion as it was much cheaper.

The occurrence of malathion as a substitute for parathion as being less poisonous was soon followed by its use on citrus. It was found to be less effective than parathion (Carman, 1954). Malathion was however, very effective against the soft scales more so than parathion. Programs soon followed employing both products and some firms offered a mixed parathion/malathion insecticide. The standard rate for parathion against scales was ·05% up to ·075% but for malathion the rate was 0·1%.

Other phosphorus insecticides soon came under trial in an attempt to replace parathion with something less poisonous. For a time interest centred on Ethion, a new phosphate compound of low mammalian toxity and later on Trithion which was however toxic. Towards the end of the 1950's citrus growers were beginning to return to oil sprays of ½–1% strength mixed with a phosphate insecticide, notably parathion although using oil at 1% almost any phosphate would be suitable. The combination was also superior to oil used alone. Many combinations were tried in all the principal citrus-growing regions of the World.

The systemic insecticides such as demeton-methyl and dimethoate proved totally ineffective against scale insects, presumably because the rate of uptake of sap by the scale was too slight for a toxic dose to be imbibed.

Low volume spraying of citrus trees has never been accepted by growers—only high volume drenching sprays has been considered suitable. Presumably the density of the foliage on established trees, reaching right down to the ground, and the depth into the tree to which the scales penetrate, renders low volume inadequate. Certainly, with the probable return to white oil, high volume drenching sprays are essential as such sprays cannot be applied low volume.

REFERENCES

CARMAN, G. E., *Calif. Citrograph,* **36,** 307 (1953)

CARMAN, G. E., *Calif. Citrograph,* **38,** 205 (1954)

DE ONG, E. R., KNIGHT, H. and CHAMBERLAIN, J. C., *Hilgardia,* **2,** 351 (1927)

ESSIG, E. O., *A History of Entomology,* Macmillan (1931)

MALLY, C. W., *J. Sci. S. Africa,* **12,** 95 (1915)

## Fam. 4. *Pseudococcidae.* Mealybugs

There are several species found on citrus. They are important pests, second in importance to the scales.

*Pseudococcus gahani* Green

*Pseudococcus citri* Risso

These two species are among the most important mealybugs on citrus. They are widely distributed throughout the World. They also live on many other host plants, including vines, coffee, cocoa and many other ornamental plants.

Mealybugs are soft-bodied and mobile, usually distinctly segmented but characterised by their being covered with white mealy wax, often extended into long lateral filaments. There are both males and females, the male being winged with one pair of wings.

Eggs are deposited in ovisacs which form large cottony masses. The eggs hatch and the young crawlers are at first free of wax. They spread over the tree and infest the twigs, fruit and foliage. A mealybug infestation consists of individuals in all stages of development. Several generations occur in the course of a season. Copious quantities of honey-dew are produced as in the case of the soft scales. The fruit on the trees thereby becomes soiled by moulds growing on the sweet and sticky deposit. Large numbers of eggs, usually 500 or so, are deposited by the females so that the mealybug infestations usually assume enormous proportions as in the case of scale insects.

METHODS OF CONTROL

Mealybugs are susceptible to all the sprays directed against scale insects especially to oil sprays. Parathion and malathion are effective but the waxy covering must be wetted.

Normally, mealybugs are kept in check by parasites and predators. They are soft-bodies and relatively stationary so that they are easy prey. Many ant species find mealybug attractive and attend them assiduously keeping at bay predators such as Coccinellids. Even so Lacewing Flies, Syrphid larvae and many hymenopterous parasites take a steady toll of mealybugs. In California, the Coccinellid *Cryptolaemus montronzieri* Muls was introduced in 1892 and it is still regarded as the chief predator of mealybugs. These insects are locally known as 'crypts' and are reared artificially. The same insect was also introduced into Palestine and Egypt without success.

Fam. 5. *Aleyrodidae.* White-flies

*Dialeurodes citri* R. & H.

This is the principal species of white-fly attacking citrus. It is known as the Citrus White-fly and occurs in California, Florida and the neighbouring states. It also occurs in the Middle East and Europe but it is not regarded as being of economic importance there. It lives on many other plants.

White-flies are best known in the adult stage, both the males and females being tiny moth-like insects, with white mealy wings. They are true *Hemiptera* in that they suck cell sap and throw off copious quantities of honeydew. They live usually on the leaves rather than the fruit and branches. The females deposit up to 150 eggs on the undersides of the leaves. The eggs are yellow and fastened to the leaf by means of a short stalk. The eggs hatch and crawlers spread to all parts of the plant. They soon choose a spot to settle and become immobile while they suck sap from the plant tissues. Eventually, the nymphs, which are now quite scale-like, become fully fed and proceed to the adult stage after a short period of rest. The adult insect emerges from the scale by escaping from the dorsal surface. The last nymphal instar is often called a pupa (incorrectly). Several generations can occur in a season. The insect overwinters in the adult stage.

*Aleurocanthus woglumi* Ashby

This is the Citrus Black-fly which is an important pest of citrus in India and the Far East. It does not occur in either the U.S.A. or the Mediterranean region. It occurs in Central and South America and in the Caribbean Islands. A chance entry into the U.S.A. was always possible and one such happened in 1934. The infestation was eliminated by oil sprays. Although the insect is a true white-fly its appearance is black to blue-black, due to its excretions.

The life-cycle is similar to that of *D. citri.* The eggs are deposited in a circle or spiral. The nymphs are dark becoming black at the final instar. They are covered with marked spines.

METHODS OF CONTROL

White-flies are kept in check by methods used against other citrus insects. Spray oils and synthetic insecticides such as parathion and malathion are all highly effective against the nymphal stages.

Fam. 6. *Aphididae*

Several species of aphid occurs on citrus. None are important as pests. The best-known species are the following.

*Toxoptera aurantii* Fonsc.

This is the Black Citrus Aphid. It occurs in all citrus-growing regions of the World. It is shiny black to brown. It inhabits the terminal growth causing leaf-curl. It lives on many other plants besides citrus but appears to be confined to citrus in the Mediterranean region. As can be said for other aphids, it prefers temperate and moist conditions and dies out in hot dry climates. *Toxoptera* appears to reproduce entirely viviparously—that is, no eggs are deposited and no sexual phase occurs although males are known.

*Aphis gossypii* Glover

This is the cotton or melon aphid. On citrus it is always grey in colour to dark grey. No sexual forms occur on citrus where reproduction is entirely parthenogenetic. It also lives on the young terminal growth.

*Virus Diseases of Citrus and their relation to Aphids.* The virus diseases, which go under the name Tristeza, occurs both in the Mediterranean and in the U.S.A. These diseases can be transmitted by aphids. Even so it is still doubtful if the diseases are spread in this way in all countries. The solution to the Tristeza problem certainly does not lie in aphid control, as is sometimes imagined, but rather in cultural practices especially in the use of proper rootstocks.

## THYSANOPTERA

*Scirthothrips citri* Moult.

The Citrus Thrips belong to the order *Thysanoptera* and is the first pest described that does not belong to the *Hemiptera*. These little insects are considered to be very important pests of citrus in all the U.S.A. citrus areas especially in the hot and dry regions. Thrips cause damage to the skin of the fruit especially to oranges, taking the form of scabby dry areas, particularly round the stem end (Fig. 4.12). This damage reduces the market value of the fruit and is in fact, caused when the fruit is quite young. The thrips feed under the petals and sepals, puncturing the cells. As the fruit fills out, the cells dry up, leaving a scab. Some damage can also be caused to the buds and leaves.

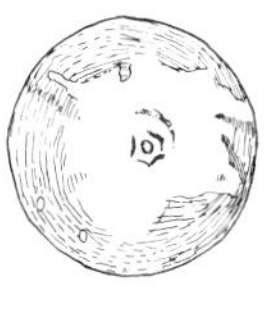

*Fig. 4.12. Thrips damage to oranges*

The eggs are inserted into the leaf tissues. The nymphs appear after winter which is passed in the egg stage. After feeding, the nymphs drop to the ground to complete the change into the adult insect. All the forms are yellow in colour and are smaller than the flower thrips usually found on citrus at blossom time. Several generations can occur in a year.

### METHODS OF CONTROL

In the U.S.A., treatment of thrips was formerly carried out with sulphur, usually lime-sulphur which was very effective. Sulphur can also be used as a dust against thrips and even today treatment of citrus against thrips is still carried out by this means in some Mediterranean countries. Sulphur dust can also be applied by aeroplane.

The disadvantage of sulphur dusting lies in its incompatibility with oil spraying. Sulphur must not be applied within 21 days of oil spraying and visa versa. The advantage of sulphur lies in its cheapness, in addition, it is also effective against the Citrus Rust Mite and the Citrus Bud Mite.

In the U.S.A., sprays containing tartar emetic were widely adopted in the 1930s. This spray was based on potassium antimonyl tartrate and was used with sugar. Its effect was short lived and thrips became resistant to it after a few years. This chemical is in fact mildly toxic to human beings. It was replaced by nicotine and later, in the post-war period, with DDT.

Other species of Thrips also attack citrus causing the same type of injury. The common greenhouse thrips, *Heliothrips haemorrhoidalis* Bché. is the most injurious in the Mediterranean region. Other species on citrus also occur in South Africa and Australia.

## ACARINA

The three most important species of mites which attack citrus are as follows.

*Paratetranychus citri* McG. The Citrus Red Mite.

*Phyllocoptruta oleivora* Ashm. The Citrus Rust Mite.

*Aceria sheldoni* Essig. The Citrus Bud Mite.

The Citrus Red Mite is the counterpart of the Fruit Tree Red Spider and the Two Spotted Mite which occur on deciduous fruit. The other two species belong to the family of mites called the *Eriophyidae* or vermiform mites, possessing only two pairs of legs instead of the usual eight pairs. The body is also elongated and the mite is not visible to the naked eye.

### *Paratetranychus citri* McG.

This is a similar mite to the deciduous fruit species belonging to the *Tetranychidae*. It is evidently different from *Panonychus ulmi* which it resembles although some workers doubt if there is any real difference. The Citrus Red Mite proper occurs in the U.S.A., Japan, South Africa and Israel. In other countries of the Middle East, the species of red mite on citrus is doubtful. Bodenheimer (1951) talks of the Oriental Red Mite *Anychus orientalis* Zacher as the principal mite on citrus in Israel and Egypt. This, in fact, may be a variant of *Tetranychus telarius*. It has recently been re-named *Eutetranychus orientalis* Klein. Undoubtedly the correct identity of the species has still to be worked out.

The abundance of the Citrus Red Mite fluctuates from year to year and from region to region. It is particularly prevalent in drier regions. The life cycle is similar to that of *Tetranychus telarius* on deciduous fruit in that the eggs and other stages occur on the foliage and fruit. Many generations occur in the course of a season depending on the temperature. The mites feed on the foliage causing it to assume a silvery appearance. Similar injury can also be caused to the fruit, lowering its market value. Severe infestations generally affect the health of the tree which tends to defoliate and drop its fruit.

### METHODS OF CONTROL

According to Lewis (1957) mites have in recent years in California, demanded more attention than red scales. More money has been spent on mite control than on any other pest if all mites are included. The reason for this state of affairs is the departure from oil spraying and a change to other chemicals, notably parathion which has upset the effects from biological control. Formerly, the mites were kept in reasonable check by natural enemies.

Citrus Red Mite and certain related mites were always controllable with white oil used at $1\frac{1}{2}\%$ as recommended for red scale. With the advent of parathion for red scale in 1951 the red mites quickly developed resistance to phosphate sprays of this kind. An account of the change in chemicals used on citrus, particularly for mite control, is given by Jeppson (1964). For mite control specifically, dinitro compounds were used in the 1930s and for about twenty years later. The occurrence of resistance of red mites to parathion led citrus growers to switch to systemics notably to demeton (Systox), a highly poisonous compound. Demeton possessed powerful mite killing properties but in two years the mites became also resistant to this chemical. Then followed a period when chlorfenson and Aramite were used. These compounds had also been exploited on dedicuous fruit, on which they were highly effective against red mites as well as being non-poisonous and non-injurious to the natural mite enemies. Chlorfenson was effective against mite eggs and Aramite against the active stages—a powerful combination. Extensive use of these compounds led to the development of mite resistance after six or seven years. The failure meant that all available mite-killing chemicals were no longer effective. Other compounds, such as dicotol (Kelthane) and tetradifon (Tedion), were introduced but resistance to them was soon observed. At present, new compounds are under trial, notably those of the carbamate group as being the only new type available. Where the race will end no one can know.

The Citrus Red Mite appears remarkable in its power to develop resistance to new compounds. Jeppson and his associates (1958) describes the occurrence of resistance in California to organo-phosphate compounds. It is probably a result of the speed of reproduction. Mutant resistant forms are rapidly produced and selected by the continuous use of different chemicals. Phosphate resistant mites were highly resistant to Trithion to the extent of x30,000 the normal dose was required to kill them—a figure obtained by interpolation. Resistance to malathion was only x9. Many figures of this type have been reported. The only solution to the problem appears to be a return to oil sprays to which no form of resistance has so far been observed.

### *Brevipalpis lewsi* Eb. & P.

This is the Citrus Flat Mite. This mite is similar in the damage it causes to the Citrus Red Mite. Its life-cycle is also similar. Sulphur is effective against it, otherwise it is kept in check by the normal routine sprays used on citrus.

### *Phyllocoptruta oleivora* Ashm.

This is the Citrus Rust Mite and is a native and inhabitant of the Middle East. It is a particularly important pest of citrus in all the eastern Mediterranean region. It also occurs in California and Florida, where it is often ranked as a pest. It is also present in the South American citrus-growing countries.

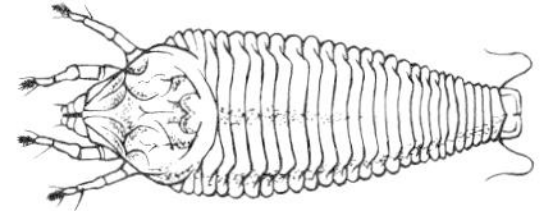

*Fig. 4.13.* Phyllocoptruta oleivora

The mites are minute, invisible to the naked eye but discernible with a strong lens (Fig. 4.13). They occur in countless millions on the trees. They have two pairs of legs at the front and a pair of sucker-like feet at the rear. Reproduction takes place continually and increases in the warmer months. Although the mites are parthenogenetic, eggs are laid.

There are two immature stages. All stages are yellow in colour. It is estimated that as many as 30 generations can occur in a year. The mites puncture the cells of the leaves and fruit so that they dry out. This causes a blemish on the fruit known as 'russetting' (Fig. 4.14). This injury lowers the market value of the fruit. Trees badly affected with rust mite produce less fruit in weight. Leaf fall can also occur. Lemons seem to be particularly susceptible.

#### METHODS OF CONTROL

Fortunately the rust mite is easily controlled by sprays and dusts containing sulphur which is still the standard remedy. In the

*Fig. 4.14.* Phyllocoptruta oleivora *(damage to orange)*

Middle East, sulphur dust is usually employed. Application is made when the fruit is small, pea-size in fact, otherwise injury may occur before the mites can be eliminated. Sulphur dusting however, is not without a hazard and fruit can be burnt in hot weather. Lime-sulphur spray is also very effective at the low dose of 1%. Oil sprays do not control rust mite. Lime sulphur also checks scale insects so that an early spray against rust mite starts the control of scales.

In recent years, the fungicide dithane (zinc ethylene bis dithio carbamate) has been used successfully against rust mite both in Florida and in the Middle East at 1 lb (of 65% wp) per 100 gal. This has the advantage of being less harsh than sulphur on the trees and furthermore, it is miscible with oil sprays.

Organo-phosphate acaricides, which are effective against the Citrus Red Mite, are ineffective against rust mite. On the other hand, non-phosphate acaricides have been used with success probably because of their sulphurous nature. Such materials are chlorobenzilate and chlorfenson.

### *Aceria sheldoni* Ewing.

The Citrus Bud Mite (Fig. 4.15) is similar to the Rust Mite but affects the buds which are distorted. It inhabits the eastern Mediterranean but is far less important than the rust mite. It also occurs in Australia and in 1937 was found in California.

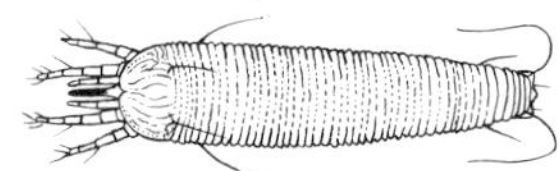

*Fig. 4.15.* Aceria sheldoni

The life-cycle of the bud mite is similar to that of the rust mite but it inhabits the buds causing malformation of the leaves and flowers when the buds open and the parts expand. Thousands of mites may be clustered in each bud, leading to a total abortion of the growth. Lemons are especially susceptible. The mite ceases to injure the tree after the bud stage has passed.

#### METHODS OF CONTROL

Oil sprays are effective against the bud mite and should be used before the new buds open. This is usually in autumn or late spring. Lime-sulphur is also effective but application cannot be delayed until the period of rust mite control. For severe infestations, two applications are recommended. Non-phosphate acaricides mentioned under rust mite are also effective.

### *Calacarus spp.*

This is yet another Eryiophyid mite occurring on citrus. It causes the trouble known as Concentric Ring Blotch. It was first noted in South Africa in 1955. Sprays of lime-sulphur at petal-fall are completely effective.

## DIPTERA

The only pests of citrus fall in the family *Trypaetidae* or fruit flies. There are several species of importance as follows.

*Ceratitis capitata* Wied. The Mediterranean Fruit Fly is the most important and has been described under deciduous fruit.

*Anastrepa ludens* Loew. This is the Mexican Fruit Fly which occurs in Central and South America. It has a much more restricted range of host fruits than has the Mediterranean Fruit Fly.

*Chaetodacus tryoni* Frag. This is the Queensland Fruit Fly of Australia. It appears to be confined to Queensland.

### *Ceratitis capitata* Wied.

Although *Ceratitis* attacks citrus fruit its favourite is the peach. It is notorious in the U.S.A. on account of its occurrence and eradication in Florida in 1929. The campaign started on April 6th and by November 15th 1930 the Fruit Fly had been eradicated. The total cost is given as over $7 million. During this period, fruit suitable for hosts for the fly were ruthlessly destroyed and vast quantities of poison bait against the adult flies used.

On citrus, the Mediterranean Fruit Fly is an important pest in that region and in South Africa where action against it must always be taken. It also occurs in other parts of Africa as well as in Australia and South America. It is absent from India and the Far East. The insect has been recorded for over 100 years.

Oranges are much more susceptible to attacks than other citrus. Lemons and grapefruit are scarcely attacked at all. Mortality of the larvae occurs in the rind of such fruit often amounting to 100%. Citrus is not an ideal host for the fruit fly but nevertheless losses can be considerable. Attacked fruit often falls off even after the preliminary puncture by the female fly. Afterwards bacteria and other disease organisms may enter these punctures and spoil the fruit. The abundance of the fruit fly is determined by the availability of ripe fruit on which it can maintain itself.

*Plate 4.12. Base of citrus tree affected by brown rot gummosis (A Plant Protection photograph)*

### METHODS OF CONTROL

This has been already outlined under Deciduous Fruit. The procedure is essentially the same and consists of the elimination of alternative fruits within the citrus area which can serve as hosts until the citrus becomes ripe. Likewise, infested fruit, after it has fallen, should be removed from the orchards. Biological methods of control have not been successful.

REFERENCES

JEPPSON, L. R., *Calif. Citrograph,* **49,** 303 (1964)

JEPPSON, L. R., JESSER, M. J. and CAMPLIN, J. O., *J. Econ. Entomol.,* **51,** 232 (1958)

LEWIS, H. C., *Calif. Citrograph,* **42,** 232 (1957)

## Brown Rot Gummosis or Foot Rot (*Phytophthora* spp.)

Brown rot gummosis, or foot rot, is one of the most widely distributed of all citrus diseases; the two alternative names describing the two most obvious symptoms of the trouble. The attack on the stem usually occurs within one to two feet of the ground (Plate 4.12) and results in the exudation of gum, but as the gum is soluble in water it may be washed off in wet weather. When the roots are affected, the injury can be seen on the bark of the upper part of the rootstock. The diseased bark is usually invaded by other organisms which cause a wet rot with a sour smell.

The variety of symptoms and the different reactions of the orange, lemon etc. made it difficult to identify the pathogens involved. In the early 1920s the culture of various fungi and their inoculation into citrus stems demonstrated that three species of *Phytophthora* were the main culprits. Subsequent work showed that the two commonest species were *P. nicotianae* B. de Haan var. *parasitica* (Dastur) Waterh. and *P. citrophthora* (Sm. and Sm.) Leonian, with the less frequent *P. palmivora* (Butl.) Butl. in third place.

As indicated above, brown rot gummosis

is found in most of the places where citrus is grown. In the last century before control measures were known, it caused very serious losses in California and Florida, but the most dramatic and serious outbreak occurred in Sicily where the disease known there as mal di gomma, wiped out all the citrus trees between the years 1863–70. In addition to the Mediterranean area, the disease was also found in Australia and South Africa.

The species of *Phytophthora* responsible for brown rot gummosis are all normal inhabitants of the soil. They produce lemon-shaped sporangia which, if put into water, quickly release the mobile spores which soon settle down and germinate. Water is thus essential for infection of the stem or roots. This coincides with the practical observation that outbreaks of the disease are liable to occur when there are long, wet periods, either due to high rainfall, or excessive irrigation.

The entry of the fungus into the bark is facilitated by wounds, or by the presence of cracks caused by the growth of adventitious shoots. Direct entry through healthy bark can take place if moisture is present, due for example to mulching materials or weeds in contact with the stem.

The first signs of the disease on the bark are discoloured spots with a water-soaked appearance. These gradually enlarge, but the progress of the disease may be temporarily halted. As the disease spreads in the bark of the stem, gum is exuded. If, as is usual, the stem is girdled, the tree goes into a characteristic decline. The foliage turns yellow, the shoots die back and there is a marked decrease in the size of the fruit. When the attack is severe, the trees may die within a year of the onset of the disease, but it is often longer.

## METHODS OF CONTROL

The first step in controlling brown rot gummosis was the empirical observation that the various rootstocks used for the citrus trees differed in their susceptibility. Following the Sicilian epidemic of mal di gomma, citrus trees on the island were gradually replanted on sour orange root-stocks. The root system of this kind of orange is resistant to invasion by the *Phytophthora* species, thus making it possible to grow oranges, etc., in contaminated soils.

The increasing losses of citrus trees in California during the 1880s led the growers to study the problem. The Committee of Investigation found that gum disease was the most serious cause of loss, that over-irrigation was the main pre-disposing cause and that lemon trees on lemon root-stocks were the most frequently affected. Towards the end of the decade, the importance of the European usage of the resistant sour orange root-stocks was recognised and led to their increased use in California.

Some fifty years went by before these facts were scientifically investigated at the Riverside Citrus Experiment Station in California. The whole range of root-stocks was tested by inoculating the bark with *P. citrophthora* and measuring the size of the lesion. The experimental work confirmed the practical observation that the lemon was the most susceptible of all the root-stocks and the sour orange the most resistant.

It would be misleading to suggest that this work solved the citrus root-stock problem as other factors, such as the behaviour in various kinds of soil, compatibility with the scion and reaction to virus diseases, must also be taken into consideration. The work was, however, an important step in the techniques for screening new root-stocks.

Due to differences in environmental conditions and possibly to variation in the strains of the fungi concerned, there is no general agreement on the exact order in which the root-stocks should be placed. A good general guide however is provided by the Florida rating starting with the most susceptible: sweet lime, lemon, acid lime, sweet orange, grapefruit, rough lemon, Cleopatra mandarin, sour orange and trifoliate orange as the most resistant.

Fungicides also have a part to play in protecting the stem and upper part of the roots from *Phytophthora* attack. The early work with Bordeaux Mixture showed that the genus *Phytophthora* was very susceptible to copper fungicides. Many programmes based on Bordeaux Mixture have been recommended, but the underlying principle is the same, to kill the spores before infection has taken place. This can be done by spraying the stem with a 12–12–100 Bordeaux Mixture or its fixed copper equivalent, starting before the onset of the rainy season. One application is usually enough, but it can be repeated if it is thought necessary.

Brown rot gummosis has thus led to a fundamental change in citrus growing. The use of seedlings has been replaced by the propagation of clonal varieties on resistant root-stocks. It is also advisable to bud well above ground level, so that the stem which may be susceptible is clear of mud-splashes, which may contain the root rot spores. Should these precautions be insufficient, copper fungicides can be used to give additional protection.

### Melanose (*Diaporthe citri* [Fawc.] Wolf)

In contrast to brown rot gummosis with its long history, melanose is a relative newcomer, having been first seen in Florida in 1892. Only four years later it was known that the application of Bordeaux Mixture would give partial control of it.

Melanose is a fungous disease which can cause very heavy losses because it disfigures the fruit of all varieties of citrus, particularly grapefruit. Fruit infected with melanose shows numerous small raised spots, reddish-brown to black in colour. The protruding spots give the surface a sandpapery feel. The spots often have a definite pattern, according to the way in which the spores were distributed over the surface. The form known as 'tear-stain melanose' follows when rain or dewdrops spread the spores over the surface. Heavy early infection causes the tissue to thicken and harden. As the fruit grows this cracks, giving rise to the mudcake pattern.

The fungus also lives on the foliage and on the shoots. In both cases the spots are small, amber to dark brown in colour. Both leaves and shoots feel rough as the spots are slightly raised above the surface.

Melanose is very widely distributed, occurring in most of the citrus-growing countries. As moisture is necessary for infection, and the fruit is only susceptible for about four weeks after petal-fall, the disease is worst in regions with an early summer rainfall such as Florida.

The study of the life history provided the essential key to the successful control of the disease. Two types of spore were found. The sexual spores are produced in perithecia which develop in decaying shoots on the ground. This phase is unimportant compared to the sexual stage which is found on the dead shoots in the tree. Such shoots bear large numbers of pycnidia from which the spores ooze out in wet weather. Raindrops and splashes spread the disease throughout the tree.

#### METHODS OF CONTROL

The discovery of the source of the spores made it economic to control the disease. All dead shoots must be cut out to reduce the amount of inoculum. When this has been done a single copper fungicide spray containing the equivalent of 14 oz of metallic copper per 100 gals of water put on within one to three weeks of fruit set will control the disease.

### Black Spot (*Guignardia citricarpa* Kiely)

Citrus black spot is a serious disease in the areas where it occurs because the fungus has a latent stage on the immature fruit and then becomes active as the fruit ripens causing black spot lesions. This presents a real problem to the grower and the pack-house, who despatch apparently clean fruit but which arrives at its destination severely disfigured.

A study of the distribution maps of the fungus (C.M.I., 1961) shows that the range of the fungus has increased during the past twenty years. It was first described in

Australia in 1899, but it is now to be found in China, Japan, South Africa and South America. It is particularly serious in New South Wales, Natal and the Transvaal.

The fungus lives on the foliage, shoots and fruit. Spore production takes place on the dead leaves. The pycnidia produce the asexual spores which depend on water for their distribution, while the ascospores from the perithecia are air-borne. It seems probable that the ascospores are chiefly responsible for the fruit infection.

The study of the life history of the black spot fungus has recently been complicated by the discovery of a closely related *Guignardia* species which also lives on citrus but does not form black spots on the fruit (McOnie, 1964).

### METHODS OF CONTROL

Many trials have been carried out to find the best method of controlling the disease because of the heavy losses which result from its presence. The value of Bordeaux Mixture for this purpose has long been known. Research has been concentrated on finding the optimum timing and concentration of the copper fungicide to protect the fruit during the twenty susceptible weeks after petal-fall.

The addition of zineb to the spray programme has been a very welcome one, as it will remove the danger of excessive contamination of the soil with copper.

In New South Wales, Bordeaux Mixture at 5–5–100 plus 1 qt of emulsified spraying oil is preferred for the first spray followed by two zineb sprays at 2 lb per 100 gal. The first spray is put on at petal-fall, with the other two 6 and 13 weeks later (Kiely, 1963).

In South Africa, the standard recommendation has been Bordeaux Mixture at 2–1–80 plus $\frac{1}{2}$ gal of emulsified white oil put on at two-thirds petal-fall and then repeated twice at intervals of 6 weeks. Recently cuprous oxide formulations at 1 to 2 lb per 100 gal have given excellent results and zineb is also being used to reduce the copper deposited on the soil. There is also a preference for zineb at the beginning of the programme and a copper fungicide at the end.

REFERENCES

C.M.I. *Distribution of Plant Diseases,* No. 53 (3rd Edn.), Commonwealth Mycological Institute (1961)

KIELY, T. B., *Agr. Gaz. N.S. Wales,* **74,** 11, 652 (1963)

MCONIE, K. C., *Phytopathology,* **54,** 1, 40 (1963)

## Citrus Tristeza or Quick Decline

During the 1930s and 1940s, the South American citrus growers, particularly those in Brazil and the Argentine, suffered the appalling loss of some 20 million trees due to the incursion of Citrus Tristeza.

Tristeza, which is now known to be due to a virus complex, only affects certain scion/rootstock combinations. The susceptible scions are sweet orange, grapefruit and tangerine when on sour orange and grapefruit stocks. Affected trees have yellow leaves at the ends of the shoots which later shrivel and fall off. The loss of foliage is accompanied by loss of rootlets which may be responsible for the general symptoms of starvation shown by the tree (Coloured Plate 7). The trees go downhill rapidly and may die within three months of the onset of the disease. Descriptions of the death of citrus trees in South African and Australian nurseries during the 1890s would suggest that the Tristeza virus was responsible, but as the susceptible trees were eliminated when very young, opportunities for its further spread were eliminated. Three factors appear to have contributed to the South American calamity, the virulence of the virus, the extensive use of the susceptible sour orange rootstock and the presence of the very efficient aphid vector *Aphis citricidus.*

The symptoms shown by affected trees are due to the action of the virus in killing the food-conducting vessels in the bark near the scion/stock union. This prevents the food materials synthesised in the leaves being translocated to the roots, which die, cutting off the supply of both water and mineral salts, causing starvation of the leaves.

### METHODS OF CONTROL

In those parts of the world where Tristeza is known to be serious, the only action that can be taken is the use of tolerant rootstocks such as sweet orange, rough lemon and Cleopatra mandarin. If for some reason sour orange rootstocks have to be used, it is essential that virus-free bud-wood is used. Such trees, however, always run the risk of infection if the vector is present as none of the existing insecticides can kill the aphis before it has transmitted the virus.

## FRUIT ROTS

Common green mould (*Penicillium digitatum* Sacc.)
Blue contact mould (*Penicillium italicum* Wehmer)

Some thirty different species of fungi are recorded as causing rotting of citrus fruits. The chief offenders are two species of *Penicillium,* the common green mould and the blue contact mould, which get into the fruit through wounds and produce a white mycelial growth on the surface of the fruit around the point of entry. Spore production soon begins, the spore masses being olive green in colour with the common green mould and the greenish-blue with the contact mould. Both fungi can spread from a rotting fruit into a healthy one if they touch each other, but this happens frequently with the blue contact mould, hence the name. The two moulds have a world-wide distribution and are found wherever there are citrus fruits, in the plantation, in the pack-house and in the markets. Their spores blow about and will infect any skin-damaged fruit.

### METHODS OF CONTROL

The first step in preventing losses from these two moulds is obviously care of the skin of the fruit during picking, transport and packing. This must be backed up with some form of skin sterilisation to kill any mould spores present, a subject which has been reviewed by Turner (1959).

The disinfection of citrus fruits is most commonly carried out by dipping in a fungicidal bath or by wrapping in paper impregnated with a volatile fungicide. The treatments are used alone or in combination.

The chemicals used in the dipping bath are borax, which was one of the first, and sodium o-phenylphenate (SOPP) which is the most popular material for this purpose. Borax is effective at a concentration of 5% to 8%, but it is not easy to dispose of the spent solution because of its toxicity to vegetation. SOPP is used at 1% to 2% but the solution must be kept strongly alkaline with either caustic soda or hexamine to maintain a pH of 12. The pH must be held at this level to prevent the release of the free phenol which is liable to damage the fruit skin. SOPP is also used as an additive to the wax with which the fruit is coated before packing.

The fumigant diphenyl, which acts as a fungistat, is very effective against the *Penicillium* rots. Wrapping papers impregnated with it are extensively used, either as a supplement to the dip treatment, or as the main defence.

It is of interest that strains of *Penicillium* have been found in California which are unaffected by standard concentrations of diphenyl (Duran *et al.,* 1962). Resistance of fungi to fungicides is very uncommon under field conditions, but is known to occur in culture in the laboratory.

None of the existing treatments to prevent citrus fruit decay is ideal and improved methods are being sought particularly at the Riverside Laboratories of the University of California, where many compounds are being evaluated for this purpose.

REFERENCES

DURAN, R. and NORMAN, S. M., *Phytopathology,* **52,** 361 (1962)

TURNER, J., *Outl. Agric.,* **2,** 229 (1959)

The vine has played an intimate part in the life of the people living round the Mediterranean from the earliest days. Although fresh grapes and dried grapes in the form of raisins and currants are important articles of commerce, the main acreage is devoted to the culture of wine grapes.

The vine is well adapted to a Mediterranean climate, requiring good rains during the winter and a hot, mainly dry, summer. A large proportion of the world's vineyards (66%) are in Europe where there are 16·3 million acres. Of these, 3·5 million acres are in France, 4·2 in Italy, and 4·5 in Spain (F.A.O., 1964). Vines also grow well in other areas of the world with a suitable climate, such as that in the western Cape Province of South Africa, Victoria and South Australia, California and Chile.

In Europe, vines absorb more insecticides and fungicides than any other crop. Diseases are more important than pests and copper and sulphur fungicides have been used on vines for many years. Little change in traditional techniques has taken place in the use of these materials over the years. The two principal pests in Europe are the Grape Berry Moth and La Cochylis, which are found in all countries to a greater or lesser extent. In the U.S.A., the grape leaf-hopper is the most important pest. The problem of *Phylloxera* occurs everywhere but has been well solved by the use of proper rootstocks.

Although there are numerous diseases which attack vines, two are of outstanding importance, vine downy mildew, and powdery mildew. The historical aspect of both these diseases has been described by Large (1940).

Detailed information on vine diseases in France is given in Lafon's handbook on the subject (Lafon *et al.*, 1955). Books on diseases of fruit crops usually include a chapter on vines, as for example that by Anderson (1956).

REFERENCES

ANDERSON, H. W. *Diseases of Fruit Crops,* McGraw-Hill Book Co. Inc. New York (1956)

*F.A.O. Production Year Book 1963–64,* Vol. **18,** *F.A.O.* Rome

LAFON, J., COUILLAUD, P., and HUDE, R., *Maladies et Parasites de la Vigne,* Librairie J. B. Baillière et Fils, Paris (1955)

LARGE, E. C. *The Advance of the Fungi,* Jonathan Cape, London (1940)

## LEPIDOPTERA

### *Polychrosis botrana* Schiff. *(Eucosmidae)*

The insect is the Grape Berry Moth. It is also known as Eudemis in France. It is a well-known pest in Europe, especially in the southern countries. It occurs also in Egypt, north Africa and in Japan.

In the U.S.A., *P. riteana* Clem. is presumably the same species. The caterpillar is small,

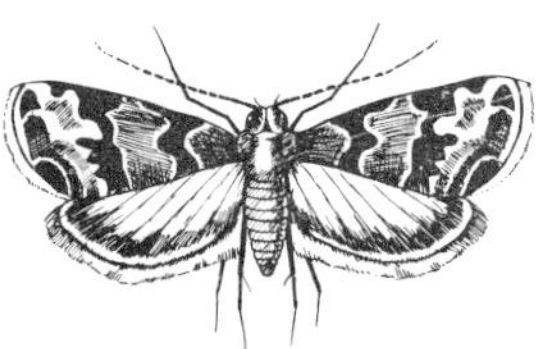

*Fig. 4.16.* Polychrosis botrana *(adult)*

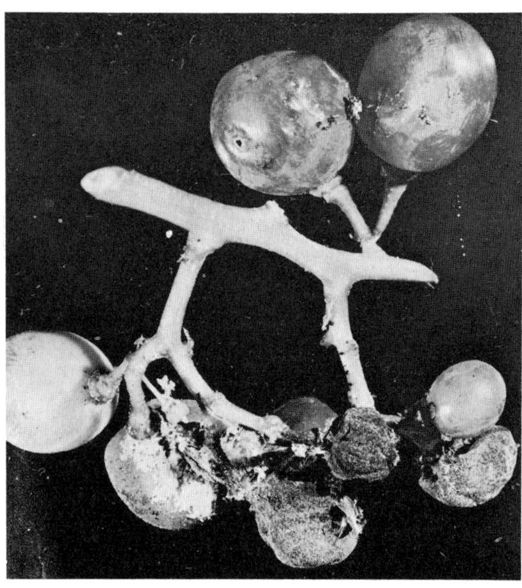

*Plate 4.13. Damage to grapes by caterpillars of Polychrosis botrana, France (Jean Vincent, Versailles)*

greenish-grey in colour and the pupa occurs in a cocoon in the foliage.

The adult moths are small and grey (Fig. 4.16). The female deposits 50–60 eggs on the flowers or fruit, usually at the end of May. The caterpillars feed on the developing fruit, webbing the clusters together with threads of silk (Plate 4.13). Feeding occupies about 5–6 weeks and there is usually a second generation. In this generation, the pupae fall off the vine on to the ground still webbed in the leaf and so pass the winter. Under very warm conditions, a partial third generation occurs.

The moth occurs on both cultivated and wild grapes. The intensity of attack varies from year to year and from generation to generation, evidently due to local climatic variations. The insect prefers warm and dry conditions and under such is able to deposit the maximum number of eggs.

### *Clysia ambiguella* Hueb. *(Phalonidae)*

This is a similar insect to *Polychrosis*. It is known in France as La Cochylis (there is no English name). The adult has pale yellow fore-wings, with a wide dark band across each (Fig. 4.17). It is mainly an insect of the more

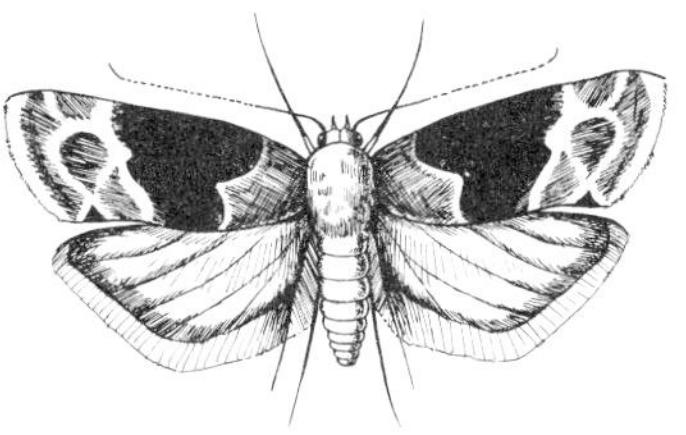

*Fig. 4.17.* Clysia ambiguella *(adult)*

northern districts. It occurs in all the vine-growing countries in Europe and is also found in north Africa, Japan, Afghanistan and parts of Brazil. As with *Polychrosis*, it resembles in habit other *Tortricidae*.

The life-cycle is very similar to that of *Polychrosis* but the caterpillars are easily distinguished, those of *Clysia* being yellowish-red. The head capsule and plate on the first segment of the thorax is brown to black whereas on *Polychrosis* they are light yellowish-brown. The caterpillar of *Clysia* does not jump and wriggle as does that of *Polychrosis* when disturbed. The caterpillar of *Clysia* is also slightly larger.

*Clysia* prefers humid conditions as well as warmth and will lay few eggs if the temperature falls below 20°C (Paillot, 1942).

### METHODS OF CONTROL

The only way to control the caterpillars of Eudemis and La Cochylis is by spraying with an insecticide. Formerly, lead arsenate was used and sometimes nicotine against the eggs. Later DDT became preferred. Application is made at the peak of the flight period which can be determined by baiting with cyder and sugar. DDT is used at 0·1% applied as a spray, using about 1,000 litres per hectare. The treatment is repeated 10 days later. In regions specialising in table grapes, rotenone is often used to avoid undesirable residues on the fruit. Rotenone is the active part of the insecticide *Derris elliptica* and is extracted from the roots of the plant.

Against La Cochylis, DDT can also be used but parathion at ·02% has been found to be very effective as well as preventing a build-up of mites. Moreover insect resistance to DDT has been found to occur in some parts of Germany where this insecticide has been used for many years on vines. Other insecticides are also effective, such as carbaryl at 0·1% but *Bacillus thuringiensis* possesses evidently little toxicity to these species. More than one round of spraying is usually necessary against both these insects, the second in mid-July.

### *Sparganothis pilleriana* Schiff. *(Tortricidae)*

This insect is another similar caterpillar on vines, known in France as La Pyrale. In Germany, it is more common than *Polychrosis* but is often only of secondary importance. The caterpillar is primarily a foliage feeder and when fully grown, is green with a black head. The moths are larger than those of *Polychrosis* and *Clysia* with the fore-wings pale yellow, carrying three transverse dark bands. Eggs are laid in a mass of 50–60, light green in colour. The young caterpillars take scarcely any food and prepare to pass the winter under the bark of the vine stock. The tiny caterpillars emerge the following year and begin at once to feed on the young foliage. By the end of June, they are fully grown and pupate in a folded leaf. The moths emerge later after about 14 days. There is only one generation each year.

## METHODS OF CONTROL

The old practice was to treat the vine stock in winter with a strong solution of lead arsenate to prevent the emergence of the caterpillars. DNOC can also be used for this purpose but the most effective material appears to be oleo-parathion. Spring treatment is also possible with DDT as for *Polychrosis* application being made at the beginning of bud movement.

## HEMIPTERA

### *Phylloxera vitifolii* Fitch *(Aphididae)*

This is the Vine Phylloxera. The species is sometimes known as *P. vastatrix* Planchon. It is a close relative of the true aphids, possessing sucking mouthparts and reproducing parthenogenitically. Some research workers consider that the *Phylloxera* are a sub-family of the *Aphididae,* differing from

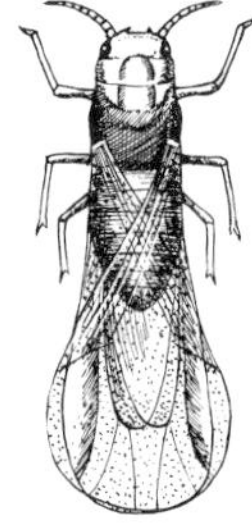

*Fig. 4.18.* Phylloxera vitifolii *(winged form)*

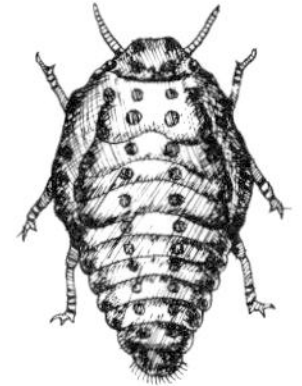

*Fig. 4.19.* Phylloxera vitifolii *(wingless form)*

true aphids in that eggs are deposited by the females; aphids normally reproduce by depositing living young—the egg stage occurring only once in the life-cycle. In both methods, the males appear only before the deposition of the winter egg (Figs. 4.18, 4.19).

The Vine Phylloxera threatened the total extinction of the vine-growing industry in France in the last century, at least 1,500,000 hectares were destroyed. A similar situation occurred in California. The insect appears to have been introduced into France from America about 1860. By the end of the century, it had spread to the entire vine area of France. Whole districts ceased production and the peasant population was forced to move elsewhere.

Today the Vine Phylloxera can be found in most vine-growing parts of the world in north Africa, South Africa, South America, Australia, Mexico and the Middle East but it no longer constitutes the threat to the industry as it once did.

The life-history of the Vine *Phylloxera* is very complicated as the insect occurs in several different forms. Furthermore, the behaviour of the insect on American vines differs from that on European vines *(Vitis vinifera)*.

The cycle begins with the hatching of the egg which has been present on the vine stock all the winter. This egg gives rise to the first aphid, the fundatrix, which is the forerunner of all subsequent aphids. The immature stages of the fundatrix move on to the leaves where they feed and form galls or pustules, which are little excrescences open on the underside and in which the aphids live (Plate 4.14). Reproduction continues on the leaf surface and more galls are formed. All aphids are yellow in colour and are all females, depositing eggs within the gall. This phase of the life-cycle is relatively unimportant although sometimes the entire leaf surface is covered with galls.

Later generations of aphids, after a period of reproduction on the leaves, descend to infest the roots. The forms that live on the roots also make galls or nodules on the root system. About the third generation in the year aphids with wings are produced which rise to the surface of the soil and fly back to the leaves. From the eggs deposited by these winged forms, the sexual generation is produced, males and females both wingless. The sexual forms mate and each female lays one winter egg on the wood of the vine stock which hatch the following year.

*Plate 4.14. Leaf pustules caused by Phylloxera vitifolii, France (Jean Vincent, Versailles)*

The life-cycle on the European vine is very different. Firstly, there are no leaf-living forms at all. If the winter eggs occur on the stock, the fundatrices are unable to colonise the leaves and even if they do succeed for a short time, they soon die out. The roots of the European vine are extremely susceptible and are infested by *Phylloxera* flying from the American vine. Reproduction occurs on the roots, galls and nodules being formed. In due course, winged aphids arise, come up to the surface of the soil, usually from June onwards, and fly back to the leaves but, as before, are unable to live upon them and die out. No winter eggs are laid.

The attack of *Phylloxera* on European vine is entirely sub-terranean and is transported on plants from place to place. On attacked plants, the leaves turn yellow and fall so that plants may often be killed outright. The *Phylloxera* which are yellow, continue to reproduce indefinitely on the roots in their galls, slowing up in the winter and starting again as the soil warms up in the spring. Each female produces about 100 eggs, all lemon-yellow in colour.

## METHODS OF CONTROL

The effective control of the Vine Phylloxera was brought about by grafting the European vines on American rootstocks. In planting such grafts, it is important that the scion wood (i.e. the European) is above soil level otherwise it will root down and become infected.

*Phylloxera* is a native of the U.S.A. but in the eastern area the root form is virtually absent, presumably because the varieties are immune from attack. It is the rootstocks from these vines which are used for grafting in Europe. On the Pacific coast of California, both the leaf form and the root form occur, but resistant rootstocks are employed as in Europe. Many hybrid rootstocks immune to *Phylloxera* are also now available.

In the past, carbon disulphide was injected into the soil to kill the *Phylloxera* before new plantings were made. This treatment also killed the vines. The leaf-infesting forms can of course be eliminated by sprays.

## *Pseudococcus citri* Risso *(Coccidae)*

This insect is the Citrus Mealybug, which also infects vines. It occurs in very many parts of the world, especially in sub-tropical vine-growing regions such as Egypt and Israel. It is common in South Africa. In the U.S.A., the Grape Mealybug is known as *Pseudococcus maritimus* Ehe.

The life-cycle is quite straightforward. *Pseudococcus* is a white mealy insect covered with wax. Eggs are deposited in cottony masses. The newly emerged nymphs are yellow and quickly disperse over the vine. They develop wax and become similar in appearance to the adults. Several generations may occur in a year.

The mealybugs feed by means of a proboscis and suck up cell sap. They absorb so much that some must be thrown off unchanged. This is the source of the sugary sticky deposit which covers the leaves and fruit and encourages the growth of moulds. In the winter, the adults hibernate on the vine.

### METHODS OF CONTROL

On vines, where mealybugs are important pests, it has been necessary to resort to spraying. The most effective insecticide is parathion applied at ·02%, but spraying should be stopped within three weeks of picking the fruit. Malathion can also be used. At least ·05% is necessary and it is still not so effective as parathion.

In California, predatory and parasitic insects have been introduced to control the mealybugs on citrus. No attempt has been made to control mealybugs elsewhere by such means and certainly not on vines, except in South Africa. Here it was found that the mealybugs on vines were protected from their natural enemies by the ant, *Iridomymex humilis* Mayr. (Durr *et al.*, 1958). This ant could be kept off the tree by soil application of aldrin at 4 lb per morgen ($2\frac{1}{2}$ acres). With the elimination of the ant, the mealybugs disappeared.

### *Erythroneura comes* Say. *(Typhlocybidae)*

This insect is the Grape Leaf Hopper—a very important pest of grapes in the vineyards of the U.S.A. It appears to be an insect of American origin and does not occur elsewhere. It has always been present on vines. It causes injury by reducing the assimilating surface of the leaf so that the quality and yield of the fruit is reduced.

The life-cycle begins as the vines come into leaf. The adults emerge from hibernation among the fallen leaves and other places of shelter. Soon females are depositing eggs on the undersides of leaves, inserted into small slits. The nymphs are pale green and suck the sap from the leaf as also do the adults. The nymphs take 3–5 weeks to grow and become adult, both forms are extremely active. Two or three generations occur in a season.

### METHODS OF CONTROL

Spraying of vines is the only method by which the Grape Leaf Hopper can be eliminated. The adults and nymphs are susceptible to DDT which is the most effective insecticide (Taschenberg, 1957). A single application of DDT at 0·1% gives protection to the leaves for about one month. Other insecticides are also effective, notably parathion and carbaryl.

Formerly nicotine sprays and dusts were used as well as winter treatment to clear up the hibernating places.

REFERENCES

DURR, H. J. R., JOUBERT, C. J. and WALTERS, S. S., *S. African J. Agr. Sci.*, **1**, 75 (1958)
PAILLOT, A., *Ann. Epiphyties*, **8**, 121 (1942)
TASCHENBERG, E. E., *J. Econ. Entomol.*, **50**, 411 (1957)

## ACARINA

Several species of mites occur on vines. The most important are:

*Tetranychus pacificus* McG. is the species on vines in California. In Europe, the mite is called *T. telarius* L. This species overwinters in the soil. It occurs widely on weeds from which it eventually makes its way to vines. Many generations can occur in a year.

*Panonychus ulmi* Koch. This species occurs on vines but is not very important on them. It overwinters as an egg on the wood of the stock and moves on to the foliage in the spring.

*Eotetranychus carpini* Oudm. This is another red mite and occurs throughout France and Italy on vines. It is said to be the most injurious species. It overwinters in hibernation on the vine stock. About 5–6 generations occur during the season.

*Eriophyes vitis* Pgst. This is a leaf mite causing the malady known in Europe as Erinose. The mite also occurs in the U.S.A., South Africa and Australia. The mites are extremely small and vermiform in shape with two pairs of legs only, carried at the front. The activity of the mites make blisters or shallow depressions on the leaf surface and marks the leaf stalks and tendrils of the vine. The leaf depressions are purplish to red.

*Phyllocoptes vitis* Nal. This is a similar mite to the foregoing but found principally on older vines. It overwinters on the vine stock and re-infests the foliage in the spring. On the foliage, the mites cause superficial damage where the cells are punctured and dry out, causing a silvery appearance. The attack is very evident during the spring as the new leaves and new growth is slow and stunted.

*Tetranychus viennensis* Zacher. This is similar to *T. telarius* as it over-winters as females on the bark. It moves on to the foliage in April where usually four generations are passed.

### METHODS OF CONTROL

Normally, it is not necessary to take action against mites on vines. Where dusting or spraying with sulphur is carried out against powdery mildew *(Oidium)* all the species are kept in check.

The use of DDT against the Grape Berry Moth has intensified the problem of mites on vines. For this reason, parathion or malathion is preferred to DDT in order to bring about some control of mites at the same time.

Rambier (1958) states that mites are important pests of vines in France in some years and the most damaging species is *Panonychus ulmi*. He suggests that the best chemical is methyl demeton.

REFERENCE

RAMBIER, A., *R.A.E.* **48,** 108 (1958)

## VINE DISEASES

### Vine Downy Mildew *(Plasmopara viticola* [Berk. and Curt.] Berl. and de Toni)

This fungus is a native of the U.S.A., but it was not until 1878 that it was recognised in France. It is highly probable that it crossed the Atlantic on the American rootstocks which were being imported for top grafting with the famous European grape vines. The importation was necessary as the European rootstocks had become infested by a root infesting aphis called *Phylloxera* which was also of North American origin. The *Phylloxera* damaged the vines by destroying the roots and after two seasons of attack, the vines were often killed. The only way in which the growers could save their vines was by using aphis-resistant rootstocks. It was a curious mischance that the rescue of the vines from destruction by insects led to the introduction of an almost equally devastating disease.

Vine downy mildew was well-known in the U.S.A., and its life history had been studied. It did little damage to the luxuriant American vines, but on the less vigorous European vines the effect was most destructive, particularly if the attack began early in the season.

The fungus is capable of attacking all the young parts of the vine. The fungal fructifications soon develop on the infected parts and can be seen by the naked eye as a whitish

*Plate 4.15. Vine leaf with downy mildew fructifications, France (Jean Vincent, Versailles)*

mould on the underside of the leaves (Plate 4.15) or on the surface of the shoots and inflorescence. The diseased tissues later turn brown and die.

The severity of the attack is closely linked with the climate, when the weather is dry it is arrested, when wet an epidemic can quickly build up. The disease is therefore of particular importance in the more humid regions such as France, Italy and parts of Spain, but negligible in the drier climates of California and western Cape Province.

The disease slows down the development of the grapes, so that they do not ripen properly. If the attack is early, the grapes are generally useless, if late, the quality of the grapes is seriously reduced and may pave the way for other diseases.

Much of the life history of the fungus had already been discovered by American workers before the outbreak in France led to many detailed studies there. The fructifications consist of sporangiophores which mainly emerge through the stomatal openings, but occasionally penetrate through the epidermis. The sporangia, which are distributed by both air currents and by raindrops, when put into water, form zoospores which can swim in the drops of water on the leaf. They swim about for 15 to 20 minutes before settling down on the leaf and putting out a minute tube which can penetrate through the stomata. Most of the stomata are on the underside of the leaf, so this is where entry mainly takes place, a fact of considerable importance when considering methods of controlling the disease.

The method by which the fungus overwintered did not take much finding, for it formed resting spores, called oospores, in the dead leaves. The oospores have thick walls which help to secure their survival through the winter. In the spring when growth is beginning, the oospores produce sporangia, whose zoospores can infect the young growth.

## METHODS OF CONTROL

Professor Millardet, Professor of Botany at Bordeaux, was one of the first people to observe the outbreak of the disease in France in 1878. During the succeeding years, he studied it with care and gave much thought to possible ways of controlling it, for the permanent loss of the French wine grapes would be a national disaster. Millardet's first clue came in the autumn of 1882 when he noticed that some grapes treated with a chemical spray still possessed healthy foliage, whereas the untreated vines further away from the footpath were defoliated. He learnt from the manager of the vineyard that the vine-growers in the Médoc often spattered the vines with verdigris or a mixture of copper sulphate and lime as a deterrent to those who might steal the grapes. For two seasons Millardet pursued his investigations testing out various combinations of copper sulphate and lime and other compounds which he thought might be effective. The copper sulphate-lime mixture proved the best and the formula was published in May 1885. Millardet's Bordeaux Mixture is one of the most important discoveries in plant pathology. It saved the vines of France and was soon shown to be effective on many other serious crop diseases such as black rot of grapes in the U.S.A., potato blight and apple and pear scab, diseases for which there had previously been no control.

So important a discovery led to further research and only two years later Professor Masson announced that sodium carbonate in the form of washing soda could be used to neutralise the copper sulphate, a formula which came to be known as Burgundy Mixture.

Millardet's original recommendation was formidably strong, 8 kg of copper sulphate and 15 kg of quicklime in 130 litres of water. Experience showed that this 6% Bordeaux Mixture could be reduced to 2% without reduction in disease control. It eventually became the custom to use 2–3% when the disease was very serious, while 0·5–1% was adequate for mild attacks. Further savings could be made by using weaker sprays as the copper deposit was built up on the leaf, with a strong spray at the end for maximum persistence between the last spray at the end of

July and the harvest at the end of September onwards. As a rule about six sprays were applied between the middle of May and the end of July.

The engineers were equally busy devising machines for putting the fungicide on to the foliage of the vines. One of the most successful sprayers was that made by Vermorel, and sprayers of this type are still being made. In his design, the knapsack tank is carried on the operator's back. The pump handle held in the left hand actuates a diaphragm pump which is unaffected by corrosive liquids or abrasive solids. The spray lance carried in the right hand can be directed wherever required.

Many improvements have been introduced since the original recommendations for the control of vine downy mildew were made, particularly new fungicides, together with better timing of the sprays and more efficient machinery.

Bordeaux and Burgundy Mixtures were the supreme fungicides for the control of the downy mildew group of fungi for fifty years. Although they gave excellent disease control, they had two disadvantages, mixing was cumbersome and phytotoxicity often occurred. These disadvantages were largely circumvented during the 1930s by the introduction of various proprietary materials based on copper oxychloride, copper oxysulphate and cuprous oxide. These did not have much impact on the vine fungicide market until the post-war years when in France a mixed fungicide was introduced containing 37·5% of copper oxychloride and 15% of zineb. This preparation was simple to mix, was as effective as Bordeaux Mixture and allowed the vines to develop better foliage. The standard rate of application is $3\frac{1}{2}$ lb of product in 90 gal of water per acre, the number of rounds and their timing being the same as that for Bordeaux Mixture. The mixed fungicide has steadily made headway in France, by 1960 it was being used on about half the acreage there, and since then it has become dominant.

In Italy, an 87% zineb formulation has increasingly replaced Bordeaux Mixture. It is used at a concentration of 0·2–0·3% but due to its rather shorter persistence, more frequent applications are required. A typical programme would involve 8–10 rounds during the season. In Spain and Portugal, Bordeaux Mixture is still the preferred fungicide for vine downy mildew control.

Interest in other suitable fungicides is increasing, both maneb and captan have given good results when used on vines.

The enormous acreage of vines in Europe, the frequency of downy mildew attacks and the absolute necessity of controlling it requires very substantial quantities of fungicides. It has been estimated that in 1958 about half the copper used in fungicides was applied on vines. The vine downy mildew fungicide market is probably the most important single one in the world (Gayner, 1961).

More attention has also been given to improving the timing of the anti-mildew sprays. The factors which lead to outbreaks of the disease are mainly temperature and rainfall. It is now possible to forecast when an epidemic is likely to occur from a study of the weather conditions and the development of the fungus. An organisation has been built up in France to advise vine-growers when to spray. It has been most valuable in ensuring that the vines are protected at the time when they are most likely to be infected, and in reducing the number of sprays applied (Lafon *et al.*, 1955).

The improvement in the fungicides has been matched by better spraying machinery. Today most of the sprayers are tractor-mounted and power-operated so that except in inaccessible sites, spraying has become a matter of tractor driving.

The conquest of vine downy mildew is one of the highlights in the history of plant pathology, for it saved the great vineyards of Bordeaux, Burgundy and the Rhine, and preserved the noble vintages for the pleasure of mankind.

REFERENCES

GAYNER, F. C. H., 'Fungicide Usage in World Agriculture', *Fungicides in Agriculture and Horticulture,* 27, Society of Chemical Industry, London (1961)

LAFON, J., COUILLAUD, P. and HUDE, R., *Maladies et Parasites de la Vigne,* Librairie J. B. Baillière et Fils, Paris (1955)

## Vine Powdery Mildew (*Uncinula necator* [Schw.] Burr.)

In 1845, not only was potato blight recognised as having crossed the Atlantic, but also a disease of vines, powdery mildew, which was first seen in Europe on some vines near Margate. It reached France in 1848 and then spread steadily throughout the Continental vine-growing areas. It is now found wherever grapes are grown.

The fungus lives on both the leaves and fruit. It is easily seen as the mycelium and mass of conidiospores give the attacked parts a white floury appearance. The conidiospores, which are produced in enormous numbers, spread the disease from plant to plant, and when weather favours it, epidemics quickly build up. Light outbreaks do not cause much loss of fruit, but severe attacks not only damage the foliage, but cause the fruit to distort and crack, opening the way for other fruit-rotting fungi.

The fungus appears to survive the winter in two ways, as a persistent mycelium on the shoots and by perithecia, the perfect fruits, which can sometimes be seen in the autumn as small black spheres on the infected leaves or shoots. The relative importance of these two modes of overwintering is uncertain, as perithecia are often absent. In the spring, the perithecia burst, releasing the ascospores and the mycelial pads produce conidia. Both types of spore can infect the young growth if they alight on it, thus initiating the disease cycle once more.

### METHODS OF CONTROL

The original outbreak at Margate occurred in a garden managed by Mr. Tucker. He was accustomed to use sulphur on his peach trees and tried out the same remedy on the vines, with great success. He reported his results to the gardening press and received the distinction of having the mildew named after him as *Oidium Tuckeri*.

It was a notable event in the history of plant pathology that the remedy for vine powdery mildew was discovered before the disease reached France, thus enabling the vine-growers to avert a catastrophe.

Mr. Tucker's sulphur remedy is still used very extensively throughout the vine-growing areas of Europe though it is now used mainly as a dust rather than a spray. The sulphur is so effective that two or three dustings during the season are usually sufficient to keep it in check. The large acreage of vines and the repeated applications use a very large proportion of the total quantity of sulphur used for fungicidal purposes.

The main value of sulphur is as a protectant, which means that the first application ideally should be put on before the onset of the disease. A curative material such as dinocap would have obvious advantages as it would enable the grower to postpone the first application until the disease is actually seen. Advantage is taken of this in Germany where the high value of wine grapes justifies the use of dinocap.

## Black Rot (*Guignardia Bidwellii* [Ellis] Viala and Ravaz)

Black rot is the most important vine disease in the U.S.A., the country of its origin. It is now found in many of the vine-growing areas in the world, but is absent from Italy, South Africa and Australia. It takes its name from the diseased fruits, which are shrivelled and black at the time when the healthy berries are ready for harvesting.

The main losses from black rot come from its effect on the fruit, which is susceptible for much of the growing season. Soon after the berry has been infected, the lesions appear. These are very obvious because the spots are whitish surrounded by a dark ring. The fungus spreads rapidly through the berry causing it to shrink and blacken. Losses can also be caused by attacks on the young inflorescence but this, however, is not so noticeable because it prevents the fruit from setting.

The economic importance of black rot can be judged from estimates in the United States that it causes losses of about 20% in the south, up to 10% in the north, and negligible in the dry climate of California.

The damage to the fruit tended to obscure the fact that the fungus also attacks all the growing parts of the vine. The first symptoms on the leaves are small reddish spots which later turn brown in the centre with a dark margin. Small black dots, which are the pycnidia, can usually be seen near the margin of the older lesions.

The pycnospores exude from the pycnidia during wet weather and depend on raindrops and splashes for their dispersal. They are produced in very large numbers, so that the vine can become heavily infected in wet seasons.

The perithecia which are present on the mummified fruits enable the fungus to survive the winter. In the spring the asci mature over a long period, with the result that the ascospore discharge continues into the summer. The ascospores are airborne and can therefore be carried considerable distances, facilitating the wide dispersal of the fungus. Those which alight on any growing part of the vine can infect it, thereby starting the next cycle.

### METHODS OF CONTROL

The early trials of Bordeaux Mixture against vine downy mildew showed some indication that the treatment was also reducing losses from black rot. Improved control was obtained with better timing of the sprays. Copper fungicides were the only effective products against black rot until the coming of the dithiocarbamates. A typical organic fungicide programme would be three rounds of ferbam, starting just before bloom, repeating the application immediately after bloom, and then again 7–10 days later. The ferbam is used at the rate of 2 lb per 100 gal (Anon., 1962).

REFERENCE

Anon., *New York State Insecticide and Fungicide Conference, 1962,* Cornell University, New York (1962)

## OTHER VINE DISEASES

### Anthracnose *(Elsinoe ampelina* Shear) and Bacterial Blight (*Erwinia vitivora* [Bacc.] Du Pless.)

As the preceding accounts have already indicated, the relative importance of the different vine diseases varies considerably from region to region. An interesting example of this is found in the Cape Province of South Africa, where the dominant problems are anthracnose, powdery mildew and bacterial blight in certain localities, but vine downy mildew although recorded is of negligible importance.

Anthracnose can infect the stems, foliage and fruit of the grape-vine. On the stem, the disease forms spots which can enlarge and girdle the shoot eventually killing it, while on the foliage the spots are greyish and irregular in shape. On the fruit, the spots are initially light brown in colour, but with age they grow in size, turning grey in the centre surrounded by a dark red ring.

The fungus overwinters in the canes and in the spring produces conidia which are dependent on moisture for their dissemination. The conidia can infect the new growth and the resultant lesions may add to the output of spores.

Anthracnose is of economic importance in North America, Chile and the Cape Province of South Africa.

The disease is not usually a troublesome one in areas where copper fungicides are regularly used to control vine downy mildew but if this is not done, as in the Cape, a dormant spray about three weeks before budburst is applied. Both 10% lime-sulphur and 5% copper sulphate solutions are effective for this purpose. In the Cape this is followed up by three sulphur dustings during the growing season.

Bacterial blight has been recorded from all the major European vine-growing countries, South America and South Africa, but not from North America. The South African name 'vlamsiekte', literally flame sickness, is descriptive as the affected bushes look as though they had been scorched by fire. The disease is serious because if unchecked it can lead to the death of the vine.

The bacteria are to be found in large numbers in the conducting vessels in the wood, but are also present in the inflorescence and foliage. They appear on the surface of the leaves and shoots during wet weather and may be distributed naturally or by the workers in the vineyard. Entry into the vine is mainly through wounds but can also take place through the leaves.

It is thought that bacterial blight was virtually eradicated in Europe by the very extensive use of copper fungicides. The South African use of sulphur-based fungicides which were effective against anthracnose and powdery mildew thus allowed the bacteria to multiply unchecked. Once the correct diagnosis of the reasons for the severity of the bacterial blight in South Africa had been made, it was a simple matter to use copper fungicides in areas where their additional cost was justified.

Olives are a Mediterranean crop, especially in the coastal regions, and are grown either for oil, or for eating. The principal olive-growing countries are Spain, Portugal, Italy, Greece, Crete, Cyprus, Turkey, Lebanon, Syria, Jordan, Israel, Yugoslavia, Egypt, Algeria, Morocco and Tunisia. Some olives are also grown in the Argentine and in the U.S.A. but by far the biggest area is in Spain and Italy together, with a total of about 10 million acres.

The olive tree can grow to a great age. In Spain, there are vast areas devoted entirely to olives but, as in all countries, there are also many scattered and isolated trees growing along the roadsides and in villages. This wild-growing nature of the olive makes the control of certain pests much more difficult as such trees are omitted from any organised scheme of treatment.

The principal pests of olives are the Olive Moth and the Olive Fly, although there are many pests of minor importance.

In spite of its warm, sunny habitat, two diseases—olive leaf spot and a bacterial disease, olive knot, sometimes cause heavy losses. Both diseases are the subject of much research work in Italy. The easiest access to this work for the English-speaking reader is through the Review of Applied Mycology.

## LEPIDOPTERA

### *Prays oleellus* Fabr. *(Hyponomeutidae)*

This insect is the Olive Moth. It is probably the most important pest of olives, especially in Italy, Spain and in Turkey. It occurs in all the Mediterranean olive-growing countries.

It is a small grey moth (Fig. 4.20), which is on wing during the flowering period of the tree. Eggs are deposited in the flowers and also on the young fruit. The tiny caterpillar feeds on the flower organs, especially the pistil and ovary and later attacks the young fruit. In some years 50% of the flowers are destroyed and followed later, by a heavy fall of fruit.

The life-cycle begins with the moths flying in May and June when the females deposit eggs which are flattened and plate-like. Over 300 may be deposited by a single female. The caterpillars pupate among the flowers and young fruits and a second generation occurs. This time the females deposit their eggs on the stalks of the fruit and the caterpillars eat into the fruit. They progress to the stone, which they enter in order to devour the kernel, leaving a characteristic hole at the top. Attacked olives fall to the ground. A third generation of moths occurs in September and October, the moths depositing eggs on the foliage. The caterpillar develops slowly, feeding on the leaves. They are fully grown by April and pupate in cocoons spun within the olive leaves.

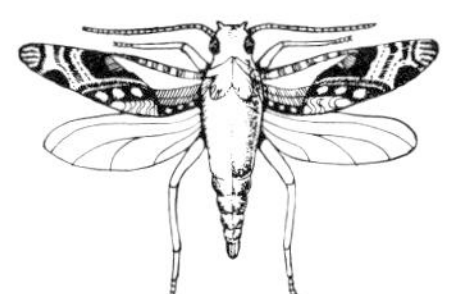

*Fig. 4.20.* Prays oleellus *(adult)*

#### METHODS OF CONTROL

In Spain and in Turkey, the standard method of control is by using DDT 10% dust just after the beginning of flowering. This reduces the numbers of the first generation which influences the strength of the second. It may be necessary to repeat the DDT treatment if the crop promises to be a good one and has been little damaged by the first generation. Attempts have been made to control *Prays* by means of insecticides applied against the overwintering generation. Parathion at 0·1% gave good results (Antongiovanni, 1958) and Rogor is also effective when used at this time and is also the usual treatment against Olive Fly.

Dusting is often preferred to spraying because it is easier to carry out on big trees with hand-operated equipment.

## DIPTERA

### *Dacus oleae* Gmel. *(Trypaetidae)*

This insect is the notorious Olive Fly. It is a small two-winged fly (Fig. 4.21) which causes maggoty olives because of the presence of larvae or maggots within the fruit. It attacks no other fruit but it is similar in activity to the Mediterranean Fruit Fly *Ceratitis capitata* Wied. which attacks citrus, peaches and other fruits. *Dacus oleae* occurs throughout the region especially in Italy. About 20% of the

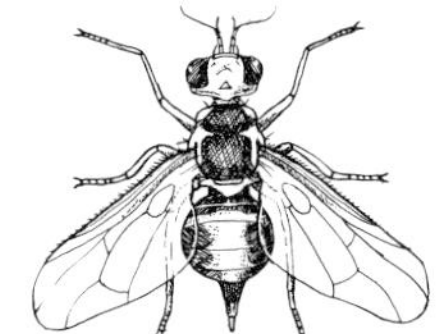

*Fig. 4.21.* Dacus oleae *(adult)*

olives are attacked and, where attacks are heavy, they are unsuitable as table olives. Oil can still be expressed from attacked fruit and the poorest quality used in industry.

The adult flies emerge from the soil in the spring and the females deposit eggs on the fruit. About 200–300 eggs are laid by each female. The skin of the fruit is pierced by the ovipositor of the female fly and an egg inserted, one per fruit. The larvae feed on the pulp of the olive fruit, which subsequently falls to the ground, and pupates therein

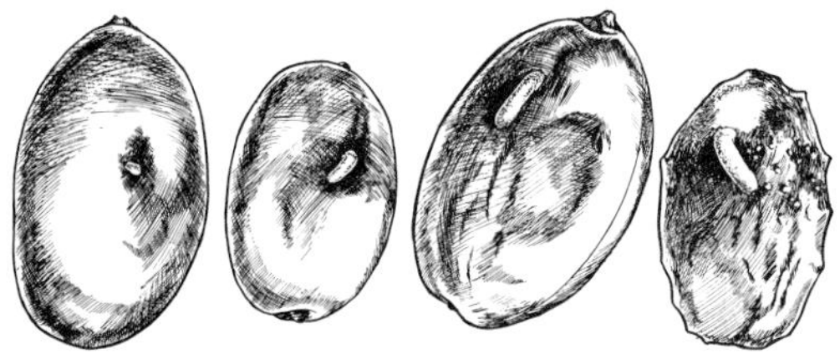

*Fig. 4.22. Larvae of olive fly in fruit*

(Fig. 4.22). A second and sometimes third generation occur. At this stage, enormous numbers of flies are prevalent and the attack on the olive becomes progressively more severe. Olive flies do not like excessive heat, which slows up the attack. The fully-grown larvae from later generations often pupate in the soil from which the flies emerge the following year. This habit is set off by the advent of colder weather.

### METHODS OF CONTROL

The problem of Olive Fly has received a great deal of attention especially in Italy. Very many insecticides have been tested against the insect. Formerly, little could be accomplished other than picking off the attacked fruit, largely to avoid heavier attacks by later generations. Baiting of flies has always been popular, usually with baits poisoned with sodium arsenite sprayed on to the foliage. Regular spraying at weekly intervals was necessary using ½ litre of spray per tree, consisting of the following mixture:

| | |
|---|---|
| Molasses | 95 lb |
| Sodium Arsenite | 2 lb |
| Water | 2 pt |

This spray concentrate was diluted 1 pt in 9 pt and sprayed on to the trees in water. This is Berlese's bait used in Italy. The timing of the bait spray was determined by fly traps consisting also of bait held in bottles suspended in the trees.

Over the last 10 years cover-spraying, that is complete overall spraying of the trees, has become popular. Formerly, DDT was used. Later BHC and dieldrin were tried but the best insecticide for this treatment is undoubtedly parathion. The effect of DDT and similar compounds was on the adults which picked up the toxic deposit from the branches and foliage (Russo, 1957; Peretz and Plant, 1953).

Parathion was extremely effective against Olive Fly because it was toxic to the larvae, even after they had penetrated into the fruits. Residue of parathion in olive oil was a disadvantage but this was shown to present no hazard at 25 ppm and, if it did not exceed 3 ppm, was quite safe (Aiazzi-Mancini, 1957). Obviously, less toxic effective chemicals were needed and one of these was found in 1957 by Pelligrini known as dimethoate (Rogor) which, at ·03%–·06% gave very high mortality of the larvae due to a long residual action. The product also gave a heavy kill of adults. Residues in the oil from 3 sprays never exceeded 1 ppm while the compound itself was non-toxic to humans. Similar results were also obtained in Jugoslavia (Tominic, 1960) and in Greece (Orphanidis, 1958).

Russo and Santoro (1958) attempted to reduce the parathion content of the olive oil, where this chemical was used, by mixing copper sulphate at 0·2% in the spray. These investigators also found that dimethoate was in fact superior to parathion.

The latest chemical to be examined for effect against Olive Fly in field trials is fenthion (Lebaycid) which has been tested on a considerable scale. This is another non-toxic compound with a very long residual action. Very high mortalities of adults have been obtained (Tominic, 1962; Kolbe, 1960).

The position at the moment seems to be in favour of the use of spring sprays directed against the adults. For this purpose, fenthion is especially suitable. For later sprays, in October and September, dimethoate is preferred. Bait sprays can still be recommended. Formerly, the attractant was often ammonium sulphate but, in recent years, protein hydrolysate, developed by Steiner in Hawaii, has been found successful for this purpose (Orphanidis, 1959).

REFERENCES

AIAZZI-MANCINI, M., *R.A.E.*, **45**, 298 (1957)
ANTONGIOVANNI, E., *R.A.E.*, **45**, 242, 296 (1946)
KOLBE, W., *Hofchen Briefe* I, 52 (1960)
ORPHANIDIS *et al.*, *R.A.E.*, **49**, 324 (1958)
ORPHANIDIS, P. S., *R.A.E.*, **50**, 237 (1959)
PELLEGRINI *et al.*, *R.A.E.*, **51**, 39 (1958)
PERETZ, I. and PLANT, N., *F.A.O. Bull.*, **1**, 101 (1953); *R.A.E.*, **45**, 298 (1957)
RUSSO, G., *R.A.E.*, **45**, 133 (1957)
RUSSO, G. and SANTORO, R., *R.A.E.*, **50**, 46 (1958)
TOMINIC, A., *Pflz. Nachr.*, **15**, No. 4 (1962)

## HEMIPTERA

### *Saissetia oleae* Bern. *(Coccidae)*

The Olive Black Scale is the most important of several scales which occur on olives. It is common throughout the Mediterranean region but is far less notable as a pest than *Prays* or *Dacus*.

*Saissetia oleae* occurs on many food plants, notably citrus but must not be confused with the Citrus Black Scale; *Saissetia* is much larger, humped and carries a discernable H-mark on the dorsum. *Saissetia* prefers a warm, humid climate and is unable to survive at high temperatures. The scales live on the twigs of the tree but shed large quantities of sticky sugary substances which falls on the leaves and fruit. On this, black moulds are able to flourish, dust collect, leading to a soiling of crop and a reduction of its market value.

Enormous numbers of eggs are produced by the females. The crawlers emerge from beneath the shelter of the scale and scatter over the tree. These crawlers can easily be picked up and transported to other trees on the feet of birds and even on other insects. Crawlers can also be spread by wind.

*Saissetia* is unarmoured (see Citrus) and retains its legs until maturity. Usually, there are two generations each year but males are rarely seen. Various parasites and predators help to keep the insect in check.

#### METHODS OF CONTROL

The measures against black scale on olives are seldom put into effect, as the infestation is rarely severe enough to make treatment necessary. In regions where the climate is favourable for its multiplication, treatment with white oil emulsion at $1\frac{1}{2}\%$ can be carried out if so desired.

This is a standard spray used on citrus and is readily adopted on olives. It is usually applied in the winter.

## THYSANOPTERA

### *Liothrips oleae* Costa

The thrips on olives are of minor importance although well-known as pests.

*Euphyllura olivina* Costa *(Psyllidae)*

This insect is the Olive Psylla. It is seldom an important pest. It is recognised by long wax filaments which it produces and is sometimes known as 'olive cotton' as a result.

## Olive Leaf Spot (*Cycloconium oleaginum* Cast.)

The olive leaf spot disease is important because severe attacks result in partial to complete defoliation of the tree, which seriously reduces the crop in the following season.

The symptoms are easily seen as the fungal spots on the upper surface are dull green to almost black in colour. The spots, which are circular, vary in size from 2 to 10 mm in diameter. As the disease progresses the leaf blade turns yellow and drops off. The dark coloured spots on the yellow leaf have a slight resemblance to the pattern on the tail feathers of the peacock, hence the alternative name for the disease of peacock spot.

The fungus is disseminated by conidiospores which are produced on the lesions. Infection can take place at any time of the year, except when it is particularly hot or cold (R.A.M. 1961). The optimum time for infection is in the autumn when the incubation period takes 30 to 50 days. The leaves infected in the autumn remain on the tree during the winter, but fall off in the spring and early summer, sometimes leaving the tree almost leafless.

The disease is found around the Mediterranean, in Eritrea, South Africa, California, the Argentine and Chile (C.M.I., 1949).

### METHODS OF CONTROL

Although the fungus can be checked with a variety of fungicides, such as ziram and mixtures of captan and copper oxychloride, those containing copper are the most effective.

The timing of the spray varies with the latitude. For example, in Italy the olives in the south and in the Italian islands should be sprayed during February, in the centre of the country in early March, and in Liguria in late March (R.A.M., 1960). When the attack is very severe, additional sprays of either copper sulphate or copper oxychloride are put on in the autumn. These act as a defoliant and thus reduce the inoculum in the spring.

Although the control measures have been worked out, their adoption has been slow, mainly due to the difficulties of spraying the olive trees which are frequently grown on rough terrain, or steep slopes.

REFERENCES

C.M.I., *Distribution of Plant Diseases No. 183,* Commonwealth Mycological Institute (1949)

R.A.M., *Rev. Appl. Mycol.,* **39,** pt. 5, 264 (1960)

R.A.M., *Rev. Appl. Mycol.,* **40,** pt. 5, 320 (1961)

## Olive Knot (*Pseudomonas savastanoi* [Smith] Stevens)

Olive knot is a bacterial disease which causes knots or tubercles to develop on the young shoots. Not only does the infection check the growth of the shoots but it usually results in their death. The bacteria can also invade the leaves, causing premature leaf drop.

The bacteria, which ooze out of the tubercles in wet weather, can only enter the shoots through openings in the bark such as those provided by fresh leaf scars or hail damage (Dowson, 1957). It is thus important to avoid injury to the bark during either pruning or picking.

The distribution of the disease is somewhat similar to that of the leaf spot as it is found in the Mediterranean region, in California and the Argentine, but it has not been recorded in Eritrea, or South Africa (C.M.I., 1947).

It is not usual to put on sprays for the control of olive knot, but any copper fungicides put on against the leaf spot disease will also have some effect on it.

REFERENCES

C.M.I., *Distribution Maps of Plant Diseases No. 135,* Commonwealth Mycological Institute (1947)

DOWSON, W. J., *Plant Diseases due to Bacteria* (2nd Edn.), 131, Cambridge University Press (1957)

# V PLANTATION CROPS

## COFFEE

Some 13 million acres are devoted to coffee-growing, a clear indication of its importance as a world crop. It is fairly easy to grow and harvest and has thus become a popular peasant crop in contrast to tea which is usually grown in large plantations.

The industry is mainly concerned with two species of coffee, *Coffea arabica* which is indigenous in Abysinnia, and *robusta (C. canephora)* which is a native of the equatorial forests of Central and West Africa. About 90% of the world's coffee is *arabica,* which when well grown and correctly processed is accepted as being the finest type of coffee. *Robusta* coffee is not so highly rated, but it is in increasing demand as a raw material for the manufacture of soluble coffees. As so often happens, *robusta* is a heavier yielder and is more resistant to disease than the higher quality *arabica.*

Coffee is grown in many countries of the world but probably the best-known coffee-producing country is Brazil. Brazil does, in fact, produce over 40% of the world's coffee. The Central and South American countries are great coffee producers; coffee is often the main export crop from places like Costa Rica, El Salvador, Nicaragua, and Guatemala. Some coffee is grown in India and the Far East but probably the next most important area is in Africa, principally the Ivory Coast, Kenya, Uganda, the Congo and Angola. Indonesia was formerly the most important source of coffee on world markets but coffee rust disease weakened its eminent position which is now held by Central and South America. The world area under coffee is bigger than that for cocoa (8 million acres) and much bigger than that for tea (about 2¼ million acres).

There are few important pests of coffee and these appear to be divided into two groups—those in the Western Hemisphere, and those in Central Africa. Only the leaf miner, *Leucoptera coffeella,* is common to both. Probably the best-known coffee pest is the berry borer, *Stephanoderes hampei*, which is found both in Central Africa and in Brazil. The best account of coffee pests is to be found in the Kenya Coffee Board publication (Coffee Research Services, 1961).

The most important disease of coffee is the well-known leaf rust which had the most devastating effect on the fortunes of Ceylon during the last century, helped to turn the English into a nation of tea drinkers and is still a limiting factor to the production of coffee in the countries where it occurs. The disease does not occur in Central and South America, an advantage which has assisted this region to become dominant in world coffee production.

Only one book has been published dealing solely with coffee diseases (Bally, 1931) but the subject has been dealt with thoroughly in two recent books on coffee-growing by Wellman (1961) and Haarer (1956). The Kenya Coffee Board has published a loose-leaf illustrated book describing the coffee diseases together with recommendations on methods for their control (Coffee Research Services, 1961).

REFERENCES

BALLY, W., *Handbook voor de Koffiecultur. Part I, De Ziekter van de Koffie,* De Bussy, Amsterdam (1931)

Coffee Research Services, Kenya, *An Atlas of Coffee Pests and Diseases* (1st Edn. April 1961 with new sheets 1963), The Coffee Board of Kenya, Nairobi (1961)

HAARER, A. F., *Modern Coffee Production,* 275, Leonard Hill (Books) Ltd., London (1956)

WELLMAN, F. L., *Coffee,* 250, Interscience Publishers Inc., New York (1961)

## COLEOPTERA

### *Stephanoderes hampei* Ferr. *(Scolytidae)*

This is the Coffee Berry Borer which is probably the most consistant pest of coffee. The beetle belongs to the family *Scolytidae* which are usually bark beetles and wood borers. It is a tiny beetle, cylindrical in shape, round at the head and rear end. It occurs throughout the coffee-growing areas of the world except those of Central and South America and the Caribbean. Brazil is an exception and control measures are still actively carried out against it.

Eggs are deposited in coffee fruits especially those most advanced. The larval stage, which is a small white, legless, curved grub, remains in the berry. The larva pupates in the berry which may or may not fall. The beetles survive when no coffee fruits are available in fallen berries. In bad attacks up to 50% of the fruit is attacked.

*Stephenoderes* is also capable of attacking trees including cocoa boring into the wood like a true bark beetle.

#### METHODS OF CONTROL

Formally the only way to control berry borers was by carrying out a complete and total clean up of coffee plantations by removing all fallen berries. This practice considerably reduces infection. More recently the insecticide BHC has been used against berry borers in Brazil. Dust was preferred and 1% dust was used successfully against berry borers as early as 1947 (Sauer *et al.,* 1947; Seixas, 1947). The rate of use was 40–50 kg per 1,000 trees, two applications usually being given when the beetle was leaving the old berries, usually November onwards in Brazil. Even in recent years BHC dust has been used by Pigatti and Pereira (1960).

Brazil appears to be the only country where action is taken against berry borers, called 'Broca' in that country, although early work on BHC formulation was also carried out in the Congo. It must be noted here that BHC and its pure form of gamma BHC (lindane) possesses the property of causing a taint to *arabica* coffee as reported by Wallis (1959) in Kenya. The taint was described as 'bricky flavour'. It seems likely that *robusta* and *liberica* coffee are either not so affected or no taint has been reported from Brazil. Other effective insecticides are endrin and endosulphan.

### *Anthores leuconotus* Pasc. *(Cerambycidae)*

This is the White Coffee Borer of East Africa. It attacks the trunk and main branches of the coffee bush, usually arabica coffee. The bore-hole weakens the tree and causes the branches to die back, so that the food supply fails. The adult beetle is large and flat. It is called a Longhorn on account of possessing very long antennae, a characteristic of the family.

Eggs are deposited in holes in the trunk made by the female, and hatch into larvae which enter into the bark of the trunk immediately. The larval life extends to 18 months, but starts by the larva boring around the stem, girdling it in fact. Later, as the larva increases in size, it enters the trunk proper and the main branches. Pupation occurs near the surface in a bore hole and the adults escape on emergence.

These general characteristics are shared by other species of borers whose activity is not necessarily confined to coffee.

*Tragocephala spp.*—also occur in Africa and attack forest trees.

*Bixadus sierricola* White—occurs in West Africa.

*Xylotrechus quadripes* Cav. is the yellow headed borer of Africa.

A good account of the present situation in East Africa in respect to *Anthores* is given by Tapley (1960) who also worked out the method of control. Tapley estimated that in a badly infested coffee plantation there were 6,000 beetles to the acre. The effect of the population was to reduce the usual yields but perhaps the trees could survive, in fact the coffee, if grown under good conditions and if well maintained could tolerate this level of infestation. Young trees of one to two years old would succumb to borer attack.

*Anthores* also attacks forest trees as alternatives to coffee as do other species of the *Cerambycidae*.

### METHODS OF CONTROL

Tapley gave precise recommendations for the use of insecticides against *Anthores*. He found that dieldrin was the most effective insecticide and 0·5% used at 18 gal per acre of 540 trees. Application should be made in November, especially to young trees by painting the trunk. DDT has, evidently, not been effective.

### *Xyleborus spp. (Scolytidae)*

These little beetles are true bark beetles in coffee. Several species attack coffee in different parts of the world, but cannot be regarded as important pests.

## HEMIPTERA

### *Antestia lineaticollis* Stal. *(Pentatomidae)*

This insect occurs in Kenya where it attacks the young berries, the shoots and sometimes even the foliage of *arabica* coffee. It also occurs in other coffee-growing regions of Africa notably in the Congo. It does not appear to occur elsewhere. Leston (1952) proposed the name *Antesticollis* for this genus.

*Antestia* (Plate 5.1) is a large insect which pierces the young coffee berries with its

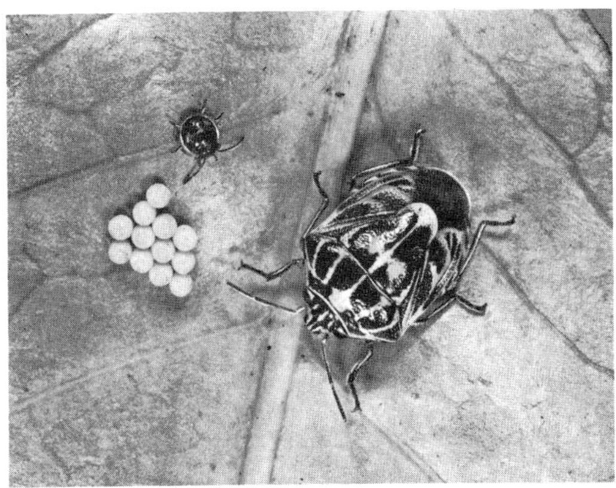

*Plate 5.1. Antestia lineaticollis with eggs on leaf, Kenya (A Shell photograph)*

proboscis thereby causing them to cease development and fall off. Others are marked by the feeding punctures and many shrivel. When shoots are attacked, the stunting of the growth forces other buds to break resulting in a forest of new growth which impairs flowering. Two bugs per tree can cause economic damage. The whole life-cycle can be completed on coffee and several overlapping generations can occur in a season. Many eggs are deposited by each female on the foliage in groups of 10 to 20. The nymphs become very active and feed on the flowers and berries as do the adults.

*Antesia* can also live on other food plants but according to Kirkpatrick (1937) only members of the *Rubiaceae*.

METHODS OF CONTROL

Many attempts have been made to control *Antestia* on coffee in Kenya but no insecticide has given complete satisfaction. Sprays and dusts based on BHC were quickly ruled out when it was shown that BHC caused 'bricky flavour' in *arabica* coffee.

DDT at 0·1% as an emulsion spray was very effective against *Antestia* but after a period of use tended to increase the numbers of *Pseudococcus* and *Habrochila* presumably by killing predators. An effective insecticide of limited persistence was needed leading to the idea of pyrethrum application to bring about a knock-down of the bugs which were arranged to fall on to a carpet of DDT 5% dust under the tree (Crowe *et al.*, 1961).

Various insecticides have been used against this insect each falling in and out of favour. At present parathion at ½ lb per acre is recommended in Tanganyika and malathion in Kenya. In the Congo, BHC was recommended by Decelle (1955) who claimed that no taint in the coffee was detected.

*Lygus coffeae* China *(Miridae)*

This is another bug found in African coffee. It is much smaller than *Antestia* and belongs to a different family but its effect is similar. Direct action is not taken against this insect but presumably measures used against *Antestia* would also serve for this bug, i.e. DDT at 0·1%.

*Habrochila placida* Horn *(Tingidae)*

This is a lacewing bug in Kenya (Fig. 5.1). The adults are tiny insects with square wings with a reticulated network. Economically, they are seldom important but on coffee they developed after blanket spraying with DDT against *Antestia*. The nymphs also live upon the coffee foliage sheltering on the underside of the leaves. If numerous, the lacewing bug can cause severe defoliation.

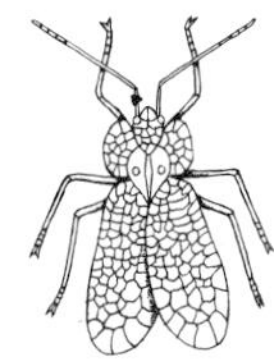

*Fig. 5.1.* Habrochila placida *(adult)*

Action is seldom necessary but sometimes insecticides are needed to remove a severe infestation. Probably malathion is the most suitable insecticide being non-persistant and safe to use. It should be used at 1 pt per acre of 50% emulsion repeated after 21 days. Other insecticides are also effective including DDT and parathion.

*Pseudodoccus citri* Risso *(Coccidae)*

This is the Citrus Mealybug which occurs on coffee in Africa. Another species *P. kenya* Le Pelley is sometimes present. These insects are normally unimportant being kept in check by predators. Following the use of DDT the species began to increase in number. *Pseudococcus* throws off large amounts of honey-dew, a sugary substance which soils the fruit and contaminates the foliage. Sooty moulds also grow on this substance.

METHODS OF CONTROL

Local control has been achieved by the introduction into Kenya of the parasite *Anagyrus kivuenvis* Comp. *(Encyrtidae)* from Uganda.

The problem of *Pseudococcus* is aggravated by the presence of ants of the genus *Pheidole* which attend and protect the mealybugs, extracting from them the sugary fluid. Some control of the ants has been attempted (Le Pelley, 1953) with a view to allowing the parasite a clear field of action. Ants, ascending the coffee trees, can be prevented by applying insecticides to the lower trunk. Gamma BHC is ruled out in Kenya and the most effective insecticide is dieldrin used at 1·5%. Ants are kept out of trees by this treatment for at least a year.

### *Coccus viridis* Green *(Coccidae)*

This is the Coffee Green Bug or Green Scale on account of the adult being bright green in colour. It occurs everywhere especially in India where it is an important pest. In Africa it is called *C. africans* Newst. and is probably the same insect. It occurs on coffee, tea, citrus and many other tropical plants.

It is a soft scale, meaning that the waxy covering of the female scale is not hardened. In common with other scales, sap is extracted from the plants by means of a long, deeply-penetrating proboscis. The scale occurs both on leaves and branches and, when numerous, can affect the growth of the newer part of the tree. *Coccus viridis* also throws off a copious quantity of honey-dew which forms a good medium on which fungi can grow, choking the aspiration of the foliage.

There are no male insects, the scale being parthenogenetic (i.e. reproducing without the intervention of the male). No eggs are laid; the young forms emerging from beneath the female scale and spreading over the tree. About three generations a year can occur.

Many ants attend *Coccus viridis* to imbibe excretions especially the large tree-nesting species of *Oecophyllus*. This ant is a vicious biter and makes all manual work in infested plantations uncomfortable.

#### METHODS OF CONTROL

Where necessary *Coccus viridis* can be eradicated by insecticidal sprays. Formerly nicotine and soap was used but on a plantation crop such as coffee, such a treatment is difficult to carry out. Modern insecticides have made the control much simpler. A favourite product in India was TEPP, a short-lived phosphorus insecticide. This has now been replaced by malathion which is safer to handle, used at 1 pt per acre of a 50% emulsion.

## HYMENOPTERA

### *Formicoidea*

Many species of true ants occur in coffee but not as pests, in the accepted meaning, only as nuisances. Some have already been noted—*Pheidole* and *Oecophylla*. In South America, ants are especially numerous and annoying in coffee and in fact can at times become dangerous to the pickers. The use of insecticides in coffee has reduced this hazard especially when directed against certain ant species. One of the best insecticides against ants is gamma BHC but this is not allowed in Kenya on *arabica* coffee. Dieldrin is an alternative but not as an application to the foliage, only to the base of the trunk.

Mention must be made of the group of ants known as 'leaf-cutters' and sometimes as 'parasol ants', usually species of *Atta* or *Azteca*. These ants live in nests in the soil, feeding on fungi which grow on decaying leaves. Pieces of leaf are brought into the nest by the ants themselves which they have also cut out of the leaves of trees. A procession of worker-ants, each bringing a small piece of leaf, has given rise to the name 'parasol' ant. When numerous, the leaf-cutting habits of the ants can cause partial defoliation.

*Atta sexdens* L. and *Atta cephalodes* L. *(Formicoidea)* are two species found in Central and South America especially notorious for their activity, *A. sexdens* being common in Brazil.

#### METHODS OF CONTROL

Many attempts have been made to control ants in the open but probably the most practical is the treatment of tree bases with dieldrin at 1·5% strength; insecticidal dusts are not permanent enough. Attempts to find and treat nests, usually with BHC dusts, have been successful but normally the procedure is too difficult and time consuming. The idea of using smoke generators in nests also was successful but came to nothing. Insecticide application to coffee foliage usually reduces the ant population significantly.

LEPIDOPTERA

## *Leucoptera coffeela* Guer *(Lyonetidae)*

This is one of the very few lepidopterous pests of coffee. It is known as the White Leaf Miner. It is a tiny moth, found in the West Indies, Central and South America and in parts of Africa. It is recorded from Ceylon but not from India. The larvae mine between the upper lower epidermis of the leaf.

The life-cycle has been given by Box (1923) and later by Notley (1949) both from East Africa observations. The eggs are deposited at night principally on the upper leaf surface. The larvae enters the leaf directly making a small circular mine which is gradually enlarged over a period of 3 to 5 weeks. There may be other mines in the same leaf which eventually join up. Before pupation the larva quits the leaf, descends on a thread and makes a cocoon for pupation beneath a fresh unattacked leaf.

Box states that over 50% of the leaves of any coffee become mined. Severely mined leaves fall off but in any case the assimilating surface of the tree is reduced. Eggs are found continually on coffee but the peak of deposition in Kenya occurs in November and December.

Notley (1956) describes *Leucoptera coffeina* Wasbu. a similar insect in Kenya which prefers shade whereas *L. coffeela* prefers exposed coffee.

### METHODS OF CONTROL

While *Leucoptera* is attacked by many parasites there was virtually no control of the insect until the advent of insecticides. Spraying or dusting against leaf miner is practised in Brazil and also in East Africa. Many insecticides have been tried including gamma BHC, dieldrin and parathion. Variable results have occurred, some observers reported good results with parathion and others poor results. At present diazinon at 0·17% appears to be in favour. Fenitrothion (Sumithion) is also being used.

REFERENCES

BOX, H. E., *Bull. Entomol. Res.*, **14,** 133 (1923)
CROWE, T. J., JONES, G. D. and WILLIAMSON, R., *Bull. Entomol. Res.*, **52,** 31 (1961)
DECELLE, J., *Bull. INEAC.* **4,** 67 (1958)
KIRKPATRICK, T. W., *Trans. R. Entomol. Soc. Lond.*, **86,** 247 (1937)
LE PELLEY, R., *Mon. Bull. Coffee Bd. Kenya*, **18,** 569 (1953)
LESTON, D., *R.A.E.*, **42,** 50 (1952)
NOTLEY, F. B., *Bull. Entomol. Res.*, **39,** 399 (1949)
NOTLEY, F. B., *Bull. Entomol. Res.*, **46,** 899 (1956)
PIGATTI, A. and PEREIRA, J., *Biologico*, **26,** 206 (1960)
SAUER, H. F. G., DUVAL, G. and FALANGHE, O., *Biologico*, **13,** 205 (1947)
SEIXAS, C. A., *Biologico*, **13,** 215 (1947)
TAPLEY, R. G., *Bull. Entomol. Res.*, **51,** 279 (1960)
WALLIS, J. A. N., *World Crops*, **11,** 321 (1959)

# DISEASES

## Coffee Leaf Rust (*Hemileia vastatrix* Berk. and Br.)

The coffee leaf rust fungus is found on its host plant in Abyssinia and Uganda and the evidence suggests that this was the original home of the disease which has had such profound effects upon the coffee industry.

The fungus is a member of the rust family and attacks the foliage. The disease is serious because it causes defoliation and consequent loss of crop. These aspects are all illustrated by the history of its occurrence in Ceylon, a story which has been told by Large (1940). The later spread of the disease and the outlook have recently been described by Rayner (1960).

Coffee was introduced into Ceylon about 1700, conditions favoured its development and by the middle of the nineteenth century the country had become one of the most important coffee-growing areas in the world. But in 1869 a fungus was found on coffee leaves in the Botanical Gardens at Peradeniya. It spread rapidly throughout the coffee gardens of the Island. The danger was not at first appreciated but by 1878 the truth was obvious, for the yield of dried coffee beans had fallen from 4·5 cwt to 2 cwt per acre. The disease continued unchecked, and by 1890 nearly 90% of the coffee estates had been abandoned.

A little fungus was thus responsible for the destruction of the coffee industry in Ceylon, for the necessity for many of the inhabitants to emigrate, and the shortage of coffee in England which led to a growing taste for tea. Fortunately for Ceylon it was found that tea grew well there, and the change has been permanent.

The symptoms of coffee rust are easily seen. On the upper side of the leaf the disease causes pale green spots which are so numerous in severe cases that the plantation has a yellowish appearance before leaf drop gets under way On the underside can be seen the spore masses which are orange-yellow in colour. (Colour Plate 8.) The numbers produced are enormous, one cluster of spores is estimated to contain about 150,000 spores.

Knowledge of the life-cycle of leaf rust will always be associated with one of the great plant doctors of the last century, Marshall Ward, who went to Ceylon in 1880. He observed that the spores on germinating sent out a germ tube which crept over the surface of the leaf until it reached a stoma through which it could enter. No stomata are found on the upper surface of coffee leaves and thus infection can only take place on the underside. After entry the mycelium ramifies through the leaf causing a lesion. In a few weeks' time reproduction begins with the formation of spores outside the stomata.

Until recently, it was generally accepted that the spores were released in dry weather and distributed by the wind, but fresh work in Kenya suggests that there is also another mode of dispersal. The new observations show that splashes from raindrops collect on the undersides of the leaves until they coalesce and fall off onto the lower leaves carrying the spores with them. From there further raindrops can cause splashes which will carry the spores onto the undersides of other leaves (Nutman *et al.*, 1964). Moisture is essential for spore germination, so that epidemics of leaf rust only occur in wet weather.

The evidence thus strongly suggests that there are two modes of dispersal of leaf rust spores, by wind and by rain splash, but their relative importance has still to be determined.

How the disease travelled from Abyssinia to Ceylon is a mystery. It has been suggested that the spores were carried by air currents, alternatively it may have been due to the importation of infected material. From Ceylon it eventually jumped to Sumatra and Java in 1876, to Fiji three years later, and subsequently to the rest of the Asiatic coffee-growing countries. It has also spread southward to Natal and in more recent years to the east, arriving in the British Cameroons in 1951 and in the Ivory Coast a year later. The way in which the leaf rust got to the Ivory Coast poses an interesting problem, as it is at least 600 miles from the Cameroons, the nearest known source. It is not thought to have been due to the import of infected materials as this had been excluded by plant quarantine regulations. It could be explained, however, on the basis of direct aerial dissemination of the spores, either by themselves or on the bodies of insects (Rayner, 1965).

The presence of leaf rust in West Africa is a terrible potential threat to the world's main coffee producing areas in Central and South America. There are times when the wind blows from the infected West African areas to the American coffee-growing regions, so the possibility of its transmission is a very real one. It is also known that the Arabica varieties grown in America are highly susceptible to *Hemileia* and the weather very favourable to its development. The steps which have been taken to deal with this fearful threat are described later.

The steady spread of the leaf rust throughout Africa and Asia had two consequences, the development of coffee-growing in areas free from the disease, in particular Central and South America, and a gradual increase in the planting of resistant varieties. Brazil which has always been a leading coffee country became dominant after the destruction of the Asiatic coffee bushes, and during the early part of the twentieth century produced roughly 70% of the world's coffee. Since then the other South American countries, particularly Colombia, El Salvador, Guatemala, Costa Rica and Mexico have expanded their production, with the result that their share has risen to about 40%, Brazil's has fallen to 40%, while only 20% comes from Africa and Asia. This distribution demonstrates the long-term effect of coffee rust.

## METHODS OF CONTROL

As indicated in the introductory section, the Robusta coffees are more resistant to disease than the Arabicas. In areas where the leaf rust is endemic, Robusta has been planted as it is more rust-tolerant. Robusta is thus the dominant variety in Uganda, is popular in Tanganyika and has been grown since 1900 in Indonesia. The acreage devoted to Robusta is still relatively small because of the world preference for the Arabicas which have usually been produced in excess of world demand.

Marshall Ward in his study of the disease investigated the possibility of using fungicides to control rust. At that time sulphur was the only known foliage fungicide and experiments showed that in the form of lime-sulphur it gave a partial control of the disease and a modest increase in yield, but the results were not good enough to have any effect on the survival of the industry. Marshall Ward however, made a fundamental contribution to the science of plant protection by pointing out that the only time when the fungus was vulnerable was during the germination of the spores before the germ-tube had entered the stoma and thus reached safety. He postulated that the fungicide must be present on the leaf before the spores germinate. The principle of protective spraying is still valid for most of the fungicides in use today.

Later research has shown that copper fungicides are more effective than lime-sulphur for the control of leaf rust. Bordeaux Mixture at a concentration of 5–5–100 was found to give good results in India and also in Kenya. Subsequent work in Kenya has shown that the success or failure of the spray programme depends on the timing of the sprays. It is essential to put on the first spray before the rains begin and follow this up with two more sprays at intervals of about three weeks. Any of the fixed coppers containing 50% of copper have been found suitable. They are used at the rate of 5 to 8 lb per acre and applied high or low volume (Plate 5.2) (Nutman *et al.*, 1964). The effectiveness of the spray programme is related to the amount of copper deposited on the foliage and not to the volume of water in which it is applied (Firman *et al.*, 1965).

In other parts of the world spraying against leaf rust has been ineffective. This is particularly true of countries such as Ceylon and

*Plate 5.2. Coffee spraying in Kenya (A Plant Protection photograph)*

Indonesia where the climate is very favourable to leaf rust. The absence of a dry season enables the fungus to continue growing throughout much of the year and thus the amount of disease remains at a high level. Successful spraying for leaf rust control is at present limited to those areas where a dry season reduces the amount of inoculum.

An unexpected side-effect of the copper fungicide applications was the 'tonic' effect which was observed in both India and East Africa. It has been found that copper sprays put on when the trees are in maximum growth improve the colour of the foliage, prolong the life of the leaves and increase the yield by as much as 4½ cwt per acre. The reasons for the beneficial effects are uncertain, but it is suspected to be due to the control of hidden fungal infections.

The resistance of the Robusta coffees to leaf rust has already been mentioned and its increasing use in countries such as Java where it is impossible to grow Arabica because of the incidence or rust. Rust resistance is not limited to different species of *Coffea* but some varieties of Arabica also show it in varying degrees. The first use of this was in Mysore, Southern India, where an investigation on resistance was followed up by a deliberate breeding programme which eventually produced a new commercial variety which was not attacked by the four physiological races recognised there.

This work proved that the threat to the coffee in the New World might be met by the breeding of resistant varieties, provided that it was started in time. Wellman, who was working at Turrialba, Costa Rica, thought that it was inevitable that some day coffee rust would cross the Atlantic. He advocated the setting up of a research station to investigate the coffee rust races and to carry on a breeding programme. Such an organisation has now been formed at the Coffee Research Centre near Lisbon, Portugal, with funds supplied by the Foreign Operations Administrations Organisation (F.O.A.) of the U.S.A., the Portuguese Overseas Ministry, the Coffee Board of Portugal and some other supporters.

In the early stages, work was concentrated on collecting together coffee varieties from all parts of the world in order to test their reactions to the various races of rust. So far 23 distinct races of rust have been identified and in addition Arabica varieties have been found which under laboratory conditions are resistant to the disease. These have been distributed to various coffee research stations for field trials in order to find out whether they are susceptible to hitherto unknown strains. The raising of resistant varieties is also being carried out in Kenya (Hanger, 1961).

Fortunately, coffee rust does not appear to have a sexual stage, so it is unlikely to produce as many races as have arisen with the cereal rusts. There is therefore hope that the programme will be successful.

REFERENCES

FIRMAN, I. D. and WALLIS, J. A. N., *Ann. Appl. Biol.*, **55**, 123 (1965)

HANGER, B., *Ann. Rep. Kenya Dept. of Agric.*, 66 (1961)

LARGE, E. C., *The Advance of the Fungi*, Jonathan Cape, London (1940)

NUTMAN, F. J. and ROBERTS, F. M., *Outl. Agric.*, **4**, 72 (1964)

RAYNER, R. W., *World Crops*, **12**, 187, 222 and 261 (1960)

RAYNER, R. W., Personal Communication (1965)

## Coffee Berry Disease (*Colletotrichum coffeanum* Noack)

In addition to contending with coffee rust, the Arabica coffee growers of Kenya have also had to deal with coffee berry disease, which has been rated as their worst disease.

The disease provides an example of the way in which a fungus can change its mode of life. The fungus normally lives as a harmless saprophyte on the bark of coffee trees, but around 1922 a mutant appeared which was parasitic, and could attack the flower and berries in all stages of growth (Rayner, 1952). On affected berries the first symptoms are dark brown lesions which usually spread ending with the death of the berry (Coloured Plate 9). The dead berries shrink a little but do not fall off, so that they are easily seen.

The disease is spread by conidiospores which can be seen as pink masses on the brown lesions on the berries. The disease increases rapidly and causes very serious losses. Soon after the original outbreak, some of the worst affected farms at high altitudes were abandoned, but even those in better sites lost as much as 50% of their crop. At first it was regarded as a mist-belt disease, but since then its distribution has extended to most of Kenya and also to Uganda where it is a potential threat to Arabica coffee there.

### METHODS OF CONTROL

The first attempt at controlling the disease aimed at protecting the berries with a copper fungicide, but this was a difficult and expensive programme as the berries are present on the trees for about nine months. A new and more effective approach to its control has come from a thorough investigation of the fungal life-cycle (Nutman *et al.*, 1964). The fungus, in addition to living on the berries, also lives on the freshly formed bark on the young shoots. Fructifications (acervuli) are formed on the shoot and produce quantities of conidia. The relative output of spores from shoots and berries was measured. The figures showed that the shoots were producing 20 times as many spores as the fruits. These results suggested that the aim should be to suppress spore production from the shoots rather than direct fungicidal protection of the berries.

This has been successfully accomplished in the monsoon districts of Kenya using the standard 50% copper formulations. Three sprays are applied at intervals of about three weeks starting in mid-February. The fungicide is used at the rate of 7 lb per acre and was originally recommended for high volume application at not less than 160 gal per acre in order to spray the shoots, a difficult target. Recent investigations have indicated that effective control can also be obtained using low volume mistblower application provided that the dosage of fungicide per acre is maintained (Wallis *et al.*, 1965). If properly executed this programme has been most effective and reduced the inoculum to such a low level that the crop remains disease free.

REFERENCES

NUTMAN, F. J. and ROBERTS, F. M., *Outl. Agric.*, **4,** 72 (1964)

RAYNER, R. W., *E. Afr. Agr. J.*, **17,** 130 (1952)

WALLIS, J. A. N. and FIRMAN, I. D., *Ann. Appl. Biol.*, **55,** 139 (1965)

## American Blight (*Mycena citricolor* [Berk. and Curt.] Sacc.

Although the coffee growers in tropical America do not have to contend with either of the preceding diseases, they also have their disease problems. Two call for discussion—American blight or leaf spot known in Latin America as 'ojo de gallo' and Koleroga or thread blight.

The American blight fungus belongs to the toadstool family, but it is parasitic, unlike many of its relations such as the mushrooms which are saprophytes. *Mycena citricolor* is also unusual in the very large number of different plants which it can attack. It is recorded as living on no less than 500 species including quinine trees, cocoa and citrus.

It damages coffee as the infected leaves drop off (Plate 5.3), the tips of the side branches may be killed and the coffee cherries damaged. In areas which favour the disease, the loss of crop may be as high as 90%. It is responsible for average losses of 20% in Costa Rica and Colombia. It has also been responsible for the destruction of coffee plantations in Mexico, Guatemala and Brazil.

*Plate 5.3. Defoliation of coffee bush caused by American blight (A Plant Protection photograph)*

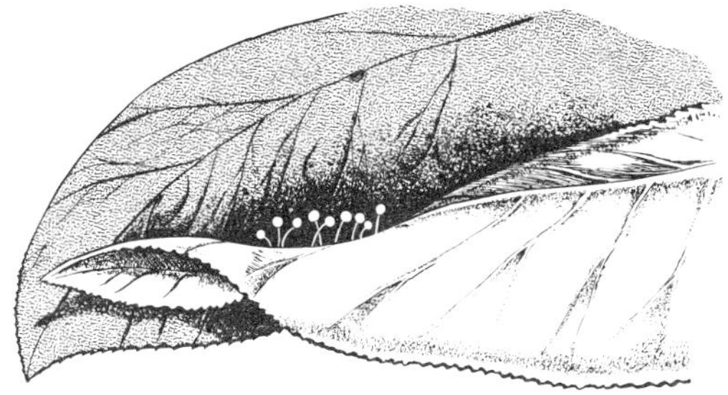

*Fig. 5.2. Gemmifers of American Blight of Coffee*

The disease causes blackish-brown spots on the leaves. The fungus quickly reproduces itself vegetatively by forming small round yellow balls on short stalks. The little balls, known as 'gemmifers' (Fig. 5.2) remain on their stalks until released by raindrops or removed on the clothing of workers. The fungus also produces miniature toadstools with stalks about $\frac{3}{8}$-in long and golden yellow caps. This phase is rarely seen on coffee.

METHODS OF CONTROL

The disease is most damaging in humid areas, particularly where coffee is grown in shade. The incidence of the disease has been greatly reduced by cutting down shade trees and this cultural method has often made fungicidal spraying unnecessary.

For many years copper fungicides were used in attempts to control American blight. These have now been superseded by lead arsenate, particularly in Costa Rica although the original observation was made when it was used as an insecticide in Colombia. The lead arsenate is used at the rate of 3 lb per 100 gal of water, plus a sticker. It is applied about three times a year, first in April or May when the rainy season begins, again in July, and in September.

## Koleroga or Thread Blight (*Pellicularia koleroga* Cooke)

Koleroga is a serious problem in many coffee-growing countries ranging from the Americas to India. Its seriousness can be gauged from the fact that it can cause crop losses of up to 60% and it has been suggested that it would pay to control it on some 2·5 million acres devoted to coffee (Wellman, 1955).

The fungus persists from one wet season to the next in dormant threads attached to the underside of coffee branches. A few weeks after the beginning of the wet season the fungus starts to grow again until it reaches the leaves or green fruit. The fungal growth then changes and forms a white web on the underside. The attack causes the leaves to turn black and shrivel but they do not fall off as they are suspended by the fungal threads. The disease can thus cause severe defoliation and hence reduction in crop.

METHODS OF CONTROL

The disease can be controlled by a variety of materials—Bordeaux Mixture, cuprous oxide and lead arsenate are all effective. Those growers who are accustomed to spraying usually put on two to three rounds of spray at intervals of about a month. The first spray is timed to protect the foliage and fruit against infection by the fungus as it resumes activity after the dormant season.

REFERENCE

WELLMAN, F. L., *Pesticides and Tropical Agriculture,* 43, Advance in Chemistry Series, No. 13, American Chemical Society (1955)

## OTHER DISEASES

In all the coffee-growing areas, die-back of the shoots is liable to be a problem. Its exact nature is not clearly understood, but it appears to be associated with over-bearing and is more serious in unshaded than in shaded plantations. While die-back can be caused by mineral deficiencies, it is believed that the main cause is a shortage of organic compounds synthesised by the leaves. Thus it is important to maintain the vigour of the bushes with good cultural practices. Should young trees be affected, the crop must be removed to prevent long-term damage.

As with other tree crops, root-rots are sometimes troublesome. *Armillaria* (*A. mellea* [Vahl ex Fr.] Kummer) is probably the most damaging, particularly in East Africa, but it is rarely seen in Central and South America. In the Americas various species of *Rosellinia* are the most frequent cause of root disease. They often occur when coffee is planted in freshly cleared forest land. Control is based on the grubbing of infected bushes, taking care to remove as much of the root system as possible in order to prevent the disease spreading.

Tracheomycosis is a lethal disease which is at present limited to Central and West Africa. The devastation which it can cause is illustrated by the destruction of some 25,000 acres of coffee in French Equatorial Africa during 1946. Tracheomycosis is caused by *Gibberella xylarioides* Heim & Saccas, one of the vascular wilt fungi. The leaves of attacked bushes turn yellow often on one side, followed by wilting and collapse. The fungus enters the bushes either through wounds at the base of the stem, or through roots near the surface. At present the only control is the prompt removal of infected plants, but there are hopes that the plant breeder may be able to raise resistant varieties.

An African disease called zebra or striped bean is of interest. Affected beans show brown stripes on the parchment covering which surrounds the bean itself. The discoloration is of no great importance, but it is accompanied by loss of flavour or even rotting of the bean. The disease is caused by *Nematospora* spp. which enter the berry through the feeding punctures of *Antestia lineaticollis*. The disease can be avoided by killing the *Antestia* with insecticides such as malathion.

# COCOA

The cocoa tree came originally from the tropical rain forests of Central and South America. The cocoa beans were used by the Maya Indians as a pleasant foodstuff and were also appreciated by the Spanish invaders. As might be expected, cocoa-growing first developed in the American tropics, and at the beginning of the twentieth century some 80% of the world's cocoa was produced there. Since then the centre of world cocoa production has moved to West Africa which now grows about 60% of the world crop. This change was mainly due to low prices and disease making the Central American cocoa estates uneconomic, whereas the West African grower is usually a subsistence farmer and thus able to survive when the returns from cocoa are small.

Exact acreage statistics for the world acreage of cocoa are not available. A rough estimate would suggest that cocoa occupies about 8 million acres, based on the knowledge that the world production of dried cocoa averaged 835,000 tons during the years 1955–59, and on the assumption that the average annual yield is about 200 lb per acre.

Ghana is the foremost cocoa producer with about one-third of the total acreage, but the other West African territories—Nigeria, the Ivory Coast and the Cameroons—are all large producers. Cocoa is also grown in other parts of the world, notably in South and Central America and the Caribbean Islands. Brazil almost equals Nigeria in production, followed by Ecuador, the Dominican Republic, and Mexico. Only a very small quantity is grown in Asia.

The most important pests of cocoa are capsid bugs *(Miridae)* which are dominant in West Africa, but do not occur elsewhere. Information on cocoa pests is to be found in the reports of the Central Cocoa Research Institute at Tafo in Ghana, and in the collective papers given at the various cocoa conferences. A good account of pests is given by Urquhart (1961).

The most important cocoa disease in South America is the witches' broom disease, which was partly responsible for the decline of cocoa growing there. In West Africa, a complex of virus diseases usually referred to as swollen shoot, is a very serious threat to cocoa culture.

The world's cocoa diseases have been reviewed by Urquhart (1961) in his book on this crop. Detailed information on the cocoa diseases in Ghana is to be found in *Agriculture and Land Use in Ghana* (Wills, 1962). Both sources have been consulted during the preparation of this Section.

REFERENCES

URQUHART, D. H., *Cocoa* (2nd Edn.), 163, Longmans, Green & Co., London (1961)

WILLS, J. B., *Agriculture and Land Use in Ghana*, Oxford University Press, London (1962)

## HEMIPTERA

*Sahlbergella singularis* Hgl.
*Distantiella theobroma* Dist.
*Bryocoropsis laticollis* Schum.
*Helopeltis bergrothi* Reut.
} *(Miridae)*

These four species, known as capsid bugs, are responsible in West Africa for causing much damage to cocoa and having marked effect on the growth of the tree. All four species are found in Ghana where *Sahlbergella* and *Distantiella* are the most common, but in Nigeria, *Sahlbergella* predominates and *Distantiella* occurs only locally. *Helopeltis* and *Bryocoropsis* are common in Ghana but much less in importance. Elsewhere in the cocoa-growing areas of the world only *Helopeltis* occurs. All species fly readily in the adult stage.

*Sahlbergella* and *Distantiella* are large, dark brown robust capsids with knobbed antennae (Fig. 5.3). *Bryocoropsis* is very similar but *Helopeltis* is a slender orange-coloured capsid with long legs and very long antennae. All possess toxic saliva which is injected into the plant tissues when feeding and causes a dark spot to appear at the point of entry. Eggs are laid in the soft tissues of the pod

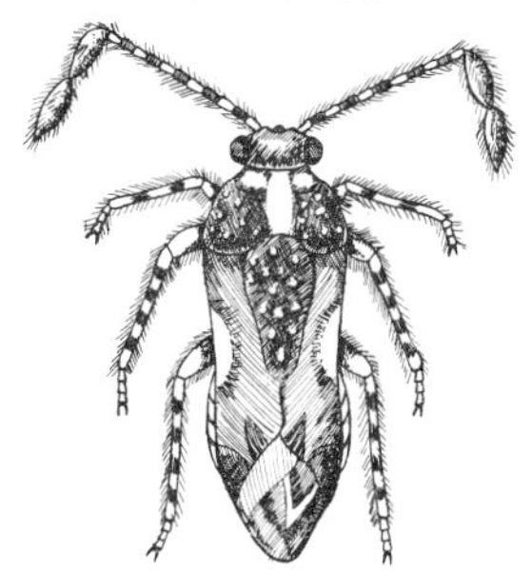

*Fig. 5.3.* Sahlbergella singularis *(adult)*

*Plate 5.4. Top: injury to cocoa plantation by capsid bugs, Ghana. Bottom: normal cocoa*

and young shoots which are green with young brown bark. The immature stages or nymphs, are wingless, carry toxic saliva and try to remain hidden on the trees within the leaf and branch axils. The whole life-cycle takes about 4–6 weeks to complete and several generations occur in a year (Cotterell, 1928 and 1943).

In Ghana and Nigeria damage to the cocoa tree is caused by the capsids feeding on the young new growth. As a result of the feeding punctures, caused both by adults and nymphs, the shoots are checked, black spots develop on them and they die back. To understand the meaning of this damage it must be understood that cocoa grows in a series of 'flushes' in which new growth is pushed out, especially after rains in late summer and autumn. It is this new growth which is prevented from developing properly and the natural growth of the cocoa tree is held up and no proper branch structure produced. The young cocoa tree also suffers and is permanently prevented from bearing pods. Capsids also breed and feed on pods causing a large number of black spots to appear near the base.

When cocoa is badly attacked by capsids there is a complete loss of leaf and the ground is exposed to the sky whereas normally cocoa produces a continuous canopy of foliage shading the ground from above (Plate 5.4). The shedding of the leaves is associated with die back of the shoots which are often invaded by a fungus *Calonectria* and which can kill the shoots (Kay, 1961). Heavily attacked cocoa is called 'blast' and the shoots show a characteristic injury known as 'hammer knock' in which the surface of the shoot is covered with small shallow depressions. In Ghana, Nigeria and the Ivory Coast the loss of yield of cocoa due to capsids is probably more important than losses from 'Swollen Shoot' virus. Box (1943) early recognised the importance of these insects.

## METHODS OF CONTROL

An attempt to control capsids was first made in Ghana on young cocoa. DDT was applied to the branch junction called the 'Jorquette' where capsids liked to shelter. A 25% DDT liquid was used at 5% strength in water applied with a sprayer or a brush.

The control of capsid on mature trees presented a difficulty because of their height. This was overcome in Ghana by using portable mist-blowers which delivered only 5 gal of water per acre (Plate 5.5). Trees could by this means, be effectively sprayed as the air-stream of the machine carries the spray high into the trees. Early work established that the best insecticide was 20% gamma BHC miscible liquid at 1 pt per acre (i.e. in 5 gal water). Two applications of an interval of 1 month are made, at 4 oz gamma BHC per acre repeated later at 2 oz per acre. The first double application is made in June and July (Stapley and Hammond, 1959). In Nigeria, successful application was made with a knapsack sprayer, using 10 gal per acre (Donald and Thresh, 1957).

The Ghana Government instituted large-scale spraying operations in 1957 which resulted in spectacular increases in yield. The total yield of all cocoa in Ghana recorded in 1960 was twice that of any previous year.

Dust insecticides can also be used but, in Ghana, they were found to be inferior to sprays. A dust of 5% BHC used at 10 lb per acre gave good results. In the Cameroons, dust seems to have been preferred.

Further trials were carried out with alternate insecticides to gamma BHC (Taylor, 1957). It has shown that endrin was the most effective insecticide even at 1 oz per acre but its high toxicity to man rules it out. Aldrin was not quite so effective as gamma BHC at the same rate of 4 oz per acre and both were more effective than dieldrin. Heptachlor and malathion were ineffective.

*Plate 5.5. Spraying with mistblowers against capsid bugs, Ghana*

In spite of considerable spraying in Ghana with gamma BHC few side effects have been noticed. The restoration of the foliage through the elimination of capsids have evidently improved the setting of the flowers. The insecticide treatment with gamma BHC had also removed undesirable ants from the trees especially *Oecophylla* and also reduced the ant population on the ground. In some places an increase of *Earias insulana* (or *bilaga*) Wlk. occurred following dieldrin application. This insect is sometimes found boring into the terminal growth of young cocoa trees. More important is the increase noted of *Marmara* spp. *(Lithocolletidae)*, a pod miner, especially after the use of aldrin, dieldrin, and endrin. The larva of this insect mines in the surface tissues of the pod. While this has no effect on the cocoa beans within, the appearance of the ripe pods, which are usually yellow at harvest, is spoiled and the dark brown mines cover the pod completely so that the ripeness of the pod cannot be judged.

Certain species of *Amblypelta* (Coreidae) cause similar damage in the Far East in the new cocoa plantations of New Guinea and the British Solomon Islands (Brown, 1958).

## SWOLLEN SHOOT OF COCOA

The great problem in cocoa of the last twenty years has been swollen shoot—a virus disease, the symptoms of which are a thickening of the bases of the new shoots. This disease was discovered by Posnette (1940) and it was thought to threaten the whole of the cocoa area of West Africa. On the advice of the Commission of Enquiry in 1948 a policy of cutting out infected trees was adopted. All trees showing leaf symptoms of the disease and those within five yards of them were cut down and burnt. This policy led to 63 million trees being cut out over the eleven-year period 1946–57 in Ghana alone which was about 10% of the total number of cocoa trees in the country (Hammond, 1957). In Nigeria from 1946–50 a total of 1,500,000 trees were cut out but thereafter large areas were abandoned as being too heavily infected. Over the following years about 300,000 trees were cut out up to 1957 (Lister and Thresh, 1957). Farmers were compensated for the loss of trees and encouraged to plant up young ones.

In the meantime, the method of transmission of the disease was investigated. It was shown that the chief vector of the virus was the mealybug *Pseudococcus njalensis* Laing, a species inhabiting many parts of the tree including the pods. This insect is relatively immobile but is attended by ants, especially of the genus *Crematogaster*. These ants transfer the mealybugs from tree to tree as well as protecting them while reproducing under tents. The object of the attention given to the mealybugs by the ants is to secure a drop of sweet liquid exuded by them. If not removed this liquid would foul the breeding places of the mealybugs, so the benefit is mutual.

Early attempts to overcome mealybugs were made with the systemic insecticide 'Dimefox' following a visit by representatives of industry who went to advise on the swollen shoot problem in 1947. Dimefox was injected into the trunks of the tree (Hanna *et al.*, 1955). A very good reduction in mealybug numbers was obtained but about 1 g per tree was needed. Persistence of the insecticide was about two months. Unfortunately in spite of good mealybug reduction, no change in the swollen shoot position could be demonstrated. This method finally fell into disrepute on the grounds of cost and toxic hazard; the method of application was far too slow and laborious.

Spraying against mealybugs even at 600 gal per acre with parathion and other insecticides was ineffective. A further insecticidal approach to the problem was made by using a heavy dosage of dieldrin to eliminate the ant population. The principle was that the mealybugs would be unable to survive without ants as with the removal of the ants mealybugs foul their own breeding grounds. The use of dieldrin was completely effective in removing the ants but led to a spectacular increase in the shoot borer *Eulophonotus myrmeleon* Feld. *(Cossidae)* which appeared in about 50% of the main trunks and branches. Obviously the experiment would need to run for several years before the effect on swollen shoot would be evident.

Thresh *et al.* (1960) showed in Nigeria that by spraying badly affected areas with gamma BHC the cocoa came back into bearing. Areas that had been abandoned, as containing too many trees affected with swollen shoot to be cut out, gave yields again after spraying. Obviously the spraying eliminated the capsids which had devastated the abandoned cocoa and were killing the trees faster than the swollen shoot virus.

## THYSANOPTERA

### *Selenothrips rubrocinctus* Giard *(Thysanoptera)*

Thrips are common on cocoa and occur at flowering time as they do on many other plants including coffee, citrus and certain deciduous fruit. This species occurs in South America, the West Indies, West Africa, particularly in Sao Tome, and the Far East. It is relatively unimportant on cocoa except during drought.

Thrips are small black insects with narrow fringed wings. They fly readily and frequent flowers of all kinds. The immature stages are nymphs and are invariably yellow in colour. If numerous, thrips can cause much loss of leaf surface due to the loss of sap from punctured cells. They live on the undersides of leaves which they cover with brown spots or specks of fluid discharged from the body. Damage can also occur to the pods. This happens at flowering time and, as the pod expands, shows up as a brown marking. This, however, does little more than spoil the appearance of the pod and is not sufficient to upset harvesting. In Trinidad, thrips damage is said to assume greater importance and cocoa trees suffer from defoliation. Action is seldom taken against thrips in cocoa but its incidence in West Africa was reduced to negligible proportions following the introduction of spraying against capsids.

## LEPIDOPTERA

Pod borers and pod miners are also unimportant except a species of *Marmara,* already mentioned as increasing following spraying against capsids. The cocoa moth, *Acrocercops cramerella* Sn. was a major pest of Java when this area produced the most cocoa in the world. The larvae tunnel in the pod and enter into the beans spoiling them at harvest.

Shoot and trunk borers are usually unimportant but reference has been made to the rapid increase of *Eulophonotus,* a trunk and branch borer, following heavy spraying with dieldrin against ants. The longhorn beetles *(Cerambycidae)* also attack cocoa as they occur in many forest trees. In North Borneo, new planting of cocoa was heavily attacked by a species of *Tragocephala* which girdles the young trunk at the first jorquette. It is difficult to prevent such attacks but monthly spraying or painting the trees at the jorquette with strong DDT is recommended. Other species are also reported causing similar damage, notably species of *Sterrastoma* in the West Indies and South America and of *Glenea* in Java.

## HYMENOPTERA

### *Formicoidea*

These are true ants and are normally of no importance as pests of cocoa. They are denizens of the forest and abound in innumerable species. Reference has been made to the association of *Crematogaster* with mealybugs on cocoa. Reference has also been made to the Parasol Ants on coffee in South and Central America. In Brazil, the 'Enxerto' ant is said to be a serious pest of cocoa in its own right. This species is *Azteca paraensis* Forel which makes nests in the trees, stripping off material from pods and shoots in building up the nest. This in itself causes damage to the trees and pods, especially when the ant is numerous. It also possesses a powerful sting.

### METHODS OF CONTROL

This is seldom attempted but one of the best and most active insecticides against ants of all kinds is gamma BHC. By blowing gamma BHC into the nest, the ants are made in time to abandon it. It has already been stated that spraying against capsids with gamma BHC in West Africa brought about a marked reduction in the ant population. Dieldrin can also be used but only as a tree-base spray otherwise undesirable effects can be produced.

## COLEOPTERA

### *Xyleborus morstatti* Hg. *(Scolytidae)*

This is a bark beetle, a normal inhabitant of the forest, but it will attack young cocoa newly planted, especially if the young trees suffer from a check. The adult beetle, which is very small and bullet-shaped, bores directly into the wood of the stem, usually about half-way from the soil to the growing point. Normally, the female beetle lays eggs in the bore-hole which develop into young larvae but, in cocoa, this does not always happen. Sometimes eggs are laid and larvae follow but the stem of the young tree is weakened anyway and dries out above the point of attack. No method of control has been worked out but treatment of the stem with dieldrin after planting out is suggested.

REFERENCES

BOX, H. E., *Memor. Cocoa Res. Sta. Tafo.,* Nos. 9 and 12 (1943)

BROWN, E. S., *Bull. Entomol. Res.,* **49,** 543 (1958)

COTTERELL, G. S., *Gold Coast Dept. Agr. Bull.,* **3** (1926)

COTTERELL, G. S., *Rep. Centr. Cocoa Res. Sta. Tafo.,* 46 (1943)

DONALD, R. G. and THRESH, J. M., *Rep. Cocoa Conf. London* 119 (1957)
HAMMOND, P. S., *Rep. Cocoa Conf. London,* 110 (1957)
HANNA, A. D., JUDENKO, E. and HEATHERINGTON, W., *Bull. Entomol. Res.,* **46,** 669 (1955)
KAY, D., *Tech. Bull. W. African Cocoa Res. Inst.,* **8** (1961)
KAY, D., LONGWORTH, J. F. and THRESH, J. M., *Proc. 8th Intern. Amer. Cocoa Conf. Trin. Tob.,* 224 (1960)
LISTER, R. M. and THRESH, J. M., *Rep. Cocoa Conf. London* 132 (1957)
POSNETTE, A. F., *Trop. Agr. Trin.,* **17,** 98 (1940)
STAPLEY, J. H. and HAMMOND, P. S., *Emp. J. Expt. Agr.,* **27,** 343 (1959)
TAYLOR, D. G., *Rep. Cocoa Conf. London,* 125 (1957)
WILLIAMS, G., *Bull. Entomol. Res.,* **44,** 101 (1953)

## DISEASES

### *Swollen Shoot Disease*

The most serious problem facing cocoa producers in West Africa is the menace of virus disease. This is illustrated by the history of its incidence in the Eastern Region of Ghana where the output of dry cocoa fell from 116,000 tons in 1936–37 to 38,000 tons in 1955–56. Other factors such as capsids contributed to this reduction, but the decline is a vivid demonstration of the damage which can be done by virus diseases (Dale, 1962).

So far, some fifty distinct viruses have been distinguished at the West African Cocoa Research Institute. The symptoms may appear on the shoots, roots, foliage and pods. The typical symptoms and those which were first recognised in 1936, are the swellings on branches and twigs (Plate 5.6), hence the usual name, swollen shoot disease. Later investigation showed that swellings also occurred on the roots. The symptoms on the leaves are variable but a frequent sign, particularly on young leaves, is the outlining of the veins by a narrow red band. The symptoms on the pods are uncommon, but light and dark green mottling has been observed. Affected pods are smaller than healthy ones and may contain only half the normal quantity of beans.

The swollen shoot virus complex is serious because many of the isolates are lethal, the time taken to kill the trees varying from three to six years, and in some cases, even longer.

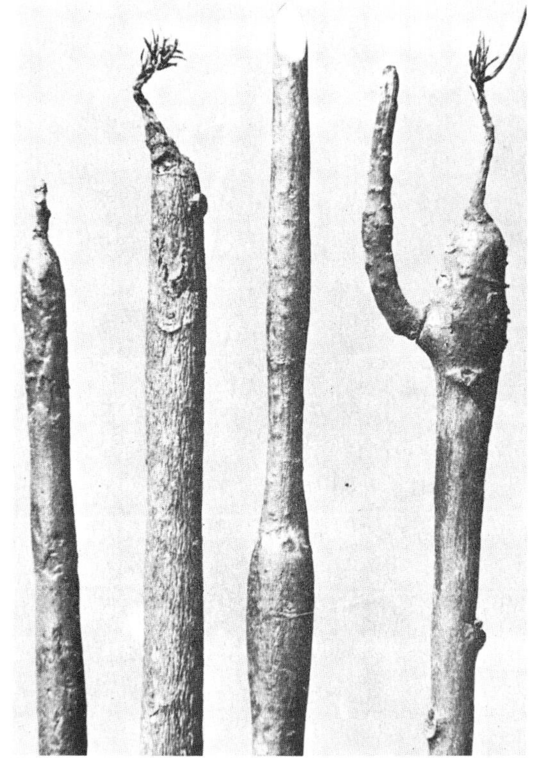

*Plate 5.6. Effect of cocoa swollen shoat virus on stems and chupons, Ghana (T.W. Tinsley, Oxford)*

After the discovery had been made that swollen shoot was due to a virus, the search began for the insect vectors. Various species of mealybugs were found to be the culprits. Some sixteen species have been found capable of transmitting one or more of the cocoa viruses. The exact status of each vector has not yet been determined but *Pseudococcus njalensis* is rated as the most important one in Ghana. Two other species of *Pseudococcus, P. hargreavesi,* and the other un-named, as well as *Planococcus citri,* have all been found to be efficient vectors. The number of mealybugs on the cocoa trees is variable but is often less than 100. The direct damage done by their feeding is small, and it is their ability to transmit disease which makes them so important.

As the virus story was gradually unfolded, it was clear that the mealybugs could carry the virus to both the indigenous plants and the crops. A large number of related species was therefore screened to determine whether or not they could be infected with the virus, and a survey was also made to find out which of the indigenous trees were carrying viruses which could be transmitted to cocoa. In the course of this work it was discovered that a small forest tree, *Cola chlamydantha,* which is common in parts of West Africa, is often infected with viruses of the swollen shoot type. The tree is found as a shade tree in cocoa plantations and is one of the hosts for *Pseudococcus njalensis.* There is therefore good reason for believing that the mealybugs carry the viruses from the *Cola* tree to the cocoa trees and vice versa. The cocoa viruses found in West Africa do not occur in Central America, so that there is now good circumstantial evidence for believing that the viruses were present in the indigenous flora before cocoa was introduced. It is therefore probable that the attack had begun many years before it was first observed.

In 1936 when work on swollen shoot began, the outbreaks were limited but scattered over a large area. In the succeeding years, the outbreaks grew larger and fresh sites became infected, with the result that cocoa production in much of the Eastern Region has now been wiped out.

### METHOD OF CONTROL

Much thought and experiment have been devoted to controlling the swollen shoot virus complex. No method is known of curing an infected tree, so that the only alternative at present is to prevent infection. Although some virus vectors such as aphids can be kept down with insecticides, this has not been found feasible with mealybugs. The only practical way of dealing with the problem is to eliminate the source of the virus. This requires the grubbing of all infected cocoa trees, the felling of potential carriers such as *Cola chlamydantha,* and the use of virus-free seedlings for planting.

It is easy to describe the scientific principles on which the anti-virus campaign must be waged, but their practical application presents the most formidable problems. The main difficulty has been the human one of persuading the farmer to destroy trees which may still be producing a few pods. Although the farmer was paid some compensation for felling diseased trees, the campaign was politically unpopular, and was thus liable to interruption.

Cutting out was first started in 1941, and by the end of 1957 no less than 70 million trees had been cut down. The Eastern Region, where the disease is at its worst, lost 62 million trees, but losses in Ashanti, where the young plantations are to be found, were about 1·4 million. Experience has shown that the removal of infected trees is an effective method of keeping the remaining trees healthy, but whether or not it will continue to be acceptable to the farmer, remains to be seen.

The possibility of using new varieties of cocoa which will either be immune or tolerant of the West African viruses is being pursued. Collections of new varieties of cocoa have been made in Central America and their reactions to the New Juaben virus studied. Some of the varieties, particularly those from the Upper Amazon area, are showing promise. There is thus the hope that the plant breeder will eventually provide a new variety which will be unaffected by the viruses present in West Africa.

REFERENCE

DALE, W. T., *Agriculture and Land Use in Ghana,* 286, Oxford University Press, London (1962)

## Black Pod (*Phytophthora palmivora* [Butl.] Butl.)

Black pod is a common fungus disease wherever cocoa is grown. Its incidence varies considerably from country to country, but it has been estimated that it reduces the world production by 7% (Hale, 1953).

As the common name indicates, the most obvious symptom of the disease is its effect on the pods. Soon after infection has taken place, the skin of the pod turns brown round the point of entry. This quickly darkens and enlarges until the whole of the pod turns black (Coloured Plate 10). The penetration of beans inside the pod is slower and a month may elapse before they are all destroyed. When the invasion of the pod is completed, the fungus grows down the stalk and invades the flower cushions. This is an important phase as the fungus is thought to persist from one season to the next in infected cushions, from which it can invade the young pods.

The fungus is disseminated by wind-borne spores which are produced on infected pods. The sporangiophores can be seen forming a light down on the infected surface of the pod soon after the first symptoms are visible. The sporangia only germinate when the relative humidity exceeds 95%. The sporangia can develop in two ways, either by producing a germ-tube which penetrates the host, or by the production of zoospores which swim about in the film of moisture for a very short time before settling down and quickly germinating. Infection is dependent on high humidity, and there is thus a close association between the weather and the incidence of infection.

As indicated above, there is considerable variation in the losses caused by black pod. The disease appears to be at its worst in Nigeria, and the British Cameroons, where losses may be as high as 90%, in Costa Rica the annual losses are put at 50%, Bahia and Western Samoa in the 25% range (Wharton, 1962). The disease is not generally rated as serious in Ghana, the published figures would suggest that it may amount to 10–15%.

## METHODS OF CONTROL

Black pod can be kept down in two ways, culturally, and by the use of fungicides. The cultural method has been successful in Bahia, Brazil, where on some estates it is the practice to remove infected pods as soon as the symptoms of the disease are seen. As the pods are the main source of inoculum, the technique is effective. The method is rarely used in West Africa because the growers there are not accustomed to harvesting their pods more than three to four times a year.

*Plate 5.7. Spraying cocoa for blackpod control, Nigeria (A Plant Protection photograph)*

Numerous trials have shown that a fair measure of control can be obtained by using copper fungicides, but this treatment can only be justified economically when the losses are serious, for example, in excess of 25%.

Pod spraying is regularly practised in parts of Nigeria (Plate 5.7), the fungicide either being home-made carbide-mixture, or one of the ready-prepared fixed coppers. The carbide-Bordeaux is made from 1 lb of copper sulphate, 6 oz of calcium carbide, and 10 gal of water, a concentration that is referred to as 1% Bordeaux. For low volume spraying the proprietary materials such as those based on cuprous oxide are preferred. The usual concentration is 4 lb of product (2 lb of copper) per 100 gal of water.

In Nigeria successful results have been obtained by starting spraying in June and repeating the application every three weeks until the end of October. A programme of seven sprays is expected to reduce the loss from about 50% on the unsprayed trees to only 10% on the treated ones.

REFERENCES

HALE, S. L., 'World Production and Consumption 1951 to 1953', *Rep. Cocoa Conf. London 1953* (1953)

WHARTON, A. L., *Agriculture and Land Use in Ghana*, 333, Oxford University Press, London (1962)

## Witches' Broom Disease
## (*Marasmius perniciosus* Stahel)

Witches' broom disease is the most damaging malady of cocoa in South America. It is due to a fungus which causes hypertrophy of the shoots and results in their becoming stubby and nearly leafless. The cushions from which the cocoa inflorescences develop are also attacked and consequently only produce small dormant pods of no value. As the disease progresses, an increasing number of young shoots become infected until at the height of an epidemic the tree is covered with witches' brooms and there are very few healthy shoots. The fungus can also penetrate the pods and the beans in them are valueless. It is not surprising that attacks of this magnitude completely destroy the crop.

The original home of the disease was probably in the Upper Amazon valley. From there it has spread outwards to the neighbouring South American countries—Peru, Ecuador, Colombia, Venezuela and the Guianas. In the 1920s it practically wiped out cocoa growing in Surinam and has had disastrous effects on the cocoa growers of Trinidad and Ecuador. It is also infiltrating in the West Indies, reaching Trinidad in 1928, Tobago in 1939, and Grenada in 1948. Fortunately the disease has not reached Central America or the Brazilian area of Bahia, and it is not found in Africa or Asia.

The fungal fructifications are small toadstools with pale crimson caps. They grow on the dead witches' brooms but are slow to develop as they do not appear until three to six months after the shoots have died. The toadstools release wind-borne spores at night when the humidity is very high. The spores can only infect young tissues, but if this happens to be a bud, no obvious signs are seen until a flush of growth, which may be up to six weeks later. The hypertrophied shoots have only a short life of six to eight weeks, and then die.

A full account of the witches' broom disease will be found in a monograph by Baker *et al.*, 1957.

### METHODS OF CONTROL

Fungicides have not been very effective in controlling witches' broom disease, and so far the only successful method has been the removal of infected tissues. The aim is to cut out all diseased parts before the toadstools appear as the fungus can only spread by means of the spores which they produce. As the minimum time between infection and the appearance of the toadstools is about four months, cutting out is usually only necessary three times a year.

It is also hoped that the plant breeder may be able to help. The upper Amazon region has been searched for resistant varieties and two have been found to be almost immune after examination in Trinidad. The bean size of these Amazonian varieties was rather too small, so a programme has been started to produce a new variety in which it is hoped to combine good bean size with resistance.

REFERENCE

BAKER, R. E. D. and HOLLIDAY, H., '*Witches' Broom Disease of Cacao (Marasmius perniciosus* Stahel), Commonwealth Mycological Institute (1957)

Tea is an Asian crop, probably originating in southern China from whence came all supplies until about the middle of the 19th century. Afterwards it began to be cultivated in Assam, India, and considerably later in Ceylon and Indonesia. These countries are still the main tea-producing regions of the world, although some tea is now grown in Africa and South America. The world acreage devoted to this crop in 1955 was about $2\frac{1}{4}$ million acres (Eden, 1959).

The main tea-growing areas are served by two research stations, one at Tocklai, Assam, India, and the other at Telewkele, Ceylon. There is now also an African research station for tea at Kericho in Kenya.

Tea suffers from few serious pests compared with the important disease of blister blight. Probably the two most damaging pests are *Helopeltis* and red spider, and since tea is predominantly grown in the Far East, the same pests are to be found in all regions. Pests in other parts of the world are, at present, mainly local ones of minor importance.

The serious diseases of tea occur in Asia. The newer plantations in East Africa and Nyasaland, although they have their troubles, are remarkably disease-free (Kearns, 1963). The most dangerous tea disease with which planters have had to deal is blister blight. Although it was first recorded in 1868, it was relatively unimportant until 1946 when it suddenly spread to both Southern India and Ceylon. Blister blight would undoubtedly have wiped out the Ceylon tea industry had fungicides not been available. The saving of so important a part of the tea industry from destruction by blister blight is undoubtedly one of the major triumphs of plant pathology.

Root diseases are important because they can kill a tea bush at any time during its life and thus reduce the yield per acre. After the plantation has reached the end of its economic life, all the bushes are grubbed and the site replanted. This monoculture favours root disease.

In addition to the specialist literature, information on tea diseases is accessible. Hainsworth (1952) has written a book on both the pests and diseases of tea, while Eden (1958) devotes a chapter on diseases in his comprehensive book on tea. Both have been consulted during the preparation of this section.

REFERENCES

EDEN, T., *Tea*, Longmans Green & Co., London (1958)

HAINSWORTH, E., *Tea Pests and Diseases and their Control*, W. Heffer & Sons Ltd., Cambridge (1952)

KEARNS, H. G. H., *Ann. Appl. Biol.*, **51**, 358 (1963)

## HEMIPTERA

### *Helopeltis theivora* Wlk. *(Miridae)*

Formerly known as the Tea Mosquito Bug of India, the insect also occurs in Indonesia but not in Ceylon. *Helopeltis* is a slender bug but with relatively long legs. It flies poorly. The adult possesses toxic saliva and its feeding marks on the young leaves, stems and developing buds are seen as brown spots (Fig. 5.4). The young shoots and the leaves occurs on the newest growth which is the same part of the bush which is picked for processing in the tea factory. In severe attacks, the feeding of the bugs may entirely suppress development of new growth on the plucking table of the bush and whole areas of planted

*Fig. 5.4. Damage to tea shoots by Helopeltis*

tea may go out of production as the plucker is faced with a forest of bare twigs. The insect is considered to be one of the more widespread and important pests of tea.

*Helopeltis* breeds on the tea bush, eggs being inserted into the tissues normally of the soft stem, leaving only the cap of the egg with two bristles of unequal length visible. The eggs are flask-shaped, typical of this group of insects. The nymphs grow up, feeding on the tea bush but tend to hide in the daytime. During the cooler season of North India, some adult *Helopeltis* shelter in the neighbouring jungle returning to the tea in the spring. They also remain on the bark or on the ground and become active again when the bush begins to 'flush' in March. The greatest activity occurs from June to September, corresponding to the period of greatest 'flush'.

METHODS OF CONTROL

It is standard practice to spray against *Helopeltis* on tea with DDT. A 5% dust is also used but in India spraying is preferred, probably because of the machinery available. The rate of DDT is 1 lb of 50% w.p. in 40 gal of water and only the top of the bush is sprayed. Spraying should begin as soon as the damage is first noticed and is usually limited to the affected bushes and those adjacent to them, unless the damage is extensive. In some areas, especially those sheltered by neighbouring jungle, populations of *Helopeltis* can be high and overall spraying is necessary. Many variations are possible, including the so-called 'barrier-spraying', in which areas are isolated by a line of bushes 10 deep. Normally one spraying, properly applied at the outset of the damage, is quite sufficient as DDT remains effective for at least a month. Two men can spray one acre a day.

Other insecticides have been tried such as aldrin and dieldrin but are doubtfully superior to DDT and undesirable residues may occur. BHC, including gamma BHC, causes taint in the processed tea and is not to be recommended. Before the advent of DDT, the planter had to contend with *Helopeltis* unaided. Various procedures in planning and planting were examined but there is no evidence that any of them were successful. Early insecticides, such as pyrethrum, were ineffective and possessed insufficient persistence.

*Helopeltis schoutedeni* Reut. and *H. bergrothi* Reut. also occur on tea in East Africa. The young stems of newly planted tea are frequently attacked and may become cankered but at present attacks are not of economic importance. Control is easily achieved, if necessary with DDT.

ACARINA

*Oligonychus coffeae* Nietn. The Red Spider Mite

Many mites are recorded on tea. Some are serious pests and the most important is considered the Red Spider Mite which occurs in all the tea-growing countries of the Far East and is also found in abundance on tea in Africa. It is probably the most serious tea pest in India, Ceylon and Indonesia.

Red spider occurs on tea throughout the year, rising to a peak of population and then declining. Affected bushes turn red in colour and later coppery. With the coming of rain, the bushes recover, probably because many of the mites are physically washed away. Red spider feeds on the leaves of the tea bush, piercing the cells and sucking the sap. All stages are found, eggs, immature stages and adults. The mites are readily distributed either on clothing or on animals or by wind, the mite being transported on a long thread. In Northern India, where tea sheds its leaves in winter, the mites still remain upon the bush and there is no period when they are inactive (Colour Plate 11), (Das, 1962).

The intensity of red spider attack is influenced by several factors which can be enumerated as follows:

1. Weather. Red spider multiplies more rapidly under hot and dry conditions, especially drought.

2. Soil. Bushes growing in hot sandy soil are more subject to red spider attack than bushes in soils which do not dry out so readily.
3. Shade. Much tea is grown under partial shade provided by planted trees. Shaded tea is less attacked by red spider than unshaded.
4. Type of tea. Certain types of tea are more susceptible to red spider than others.
5. Defoliation after pruning. On tea subject to red spider attacks, removal of the remaining leaves after pruning reduces the residual red spider population on the leaves and delays build-up in the next season.

## METHODS OF CONTROL

Prophylactic spraying has been found to be of doubtful value and the normal practice is to apply two rounds of acaricidal sprays at the beginning of an attack. The interval between the two rounds varies from six to fourteen days in relation to the length of the incubation period of the eggs, which varies according to the temperature. Some lime-sulphur is still used but chlorobenzilate at 0·05%, tetradifon (Tedion) at 0·016% and dicofol (Kelthane) at 0·37% have been found to give adequate control in north-east India. Tolerances of residues on made tea in the case of chlorobenzilate and dicofol have not yet been established and it is recommended that the leaf from two rounds of plucking subsequent to spraying is discarded. The residue tolerance on tea for tetradifon has been set at 8 ppm by the U.S. Food and Drug Administration. East Africa recommends the use of 2 lb dicofol (18·5% w.p. per acre) or 1 pt of dimethoate (32%) applied in 10 to 100 gal of water per acre. A second spray with a minimum interval of one week between spraying and plucking is necessary.

Many other species of mites are found on tea of which the most important are:

*Phytoptus theae* Watt.—the Pink Mite.
*Phytoptus carinatus* Green—the Purple Mite.
*Brevipalpus phoenicis* Geij.—the Red Crevice Mite.
*Tarsonemus translucens* Green—the Yellow Mite.

*Brevipalpus* is similar in its effect to *Oligonychus*. It is a large mite with a brick-red colour and lays eggs in the crevices of the stem. Lime-sulphur, chlorobenzilate and dicofol have been found to be effective in North-East India and in East Africa chlorobenzilate at 10 fl oz (25%) is recommended.

*Phytoptus spp.* are *Eriophyidae.* These are minute vermiform mites with two pairs of legs only. They also cause a similar effect upon the bush.

*Tarsonemus* is a translucent mite seldom seen and is susceptible to DDT and other insecticides.

## COLEOPTERA

### *Xyleborus fornicatus* Eichoff. *(Scolytidae)*

This beetle is known as the Shot-hole Borer, a name which is derived from the numerous exit holes which occur in the wood of the branches of the tea bush when attacked by this insect. *Xyleborus* attacks many different kinds of trees displaying a preference for weakened or dying wood. On tea, as a pest, it occurs principally in Ceylon. *Xyleborus* belongs to the sub-family *Ipinae* or Ambrosia Beetles which are characterised by their habit of introducing fungi into their galleries which grow on the excrement of the beetles. Both the beetles and the larvae feed on the fungi and the tunnels turn black. The beetles bore into the bushes and make short tunnels in the wood in which the eggs are deposited. The eggs hatch into grubs or larvae which remain in the wood extending the tunnels or galleries. Pupation occurs and the beetles emerge to fly to other bushes; several generations occur during a year.

## METHODS OF CONTROL

Control is not always necessary but recently trials by Judenko (1960) have shown that dieldrin can be effective in preventing damage. He recommends 1–1·5 lb dieldrin per acre applied in 60–100 gal of water making two or three applications at intervals of a few weeks. Application is best made after pruning, and all the wood of the bush must be wetted by the spray. This gives protection for over one year.

## LEPIDOPTERA

There are many species of caterpillars which are found on the tea bush. These occur from time to time and can cause damage when large local populations occur. Several generations may occur. As a rule all are susceptible to DDT and spraying will eradicate them. The commonest species are

### *Biston suppressaria* Gn. *(Selidosemidae)*

This is a 'looper' caterpillar. It can occur in large numbers and strip the foliage. Eggs are normally laid on the wood of the bush. The moths are sluggish in habit and can be collected by hand. The caterpillars, when excessive in number, often succumb to a bacterial disease which eliminates the entire population.

### *Andraca bipunctata* Wlk. *(Saturniidae)*

This is the Bunch Caterpillar from its habit of spending the day time in clusters in the bush. Collection of the caterpillars is usually practised as a method of control.

### *Thosea spp. (Limacodidae)*

These are 'Nettle Grubs' so-called because the caterpillars possess stinging hairs. Many species occur and can be found on other plants. They constitute a nuisance to pickers rather than as direct pests of the tea bush.

### *Homonae coffearia* Nietn. *(Tortricidae)*

This is known as the Tea Tortrix. It is common both in India and Ceylon. The caterpillar spins leaves together causing the shoots to bend. Sometimes every shoot in a bush is so spun up and the young leaves are unsuitable for picking. The best way to deal with this insect is to pick off and destroy the leaves which are folded together.

This caterpillar is frequently heavily parasitised by a Braconid parasite *Macrocentrus hormonae* introduced from Java into Ceylon about 1937.

## APPLICATION OF INSECTICIDES

Spraying of tea is usually carried out by hand-operated or pneumatic knapsack sprayers. In India, Ceylon and Indonesia, spraying is dominated by control measures necessary against Blister Blight. For this disease, spraying is carried out with the knapsack sprayers fitted with low volume jets so that the application rate is about 12–16 gal per acre. Only the tops of the bushes are sprayed. A similar type of application is suitable for the control of *Helopeltis* but not for pests such as red spider where more wash per bush is required. Engine-driven sprayers are seldom used in tea and the portable mist-blower has never found favour, probably because of the difficulty of operating such a machine in the density of tea plantations.

Dusts are also used in tea as for example for Blister Blight control, in Indonesia. Dusting at 5–10 lb per acre is usually carried out by means of powerful motorised dusters mounted on a cart or truck operating from roadways built along the contours.

REFERENCES

DAS, G. M., *Two and a Bud,* **9,** 17 (1962)
HAINSWORTH, E., *Tea Pests and Diseases and Their Control,* W. Heffer & Sons Ltd., Cambridge (1952)
JUDENKO, E., *Tea Quart.,* **31,** 19, 72 (1960)

DISEASES

## Blister Blight (*Exobasidium vexans* Massee)

Blister blight is a disease which mainly attacks the foliage (Plate 5.8) and to a lesser extent, the shoots of the tea plant. As the English name indicates, the infected leaves develop blisters which quickly increase in numbers until practically all the young foliage is diseased. Its appearance in Ceylon and southern India in 1946 threatened the very existence of the tea industry there.

As previously indicated, blister blight has been known since 1868 where it had been seen in Assam. In the succeeding years it was recorded in Formosa, Japan and Indo-China but the industry was able to survive. How the disease suddenly arrived in the south is not known. Since then the disease has appeared in Sumatra in 1949, Malaya in 1950, and Java in 1951. This phase of its spread is thought to have been initiated by wind-borne spores from Ceylon.

The arrival of blister blight in Ceylon made it necessary for the Tea Research Institute there to devote much of its energies to a more detailed study of the disease and particularly to methods of controlling it (Portsmouth, 1961). It was found that the majority of the infections take place on the upper surface of the leaf, germination being favoured by moderate temperatures and high humidity. The first symptom is the appearance of a transluscent spot within 6–10 days of infection. After this the blister forms on the underside of the leaf, and about 7 days later the epidermis ruptures and spores are released. It has been found that the spores are forcibly shot clear of the hymenium (Fig. 5.5) and are then carried by the wind. Spore discharge continues for 7–10 days, during which time a single large blister may produce several million spores. The total quantity of spores produced by one infected bush is thus absolutely enormous, and explains the speed with which the disease can build up to an epidemic when weather conditions favour it. As the blister ages, it turns black and dies. The fungus has no resting stage and is thus

*Plate 5.8. Tea-foliage with blister blight pustules, Ceylon (Tea Research Institute of Ceylon)*

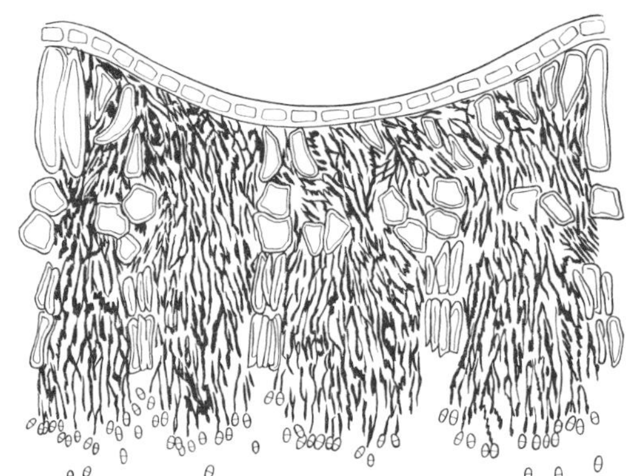

*Fig. 5.5. Transverse section of hymenium of blister blight of tea*

*Plate 5.9. Dusting tea for blister blight control, Indonesia (Dr. Churchward, Indonesia)*

dependent for its survival on continued growth throughout the year.

METHODS OF CONTROL

Research on methods of control was also actively prosecuted. The discovery that the spores were extremely susceptible to copper fungicides was an important one, and enabled the research workers to concentrate on the formidable problem of application. The Ceylon tea plantations are frequently planted on steep slopes which make mechanical spraying impossible, and the use of large volumes of spray fluids very difficult.

The problem was eventually solved by the use of pneumatic knapsack sprayers which are charged mechanically and then carried on the back of the sprayman through the plantation. The standard rate of spray eventually settled down to 6 oz of copper fungicide in 15 gal of water per acre. The most widely used copper fungicides are based on cuprous oxide and on copper oxychloride.

Trials were carried out comparing yields from plots sprayed at 7 and 14 day intervals. The best results were given by weekly spraying. It was also important to keep down copper residues and this was best done by spraying immediately after the tea had been picked. In Ceylon picking is usually carried out every 9–10 days, so that the programme has now settled down to routine spraying as soon as possible after plucking. This generally necessitates about 15 sprays each year.

Control using copper fungicide dusts was also investigated, as dusting would be very attractive in areas where water supply was difficult (Plate 5.9). It was found to be necessary to dust every 5 days to get as good a control as was given by spraying every 10 days. Spraying is usually more effective than dusting so that spraying will be preferred in the wetter areas where the disease is difficult to control, and dusting in the drier areas where it is easier.

The research findings were publicised in Ceylon in 1950 and made such rapid headway that by 1955 it had become routine practice on some 250,000 acres of tea which were affected by the disease.

The anxiety caused by blister blight was intensified by the memory that the coffee plantations in Ceylon were destroyed by leaf rust in the 1870s. It is a measure of the advance of plant pathology that the tea industry was brought through a serious setback in an astonishingly short time.

REFERENCE

PORTSMOUTH, G. B., *Outl. Agric.*, **2**, 81 (1961)

## *Root Rots*

As already indicated, root diseases of tea are a serious problem in most of the tea-growing areas of the world. At least nine different fungi are accepted as sufficiently lethal parasites to kill tea bushes. It is, however, not necessary to discuss each disease in detail as they have certain characteristics in common and are all dealt with on the same general principles. Two examples will therefore suffice, *Ustulina* root rot (*Ustulina deusta* (Fr.) Petrak) and *Armillaria* root rot (*Armillaria mellea* (Vahl ex Fr.) Kummer).

*Ustulina* root rot is thought to be the most serious root disease in northern India, and is common in India and Ceylon. Bushes, the roots of which have been attacked by the fungus, are suddenly killed. If such bushes are cut down leaving only a stump, the fungus will grow over the collar, developing a white felt-like covering which later turns black, hence the common name charcoal stump rot for this disease. When the diseased roots are dug up irregular black patches can be seen on the outside, and if the bark is removed, white fan-shaped patches of mycelium can be found.

The fungus spreads from a diseased bush to a healthy one by means of hyphae which penetrate the healthy root when it comes in contact with an infected one. The fungus persists in the soil, living on infected dead roots which remain as a source of inoculum.

The fungus also produces spores on the black fructifications round the collar. The spores, which are produced in great numbers, are dispersed by the wind and mostly perish, but if they land on the cut stump of a shade-tree, they germinate and the mycelia then spread through the root system.

### METHODS OF CONTROL

No fungicides are as yet available for preventing underground infection, neither can they be used on a large scale for soil sterilisation. Plantation hygiene is thus the only method which can be used. It is the accepted practice to grub dead bushes and to remove as many roots as possible.

*Armillaria* root rot is a common parasite of tree roots in both the temperate and tropical regions. It is a serious trouble in East African and Indonesian plantations but is infrequent in India and Ceylon.

The foliage on bushes affected by *Armillaria* turns yellow and soon afterwards wilts and dies. Examination of the collar of the bush usually shows longitudinal cracks, and removal of the bark from the roots normally discloses a mass of white mycelium on the surface of the wood. Black, root-like strands, called rhizomorphs, can be found spreading extensively over the root surface, under the root bark, or in the soil nearby. It is these which have given rise to the popular name, boot-lace fungus. *Armillaria* rhizomorphs can be frequently observed living on the surface of forest trees and planted mature tea without apparently causing damage.

### METHODS OF CONTROL

The *Armillaria* problem has been carefully studied in both East Africa and Malawi. Losses from this cause were frequent when tea was planted on newly-cleared forest land. It was known that *Armillaria* could only live on roots high in carbohydrates. Leach in 1939 carried out trials in Malawi of ring-barking trees for some months before felling, the removal of the bark preventing the downward translocation of carbo-hydrates. The scheme effectively prevented the fungus from developing on the roots of dead trees (Goodchild, 1958). Further investigations in Kenya have shown that *Armillaria* is a common associate of tree roots and that they become very susceptible to attack after the tree has been felled. Ring-barking of forest trees before felling is also practised in Kenya. It has not proved quite so effective there as in Malawi but still markedly reduces the incidence of *Armillaria* in the following tea crop (Gibson *et al.*, 1961).

In recent years, the practice of killing trees before felling has become general in East Africa, both for forest trees and in the routine removal of shade trees of *Albizzia* and *Grevillea*. It is done by cutting a 'frill' in the bark near the base of the stem, and the pouring of a dilute solution of 2, 4, 5-T into it. The chemical is applied 6 to 18 months before the trees are removed. Reduction of starch reserves in the roots by this method is rapid, and the risk of *Armillaria* infection following removal of the tree is reduced. In the case of *Grevillea* shade trees, current practice is to kill the tree by this method and afterwards remove the dead trunk at ground level, leaving the roots in the soil (T.E.P., 1966).

Should a tea bush become infected by *Armillaria*, it and its immediate neighbours must be grubbed and all the roots burnt.

REFERENCES

GIBSON, A. S. and GOODCHILD, N. A., '*Armillaria mellea* in Kenya Tea Plantations', *Rep. 6th Commonwealth Mycol. Conf. 1960* (1961)

GOODCHILD, N. A., '*Armillaria mellea* (Vahl) Fr.', *Proc. 5th Conf., Tea Res. Instit. E. Africa,* 19 (1958)

T.E.P., *Tea Estate Practice,* Tea Research Institute of East Africa (1966)

## Black Rot (*Corticium theae* Bernard and *C. invisum* Petch)

Black rot is a leaf disease which is common in north-east India. It is caused by two closely related species of *Corticium* which differ mainly in the way in which they overwinter.

Black rot is a summer disease which spreads through the plantation in warm, moist weather. The first symptoms are small dark necrotic spots which quickly coalesce forming larger patches. Eventually the leaf is killed and drops off. Leaves dropping on to healthy ones infect them also as the mycelium soon spreads the disease. Although contact increases the disease, basidiospores formed on the underside of the leaves are the main method of dissemination. These spores can be airborne or they may be carried on the clothing of those working in the plantation.

Both fungi overwinter on the bush, *Corticum invisum* forming small hard brown sclerotia, and *C. theae* dormant mycelical strands which adhere to the branches. After the rains have started in the spring, the resting phase of both fungi send out hyphae which creep along the branches until they reach a leaf, thus starting the summer cycle.

### METHODS OF CONTROL

To prevent black rot, it is important to prevent leaf infection in the spring. This is done by spraying with a copper fungicide and repeating the application a fortnight later.

## Red Rust (*Cephaleuros parasiticus* Karst.)

Red rust of tea is a curiosity among plant diseases. It is not caused by one of the rust fungi but by an uncommon pathogen, a parasitic alga. The name red rust was given to the disease because the fructifications form bright orange red patches on young stems and leaves.

The disease is an important one in India and is frequently found in Ceylon. It is responsible for killing some of the young shoots with the result that the weakened tea bush does not suppress the weeds beneath it. Thus the disease not only directly reduces the yield of tea, but makes extra weeding necessary. The trouble can also be very long-lasting, the disease persisting in localised patches for 15–20 years after planting.

The red rust spores are produced in enormous numbers during the period between the end of April and early June. They are dispersed by the wind, and when they land on a suitable host, germinate and penetrate into the tissue. Not only is the tea plant infected, but some of the green manure crops used in tea plantations, such as medeloa *(Tephrosia spp.)* and the leguminous shade trees *(Albizzia spp.)* are very susceptible. There is thus no lack of sources of infection in areas where the disease is present.

The alga on penetrating the host forms a thallus under the epidermis where it can be seen as a dark patch. The thallus is variable in size, varying from as little as 1 mm to as large as 5 cm. If the attack is heavy, the shoots are killed. With lighter attacks the shoots survive but the leaves develop characteristic yellow patterns in the following spring. As indicated above, the fructifications are produced in early summer, approximately a year thus elapsing between infection and spore production.

### METHODS OF CONTROL

From what has been said, it will be clear that once infection has taken place, the alga is protected from any spray treatment. The only possible way of controlling the disease is to kill the spores before infection has taken place. This is done by spraying the tea bushes with a fungicide containing the equivalent of 50% of metallic copper at a concentration of 2½ lb per 100 gal of water. The first application is made when spore production is beginning, and is repeated 3–4 weeks later. The aim is to get a rainfast, protective deposit of copper on the growing shoots as these are the only susceptible parts of the bush.

In addition to spraying, any cover crops infected by red rust must be removed well before spore production begins. If this is not done, the inoculum produced is so large that the tea will be heavily infected and show very severe symptoms a year later.

The casual consumer of a banana in Europe or North America might be surprised to learn that world production of bananas was estimated at the very substantial figure of 20 million tons in 1955. This quantity is much larger than might be expected, due to the fact that most of the bananas grown, some 17 million tons of all varieties, are consumed locally, and only 3 million tons, about 15% enter into world trade.

The banana is a truly tropical plant as it can only be grown commercially in those parts of the world which are frost-free during the winter. It is believed to have originated in south-east Asia, where it was probably a source of food for man from the very earliest times. From Malaysia it spread to India and East Africa, both countries where it is an important contributor to the food supply. The Portuguese were responsible for taking the banana to the Canary Islands in the fifteenth century and to the New World a hundred years later. The banana, with only a short natural storage life, could not be exported to the temperate zone until fast sailing ships had been built. The coming of steamers, and particularly the introduction of refrigeration, allowed the trade to develop into the huge industry it is today.

Although the export trade started modestly, the increasing quantities required called for a steady supply of fruit, a requirement most readily met by the development of large uniform plantations. Such units were developed in the Caribbean, particularly Jamaica, and later in the countries bordering the Pacific coast of Central America.

The most important commercial variety of banana is 'Gros Michel', which is ideally suited to the export trade. It has many attributes which have contributed to its popularity. It is easy to handle during transportation due to its compact finger habit, with the 'hands' fitting tightly to the main stem. The bunches are large and uniform, and although harvested while still green, ripen evenly to a beautiful golden yellow.

Bananas are usually grown in large plantations without crop rotation, a system which suits man, but which also creates conditions very favourable to fungi. Two fearful epidemics, Panama disease, and leaf spot, have struck the 'Gros Michel' variety. How these diseases have been fought and the changes they brought about, is one of the many fascinating chapters in plant pathology.

The banana diseases have been comprehensively described by Wardlaw (1961), and a chapter on the subject is to be found in Simmonds' (1959) book on banana growing. Simmonds cites 182 insect pests found attacking bananas, together with 7 mites and 6 eelworms. He then selects only five major pests, all insects, four of which are specific to bananas, which he considers are important. It is, in fact, doubtful if any pest is of real significance in banana production in comparison with the over-riding importance of diseases.

REFERENCES

SIMMONDS, N. W., *Bananas,* Longmans, Green & Co., London (1959)

WARDLAW, C. W., *Banana Diseases,* Longmans, Green & Co., London (1961)

## COLEOPTERA

### *Cosmopolites sordidus* Germ. *(Curculionidae)*

This is the Banana Borer. The insect is a weevil, in appearance like a large version of the Grain Weevil. It is present in all the banana-growing areas in the World.

The weevil bores into the base of the banana stem. Eggs are deposited in the stems and the larvae arising continue to live within the stem making endless tunnels. Several generations occur during the year and the insect is evidently specific to the banana genus. It is indeed doubtful just how much damage is caused by *Cosmopolites.* Obviously if large numbers occur considerable tunnelling of the stems can occur, which must weaken the plant but it is obvious that a vigorously growing banana can tolerate many borers (Colour Plate 12). The weevils can live for a time in cut stems, that is, those felled after producing a bunch of fruit.

### METHODS OF CONTROL

Cultural control has really been the only method practised. This method consists in cleaning up banana plantations by removing fallen and felled stems which can harbour the weevils. The removal of trash (fallen leaves) and weeds also prevent weevils sheltering in plantations. It is also notable that cut stems can be used as traps for weevils if removed at intervals and replaced by fresh pieces of stems about 1–2 ft in length. In planting new areas suckers should be free from weevil otherwise the insect is transported to the new ground at the beginning.

Biological control has been attempted in many areas especially in the Pacific Islands with little success. The predatory beetle *Plaesius javanus* Er. *(Histeridae)* from Java has been mostly used.

Probably the only successful chemical control is that reported by Whalley (1957) in Uganda who used 0·5% dieldrins dust applied around the base of stools at about 1 cwt per acre. This dust persisted for 2½ months and completely prevented infestation. Similar results have been reported by other workers notably Leach (1958) in Jamaica and Simmonds (1953) in Trinidad.

Even so the dust treatment has never been adopted as a routine treatment by banana growers, in spite of much publicity. BHC is phytotoxic to banana roots and should not be used.

### *Pentalonia nigronervosa* Coq. *(Aphididae)*

This is the banana aphid. It occurs in all the principal banana-growing countries except Africa. As a pest, it is of no importance as its feeding has little effect on vigorous banana stems and it tends to occur at the edges of leaf folds. On nursery plants, it may be more important but interest in *Pentalonia* lies in its ability to transmit the virus disease Bunchy Top. It is doubtful if this is the main means by which the disease is spread.

Very strenuous efforts to eliminate the aphids were made in the abaca plantations of North Borneo by spraying (Mapother and Tapscott, 1959) but it is doubtful if the action was justified. Other aphid species not specific to bananas in the Philippines are said to transmit mosaic.

*Ceramiolia viriolis* Douse also causes leaf damage in Ecuador and it is customary to add insecticide to the fungicidal sprays for the control.

The root nematode *Radopholis similis* is said to be responsible for damage to bananas in some areas but this is doubtful.

REFERENCES

LEACH, R., *Farmer,* **62,** 204 (1958)

MAPOTHER, H. R. and TAPSCOTT, A. K., *Ann. Rep. Long Ashton,* 142 (1959)

SIMMONDS, H. W. and SIMMONDS, F. J., *Trop. agr. Trin.,* **30,** 216 (1953)

SIMMONDS, N. W., *Bananas,* Longmans (1959)

WHALLEY, P. E., *E. African Agr. J.,* **23,** 110 (1957)

### Panama Disease or Banana Wilt (*Fusarium oxysporum* Schl. *f. cubense* [E. F. Smith] Snyder and Hansen)

The first major disease which attacked bananas was called Panama disease from the area where it first became severe, but banana wilt is a better name as it is descriptive of the symptoms. The disease has for many years been the subject of extensive research work, which has been summarised in a monograph by Stover (1962).

The most important commercial variety, 'Gros Michel', was particularly susceptible, but a few other varieties such as 'Silk' and 'Bluggoe' were equally so. Plants at any age were liable to be infected. The first symptom was a yellowing of the outer margin of the leaf, usually beginning with the older ones. Next the leaf wilts, followed by buckling of the leaf stalk, which results in the leaves

*Plate 5.10. Panama disease of bananas (A Plant Protection photograph)*

hanging down (Plate 5.10). Later, only the innermost leaf remains erect, the pseudostem being covered by a skirt of dead brown leaves. Eventually, all the aerial parts of the plant are killed but suckers form round the base. Most of these suckers also become infected with the result that there is very little recovery. Poor growth with no crop of any value may continue for a few years before the stool finally dies out.

The banana is readily propagated from the suckers, but the devastating nature of the disease was brought home to the plantation owners and peasant cultivators when it was found that healthy suckers when planted in diseased plantations became infected. It was impossible to grow bananas again on the infected sites. By 1910 in Panama, some 20,000 acres had been abandoned, and by 1931 this had increased to 50,000 acres. Similar damage occurred in other areas, particularly Costa Rica and other Central American countries. In Surinam, a new banana industry was begun in 1906, but by 1911 it had been destroyed.

Although a fungus was thought to be responsible for banana wilt, it was not isolated and named until 1910, and a further five years elapsed before all the diagnostic and experimental work had been carried out. It was then shown that the fungus was a specialised form of the well-known *Fusarium oxysporum* which can attack a wide range of plants.

Experimental work showed that the fungus, which is a soil inhabitant, enters through the rootlets, and then progresses from the root to the rhizome. Once there, progress is rapid, the fungal threads growing up the vessels in the pseudostem, and finally into the leaves.

The wilting appears to be mainly due to the production of toxic substances by the fungus, a process which occurs with other species of *Fusarium*. It does not appear that root destruction or blocking of the water conducting vessels is a major contributory factor.

## METHODS OF CONTROL

The magnitude of the problem will now be apparent—how to deal with a fungus which lives in the soil and after infection, inside the plant tissue. Chemical sterilisation is well-nigh impossible, the top six inches of soil alone weighing approximately 1,000 tons. Internal therapy is not, as yet, practicable as the fungicides in common use are insufficiently mobile for easy penetration and movement within the plant system or are phytotoxic if penetration takes place.

The disastrous nature of the disease and the difficulties of control would suggest that 'Gros Michel' might cease to be grown. This is not so. In 1957, 63% of the bananas entering the export trade were 'Gros Michel' (Simmonds, 1959). Its survival is a tribute to its pre-eminent qualities.

The most important step has been the use of disease-free suckers, not just those which appear healthy, but by the establishment of special nurseries with rigorous inspection. The specially raised suckers are then planted in disease-free areas, or in virgin soil.

The use of resistant varieties and the breeding of new ones, although attractive to the plant pathologist, have not met with universal acceptance. Many varieties of bananas are highly resistant to Panama disease, such as the well-known 'Cavendish' group which includes 'Lacatan' and 'Robusta'. 'Lacatan' in many ways appeared to be a suitable alternative, but the persistent styles on the end of the fruit, the susceptibility of the plant to wind damage, the easily damaged skin of the fruit and increased handling problems, have all discouraged its wider use. However, in some areas such as Jamaica where it was not possible to establish disease-free 'Gros Michel' plantations, the introduction of 'Lacatan' has converted a dying industry into a prosperous one.

Plant breeding although an obvious approach, is beset by two major difficulties, that of breeding a seedless fruit, for raising new varieties involves the production of banana seeds, without which new varieties cannot be bred. When this hurdle has been surmounted, as it has been, the new variety has to have the same qualities as 'Gros Michel', an objective which the plant breeder has still to achieve.

Other approaches, such as quarantine, improvement of soil conditions, use of antagonistic organisms and flood fallowing have all played their part. Flood fallowing is intended to suffocate the fungus, for like most fungi, *F. oxysporum* needs oxygen for respiration. Deprive it of oxygen and it dies.

Experiments to follow up this approach were started in Honduras in 1940, 100 acres of infected land being used. The area was divided into four plots, each surrounded by earth walls and then flooded with water to a depth of three feet for different periods of time up to eighteen months. The experiment was successful as 'Gros Michel' plants survived for about five years in the treated areas. Re-treatment however, was not so successful and profitable production was short.

The flood fallowing technique is encouraging as being the first direct attack on the fungus itself. It has, however, severe limitations. It can only be used where the soil is level, where there is a clay sub-soil to retain the water, and it is expensive.

Summing up, it may be said that banana wilt has been contained but not conquered. It exemplifies the fact that the control of the vascular wilt diseases is one of the unsolved problems of plant pathology.

REFERENCES

SIMMONDS, N. W., *Bananas*, 283, Longmans, Green & Co., London (1959)

STOVER, R. H., *Fusarial wilt (Panama Disease) of Bananas and other Musa species*, Commonwealth Mycological Institute (1962)

## Leaf Spot or Sigatoka Disease (*Mycosphaerella musicola* Leach)

The banana industry, having survived the ravages of Panama disease, was faced in the 1940s with the onslaught of another disease, leaf spot or Sigatoka disease. The story of the measures taken to repulse the attack is dramatic and has been acclaimed as 'probably one of the greatest achievements in the history of phytopathology' (Wardlaw, 1961).

The fungus, which can only live on banana foliage, was first described in Java in 1902. Its potentialities for damage were observed when there was a severe outbreak in the Sigatoka Valley in Fiji in 1913. By 1923 it had spread to Queensland, and in 1933, the New World invasion had begun with outbreaks in Surinam and Trinidad. During the following two or three years, it spread to Jamaica and to the great banana plantations in Central America, the main producing areas for the export trade. The livelihood of those dependent on the banana, from the peasant to the great banana companies, was threatened by a fungus.

The first symptoms of infection by the fungus are light yellowish spots. A small proportion of these enlarge, becoming oval, with a length of about 1 cm. The colour also changes to dark brown. Later still, the centre of the spot dies, turning light grey, surrounded by a brown ring. The ring is frequently surrounded by a bright yellow halo. The damage done by a few spots is negligible, but as an epidemic builds up, the numerous spots coalesce, killing ever larger parts of the leaf until the majority of the leaves are scorched brown and useless (Plate 5.11).

It is leaf spot development on the foliage after flowering which is important. When the flower has been thrown, no new leaves can be produced on that plant and the existing foliage is necessary for the three months which it takes to ripen the bunch up to the stage when it is harvested for export. If the leaves are not kept going for those three months, small bunches of prematurely ripened and unsaleable bananas are produced.

The fungus produces condiospores in great abundance, a fact which was known very early on. However, work on the disease in Jamaica, in the late 1930s resulted in the discovery of the perfect or sexual stage of the fungus which produces ascospores. Under suitable conditions each kind of spore produces its own typical symptoms. The conidiospores

*Plate 5.11. Leaf spot of bananas (A Plant Protection photograph)*

are waterborne and are spread through the plantation during wet and windy weather. Some fall into the cup formed by the uppermost leaf and as this is often full of water, the spores lodge along the edge of the furled leaf as it pushed upwards through it. When the spores germinate, the spots are in line, hence the name 'line spotting'. The ascospores, in contrast, are airborne and mainly attack expanded young leaves, particularly the second, third and fourth. The spores are carried upwards and lodge under the tips of these leaves, producing 'tip spotting'.

## METHODS OF CONTROL

The United Fruit Company with its great plantations in Central America was in the forefront of the battle with the disease for it was a case of conquer or perish. Initial experimental work suggested that Bordeaux mixture was the most helpful fungicide for the control of the disease. No time was wasted in installing central pumping plants and underground mains. To each main standpipes were fitted so that with the aid of rubber hoses and lances it was possible to spray each banana plant. The programme was a daunting one, for each banana leaf as it emerged at the top had to receive its protective spray of Bordeaux mixture. As new leaves appear at intervals of five to ten days, the programme called for up to seventeen sprays each year. It is a tribute to the courage and energy of those who took part in this operation, that the banana industry was saved.

Since the early days, many improvements have taken place both in the fungicides used and in the methods of application. At first the spraying had aimed at overall cover, but when it was realised that it was the young leaves which needed protection the emphasis was put on placement. Wetting agents were added to improve cover and the attack was concentrated on the youngest leaves in the centre, a technique called 'heart-leaf spraying'. The use of proprietary fungicides based on copper oxychloride or on cuprous oxide simplified the mixing and made it easier to use low volume techniques. The most important advance however was made in the French Antilles in 1952 when refined mineral oils were added with the intention of slowing down water evaporation from small spray droplets, very necessary if the small droplets are not to dry out before they stick on to the foliage. Low volume spraying cut the quantity of spray fluid from 100-150 gal per acre to 8-10 gal.

But even more important than the reduction of the volume of water was the discovery that the oil itself was acting as a fungistat and was making a most important contribution to the successful control of the disease. So effective was the oil that in some places such as Jamaica, it was used by itself, but generally it was used as a mixture with one of the fixed coppers. The quantity of oil used was originally 2 gal per acre, but currently the accepted rate is 1 gal.

Although the use of oils was a most important advance, it was not the complete answer, as repeated oil spraying is liable to scorch the leaves due to the over-dosing of the lower leaves. This is inevitable when the application from ground level has to pass through the canopy to reach the target leaves in the crown. The injury to the leaves slows down the growth rate of the bananas and thus smaller bunches are produced within the normal period of fruit development. Consequently, the search for safe and effective fungicides has been continued. Maneb, for example, has been subjected to very extensive field trials.

The progress with fungicides has been matched with progress with machines. As mentioned above, the original installations consisted of central pumping stations with underground mains. This requires heavy capital expenditure and a large labour force for the manual application of the spray. The introduction of the oils in 1952 permitted the use of a fogging technique in which small droplets form a mist around the canopy of the plantation. Not only does this ensure good cover, but it also helps to reduce spray damage, as there is no need to direct the spray at the leaves. The reduction of the volume of spray to be applied has made it possible to use motorised knapsack sprayers which are suitable for use on either large or small plantations.

The aeroplane and the helicopter are now in regular use for the spray treatment of the bigger plantations.

This brief account of the battle to control banana leaf spot has recorded changes in both fungicides and in the methods of application. It seems clear that the techniques are still in a stage of rapid evolution and judging by the past, further developments are likely to take place.

REFERENCE

WARDLAW, C. W., *Banana Diseases,* 345, Longmans, Green & Co., London (1961)

### *Bunchy Top*

Bunchy top is due to a virus disease which, so far is limited to south-east Asia, Australia, some of the Pacific Islands and Egypt. It is of great interest to plant pathologists as its conquest is one of the great victories for legislative methods of disease control (Simmonds, 1959).

As the name bunchy top suggests, the most obvious symptom of this disease is a crowding of the leaves at the top of the pseudo-stem. The earliest symptom, however, is seen on the leaf blades where dark green streaks appear on the secondary veins. The streaks vary in length, producing a dot and dash effect. Leaf changes would not in themselves be serious, but the fruit bunches are small and unsaleable.

The disease was first recorded in Fiji in 1880 and during the succeeding years, increased in intensity until 1895 when the export of bananas was only 14% of the amount attained three years previously. The next stage in its spread was in 1913 when suckers were imported from Fiji to new banana plantations in New South Wales. Unfortunately, some of the suckers were infected with the virus. As the plantations increased in number, both healthy and diseased plants were propagated. The inevitable end was reached in 1922 when 90% of the banana-growing area had gone out of production.

In 1924 the Department of Agriculture of New South Wales and Queensland set up an organisation to study the disease and to introduce control measures. When work started, there were numerous theories as to the cause of the disease, such as nutritional deficiencies, aphid damage, aphid transmission of the disease, and fungal or bacterial infection of the roots. The work undertaken under the direction of the Bunchy Top Advisory Committee in Australia steadily cleared a way through the jungle of possible causes, and its eventual findings were straightforward. The disease was due to a virus, a discovery which immediately simplified the problem. The disease was systemic, which meant that the suckers from a diseased plant would also be diseased. The disease is also transmitted by the banana aphid *(Pentalonia nigronervosa)*. The general picture of the transmission of the disease also became clear, long distance transmission was due to man planting up infected material, spread within the plantation was due to the aphid.

Consideration of control measures quickly showed that it was not possible to kill all the aphids for the aphicides available at that time were nicotine and derris which possess limited effectiveness. There was but one thing to do and that was to eliminate all diseased plants and to ensure that healthy plants were used for establishing new plantations. Legislation was passed authorising the destruction of all diseased plants and only permitting the use of officially certified stock for planting up. The appointment of the necessary officials and the enthusiastic co-operation of the farmers produced most successful results, and by 1933 the industry had been restored to prosperity.

The importance of maintaining phytosanitary control methods was emphasised two years later when there was a further mild outbreak, but tightening up the restrictions quickly checked it. The value of legislative methods of controlling virus diseases had been demonstrated for all to see.

The other virus diseases such as infectious chlorosis, mosaic disease and heart rot only call for very brief mention. They can be locally serious, but can be kept in check in exactly the same way as bunchy top.

REFERENCE

SIMMONDS, N. W., *Bananas,* 395, Longmans, Green & Co., London (1959)

## MINOR DISEASES

Virus, bacteria and other fungi are responsible for numerous other minor diseases of bananas.

They may injure the roots, the foliage or the fruit.

Moko, or bacterial wilt disease, is caused by a soil-inhabiting bacterium, *Pseudomonas solanacearum* [E. F. Smith] E. F. Smith. It has quite a wide distribution, but it is in Central America that it has caused serious losses. The bacterium enters the plant through wounds in the roots and then spreads through the plant in the vascular strands. The blockage of the conducting tissue and possibly the production of toxic substances result in wilting of the banana plant. The symptoms show some resemblance to those caused by banana wilt but differences in the colour of the leaves, premature ripening of the fruit and initial wilting of the heart leaf are indications that the disease is due to bacterial infection. Confirmation is readily obtained by cutting a section through the rhizome where the bacteria occur in great abundance if responsible for the wilt.

The most effective method of dealing with this disease is the same as that for banana wilt, namely, planting healthy setts in clean soil. It is difficult to eradicate it from infected plantations, but its spread can be minimised by the prompt destruction of any infected plants.

Few names of plant diseases are more descriptive than that of cigar-end rot, a trouble which sometimes attacks the fruit. As the name indicates, the end of the fruit turns an ashy-grey, the external appearance closely resembling the ash on the end of a cigar. Several fungi have been found associated with these symptoms, the most important being *Verticillium theobromae* (Turc.) Mason and Hughes.

The dwarf Cavendish variety is particularly susceptible, and the disease is therefore an important one in the Canary Islands. The disease is controlled by a routine removal of the styles every three or four days.

In spite of all the difficulties which have arisen as a result of the Second World War, and the advent of synthetic rubber, the natural rubber industry has succeeded in surviving and expects a continuance of a demand for its products in the future.

At first sight it would seem curious that the rubber tree, which is a native of Central and South America, is only cultivated on a large scale in south-east Asia, and to a lesser extent, in tropical Africa. Several factors have implemented the distribution of the plantations, including historical reasons, the availability of a plentiful labour supply, and the absence of the destructive disease, South American leaf disease.

The natural rubber industry is not without its fungal troubles, the most serious being those due to root diseases. Losses are also caused by secondary leaf fall, which is caused by a complex of fungi, insects and mites, and by a small group of diseases which injure the tapping panel.

The diseases of rubber have been described by Sharples (1936). The identification of rubber tree diseases in Malaya has recently been simplified by the publication of coloured illustrations of all those of importance (Hilton, 1959), together with brief instructions on their recognition and methods of control. The disease story is conveniently summarised by Edgar (1958) in his book on the culture of rubber trees.

Insect pests, as a rule, are not a serious problem for rubber planters, and accordingly a description is not included. The situation in Malaya has been comprehensively dealt with by Rao (1965).

REFERENCES

EDGAR, A. T., *Manual of Rubber Planting (Malaya)*, The Incorporated Society of Planters, Kuala Lumpur, Malaya (1958)

HILTON, R. N., *Maladies of Hevea in Malaya*, Rubber Research Institute, Kuala Lumpur (1959)

RAO, B. S., *Pests of Hevea Plantations in Malaya*, Rubber Research Institute, Kuala Lumpur (1965)

SHARPLES, A., *Diseases and Pests of the Rubber Tree*, Macmillan & Co. Ltd., London (1936)

## ROOT DISEASES

### White Root Disease (*Fomes lignosus* [Klotzsch] Bres.): Red Root Disease (*Ganoderma pseudoferreum* [Wakef.] Van Overeem & Steinm.) and Brown Root Disease (*Fomes noxius* Corner)

There are various fungi on dead roots in the virgin forest soil which can cause serious losses when the site is cleared and planted up with rubber trees. The attack on the young plantations began soon after the industry was established, and at times has been responsible for serious tree mortality. Although much can be done to limit the spread of the root fungi, they are still placed as the most important diseases of the rubber tree. On account of their importance the pathologists responsible for the health of the rubber tree have spent much of their time working out the life histories of the fungi concerned and methods of arresting their progress. Research has simplified the treatments recommended and is still finding new ways of minimising the losses.

In Malaya where the subject has been most intensively studied, the three major causes of root rot are the white root disease, red root disease, and brown root disease.

Of these three the white root disease is the most serious, both in terms of the number of trees which it kills, and the cost of controlling it. It gets its popular name from the whitish fungal strands called rhizomorphs (Fig. 5.6) which creep along the infected root. The fungus also produces hyphae which penetrate the root, eventually killing it. As the invasion proceeds, the fungus eventually reaches the collar and may develop the very characteristic bracket fructification (Fig. 5.6), orange-yellow on top and orange, red or brownish below. The brackets are usually seen at the base of the stem but may be found on large exposed roots.

The red root disease, although creamy white at the leading edge, turns red with age. The colour may be obscured by soil particles,

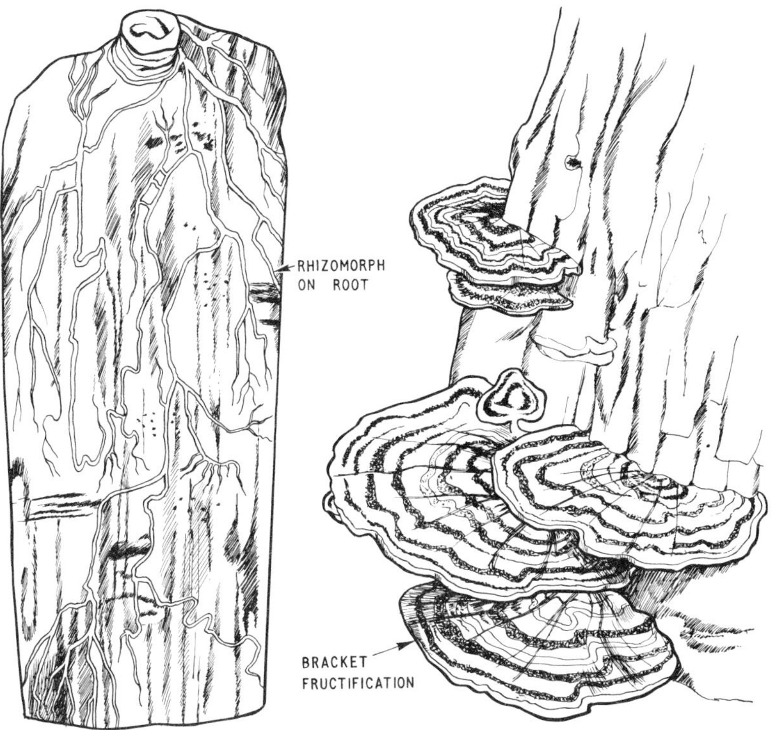


*Fig. 5.6. White Root Disease of Rubber. Left: Rhizomorphs on root. Right: Bracket fructification*

in which case they must be washed off before it can be seen. Another characteristic of the disease is that the fungus forms a continuous skin over the surface of the root. The fungul brackets are also distinct, the upper surface dark brown to black, with a white margin and white below.

The brown root disease, the least important of the three, also forms a skin on the root, but its colour is tawny brown, which becomes black with age. Fungal excretions bind the soil particles to the older infected parts of the root, with the result that the root becomes encrusted with soil particles, particularly in sandy soils. The bracket-like fructifications are more irregular than those of the two other fungi. The colour of the upper side is at first dark brown but blackens with age. The growing margin is yellowish. The underside is tawny to greyish brown.

All three diseases persist in the soil on infected dead roots. Fresly planted rubber trees remain healthy until their roots come into contact with pieces of diseased root. The fungus can then invade the root system of healthy trees, widening the source of potential infection. A plantation can thus be destroyed by the fungus, steadily spreading outwards from a few foci of infection.

### METHODS OF CONTROL

It will be seen that the heart of the problem is the removal of sources of infection. Prior to the last war, when labour was more plentiful, it was common practice to inspect the roots by excavating the soil and to remove all diseased pieces, but rising costs and shortage of labour have made it essential to use less costly methods of control.

In the post-war era, the method of inspection used depends on the age of the plantation. In young plantations which contain more trees than will be required in the final stand, the trees themselves are used as indicators of the presence of diseased roots in the soil (Anon., 1961). It is recommended that the first round of foliage inspection should be made about twelve months after planting and then repeated at intervals of not less than three months. Young trees which show foliage symptoms usually die and must therefore be removed with as much of the root system as possible. Collar inspection is then carried out on neighbouring trees and continued until a disease-free one is reached. The suspect trees must be excavated to expose the main roots and the infected roots then amputated. All cut surfaces are tarred and the visible roots treated with a tar acid fungicide.

Routine rounds of inspection are no longer required when tapping begins, as the tappers can report any trees which appear to be unhealthy. The same principles apply to mature rubber as to young trees, namely the removal of trees which cannot be saved, and the cutting out of infected roots from trees which are not too far gone.

The cost of such a programme is not justifiable on trees which are nearing the end of their productive life. At this stage, the cheapest treatment is isolation. This is done by digging a trench, usually 1 ft wide and 2 ft deep round the infected site. It is advisable to refill the trench to within six inches of the top. This prevents new roots growing below the trench and also facilitates its maintenance as it should be dug out again in about 18 months' time.

Recent research has shown that the application of a fungistat to the collar may lead to a marked improvement in the control of white root disease in young plantations (Anon., 1964). The dressing, which contains quintozene as the active ingredient, is applied to the collar and for a short distance along the roots. The quintozene prevents the fungus, which creeps along the roots, from attacking the treated area. This is of great value because, as already indicated, the rubber trees can survive the loss of some of their roots, but fungal attack on the collar is much more likely to be fatal. The latest evidence indicates that the quintozene dressing will remain effective for 2 years after application. The treatment is of particular value for young replantings since natural infections in old stumps will have virtually died out in that period (Anon., 1965).

REFERENCES

Anon., *R.R.I. Plant. Bull.*, **44,** 72 (1961)
Anon., *R.R.I. Plant. Bull.*, **70,** 8 (1964)
Anon., *R.R.I. Plant. Bull.*, **78,** 107 (1965)

## SECONDARY LEAF FALL

Various causes, including Powdery Mildew *(Oidium heveae* Steinm.*)*, Abnormal Leaf Fall *(Gloeosporium alborubrum* Petch*)*, Abnormal Leaf Fall Disease *(Phytophthora palmivora* [Butl.] Butl.), Yellow Tree Mite *(Hemitarsonemus latus)* and Rubber Thrips *(Scirtothrips dorsalis)*

The rubber tree is deciduous and at least part of the canopy is shed during the 'wintering' period. When growth begins again, the new foliage is susceptible to attack by various fungi, insects and mites. If the combined attack is severe, the young leaves are killed and drop off, a condition which has been named secondary leaf fall.

The powdery mildew, often referred to as *Oidium,* is a typical member of its family. For most of the year it is a harmless parasite on shaded foliage in the lower part of the tree, or on stray rubber seedlings. On the foliage it develops the usual floury white patches which consist of the mycelium and the chains of conidiospores. The spores are dispersed by the wind and if they settle on a suitable site, germinate and start a new infection. As with other members of the group, optimum germination takes place when the humidity is high but infection is inhibited if water is present on the leaf, or if the humidity is low. The young leaves are particularly susceptible and consequently the fresh growth after the winter provides a very favourable site for the fungus. If the conditions are also right for the germination of the spores, an *Oidium* epidemic can quickly develop. The infected leaves become purplish and then turn black before falling off.

The yellow tea mite is commonly found on rubber trees in Malaya. It feeds for preference on the young shoots and leaves. The feeding punctures, if numerous, damage the leaf so severely that it turns pale and then drops off.

The *Gloeosporium* fungus attacks both the young foliage and young shoots. Attacked leaves shrivel and eventually drop off. Infection also takes place on the young green shoots, the point of entry soon turning brown. If the lesion girdles the shoot, it will die.

The rubber thrips is a small insect which also prefers the young leaves to feed on. The thrips puncture the veins and suck the sap. Leaves damaged in this way have enlarged and darkened veins and are liable to drop prematurely.

The *Phytophthora* fungal attack on a rubber tree is mainly on the young foliage and on the fruits. The affected parts decay into a blackened, wet rot and eventually fall off. The defoliation can be severe, the trees losing between 50% and 100% of their leaves, and as a consequence, the potential rubber yield may be halved. The disease is particularly important in South India, but in Ceylon, although it is widespread, its effect is thought to be negligible (Lloyd, 1964).

### METHODS OF CONTROL

In Malaya, in spite of the variety of causes of secondary leaf fall, it is not generally thought to be economic to control it, although methods of doing so are known. In Ceylon, India and parts of Africa, however, *Oidium* is sufficiently severe to necessitate control measures. The usual programme calls for five rounds of sulphur dust at the rate of 12 lb per acre at weekly intervals. Dusting starts soon after the new growth has started and is continued while the foliage is in the susceptible stage.

Although the dusting programme is a straightforward one, the dusting of tall trees often growing on hillsides, is difficult. When the tropical climate and the skin irritation liable to result from sulphur is also taken into account, it will be seen that the application problem is a very real one. On estates which are sufficiently level for wheeled traffic, it is, of course, much simpler. But where the terrain is too uneven for this, the duster must be fitted into a light framework which can be carried by two, or sometimes, four men.

The *Phytophthora* leaf-fall disease is sufficiently serious in South India to justify control measures. Copper fungicide sprays have been shown to be effective, but as with *Oidium*, control is not easy because of the difficulty of covering the leaf canopy of tall trees (Rama Krishnan, 1961).

REFERENCES

LLOYD, J. H., 'The Control of Abnormal Leaf-Fall Disease of *Hevea* in Ceylon', *Bull., Rubb. Res. Inst. Ceylon,* **57** (1964)

RAMA KRISHNAN, T. S., *Proc. Nat. Rubb. Res. Conf., Kuala Lumpur,* 454 (1961)

## Mouldy Rot (*Ceratocystis fimbriata* Ell. and Halst.)

The latex from rubber trees is obtained by removing a thin strip of bark (tapping), the process being repeated at alternate daily intervals in order to renew the flow. Tapping is a highly skilled operation as the cut must be made as deeply as possible to within approximately 2 mm of the wood. If the cambium is damaged, either by too deep cutting, or by disease, the bark does not regenerate evenly over the tapping panel and fails to provide good secondary bark when the tapping cycle starts again in about eight years' time.

Several fungi can attack the tapping panels, the most important being mouldy rot. How this fungus got to Malaya is not known, but it was first recognised there in 1916 and four years later in Java.

The first signs of mouldy rot are small depressed lesions on the freshly cut bark. The spots soon darken and produce a greyish

*Plate 5.12. Spraying rubber tapping panel for control of mouldy rot, Malaya (A Plant Protection photograph)*

mould which is composed of mycelium and masses of spores. The spores can be airborne, but tapping knives and clothing are the main agents by which they are carried from diseased to healthy panels. The fungus can be highly damaging as it penetrates the thin layer of bark and cambium, killing both, with the results already described.

The fungus is dependent on high humidity for infection and subsequent development. Its progress is arrested during the dry season. A certain amount can be done by ensuring freedom of air movement by keeping down undergrowth, but the main defence is based on fungicides.

#### METHODS OF CONTROL

The fungicides used on tapping panels must not affect the latex, a requirement which eliminates both sulphur and copper. Materials which meet this need have been found in some of the tar acid fungicides, and one of the quaternary ammonium disinfectants. The fungicide, which is usually diluted with water, is sprayed on to the panel (Plate 5.12), the aim being to cover about 4 in above the tapping cut and about 2 in below. After several applications, the width of the band can be reduced. As the fungicides are not persistent under the tropical conditions in which they are used, and fresh bark is being continually exposed by tapping, repeated applications are necessary. If tapping is being continued, the treatment should be carried out after each tap, about twelve applications being required. If the trees are to be rested, no new susceptible bark will be exposed and the number of applications can be reduced to four or five with an interval of four days between each application.

### South American Leaf Blight *(Dothidella ulei* Henn.)

South American leaf blight attacks the wild rubber trees which occur in the tropical forests of Central and South America. In the wild, the rubber trees are scattered through the forest, with the result that the disease does not build up to damaging levels. In addition, natural selection has been in operation so that the indigenous trees show varying degrees of resistance to leaf blight.

Various attempts, such as those by the Ford and by the Goodyear companies, have been made to establish rubber plantations in Central and South America. The planting material was obtained from Asia in order to ensure good yields of latex. Unfortunately, the Asian rubber varieties were susceptible to leaf blight, and the large plantations provided ideal conditions for its multiplication. The damage done was so devastating that the plantations had to be abandoned.

The youngest tissues are the most susceptible to infection, and after the first few weeks' growth, the leaves become resistant. The infected spots turn yellowish, while the olive-green conidiospores are produced on the underside of the leaf. The conidiospores are wind-borne, and are the main way by which the disease spreads.

If the young leaf is heavily infected, it soon turns black and falls off, but if the attack is light, defoliation does not take place. As the leaf grows, the centres of the spots fall out, producing a shothole effect. The fungus also develops two other fruiting bodies, pycnidia and perithecia, but their spores do not appear to be of much importance in its life cycle.

Heavy attacks of the disease not only cause defoliation, but may also lead to die-back of the shoots. So severe a disruption of the normal functioning of the tree inevitably results in considerable reductions of latex yield.

### METHODS OF CONTROL

Although leaf blight can be controlled on a small scale by the application of fungicides, it is quite impossible to do so on mature commercial trees. The disease is therefore a very serious potential threat to the Asian rubber plantations and every effort has been made to prevent its entry. In Malaya the importation of any plant material, alive or dead, is forbidden, unless it has been authorised by the Director of Agriculture.

In Malaya, the rubber planters have been encouraged to keep a careful watch on their plantations and to report any suspicious outbreak to the Rubber Research Institute there. As there is no known method of checking the disease, plans have been made to eradicate it by spraying the affected area with 2% normal butyl ester of 2, 4, 5-T in diesel oil. In order to act as quickly as possible, it is the intention to use aircraft to apply about 1 gal of the mixture per acre.

The Malayan rubber industry has also taken long-term steps to breed leaf blight-resistant rubber trees. Such a programme involves testing the seedlings for resistance, which cannot be carried out in Malaya. The problem has been solved by the setting up in 1960 of a Dothidella Research Unit in Trinidad, in association with the Imperial College of Tropical Agriculture. The Unit has established reference collections of rubber trees and the fungus (de Jonge, 1962), and has shown that there are resistant strains of *H. brasiliensis* and of its hybrids (Brookson, 1963). There is thus a good prospect that the objective may be achieved.

#### REFERENCES

BROOKSON, C. W., *Bot. Div. Rep., Rubb. Res. Inst. Malaya for 1962*, 64 (1963)

DE JONGE, P., *Bot. Div. Rep. Rubb. Res. Inst. Malaya for 1961*, 74 (1962)

# COCONUT AND OIL PALMS

Of the very many different kinds of palms, including date palms of the Middle East, the nipa palm, betelnut and palmyra, two are of outstanding economic importance, the coconut and the oil palm.

The coconut palm is grown for the production of coconut oil which is expressed from the copra, the dried meat of the nut. It is estimated that the crop occupies some 10 million acres scattered through the tropics, often near the sea. Coconuts are grown principally in the Far East, especially in the Philippine Islands which have the largest area, but are also found in Indonesia, Malaya, Borneo, India and Ceylon. They are also cultivated in Africa in Mozambique, Tanganyika and Zanzibar, and to some extent in the West Indies in Trinidad and Jamaica. Some occur in Central America, and there is a large area in Mexico.

The oil palm grows in small groups throughout the wetter part of the West African tropics and the Congo. The estimated area in Nigeria alone is 4 million acres, so that the world total is obviously large. The fruit is an important source of vegetable oil both for local consumption and for export as one of the raw materials for the manufacture of margarine.

Few pests occur on palms, and those are usually found on the coconut palm. The most important pest throughout the Far East is the Rhinoceros Beetle. A good account of coconut pests is given by Child (1964).

It is curious that the four major diseases which have killed millions of coconut palms are all of uncertain origin. Their behaviour would suggest that they are virus diseases, but this has not yet been proved. The only fungous disease of any importance is bud rot.

The coconut diseases are well documented. There is a monograph by Briton-Jones (1940), a general survey by Martyn (1955), and a description of the diseases of unknown origin by Maramorosch (1964). There are also chapters on the subject in books on coconut culture (Menon *et al.*, 1958; Child, 1964; and Piggott, 1964).

The main cultural problems of oil palms are nutritional, but there are certain aspects of their pathology which are unusual. Of these, the most interesting is the effect of cultural methods on the incidence of disease. When the palms are grown in small scattered units, the main disease is a trunk rot, which is caused by various species of *Ganoderma*, but when they are grown in plantations *Fusarium* wilt is liable to cause serious losses. The other point of interest is a bacterial bud rot which only attacks unhealthy trees and does not infect those which are vigorous.

The literature on oil palm diseases is not extensive, and is mainly confined to journals such as that published by the West African Institute for Oil Palm Research. In this will be found a disease survey by Waterston (1953) with numerous references, and a list of all the Nigerian diseases (Bull, 1954).

REFERENCES

BRITON-JONES, H. R., *The Diseases of the Coconut Palm*, Baillière, Tindall & Cox, London (1940)

BULL, R. A., *J. W. African Inst. Oil Palm Res.* **I**, 2, 53 (1954)

CHILD, R., *Coconuts*, Longmans, Green & Co., London (1964)

MARAMOROSCH, K., *A Survey of Coconut Diseases of Unknown Etiology*, F.A.O., Rome (1964)

MARTYN, E. B., *Trop. Agriculturalist*, **32**, 162 (1955)

MENON, K. P. V. and PANDALAI, K. M., *The Coconut Palm—A Monograph*, Indian Central Coconut Committee, Ernakulam, S. India

PIGGOTT, C. J., *Coconut Growing*, Oxford University Press, London (1964)

WATERSTON, J. M., *J. W. African Inst., Oil Palm Res.*, **I**, I, 24 (1953)

## COLEOPTERA

### *Oryctes rhinosceros* L. *(Scarabaeidae)*

This is the best known pest of coconuts and is called the Rhinoceros Beetle. It occurs in the Far East, also in Africa, the Western Hemisphere and the Pacific Islands. It is a large beetle about 1 in in length, black, with grey markings (Fig. 5.7). It attacks palms of all ages but is most important in young plan-

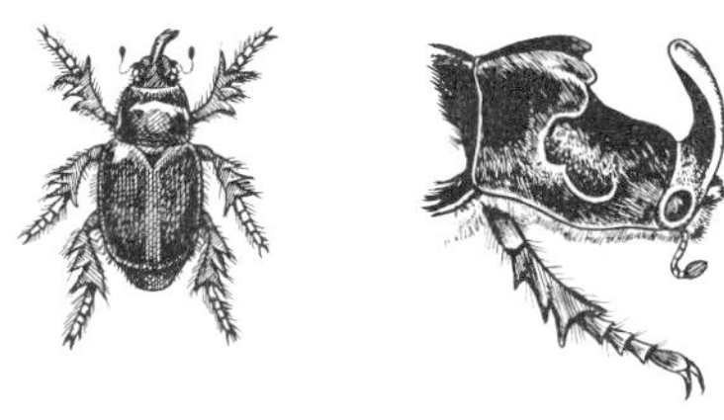

*Fig. 5.7.* Oryctes rhinosceros *(adult)*

tations. The adult beetle bores directly into the growing point of the palms, either killing the bud completely or spoiling the developing fronds which will be tattered and weakened when they expand. Even on older palms damage by *Oryctes* can be considerable, the fronds being jagged and frequently shortened when they have broken off at places weakened by the beetle feeding upon them before expansion, (Plate 5.13). The beetles live for several months and can in that time bore into many palms. Many bore-holes are made at the junction of the frond and bud. Rotting often follows the path of the bore-holes. In the South Pacific Islands, where the beetle has been recently introduced, up to 50% of young palms have been destroyed.

Breeding by adults occurs in coconut waste, on any decaying and fermenting matter such as heaps of dung or garden compost. The larvae are large white grubs, curved and fleshy, at least 2 in in length. Larvae will also breed in the decaying wood of felled oil palms, their life-cycle taking six months.

*Plate 5.13. Damage to coconut plantation by Rhinoceros Beetle, Malaya*

METHODS OF CONTROL

Direct action against the Rhinoceros Beetle is essential on young palms otherwise a good deal of replanting becomes necessary and new plantations grow unevenly. The method practised in Malaya consists of a strong wash using 1 lb in 10 gal of water of a 26% gamma BHC product. This is painted or sponged into the growing point of the young palm up to about five years old. Monthly applications may be necessary when the beetles are active. BHC mixed with sawdust in the rates of 1:9 has been advocated by O'Connor (1953) working in Fiji, applied to the crown so that the mixture lodges in the leaf bases. Treatment of compost and waste coconut heaps with BHC has also been suggested to stop breeding.

Hand-collection of adults is also possible as the beetles fly at dusk, and are quiet in the daytime. Beetles are also strongly attracted to light at night and light traps will catch larger numbers. New palms should not be planted on old sites where felled palms remain. All dead and felled palms should be split up into small pieces to dry out.

*Rhynchophorus ferrugineus* Oliv.
*(Curculionidae)*

This is the Red Stripe Weevil which lives within the trunk of palms and sometimes is numerous enough to kill them (Fig. 5.8). It can be trapped in the split trunk of the Arenga palm. A similar species *R. palmarum* L. occurs in the West Indies.

The adults and larvae of the beetle *Brontispa longissima* Gest. *(Chrysomelidae)*

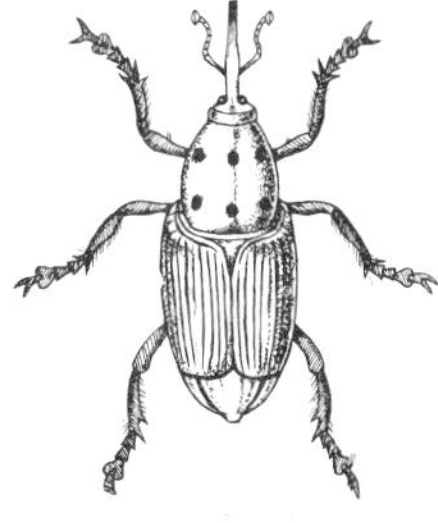

*Fig. 5.8.* Rhynchophorus ferrugineus *(adult)*

cause considerable damage to the fronds of young coconut palms in the Pacific Islands. Spraying monthly with either dieldrin at 0·15% or DDT at 0·2% was found to be an effective means of control, (Brown and Green, 1958).

## LEPIDOPTERA

Several species of leaf-feeding caterpillars occur principally on oil palms where they are probably more important than *Oryctes*. These little caterpillars can cause defoliation of the fronds (Plate 5.14), which are produced singly from the growing point, each frond taking about one month to expand fully. *Setora nitens* Wlk. *(Limacodidae)* and species of *Thosea* are Nettle Grubs—that is they possess stinging hairs.

*Artona catoxantha* Hamps. *(Zygaenidae)* is also important but possesses no hairs of the stinging type.

### *Cremastopsyche spp. (Psychidae)*

These are bagworms, so-called because the larvae construct cases of silk and extraneous matter in which they live. The larvae hang on to the foliage by thoracic legs only.

### METHODS OF CONTROL

Foliage feeding caterpillars are easily controlled with insecticides, DDT being the most suitable. The main problem is to determine whether action is necessary. Against *Setora,* the appearance of the early stages of the caterpillar should be observed and spraying carried out if the numbers exceed 10 per frond. Bagworms are far less damaging and at least 100 per frond are allowable before spraying is justified.

For application of DDT to oil palms, the portable engine-driven mist-blower is ideal. Palms seldom exceed 15 ft in height except when old, and they can be sprayed easily from the ground using about 25 gal per acre. It is of course virtually impossible to spray coconut palms which may rise to 60 ft. Dieldrin should not be used as this insecticide kills beneficial insects living on these caterpillars.

*Plate 5.14. Injury to fronds of oil palm by stinging caterpillars, Malaya*

## HEMIPTERA

### *Theraptus spp. (Coreidae)*

Mention must be made of this bug which occurs on coconuts in Zanzibar. The insects attack the infloresence and cause poor setting of the flowers. Way (1953) suggests dusting the infloresence with 0·4% gamma BHC dust at $\frac{1}{2}$ lb per palm applied by an experienced coconut tree climber.

*Amblypelta cocophaga* China *(Coreidae)* also causes nut fall in British Solomon Islands, (O'Connor, 1950).

REFERENCES

BROWN, E. S. and GREEN, A. H., *Bull. Entomol. Res.*, **49,** 239 (1958)
O'CONNOR, B. H., *R.A.E.*, **40,** 208 (1950)
O'CONNOR, B. H., *R.A.E.*, **44,** 419 (1953)
WAY, M. J., *Bull. Entomol Res.*, **44,** 657 (1953)

## DISEASES OF UNCERTAIN ORIGIN

There are four major epidemic diseases which invariably kill affected coconut palm trees.

They can conveniently be divided into two groups; those which kill quickly in less than a year, and those which are slow, taking some 2½ to 15 years. The quick group contains two rather similar diseases, bronze leaf wilt and lethal yellowing, while the slow killers are cadang-cadang and Kerala wilt.

Bronze leaf wilt, which is found in Trinidad and the Guianas, kills the palm within 4–6 months of the onset of the symptoms. The typical early signs are bronzing of two or three of the old leaves compared with only one on a healthy tree. The leaves eventually wither and hang down and there is some shedding of the green nuts.

Lethal yellowing, for which there are various other names including 'the unknown disease', has been recognised in Jamaica and the Cayman Islands for a hundred years. The first symptom of its presence is a sudden drop of all the nuts, soon accompanied by a yellowing of the foliage, but there is no early wilting as in bronze leaf wilt. Affected trees die within about 3 months. Palm seedlings replanted in the same area usually go down with the disease in 2 or 3 years' time.

The symptoms and distinctions between these two diseases are not very clear-cut, and may overlap. In the case of bronze leaf wilt there may be confusion with physiological wilt due to drought, while the symptoms of lethal yellowing vary slightly in different localities. Similar diseases are known in West Africa and opinions as to their exact identity with one or other of the Caribbean diseases have differed.

Cadang-cadang, sometimes called yellow mottle decline, occurs in the Philippine Islands where it has been present for at least 50 years, but its major ravages have occurred in the post-war years. It has been responsible for the death of 14 million coconut palms.

Affected palms have yellowish bronzed leaves. Initially the colour change only occurs on the older leaves, but as the disease progresses, the youngest leaves also show the same symptoms before they finally die, leaving a small crown of dead leaves. Bronzed leaves viewed by transmitted light show a yellow mottling.

The disease is a slow killer, the trees generally succumbing 5–6 years after the symptoms are first seen. It slowly spreads through the plantation and is therefore regarded as infectious. In the absence of a visible pathogen, it is attributed to a virus.

Kerala wilt, also known as wilt (root) Travancore, is reported to have killed 10 million coconut palm trees in Kerala State (S. India). The symptoms differ from those of cadang-cadang, and the two diseases are distinct.

With the progress of the disease, the leaves get smaller until the ultimate death of the palm in 3–15 years. The mid-rib becomes weak so that breakages often occur. The leaflets are also affected, hanging limply due to wilting, and showing chlorotic streaks in the young ones when viewed by transmitted light.

As with cadang-cadang, the cause of the wilt has not yet been determined but a virus is suspected.

### Bud rot (*Phytophthora palmivora* [Butl.] Butl.)

The first sign of bud rot is the withering of the youngest leaf, followed by the older leaves in succession. The leaves turn yellow before dying and the bud rots, giving off a very unpleasant smell. As the coconut palm only possesses one growing point, the terminal bud, its death inevitably results in the death of the tree.

*Phytophthora* species associated with bud rots have been reported from most of the coconut-growing regions of the world, but the worst epidemics have occurred in Madras. It has been observed in some areas that bad outbreaks tend to follow after hurricanes, which would suggest that the crown can resist infection unless it is damaged. The symptoms may also resemble those caused by lightning, which kills the palms in the neighbourhood of the flash to earth.

There is no remedy for bud rot and the dead trees should be felled and burnt as soon as possible as they harbour insect pests of the palms.

*Ganoderma* wilt *(Ganoderma spp.)*

Seven species of *Ganoderma* have been found associated with trunk rots of oil palms. Of these, *G. lucidum* (Leys. et Fr.) Karst. is the commonest in Nigeria, being widespread throughout the Forest Region. The wilting of the oldest leaves is the first sign of this disease, and it is quickly followed by their death. The central leaves on the crown are at first unaffected, but later turn pale green before eventually dying. The bracket-shaped fructifications are usually to be seen at the base of the stem in the later stages of the disease.

The susceptibility of the palm trees to attack by *G. lucidum* appears to vary with their age. Young trees aged 3–5 years and those over 20 are liable to go down with *Ganoderma* wilt, but those of intermediate age are resistant.

No control measures other than the removal of the diseased trees are recommended.

*Fusarium* wilt (*Fusarium oxysporum* Schl.)

*Fusarium* wilt does not apparently damage oil palms when they are growing naturally in the forest areas, but it can be a serious menace to palms grown in plantations.

At first it is not easy to distinguish between the wilts caused by *Fusarium* and *Ganoderma,* but the *Fusarium*-infected trees sometimes exhibit lemon frond symptoms in the early stages. This name describes the yellowing of a few leaflets on or near the fifteenth leaf in the crown. As the disease progresses, the wilting becomes rapid and the leaves die. The mid-ribs of some of the older leaves also break and hang down in characteristic fashion.

On cutting the trunk, the vascular bundles are buff in colour if recently infected, greyish-black if of longer standing.

The fungus, as the scientific name indicates, is closely related to the species that attacks bananas causing Panama disease, or banana wilt. As with other vascular diseases, infected trees cannot be cured, and must be removed.

It is hoped that the long-term solution will be provided by the plant-breeder. Techniques have been worked out for testing the susceptibility of oil palm seedlings to infection. Their use has shown that seedlings vary in their resistance to the disease and thus supports the hope that the breeding of resistant varieties will be feasible (Prendergast, 1963).

REFERENCE

PRENDERGAST, A. G., *J. W. African Inst. Oil Palm Res.,* **4,** 14, 156 (1963)

Bud rot little leaf disease *(Erwinia spp.)*

Bud rot little leaf is a bacterial disease which is of small importance in Nigeria, but has caused losses of 30% or more in the Kwilu/Kasai region of the Congo (Duff, 1963).

The bacterium is a normal member of the plantation microflora, but it only infects the palm tree when it is unhealthy. It is often assumed that healthy plants can resist infection better than those in poor health, but this is one of the few cases where the supposition has been proved.

The bacterium invades susceptible palms low down on the spear, causing a wet brownish patch. The infection may spread to the crown which may, or may not, be killed. If recovery takes place, the crown produces 'little leaves' which are small because the upper part was destroyed in the spear infection phase.

The disease must be kept at bay by ensuring that the palms grow vigorously.

REFERENCE

DUFF, A. D. S., *J. W. Africa. Inst. Oil Palm Res.,* **4,** 176 (1963)

# VI WEED CONTROL WITH HERBICIDES

## INTRODUCTION

Weeds must be considered as important in limiting the yield of a crop, as are insect and allied pests and fungous diseases. Weeds are very different in many ways and must be discussed from a different point of view in considering the desirable features of a herbicide. Herbicides to kill weeds are readily available; it is their application without injury to the crop which limits their use. This problem seldom arises when dealing with insect pests and fungous diseases.

First, weeds compete with the crop for air, light, water and other requirements essential to plant growth and seldom act like insect pests and diseases as parasites on the actual crop. Secondly, weeds grow in many situations and only become weeds when they occur where they are not wanted; the French word 'mauvaise herbe' or the German 'unkraut' are much more expressive. Weeds are seldom specific to the crop as are insect pests and fungous diseases. Thirdly, weeds can always be removed by hand; this is still the usual method of dealing with them in more primitive systems of agriculture, whereas the cultivator can hardly overcome an insect pest by hand except in a limited fashion and likewise, a tea planter could hardly prevent an outbreak of blister blight by means of his labour force alone. Fourthly, weeds are generally predictable, knowing the locality and the soil type, and they are hardly subject to unexpected outbreaks. Fifthly, weeds follow an orderly pattern of existence and are free from the complications of involved life-cycles such as are followed by insects and fungi which must be unravelled and understood before any attempt can be made to overcome them.

The control of weeds therefore presents a somewhat simpler picture than the control of pests and diseases, and it is more often the economic justification of weedkilling which is in doubt rather than the method of attack.

## CEREALS

Weedkilling in cereals is now an established practice in the U.S.A. and in northern Europe where MCPA and 2, 4-D have been used since 1945. In these countries, about 75% of all cereal crops are treated with hormone weedkillers. The dominant weeds are, to a large extent, similar and include the following, all of which are susceptible:

| | |
|---|---|
| *Brassica nigra* | *Raphanus raphanistrum* |
| *Capsella bursa pastoris* | *Rumex crispus* |
| *Chenopodium album* | *R. obtusifolius* |
| *Erysimum cheiranthoides* | *Senecio vulgaris* |
| *Galeopsis speciosa* | *Sinapis alba* |
| *Papaver rhoeas* | *S. arvensis* |
| *Plantago lanceolata* | *Sisymbrium officinale* |
| *Ranunculus arvensis* | *Thlaspi arvensis* |
| *R. repens* | *Urtica urens* |

The next important step came about 10 years later in the discovery of the phenoxy-butyric acid derivatives, MCPB, and 2, 4-D-B. These chemicals are more selective than MCPA and 2, 4-D in that they can be used with safety on young leguminous forage crops such as clover, lucerne and similar plants. In practice, this means that MCPB and 2, 4-D-B are preferred for weed control in cereals, where these are under-sown with a forage crop, usually grass and clover. When these plants have come up in the cereal, weed control can be carried out, whereas MCPA and 2, 4-D would have been too active and suppressed the legumes.

After 10 years of selective weed killing in cereals with MCPA and 2, 4-D, the more susceptible and 'easy to kill' weeds such as charlock *(Sinapis arvensis)* and runch *(Raphanus raphanistrum)* were reduced and other weed species become dominant. Two species are particularly noticeable namely cleavers *(Galium aparine)* and chickweed *(Stellaria media)*. These weeds were particularly important in winter wheat and had hitherto been controlled by DNOC, applied during the early spring. The appearance of a new hormone, namely methoxychlor phenoxy propionic acid (MCPP or CMPP) in 1957, permitted these weeds to be controlled in the spring. The available range of hormone weedkillers and combinations of them brought nearly all the important arable land weeds within their control.

Even so, certain weed problems still remain such as species of *Matricaria, Polygonum* and *Chrysanthemum segetum*. While species of *Polygonum* were controllable with CMPP better action was desirable. The need for a more certain control of these species would seem to be about to be fulfilled with ioxynils against *Matricaria* and pichlorans against *Polygonum*. Certain arable weeds, particularly grass weeds, are still difficult to control, notably couch *(Agropyron repens)*, wild oat *(Avena fatua)* and black-grass *(Alopecuris pratense)*. Various recommendations have been made and many new herbicides introduced but they still remain a menace to arable cultivation.

## GRASSLAND

Grass is the cheapest form of animal food and yet grassland is more neglected than any other crop. The farmer tends to pay less attention than its importance demands and grassland receives more attention from the biologist than from the herbicide specialist. In England, less than 5% of the area recorded as grassland is treated with herbicides and it is doubtful if this amount is exceeded in any other country. One of the reasons for this is that weeds themselves swell the bulk of the green herbage and the removal of these by herbicides, lowers the total yield. In many countries in Central and Southern Europe, weeds themselves seem to form nearly the total herbage of the meadows which are assiduously grazed, cut and made into hay. The idea of using longer-lived productive grasses and forage species does not seem to have been accepted. Likewise the need for fertilizers is not fully recognised.

The weedy nature of grassland, even in the more highly developed agriculture of certain Northern European countries, is remarkable and buttercups and daisies seem to be a normal ingredient of the true farm meadow. Thistles, docks, ragwort, coltsfoot and rushes become permanent features of the older grass fields, especially those lying near to farm buildings. On hill pastures, bracken becomes the dominant weed.

Weeds in grassland can be removed by the use of selective hormone weedkillers, MCPA and 2, 4-D, which will kill most of the main weeds. There is good evidence to show that the use of such weedkillers results in an increase of herbage provided that adequate nitrogen is applied at the same time. Furthermore, the herbicides MCPB and 2, 4-DB can be used where there is abundant clover which would otherwise be suppressed. One other problem exists in grassland, namely that of unproductive grasses or grass weeds such as *Agrostis stolonifera, Festuca rubra* and, on hill pastures, *Nardus stricta*. The removal of these grasses presents greater difficulty and often the only solution is to re-sow. This can obviously be accomplished by ploughing up the old sward, cultivating and re-sowing with a new seeds mixture but currently, experiments are in progress of a revolutionary character in which grassland is being renewed by the help of a herbicide. Paraquat suppresses a wide range of grasses and can be used to destroy the green herbage of a grass field by the simple and rapid process of spraying it at 1 lb per acre of ion (4 pt 'Gramoxone'). A seed bed can be prepared within a few days and the old sward re-sown with the minimum of cultivation. Progress is now being made towards drilling new seeds directly into the old sward without any cultivation at all. Chemical treatment is certainly suitable for low lying pastures and leys but the treatment of hill pastures requires further exploration. Paraquat can also be used as a selective herbicide on pastures at lower rates, as it shows a greater degree of toxicity to certain less desirable grasses such as *Agrostis* and *Poa annua* than to more desirable grasses such as *Lolium perenne* and *Dactylis glomerata.* No doubt grass weeds in grassland will receive ever increasing attention in the future.

## RICE

The use of herbicides in rice has been slow to develop probably because this crop is cultivated in small plots and still treated largely as one hand produced with little, if any, form of mechanisation. Furthermore, the traditional method of paddy growing is by transplanting, which allows time during the preparation of the land, for weed control by flooding and cultivation.

The principal weeds in paddy are water grasses, especially species of *Echinochloa (Panicum), Digitaria* and sedges such as *Cyperus* and *Eleocharis*. Weed control in most paddy growing countries has been slow to turn to herbicides, even in Western Europe, where a little paddy is grown. In Japan, PCP (pentachlorphenol) has probably been the most widely used herbicide, applied pre-emergence or post-emergence, particularly against grass weeds. At present, granular formulations of PCP are in favour and these are used normally before planting or before emergence, if seed is sown. Some interest is being shown in MCPA and 2, 4-D in many countries but these are suitable only for broad-leaved weeds. These hormones are selective in paddy, as in other cereals, but of limited value as they are ineffective against grass weeds. MCPA is safer on paddy than 2, 4-D, the use of which can lead to malformation of the ears. Broad-leaved weeds are of limited importance but some such as *Alisma plantago* occur persistently.

The advent of propanil (Stam 34 = 3, 4-dichloropropionanilide), which possesses selective action against water grasses, is the most significant step in herbicide development in this crop. Propanil is used at the rate of up to 1 gal per acre of a 35% formulation applied in 20 gal of water at the three- to four-leaf stage of paddy, the water being temporarily withdrawn. This herbicide is now widely used in many paddy growing countries of Central and South America but appears to be still under experiment in Japan. Limited quantities of herbicides are used in Thailand, but India, Burma and Indonesia have hardly begun to use them and the normal method of weeding is to pull out by hand the grass weeds after the paddy is transplanted.

In Japan, attempts are being made to mechanise the growing of paddy, both the seeding and harvesting. Such methods include direct drilling of seed without prior cultivation. This inevitably demands the use of herbicides which would appear to be essential if land is weedy. The use of paraquat to kill weeds after sowing but before emergence is such a possibility. Alternatively, mixtures of 2, 4-D and amitrol (ATA = amino-triazol) are also under investigation. The final selection of herbicides will undoubtedly depend on the weed flora and the system of cultivation undertaken.

## MAIZE

In all the big maize growing countries of the world, mechanisation is the main development, including direct drilling of the seed without prior preparation of the land. By this means, the cost of production can be reduced. In the past, seed bed preparation consisted of autumn ploughing followed by discing and further cultivations in the spring, partly aimed at weed destruction. Modern sowing techniques, with little soil preparation and subsequent inter-row cultivation, depends inevitably on chemical weed control and this need has been fulfilled by the triazine group of herbicides of which atrazine is the one most used in maize.

Atrazine (and Simazine) are selective in maize, as this plant is tolerant to them. Application is made at 3–4 lb per acre of a 50% product pre-emergence, shortly after planting. The seed bed must be smooth and weed free, as the chemical acts against germinating seeds, including those of grasses. Atrazine is not effective against deeper rooted perennials such as couch *(Agropyron repens)*. Higher rates of atrazine can be used against *Agropyron* but in these circumstances the subsequent crop after maize, such as winter wheat, may be adversely affected. The use of atrazine is leading to the idea of continuous maize growing, especially where high rates of atrazine have been used to obtain better weed control.

Various ideas are under investigation to reduce the hazard of atrazine persistence in soil, such as reducing the rate and mixing with 2, 4-D. Both MCPA and 2, 4-D can be used selectively for weed control in maize, either pre-emergence or post-emergence when the maize has reached six inches in height. For pre-emergence, 2, 4-D amine (50%) is used at 3–5 pt per acre but at only $\frac{3}{4}$ pt post-emergence. Atrazine is the dominant herbicide used in maize and in some countries, over 80% of the crop is treated.

## SUGAR-CANE

The use of herbicides in sugar-cane depends on the availability of manual labour. Formerly, weed control was accomplished by means of hoeing in the cane row and inter-row cultivation by means of a mule or horse. By these means the inter-row soil ridge was broken down and the soil redistributed. With labour becoming increasingly expensive and, in some regions, short in supply, cane growers and estate managers have begun to turn to herbicides to control weeds in their plantations.

Herbicides previously used were sodium chlorate, sodium arsenite and PCP (pentachlorphenol) in diesel oil. Modern herbicides have been extensively tested in many sugar-cane growing countries, notably in Hawaii, Mauritius, Natal, Trinidad and in the U.S.A. First to be used were the hormone weed-killers, especially 2, 4-D, which was introduced into cane growing practice both as a pre-emergence and as a post-emergence herbicide. The most favoured formulation was 2, 4-D amine containing 50% acid equivalent used at 5 pt per acre pre-emergence and $1\frac{1}{2}$ pt per acre post-emergence. When used in this way, 2, 4-D gave good control of broad-leaved weeds, as would be expected, and some control of grass weeds if applied before the seedlings emerged from the soil. Application of 2, 4-D amine could also be made by aeroplane in small volumes of water. It could also be used in cane ratoons and the whole technique was cheap and effective.

Unfortunately 2, 4-D is not basically a grass killing herbicide and, after many years of application, cane growers were faced with an ever increasing problem of grass weeds, particularly of *Cyperus rotundus* and *C. esculentus*. Other grass weeds also became important such as species of *Digitaria* and *Panicum* and, in some countries, Johnson grass, *Sorghum halepense*. A great search was then begun for alternative herbicides, especially those with greater persistence. Attention was focused on the soil herbicides of the triazine group. Simazine and atrazine were soon found to possess a selective action in sugar-cane and could be used at high rates without damage to the cane. Rates of 5–8 lb per acre (of a 50% product) were too expensive and not entirely effective against all grass species. Better weed control was obtained with herbicides of the substituted urea group, diuron and monuron used as pre-emergence herbicides. Diuron used at 4–8 lb per acre

(80% as Karmex) was particularly effective against a wide range of weeds including species of *Cyperus*. It is essential to have moist soil for the action of these residual herbicides and they are therefore particularly suitable in irrigated cane.

More recently, the bipryridyl herbicide paraquat has been extensively tested in cane in both pre-emergence and post-emergence application. Paraquat is particularly effective by contact against grasses and can be used as an overall spray at 1 lb per acre as ion (4 pt of 'Gramoxone') both in plant cane and in ratoon cane without permanent injury. Many combinations of herbicides, both contact and residual, are under trial, and will surely solve the problem. The best combination of herbicides for prevailing conditions will be chosen.

## POTATOES

The treatment of potatoes with herbicides is in its early stages. The reason for this is because the traditional methods of potato growing, which require many cultivations to ridge up the land both before and during the growing of the crop, gave adequate weed control. Recent research is demonstrating that these methods of cultivation may in fact be harmful to the crop in reducing yields but, moreover, render the mechanical harvesting of the tubers more difficult by consolidating the soil. Even so, the use of herbicides in potatoes is at present not great and only amounts to a few per cent of the area of the crop even in the most highly developed farming regions of Western Europe; it is, however, growing.

Weedkillers are now available which can be used in potatoes, notably paraquat, a contact herbicide which is applied at 10% crop-emergence but no further cultivation should be carried out in order to avoid stimulating further weed seed germination. A popular weedkiller in potatoes is linuron (the methoxy analogue of diuron) which is a persistent soil herbicide applied at 1–2 lb per acre pre-emergence to clean soil. MCPA always carried a recommendation for potatoes and was applied at 10% crop-emergence but such a treatment could in fact depress yields of some varieties. The advent of paraquat and soil residual herbicides stimulated the search for the best combination of products to replace the old traditional cultivations. Yield increases of up to 25% were achieved where the soil was undisturbed after planting. At present few herbicides are officially recommended for use in potatoes.

## SUGAR-BEET

Weed control in sugar-beet represents a challenge to the research worker, as there is need for a selective herbicide to enable the growing of this important crop to become fully mechanized. At present, the need to prepare a fine seed-bed, followed by 'chopping out', the mechanical removal of unwanted seedlings and inter-row cultivation has largely obviated the need for a chemical weedkiller. Even so, great efforts are at present being made to find suitable herbicides to be used as part of the technique of growing which is itself changing with the increasing interest in monogerm seed and precision drilling.

In 1965 in England, about 50% of the 400,000 acres of sugar-beet were treated with some form of herbicide—a steep rise over 1963 when only about 10% of the area was treated. Ideally, a herbicide in sugar-beet should be selective, so that it can eliminate the weeds in the seedling row which are the main source of anxiety and determine the ultimate yield of the crop. Several herbicides have been put forward for this purpose, mostly for pre-emergence treatments such as a mixture of OMU and BiPC (Alipur = N-cyclo-octyl NN dimethyl urea+methylprop-2ynyl N-(3 chlorophenyl) carbamate) and a mixture of IPC and Endothal. These herbicides are usually applied as a band spray covering the row only. This reduces the overall amount of weedkiller used to about one-third and concentrates the application in the seedling row where it is required.

The most recent herbicide offered for sugar-beet is pyrazon (80% PCA = 5-amino-4-chloro-2 phenyl-3 pyridazone) which can be used either pre-emergence at 5–6 lb per acre or post-emergence at 4 lb per acre. Unfortunately, these weedkillers vary in their activity and selectivity according to weather conditions—heavy rain washes the weedkiller into the soil to the detriment of the beet seedlings. Straight contact herbicides used pre-emergence such as paraquat, have not been accepted because weed control is only partial, as the sugar beet germinates too quickly and too few weeds are present for spraying. Likewise, the idea of preparing the seedbed and delaying drilling is also not acceptable as the earliness of sowing beet determines the yield of crop. Undoubtedly, this problem will be solved in order to bring about the complete mechanization of sowing, singling and harvesting.

## DECIDUOUS AND CITRUS FRUIT

The need for weedkilling in these permanent crops has never been completely established. In any case, weedkilling in the apple and pear orchards in Northern Europe and North America is merely the removal of undesirable grass and other weeds from the base of the tree-trunk. Such an action may or may not be justified, although a case could be made out for the removal of weeds in the tree row in cordon and espalier type cultures. Established apple and pear orchards are either grassed down or cultivated. In the more northern countries, grass is frequently preferred to clean cultivation, as rainfall is usually adequate and grass forms a better surface on which to carry out the routine spraying, which is all important in fruit production. The grass is mown and the cut grass allowed to rot back into the soil. Some orchards are cultivated, especially where rainfall is lower so that the grass does not compete with the tree for moisture. Such a situation is more common in peach orchards and in citrus groves, both of which are sometimes irrigated. In these circumstances, cultivation in some form is necessary to break up the soil surface and kill weeds.

The argument for the overall use of herbicides would appear to stand or fall on the effect on the soil structure and the inevitable yield of fruit from orchards treated with herbicides in comparison with those mechanically cultivated. Evidence of the beneficial effects of non-cultivation and weed control with herbicides is already available for soft fruit such as blackcurrants, raspberries and strawberries. Even so, herbicides are coming into use in orchards and citrus groves on their ability to kill weeds at the base of the tree or in the tree-row—a technique which is both cheap and effective. Preference is given to residual soil herbicides, particularly of the simazine group or the monuron group all of which are recommended in fruit orchards. Their chief merit lies in the fact that one application to a clean surface prevents weed growth for many months, provided that the surface of the soil is not disturbed. In addition, dalapon and amitrol (ATA = aminotriazol) are being used especially against grass weeds. Paraquat is also extremely useful where weeds are already established round the tree base or in the tree row and can, if necessary, be combined with a residual herbicide. As evidence accumulates, it is becoming increasingly clear that weedkilling in deciduous fruit and citrus will develop as a programme, just as insecticides and fungicides are applied to a programme drawn up at the beginning of the season, as no one herbicide will serve all purposes.

## VINES

Weedkilling in vines with herbicides is accepted with reserve, even in Europe, which is the principal vine-growing region of the world. The delicacy of vine culture, finely adjusted to avoid any possible variation in the ultimate product, is far too important to allow traditional practices to be altered without good reason. Moreover, vines are traditionally grown in small plots—the average size of a holding seldom exceeds one hectare in either France, or Italy or Spain. The normal practice in vine culture in Europe is to cultivate the soil during autumn and winter, throwing it up to the vine stock and pulling it down again in spring. All vineyards, at the beginning of the season, are weed free as a result of this practice.

Having reached this situation, vine growers are being persuaded that residual herbicides will maintain this weed-free condition for the remainder of the season. It is at present not certain how far residual herbicides such as simazine and monuron can be safely used in vines, until several years of treatment have elapsed. Paraquat, while being useful, is risky to employ after the weeds have appeared as usually, at this time, the vine is rapidly bursting into growth. Moreover, some growers like weeds to appear later in the year to remove excessive moisture from the soil to help ripen the grapes. Vines are also frequently beset with weeds difficult to kill with herbicides such as *Convolvulus arvensis* and *Agropyron repens*.

No doubt, as with other crops, herbicides in vines, at least in the tree row, will be used as the cost of manual labour increases but weedkillers will hardly take the place of family labour.

## PLANTATION CROPS

The use of weedkillers in tropical plantation crops such as rubber, oil palms, coffee, cocoa, tea, bananas and others of a similar type is relatively new but is developing fast. The speed of acceptance and establishment of herbicide practice in these crops will once again depend on the availability and cost of labour.

## RUBBER

Probably the use of herbicides in Malayan rubber represents the best example of the general acceptance of chemical weedkillers in plantation crops. It should be noted in passing that rubber is free from many of the complications which surround the use of chemicals on food crops such as bananas and secondly, in Malaya, the rubber industry is highly organized, in a country not over supplied with cheap labour.

The most important herbicide, until recent years, has been sodium arsenite, an effective contact herbicide and very cheap. Unfortunately, sodium arsenite is highly toxic to warm-blooded animals and corrosive to the skin. Even so, its efficiency as a herbicide against difficult grass weeds such as species of *Paspalum* and Lalang *(Imperata cylindrica)* made it irreplaceable until very recently. It is curious to reflect that the value of sodium arsenite as an important part of rubber cultivation, was often outweighed by its hazard of poisoning local cattle, although the rubber crop was the main source of income of the Federated Malay States.

Normally, sodium arsenite is used as a powder containing 80% of arsenic trioxide at the rate of 10 lb per acre for the first application and 5 lb for the second and sometimes further applications. Most grasses and other weeds are controllable by this treatment. Other herbicides, such as sodium trichloracetate are often used specifically against Lalang. In certain other rubber growing countries, herbicidal oils, applied by hand by wiping the weeds with an oil saturated rag, are used especially where oil is freely available. Very high rates of oil are necessary of 150 up to 400 gal per acre, to achieve effective weed control of grasses. This rate may be reduced by adding PCP to the oil.

Efforts are being made to replace sodium arsenite in Malaya with the best alternative which at present appears to be paraquat, applied in several sprays during the season. Residual soil herbicides, such as simazine, are also under trial and have, to some extent, been accepted as satisfactory.

## OIL PALMS AND COCONUTS

The control of weeds in these crops is doubtfully justified or necessary. In oil palms, it is customary to keep the base of the palm free from weeds so that the fallen nuts can be easily seen and collected. Collecting paths and circle weeding are rapidly being introduced and for their maintenance, paraquat is widely favoured as the herbicide. In coconuts, the traditional slashing of the undergrowth with cutlasses or grazing by animals seems to be the only action necessary as competition from weeds is unimportant, except in new plantings.

## COFFEE AND BANANAS

Weed control in these two plantation crops is quickly changing over to herbicides. Clean weeding with residual herbicides seems to be accepted as the best alternative to hand labour. The most favoured herbicide at the moment is dalapon (sodium dichloropropionate) which is particularly effective against grasses. Killing weeds with straight-contact herbicides such as paraquat, or herbicidal oils, is liable to lead to a build up of deep-rooted perennial grasses such as *Cynodon dactylon.*

## COCOA

Weedkilling with herbicides is seldom attempted in this forest grown crop. In Ghana, the largest cocoa producing country in the world, the young trees are planted very densely with a view to thinning them out later. Weed growth is almost totally suppressed and, what remains, is frequently the bush type of weed, more easily tackled with a cutlass. Cocoa is seldom grown as a plantation crop in open land where herbicides would be needed but, usually as a forest crop, with natural shade. Established cocoa forms a complete overhead canopy of foliage which suppresses all weed growth.

## TEA

This crop lends itself readily to the use of herbicides during the pruning period. Normally, tea bushes are so densely packed that little weed growth between them is possible and such as occurs, can be dealt with by local or spot treatment such as slashing or pulling out. Pruning opens up the bushes and the space between them so that weeds, such as *Mikania scandens,* a climbing plant, and perennial grasses, begin to flourish. At this time, the bushes are very susceptible to injury as they need all their reserves to recover from the effect of pruning. The normal practice is to dig through the tea garden by hand but this procedure disturbs the roots in the soil and often damages the closely planted bushes. Paraquat, which leaves no residues in the soil, is already being tried to replace hand labour during this period. The main danger is from spray drift on to the bushes nearby.

REFERENCE

WOODFORD, E. K. and EVANS, S. A., *Weed Control Handbook,* Blackwell Scientific Publications, Oxford (1965)

# APPENDIX

## GLOSSARY OF TECHNICAL TERMS

Acervulus — A small cushion-like body composed of conidiospores and conidia.

Adult — The fully grown insect, usually with wings.

Aecidiospore — (Aeciospore in the U.S.A.). The spore produced in an aecidium (Fig. 2.3e).

Aecidium — (Aecium in the U.S.A.). The cup-shaped fructification of the rust fungi containing tightly packed spore chains (Fig. 2.3e).

Apothecium — A saucer-shaped fructification bearing asci on the upper surface.

Ascospore — A spore which develops inside an ascus (Fig. 4.10c).

Ascus — An elongated sac containing spores, usually eight in number. The asci develop in fruiting bodies such as apothecia and perithecia (Fig. 4.10b).

Basidium — See Promycelium.

Cauda — The tail-piece at end of the abdomen of an aphid.

Chitin — The exterior body material on the insect.

Chlamydospore — A thick-walled asexual spore which usually has a dormant stage before germination.

Conidiophore — The structure carrying the conidia (Fig. 4.11).

Conidium — (Conidiospore) An asexual spore (Fig. 4.11).

Cornicles — The tube-like structures on each side of the abdomen of an aphid.

Cortex — The principal tissues of the root lying between the peripheral layer and the central endodermis.

Cyst — The flask-shaped body of the female eelworm of the genus *Heterodera*.

Dorsum — The back or upper part of the body of an insect.

Elytra — The wing cases of a beetle.

Fallow — When soil is left without a crop during the growing season.

Femora — The first part of the leg of an insect just before attachment to the body.

Fructification — A fruit body especially of the lower plants.

Gemmifer — A small mycelical ball which propagates a fungus vegetatively (Fig. 5.2).

Glume — The bract-like cover of the flower or seed in grasses and cereals.

Hermaphrodite — Animals having both male and female sexual organs.

Honey dew — A sugar substance ejected by aphids and other *Hemiptera*.

Hymenium — The layer, made up of asci and sterile hyphae, found in some fruit bodies (Fig. 5.5).

Hypha — The individual thread or filament of a fungus.

Hypocotyl — The stem of a seedling between seed and leaves.

Host — The plant, or another animal on which an insect lives.

Instar — A stage through which an insect passes between moults.

Larva — The immature stage of an insect which is dissimilar to the adult, found in beetles, flies, moths, etc.

Lesion — The wound caused by a pathogen

Mycelium — A mass of fungal filaments, for example, mushroom spawn.

Nymph — The immature stage of an insect which resembles the adult, found in aphids, capsids, etc.

| | |
|---|---|
| Oogonium | In fungi, the female organ which contains the oospore (Fig. 3.4e) |
| Oospore | A thick-walled spore formed as a result of fertilization, germinating after a dormant period (Fig. 3.4e) |
| Parthenogenetic | A method of reproduction without the intervention of the male. |
| Pathogen | A micro-organism producing disease. |
| Perithecium | A round, flask-like structure containing asci (Fig. 4.10a). |
| Phytotoxic | Injurious to plants. |
| Polyphagous | Living on many plants. |
| Promycelium | (Syn. Basidium). The structure which bears the secondary spores of the rust and smut fungi (Fig. 2.3c). |
| Pupa | The resting stage in an insect possessing a larval stage before transformation into an adult. |
| Pustule | An excrescence composed of spores and sporophores. |
| Pycnidiospore | A slime spore which develops inside a pycnidium. |
| Pycnidium | A flask-like fructification, resembling a perithecium in shape, containing asexual spores. |
| Pycniospore | An asexual spore developed inside a pycnidium (Fig. 2.3d). |
| Pycnium | A flask-like fruit body produced by the rust fungi (Fig. 2.3d). |
| Rachis | Upper part of the stem of a cereal plant bearing the ear. |
| Rhizomorph | A mass of hyphae looking like a root (Fig. 5.6). |
| Sclerotium | An irregularly shaped resting body, usually black, composed of a mass of hyphae (Fig. 3.6). |
| Silk | A substance used by insects to make cocoons. |
| Sporangiophore | The structure carrying a sporangium (Fig. 3.4c). |
| Sporangium | An organ containing asexual spores (Fig. 3.4c). |
| Spore | A single or multi-cellular reproductive body. |
| Sporidium | The spore borne on the promycelium (Fig. 2.3c). |
| Sporophore | A structure carrying a spore (Fig. 2.19). |
| Stoma (pl. Stomata) | A pore on the surface of a leaf or shoot. |
| Synthetic | Made in a chemical factory. |
| Systemic | Chemicals which enter and travel in the sap stream of plants. |
| Teleutospore | The overwintering spore, consisting of two or more cells, produced in the autumn by the rust fungi (Fig. 2.3b). |
| Thorax | The middle part of insect's body bearing the wings and legs. |
| Tiller | A side shoot arising from the base of a plant, usually in cereals. |
| Uredospore | The summer spore produced by the rust fungi (Fig. 2.3a). |
| Vector | An insect carrying a virus disease from one plant to another. |
| Vermiform | Worm-like in appearance. |
| Viviparous | Reproduction without the egg stage, as in aphids which give birth to living young. |
| Zoospore | An asexual motile cell which moves by its flagella (Fig. 3.4d). |
| Zygote | The cell formed as a result of the union of two sex-cells. |

# Index